Workers and the State in New Order Indonesia

Under the New Order, Indonesia has undergone a process of sustained industrialisation. This has led to the emergence of a new urban industrial working class more inclined to organise independently of the state. Workers have been increasingly involved in industrial unrest in the 1990s, despite stringent state controls over labour.

Workers and the State in New Order Indonesia provides theoretical analysis of the role and prospects of organised labour in late industrialising Indonesia. With the use of comparative models it argues that emerging labour movements face greater obstacles the later it is that a country undergoes industrialisation. Vedi Hadiz demonstrates how the strict labour controls in Indonesia are the legacy of the struggles between the army and the Left before the New Order and that a corporatist social and political framework continues to constrain the development of labour movements.

This book is the first major study of labour relations in Indonesia for nearly thirty years. As such it offers fresh insights on Indonesian politics and the theoretical debates on industrialisation in Southeast Asia.

Vedi R. Hadiz is Research Fellow, Asia Research Centre, Murdoch University, Australia. He has written widely, in both English and Indonesian, on social and political change in Indonesia. He is co-editor of *The Politics of Economic Development in Indonesia: Contending Perspectives*.

Routledge Studies in the Growth Economies of Asia

Workers and the State in New Order Indonesia

Vedi R. Hadiz

Asia Research Centre
Special Research Centre on Social, Political and Economic Change in Asia
Murdoch University, Perth, Western Australia
Established and Supported under the Australian Research Council's
Research Centres Program

London and New York

First published 1997
by Routledge
11 New Fetter Lane, London EC4P 4EE

Simultaneously published in the USA and Canada
by Routledge
29 West 35th Street, New York, NY 10001

© 1997 Vedi R. Hadiz

Typeset in Times by Routledge
Printed and bound in Great Britain by Antony Rowe Ltd,
Chippenham, Wiltshire

British Library Cataloguing in Publication Data
A catalogue record for this book is available from the British Library

Library of Congress Cataloguing in Publication Data
Hadiz, Vedi R.
Workers and the State in New Order Indonesia
(Routledge studies in the growth economies of Asia)
Includes bibliographical references and index.
1. Trade unions – Indonesia. 2. Labor movement – Indonesia.
3. Working class – Indonesia. 4. Indonesia – Economic
conditions – 1945. I. Title. II. Series.
HD6822.H33 1997   97–7098
331.88'09598 – dc21   CIP

ISBN 0–415–16980–1

For Juzar Hadiz

Contents

Illustrations

Acknowledgements

I would like to express my gratitude for the invaluable support provided by the Asia Research Centre at Murdoch University, without which this book would not have seen the light of day. Special thanks must be conveyed to its director, Professor Richard Robison, who supervised the Ph.D. thesis upon which it is based, and who has been both a valued friend and teacher.

Various people at or associated with the Centre have also been helpful, both academically and in other ways. I would like particularly to thank Del Blakeway, David Bourchier, Helen Bradbury, Ian Chalmers, David Hill, Kanishka Jayasuriya, Rob Lambert, Garry Rodan and Krishna Sen. I would also like to thank my former fellow postgraduates for their stimulating company and friendship.

My sincerest appreciation is extended to Frederic Deyo, Andrew MacIntyre and Ken Young, who read and commented on the original thesis, as did George Aditjondro, Mark Berger and Greg Talcott.

I would also like to thank those in Indonesia: the factory workers, too numerous to mention individually, who willingly spent their precious free time with me; friends at Yayasan SPES – Daniel Dhakidae, Hilmar Farid, Ignas Kleden and Titin; and *Kompas*, which provided financial assistance to supplement my scholarship.

Many thanks also to Fauzi Abdullah, Nori Andriyani, Saut Aritonang, Dieter Bielenstein, Edi Cahyono, Margot Cohen, Shafiq Dhanani, Sjaiful DP, Victor Fungkong, Hardoyo, Haruno, Hemasari, Nugroho Katjasungkana, Melody Kemp, Koeswari, Sutanto Martoprasono, Teten Masduki, Nikensari, Indera Nababan, Abdul Hakim Garuda Nusantara, Muchtar Pakpahan, Johnson Pandjaitan, Bomer Pasaribu, H.J.C Princen, Razif, Sadisah, Aris Santoso, Dita Sari, Bonnie Setiawan, Sjahrir, Valentin Suazo, Ari Sunaryati, Suwardi, Reshanty Tahar, the late Titis, Tosari Widjaja, Wilson, Harry Wibowo, Arya Wisesa, as well as Chris Manning at the ANU, Victoria Smith at Routledge, and Jeremy Wegstaff at *Reuters*.

My greatest appreciation is extended to my family: my wife Herlina, who put up with me and this study for all these years with love and understanding, our daughter Karla, who has reminded me of the joys and wonders of life, and my parents – Fathma Nurthiny and the late Juzar Hadiz – who encouraged my life explorations, even when they were uncertain of my direction.

Fremantle, November 1996

Glossary

AAFLI: Asian-American Free Labour Institute.

AAWL: Australia-Asia Workers Links.

ABRI: *Angkatan Bersendjata Republik Indonesia*; Indonesian Armed Forces.

ACTU: Australian Council of Trade Unions.

AFL-CIO: American Federation of Labor-Congress of International Organizations.

API: *Asosiasi Pertekstilan Indonesia*; Indonesian Textiles Association.

APINDO: *Asosiasi Pengusaha Indonesia*; Indonesian Employers' Association.

BAKERPROBI: *Badan Koordinasi Proyek Buruh Indonesia*; Indonesian Labour Project Coordination Body, established in 1968.

BAKIN: *Badan Koordinasi Intelejen*; Intelligence Coordinating Body.

BAKORSTRANAS: *Badan Koordinasi Strategis Nasional*; National Strategic Coordinating Body.

BAPPENAS: *Badan Perencanaan Pembangunan Nasional*; National Development Planning Body.

BBI: *Barisan Buruh Indonesia*; Indonesian Workers' Front, formed in 1945.

BKS-BUMIL: *Badan Kerjasama Buruh-Militer*; Labour-Military Cooperation Body.

Dewan Perusahaan: Enterprise Councils, formed in the early 1960s to give labour a voice in the running of state enterprises.

Dwifungsi: Doctrine which asserts that the armed forces have a social and political role.

EOI: Export-oriented industrialisation.

FAS: *Forum Adil Sejahtera*; Forum for Justice and Prosperity, a Jakarta-based NGO.

FBSI: *Federasi Buruh Seluruh Indonesia*; All-Indonesia Labour Federation, established in 1973.

FES: Friedrich Ebert *Stiftung*; a German-based NGO linked to the Social Democratic Party.

FKTU: Federation of Korean Trade Unions.

FORSOL: *Forum Solidaritas Buruh*; Labour Solidarity Forum.

GASBI: *Gabungan Serikat Buruh Indonesia*; Amalgamated Trade Unions of Indonesia. A BBI splinter group.

GOLKAR: *Golongan Karya*; Functional Group. The state-backed electoral vehicle established in the early 1960s by the military as a front to counter communist influence.

GSBVI: *Gabungan Serikat Buruh Vertikal Indonesia*; Amalgamated Vertical Trade Unions of Indonesia. A BBI splinter group.

GSP: Generalized System of Preferences; US government scheme to allow duty-free import of goods from selected developing countries.

Guided Democracy: Political system in place in Indonesia from the late 1950s to 1965. Established by Soekarno, it replaced the liberal parliamentary system.

HIP: *Hubungan Industri Pancasila*; Pancasila Industrial Relations. Originally HPP, *Hubungan Perburuhan Pancasila*, or Pancasila Labour Relations.

HKTI: *Himpunan Kerukunan Tani Indonesia*; Indonesian Peasants' Association.

HNSI: *Himpunan Nelayan Seluruh Indonesia*; All-Indonesian Fishers' Association.

ICFTU: International Confederation of Free Trade Unions.

ILO: International Labour Organization.

IS: *Institut Sosial*; a Jakarta-based NGO.

ISDV: *Indische Sociaal Democratische Vereeniging*; Indies Social Democratic Association; socialist grouping in colonial Indonesia.

Jabotabek: Jakarta–Bogor–Tangerang–Bekasi.

KABI: *Kesatuan Aksi Buruh Indonesia*; Indonesian Workers' United Action. Action front comprised of non-communist labour organisations set up to support New Order.

KADIN: *Kamar Dagang dan Industri*; Chamber of Commerce and Industry.

Karyawan: Term introduced by SOKSI to describe Indonesian workers, aimed at supplanting *buruh*, which had radical political connotations.

KBKI: *Kesatuan Buruh Kerakyatan Indonesia*; Populist Workers' Union of Indonesia, linked to the PNI.

KBM: *Kesatuan Buruh Marhaenist*; Marhaenist Workers' Union, linked to the PNI.

KBSI: *Kongres Buruh Seluruh Indonesia*; All-Indonesia Workers' Congress, regarded to have close links to the PSI.

Kelompok Aksi Lapangan: Field Action Groups, introduced by Minister of Manpower Sudomo in the 1980s to monitor labour problems.

KNPI: *Komite Nasional Pemuda Indonesia*; Indonesian Youth National Committee.

KONGKARBU: *Konsentrasi Golongan Karya Buruh*; Workers' Functional Group Concentration. Labour group established by SOKSI.

KOPKAMTIB: *Komando Pemulihan Keamanan dan Ketertiban*; Command for the Restoration of Order and Security, a supra-national security agency intertwined with the structure of the military, set up in the early New Order.

KORPRI: *Korps Pegawai Republik Indonesia*; Civil Servants' Corps of the Republic of Indonesia.

LPHAM: *Lembaga Pembela Hak Azasi Manusia*; Institute for the Defence of Human Rights.

LWR: *Lembaga Wanita dan Remaja*; Women's and Children's Institute of the SPSI.

MALARI: *Malapetaka Limabelas Januari*; 15 January Catastrophe. Name given to student-led anti-government and foreign investment riots taking place in 1974.

MASYUMI: *Majelis Syuro Muslimin Indonesia*; Consultative Council of Indonesian Muslims. Major Muslim party of the 1950s, banned in 1960.

MPBI: *Majelis Permusyawaratan Buruh Indonesia*; Indonesian Labour Consultative Council, inaugurated in 1969, defunct in 1973.

MTUC: Malayan Trade Union Council.

MURBA: 'Proletarian' party, originally established in the 1940s by non-PKI communists.

MUSPIDA: *Musyawarah Pimpinan Daerah*; Regional Consultative Leadership.

MUSPIKA: *Musyawarah Pimpinan Kecamatan*, Sub-district Consultative Leadership.

NASAKOM: Nationalism, Religion, and Communism; Soekarno-coined term illustrating the unity of the three major political streams in Indonesia before the New Order.

NIC: Newly Industrialised Country.

NTUC: National Trade Union Congress (of Singapore).

NU: *Nahdlatul Ulama*; Islamic Scholars Association. Major Muslim political party until fused into the PPP in 1973.

OPPI: *Organisasi Persatuan Pekerja Indonesia*; Organisation of Indonesian Workers' Associations.

OPSUS: *Operasi Khusus*; Special Operations. Military intelligence unit headed by General Ali Moertopo.

P4P/P4D: Central dan regional-level labour disputes resolution committees established in the early 1950s.

Pancasila: The Five Principles; state ideology professing belief in One God, Humanism, Indonesian Unity, Social Justice, and Consultative Democracy.

PARKINDO: *Partai Kristen Indonesia*, a Protestant political party formed in 1945 and fused into the PDI in 1973.

PDI: *Partai Demokrasi Indonesia*; Indonesian Democratic Party, established in 1973.

PFB: *Personeel Fabrieks Bond*; a colonial period sugar refinery workers' union.

PKI: *Partai Komunis Indonesia*; Indonesian Communist Party.

PNI: *Partai Nasional Indonesia*; Indonesian National Party.

PPBI: *Pusat Perjuangan Buruh Indonesia*; Centre for Indonesian Working Class Struggle.

PPP: *Partai Persatuan Pembangunan*; United Development Party, established in 1973.

PPPB: *Perserikatan Pegawai Pegadaian Bumiputera*; a colonial period pawn-shop workers' union.

PRD: *Persatuan Rakyat Demokratis*, later *Partai Rakyat Demokratis*; Democratic People's Union, later Democratic People's Party.

PSI: *Partai Sosialis Indonesia*; Indonesian Socialist Party, banned in 1960.

PUK: *Perwakilan Unit Kerja*; SPSI enterprise-level units.

Pusat Pelaksana Pencegah Konflik: Conflict Prevention Executive Centre; labour-monitoring body operating in the 1980s.

SARBUMUSI: *Serikat Buruh Muslimin Indonesia*; Indonesian Muslim Trade Union, linked to NU.

SARBUPRI: *Serikat Buruh Perkebunan Republik Indonesia*; Plantation Workers' Union of the Indonesian Republic.

SBII/GASBIINDO: (*Serikat Buruh Islam Indonesia/Gabungan Sarekat Buruh Islam Indonesia;* Indonesian Islamic Trade Union/ Amalgamated Islamic Trade Unions of Indonesia). Trade union federation linked to MASYUMI.

SBLP: *Serikat Buruh Lapangan Pekerjaan*; Industrial Sector Unions.

SBM: *Setiakawan*; Solidarity Free Trade Union.

SBSI: *Serikat Buruh Sejahtera Indonesia*; Indonesian Prosperous Workers' Union.

SI: *Sarekat Islam*; a colonial period Islamic Association and later political party.

SISBIKUM: *Saluran Informasi dan Bimbingan Hukum*; Information Channel and Legal Assistance.

SOB Pantjasila: *Sentral Organisasi Buruh Pantjasila;* Pantjasila Central Workers' Union, linked to Catholic Party.

SOBSI: *Sentral Organisasi Buruh Seluruh Indonesia*; All-Indonesia Central Workers' Organisation, linked to PKI.

SOKSI; *Sentral Organisasi Karyawan Sosialis Indonesia*; Central Organisation of Socialist *Karyawan* of Indonesia.

SPSI: *Serikat Pekerja Seluruh Indonesia*; All-Indonesia Workers' Union. (FSPSI, or SPSI Federation, from 1995.)

Tim Bantuan Masalah Perburuhan: Labour Assistance Teams, operating in the 1980s to monitor labour problems.

VSTP: *Vereeniging voor Spoor-en Tramwegpersoneel*; a colonial-period rail and tram workers' union.

YAKOMA: *Yayasan Komunikasi Massa*; Mass Communications Institute, NGO working with labour and urban poor.

YASANTI: *Yayasan Anisa Swasti*; NGO catering to women workers.

Yayasan Arek: Labour-oriented NGO based in East Java.

YBM: *Yayasan Buruh Membangun*; Foundation of Workers in Development.

YLBHI: *Yayasan Lembaga Bantuan Hukum Indonesia*; Indonesian Legal Aid Institute.

YMB: *Yayasan Maju Bersama*; Foundation for Mutual Progress.

YPM: *Yayasan Perempuan Mhardika*; an NGO catering to women workers.

YTKI: *Yayasan Tenaga Kerja Indonesia*; Indonesian Manpower Foundation.

1 Introduction

This study is about the emergence of an industrial working class in Indonesia and its implications for the maintenance of a model of accommodation between state, capital and labour characterised by the control and demobilisation of labour as a social force. Sustained industrialisation has ensured the slow, but steady, development of this class and there is little doubt that the future will see its further growth and gradual maturation, especially given the emergence of Southeast Asia as a prime site of export-oriented production. The early consequences of this fact were most apparent in the first half of the 1990s, when we first witnessed signs of the revitalisation of working-class organisation and activism, in spite of the surrounding, largely unfavourable, if not hostile, social and political terrain.[1]

Such a revitalisation has in part been manifest in an upsurge of labour unrest in centres of industrial production in Java and beyond (e.g. Sumatra). Thus, even Indonesia's conservative mainstream newspapers have recently devoted more space to reporting labour strife, sometimes conveying quite vividly such events as the mass ransacking of factory property by angry workers demanding better wages, improved work conditions or greater freedom to organise. Significantly, such images contrast starkly with those that the New Order prefers to project, invariably emphasising the successful maintenance of stability, order and harmony.

To the distress of some state planners, the surge of labour unrest has been accompanied by the proliferation of alternative, grassroots forms of organisation of the working class. These forms of organisation essentially confront the institutional arrangements of state–society relations entrenched since the early 1970s, a major feature of which has been the political subordination of labour as a social force.

It is important to place these developments in the labour area in the context of the economic and political contradictions surfacing as industrial capitalism in Indonesia matures on the one hand, and as the new Order begins to show some signs of ageing, if not decay, on the other. This is perhaps more so given that the study of labour has been largely neglected in the social and political analysis of Indonesia over the past three decades.

It is also important to consider that the emergence of the industrial working class in such a terrain will certainly have a profound effect on the range of possibilities and options that are available to it. There are huge obstacles, for example, to the development of the path of social democratic trade unionism. The international mobility of capital, particularly in the low-wage, export-oriented industries that have underpinned Indonesia's industrial development since the mid-1980s, has meant the global weakening of labour's bargaining power. Moreover, Deyo (1989) has pointed to the structural constraints to effective organisation that he suggests are inherent to these kinds of industries.[2] Equally importantly, the Indonesian working class confronts a powerful state which is predicated upon the subjugation of society-based movements and organisations, particularly those, like labour, whose history is associated with radical political movements.

Thus, there are mutually contradictory tendencies simultaneously at work in Indonesia which are affecting the course of the working-class struggle. Understanding the tension between these contradictory tendencies is not only crucial to an assessment of the future of labour, but also to an understanding of the wider dynamics of social, economic and political change in contemporary Indonesia. This is all the more important given the uncertainty that the current institutional arrangements of state–society relations can survive in their present form in relation to any post-Soeharto configuration of political power.[3]

Implicit in a study such as this is the assumption of a view of the working class as an active, rather than merely reactive, historical agency. Consequently, this may appear to some – to paraphrase Burawoy (1985: 5) – to be quite an unfashionable study of an unfashionable topic. Indeed, in recent times, students of capitalism in the advanced industrial countries seemed to have grown increasingly dismissive of the working class as 'new social movements' (environmentalism, feminism, etc.) appear to have superseded it in terms of challenging 'the cultural model . . . and hierarchical structures of contemporary Western society' (Cohen 1982: 1, xi; Lebowitz 1991: 5–6).[4] It was Gorz, who summed up the mood most succinctly when he bid 'farewell to the working class' (Gorz 1982). In response to such a tendency Burawoy has rightly claimed that studies of the working class have been 'plagued by lurches between a voluntarism in which anything is possible and a determinism in which nothing seems possible, between a naive workerism and bleak prognostications' (Burawoy 1985: 7), while noting that the latter conditions are prevailing.[5]

Others (e.g. Cohen *et al.* 1979; Munslow and Finch 1984; Munck 1988a; Southall 1988a), however, have resurrected studies of this class by shifting attention to the sometimes ill or loosely defined (Lloyd 1982: 21) newer proletariat of the 'Third World' – itself an increasingly problematic concept (e.g. Kiely 1995: 160–162; Berger 1994). Callinicos, for example, suggests that it is premature to bid farewell to the working class when the rapid industrialisation process of various East Asian countries is producing vast numbers of new proletarians (Callinicos 1995: 202–203). While Callinicos' point may be valid, studies such as these will undoubtedly be coloured by the fact that both nascent and established working-class movements all over the world confront an increasingly hostile political terrain. Indeed, at the same time that the limited gains of recent years by workers in South Korea, for example, have been noted, organised labour in the advanced industrialised countries has been on the receiving end of quite unprecedented attacks in the post-war period. These have not only undermined the very legitimacy and relevance of trade unionism,[6] but also by extension, the normative value of the welfare state itself, primarily the product of past working-class struggles.

Moreover, in contradiction to the predictions of some (e.g. Levinson 1974: 141; Frobel *et al.* 1980: 406), and the hopes of others (e.g. Labour Research Association 1984), the internationalisation of the process of production has not given rise to conditions unambiguously supportive of greater levels of international working-class solidarity (Olle and Schoeller 1987: 26–27). Indeed, the current pessimism is quite in contrast with times when it was fashionable to suggest that such a development would almost inevitably usher in a new period of greater working-class solidarity on a trans-national basis. As Southall (1988b: 18–20, 24–26) and Jenkins (1984: 50–53) maintain, its impact has been, at best, contradictory, resulting in as many conditions conducive to greater rivalry among individual, national working classes, as to the forging of greater solidarity among them. Referring to the 'New International Division of Labour',[7] they have pointed to the strong tendency for the employment of protectionist strategies by the working classes of advanced industrial countries, as a means of defending jobs against competition from low wage imports, as well as the obsession with countering the relocation of capital from 'core' to 'Third World' sites.[8] These have ensured, and perhaps in some ways, reinforced, the division of the 'global' working class along national, sometimes ethnic, lines (see also Olle and Schoeller 1987: 42–43).

This work will also appear unfashionable in the context of current developments in the study of Indonesian politics, which has been traditionally elite-centred, and of political economy, within which the working class has hardly figured at all. Indeed, while there is a burgeoning literature on the growth of the capital-owning (e.g. Robison 1986; MacIntyre 1991; Shin 1989) and middle classes (e.g. Tanter and Young 1990), as noted earlier, relatively little attention has been accorded to the emergence of an industrial working class. Significantly, some of the more fashionable perspectives on Indonesian politics have been characterised by the liberal belief in the more or less 'naturally' progressive role of an increasingly assertive bourgeoisie and/or growing new middle class. Within this liberal scheme of things, it is assumed that these classes will eventually realise democratic reforms and a loosening of the authoritarian reins.[9] It is in this connection that, for example, the deregulation of the Indonesian economy since the mid-1980s is assumed to lead inevitably to the enhancement of the abilities of 'society' – a term which, revealingly, is often used to refer only to the capital-owning and/or middle classes – to countervail the power of the state (Sjahrir 1989). Alternatively, when cold reality intrudes on this optimism – as was the case following the recent, abrupt, end of the so-called era of political 'openness'[10] – the weakness of the democratic impulse in Indonesian society is assumed to be rooted exclusively in the current immaturity of the bourgeoisie and/or middle classes.[11]

The predominance of this largely liberal problematic has resulted in the preoccupation in much of the recent literature on Indonesian politics with such things related only to a particular realm of politics: the way parliament works, the extent of the freedom of the press, the current and prospective roles of political parties and of the armed forces, etc. In other words, the 'things' that would 'normally' cater to bourgeois and/or middle-class sensibilities and concerns. Inevitably, analysis is often limited to the role of particular institutions that are also more or less recognised by the state to have a formal place within the 'legitimate' realm of political life. Not surprisingly, the politics that go on outside this delimited space is often simply ignored.[12]

Importantly, the political exclusion of large sections of society, including that of the working class, has been the major characteristic of New Order political strategy, best exemplified in its self-described 'floating mass policy'. It is in the context of such a strategy that the absence of meaningful, independent workers' organisations throughout most of the New Order ought to be understood. However, within the confines of the liberal problematic mentioned above, the struggles of the working class – which necessarily take place outside of the official institutions that occupy the 'legitimate' realm of political life – will only rarely constitute the focus of political analysis. It may be said, therefore, that the officially enforced separation of labour from politics in the New Order, has, until recently, also constituted the basis for the divorce of labour from the intellectual discourse.

Nevertheless, as mentioned earlier, the gradual maturation of capitalism in Indonesia has resulted in the slow, but distinct, development of an industrial working class. The rise of working-class action has been particularly significant given Indonesia's push to develop a more export-oriented economy, based on light manufacturing industries benefiting from the abundance of a cheap – and politically docile – labour force. Not surprisingly, it is only since this time that systematic academic attention has been given to the contemporary working class (e.g. Hadiz 1993; 1994a and b; Lambert 1993). The big gap in time between major studies on working-class politics in Indonesia – important works on the pre-New Order period do exist – has inevitably meant that there is a lot of catching up for academics to do. Though partly the product of the seemingly complete political subordination of labour in the New Order, the long-standing lack of attention to the working class has meant that academics are poorly equipped to understand the dynamics of the country's fledgling working-class movement.

The main theoretical concern of this study involves the question of the political prospects of working-class movements emerging in very late industrialising countries including Indonesia. Admittedly, I have been aware of the considerable degree of direct political relevance of this question insofar as attempts to build an independent working-class movement in Indonesia continue to take place. Indeed, the study is undertaken in the full realisation that the analysis employed, rather than being exclusively an intellectual exercise, essentially constitutes a form of *praxis* in itself. As Lloyd points out, the very act of studying the working class has inevitable political implications – by identifying a 'proletariat', one may indirectly contribute to its self-consciousness.[13] Hopefully, readers will also recognise that I have, at the same time, remained vigilant of the danger of raising 'false hopes about its strength' (Lloyd 1982: 9), an exercise which would automatically diminish any degree of political relevance that the study might have had.

Most studies of the working class, it could be argued, have been undertaken on the basis of one of the following two positions. The first is to deny much autonomy at all to the working class by portraying its fate as being totally dependent on the designs of more dominant social groups or classes, which invariably constrain that class from pursuing its interests. From this standpoint, the working class is essentially a passive, or at best reactive, participant in the unfolding of history. Commenting on world-system analysis, for example, Charles Bergquist writes that

> even those who focus on labor itself – have been wont to subordinate labor's struggles, like the class struggle generally, to the 'logic' of impersonal forces – to the demands of the world market, to the 'exigencies' of capital accumulation, to the periodicity of the famous long waves.
>
> (Bergquist 1984: 15)

In the same vein, Munck (1988a), referring to dependency-style analysis, finds great fault in the preoccupation of some authors with the impact of international conditions on national-level labour movements. This results, he argues, in the underestimation of the ability of workers to 'actively participate in the shaping of their own destinies'.[14] Significantly his assessment may be seen as an integral part of a more general critique of 'pure functionalism', which is dismissed for its 'formalistic juggling' of variables, where 'all sense of process and human agency disappears'. Against such an approach, Munck argues that the working class has to be treated as 'agents of their own history, and not simply bearers of relations of production following their predestined lot' (Munck 1988a:8–9, 21, 99).

The second position often taken is the complete opposite of the one just described. Here the working class is posited with an autonomy so great, that any useful analysis of it *in relation to* a wider social, economic and political context becomes impossible as works degenerate into romanticised accounts of sporadic, usually glorious episodes of a heroic working-class struggle. Burawoy (1985: 6), for example, refers to 'studies of workers in their brief moments of heroism' which 'have unearthed the swan songs of artisans in their battle to defend their skills against the encroachment of capital – a battle they seemed destined to lose, but which momentarily threw up radical visions'.

If in the first position the emphasis is on deciphering an overwhelming structural logic, in the second position little more is presented than 'detailed studies lacking any general perspective and isolated from their context'.[15] If in the former position 'all sense of process and human agency disappears', the latter is easily 'reduced to a sequence of events (*histoire événementielle*) where major structural transformations are subsumed by the flow of names and places' (Munck 1988a: 21).

It is hoped that readers will recognise that there has been a conscious effort throughout the study to avoid the pitfalls of both of the tendencies described above. Though 'structural' factors figure very prominently in the analysis in the following Chapters, readers will also find that the importance of political struggles and their legacy is a recurring theme throughout the study. By constantly being aware of the specific historical and structural context, however, this theme is not raised within a social and political vacuum that offers historical agencies an infinite array of options and possibilities. Thus, it may be said that while there is an effort to avoid a debilitating, formalistic 'functionalism', an equally unsound political 'voluntarism' is rejected as emphatically.[16]

Admittedly, the initial impetus for this study was the rise in 1990–91 of working-class unrest in Indonesia,[17] which continued throughout the first half of the decade. It was quite clear even at the onset that a situation could develop that would contrast sharply with the relative calm of the labour area – aside from periodic outbreaks of industrial action in the late 1970s and early 1980s – that has been maintained throughout most of the New Order period. It also became increasingly clear that state officials were treating the emergence of alternative forms of labour organisation as a political problem, as being in contradiction to the institutional arrangements of state–society predicated upon the control and demobilisation of social forces by the state.

Because of such an impetus, however, there will be criticism from some quarters that there is a bias inherent in the study toward 'organised' forms of activity by workers, and a consequent, unforgivable, underplaying of less tangible, everyday forms of working-class 'resistance' to its social and political subordination.[18] These critics will note that the bias toward organisational capacities will seem at odds with the absence, for most of the New Order, of autonomous, independent, trade unions – institutions which Munck (1988a: 103) has quite rightly called 'the basic organ of workers' self defence'.[19] They might also be concerned that this bias may result in a limited appreciation of the partly spontaneous nature of much of the thousand – some say thousands, of cases of industrial action that took place in Indonesia between 1990 and 1994. In making this criticism, they could be supported to some extent by Munck, who attacks the tendency of other writers to be more concerned with what he calls 'political history' rather than 'social history', with 'organised' rather than 'unorganised' workers, and with 'strike action' rather than 'other forms of labour protests' (Munck 1988a: 9).

There will be those, moreover, who will take exception to the fact that the study entirely focuses on industrial workers, to the detriment of the workers of Indonesia's huge urban (and rural) informal sector, of those employed in commerce and trade activities, in transport or construction, or those struggling in the little-discussed, though historically important, plantations sector. Perhaps causing more discomfort to them, the study even more specifically focuses on the limited, though growing, number of workers employed in the increasingly strategic export-oriented, manufacturing sector. Indeed, critics will be justified to point out that such workers constitute a relatively small proportion of those that may be classified under the broad rubric of 'workers' in contemporary Indonesia, and therefore, may legitimately question the representativeness of manufacturing workers.[20]

Still others will take exception to the largely Jabotabek (Jakarta–Bogor–Tangerang–Bekasi) geographical focus of this study, which they might argue, reveals the lingering influence of Jakarta-centric approaches to Indonesian politics and political economy. To add one more group of potential critics to this now rather long catalogue – there will be others who will regard the historical and comparative interest of this study to be disturbingly 'lofty' and 'removed' from the every day concerns of rank-and-file workers and those that struggle on the ground. They might also regard the relative absence of comprehensive tabulations of the widespread episodes of gross abuse of workers' rights to be suggestive of the politically suspect clinical detachment expected to characterise the impersonal approaches of academics, out to underline their 'neutrality' and 'objectivity'.[21]

It is perhaps appropriate, therefore, that some effort to deal with these inevitable criticisms is made at this early stage, though not necessarily while entertaining the notion that the brief rejoinders offered here will suffice to placate all of them. First, the important issue of the bias toward 'organisational capacities', which indeed, has wide-ranging implications. Admittedly, the emphasis placed here on organisation is rooted in the high value I attach to social movements. Thus, while recognising the importance of less tangible forms of everyday resistance than strike action – usually, though not always – the domain of anthropologists and sociologists, this interest in social movements has naturally led me to an inclination to look at them only if they form the potential basis for the development of more highly organised activity. Such an interest is in turn rooted in the conviction that any success that contemporary workers may achieve in their struggle will, to a significant degree, stem from their ability actively and collectively to exert pressure on both state and capital (again, while being aware of the specific context) to accommodate, at the least, some of their less problematic demands with regard to issues of welfare and particular freedoms. Effective organisation, to the mind of this author, is the only possible instrument of any such active and collective effort.

Does this sit oddly, though, with the absence of independent trade unions, the primary vehicle of working-class struggle, throughout most of the New Order? It is of course recognised here that in spite of the trade union aspirations of some independent, working class-based organisations, many of the vehicles involved in the working-class struggle in recent years have not been trade unions in the traditional sense. Many are instead labour-oriented NGOs, or even looser, more informal organisations, which ostensibly carry out activities as overtly unconfrontational as the promotion of workers' education, their discussion and cultural groups, or limited welfare schemes. As this study makes clear, however, whether such vehicles are adequate to sustain the working-class movement in the long run is still an unresolved question.

Clearly, the prominent role that these non-traditional agents of working-class struggle have played in the 1990s is the direct consequence of the restrictions imposed within the existing arrangement of state–capital–labour relations. However, the strategies that workers in Indonesia have adopted to deal with this situation are by no means unique. Workers in other countries and at other times have had to cope with repressive state policies and an authoritarian environment in similar ways. Useful comparisons could probably be made with the strategies which were adopted by workers in South Korea in the 1980s, where independent trade unionising was also hampered, and so-called 'third parties', often involving NGOs, came to play a prominent role. With this in mind, analogies may also be made with the strategies that workers adopted in politically repressive, pre-trade union, nineteenth-century Europe, where informal and often semi-clandestine organisations played an important role in shaping the nature of working-class politics and served as the basis for the later development of trade unionism (Geary 1981: 42–45).

It may be said that the attention given to those employed in the export-oriented, manufacturing sector is inextricably linked to the above-mentioned interest in organised social movements. The growth of manufacturing industries has brought greater numbers of young men and women into direct contact with the social relations of production embedded in the factory. It has also conjured up the development of sprawling industrial areas around major urban centres that are the site for the emergence of increasingly distinct working-class areas and neighbourhoods. There is some rationale to expect that the experience of everyday life within such a relatively new social milieu would in some ways be conducive to the emergence of significant organisational activity. There is reason to expect greater potential for organisation within these areas even while keeping in mind Deyo's reservations about the organisational capacities of working classes emerging from export-oriented industries. Thus, rather than 'representativeness', the interest has been to locate the type of worker who would be more inclined to organise.

The geographical focus on the Jabotabek area was established on the basis of related considerations. As the site of some the largest, oldest, and most advanced concentrations of manufacturing production, it is more likely that it is within its confines that the conditions conducive to independent organising activities may be present. That workers in East Java and North Sumatra have rapidly 'caught up', though, is evidence that the transformation ushered in by the process of industrialisation is spreading to other areas.[22] In spite of the geographical focus of the study, there is some good reason to suspect that there may be particular features unique to some outlying industrial areas that could actually be supportive of independent organising. Some may suggest, for example, that being further from the gaze of the central government works in favour of organising activities outside of the officially-recognised framework. Others, however, might point out that it is in the regions in particular that workers and activists are most susceptible to overt acts of violence by local state security forces, relatively removed from some of the recent, limited, reforming tendencies emanating from some sections of the central government in Jakarta. At this stage it can only be said that ascertaining what kind of situation actually prevails in specific regions requires a different kind of study with a specialised, more local-level attention.

Finally, it is necessary briefly to address those who might be somewhat disappointed with the absence from this study of 'dramatic' accounts of specific cases of abuse or infringement on the rights of individual or groups of workers – in other words the stuff that usually makes for excellent propaganda. To them, it can only be said that the choices that were made with regard to the emphasis of this study was one that involved both considerations of academic relevance and of political significance. The relative absence of such accounts is not the product of some misguided, and ultimately futile attempt to maintain some kind of 'neutrality' or 'objectivity' that transcends the subject of study, or a disinterest with the plight of 'real persons'. It is simply the outcome of a pragmatic identification of what the study seeks to contribute.

During the course of research it became evident that the kind of accounts in question, though scattered, exist in abundance, and are reasonably easy to compile with some diligence and effort. At the same time, what analysis that does exist has been excessively characterised by either pure moral indignation or a tendency toward romanticisation of the plight of the 'suffering but honourable and strong worker' – devoid of a structural and historical context. I am here referring primarily to the handful of works undertaken by my fellow Indonesians, whether researchers, activists or both. While these works have often contributed the kind of invaluable insight into the everyday hardships of contemporary workers which can only be engendered by a particular kind of intimacy and commendable commitment to subject matter, they have, unfortunately, rarely been directed at tackling the matter of greatest political urgency: the tough implications for organisational activity that arises from an analysis which places the worker within the concrete social, economic and political configuration of very late industrialising, contemporary Indonesia. Such a task is what is attempted in this study.

This introduction began with a picture of the doom and gloom which has characterised recent studies on labour. It pointed out the state of the working-class struggle in the advanced industrial countries, as well as the lack of justification for past optimism about a new period of international working-class solidarity.

Nevertheless, there remain some solid reasons not yet to 'abandon' the working class as a significant historical agency – even in this age when capitalism has apparently triumphed to a degree that has effectively muted most attempts at forging 'alternatives'. With regard to the matter of international working-class solidarity, for example, it was noted that the impact of the internationalisation of the process of production has been contradictory, rather than definitive. Thus, in spite of the obstacles mentioned earlier, there are indications that a more modest, limited level, of solidarity among sections of workers' organisations of different countries has been developing. For example, there is considerable awareness among some sections of the working-class movement in Australia that the horrid conditions of life and work of Indonesian, or Chinese, workers reinforce existing domestic pressure steadily to lower the quality of some of the conditions of life and work of the rank-and-file Australian worker in the name of international competitiveness. Similar concerns of American workers have had some impact on the foreign and human rights policies of the US government. This kind of 'solidarity' grows in large part not from purely altruistic motives, but out of self-interest. But then again this is what one refers to when one talks about 'objective' conditions for trans-national workers' solidarity. Thus, in spite of the current limitations on available options for concerted action by workers across a range of countries, many workers' organisations arguably have demonstrated some realisation, though certainly not to the degree envisaged by such former sages as Levinson, that 'struggles in each nation and each continent' are indeed 'vitally linked' (quoted in Southall 1988b: 26).

Notwithstanding some cases which appear to show conflicting interests, there is no reason to suggest that the working-class movement cannot flourish side by side with the new social movements of environmentalism, feminism, world peace and the like. This is because they are all, to a degree, directed at some critique of different aspects of a prevailing capitalist order that does not prioritise such problems as the continuing presence of massive human deprivation (in the face of the affluence of the few), of various other forms of domination and inequality, of ecological destruction and war. There is evidence that there has been increasing interaction, in some of the advanced as well as less industrialised countries, between worker activists and activists of the various new social movements, in confronting these issues. In Indonesia, for example, activists of independent workers' organisations intermingle on a regular basis with human rights and environmental activists, pro-democracy student demonstrators, and feminists. There is surely something that the working-class movement can contribute, for instance, to countervail the ignorance of some prophets of development of the disastrous ecological implications of envisaging a world order in which several billion of the world's population are eventually geared toward emulating the current consumption pattern of the West's affluent middle classes.

With specific regard to Indonesia, some of the more compelling reasons to direct some attention to the working class is argued in the course of this study. Among these, as mentioned earlier, is the virtually inevitable continued growth and development of this class. As this occurs, workers are sure to develop aspirations and make demands that the current framework of state–society relations is only minimally geared to accommodate. There is little reason to assume, furthermore, the unlimited longevity of this framework in the face of rapid social change brought about by the process of industrialisation. Workers might yet, if organised, contribute to a strengthening of the weak impulse toward democratisation, and therefore, have something to say about how that framework could be modified and redefined in the face of changing social realities.

2 Theoretical and comparative considerations
Labour and the politics of industrialisation

INDUSTRIALISATION AND MODELS OF ACCOMMODATION

The main concern of this Chapter is to explore the historical emergence of different models of accommodation between state, capital and labour within different industrialisation experiences. It is suggested here that the presence or absence of significant working-class movements has had a distinct impact on the development of these models of accommodation, which are in turn linked to the development of different types of social and political frameworks. Three models – which do not exhaust the range of possibilities – are explored here: the 'social democratic', linked with 'liberal democracies'; the 'populist', linked with 'inclusionary corporatism'; and the 'exclusionary', primarily linked with 'exclusionary corporatism'.[1]

Some of the recent work on labour has been influenced by the orthodoxies of modernisation theory, neo-classical economics and that of the New Institutionalism. In modernisation theory, particularly its earlier versions, it is assumed that 'liberal pluralism' is a natural outgrowth of economic modernisation (Hewison et al. 1993: 12). Thus, within that theory, the development of social-democratic trade unionism may be treated as a relatively unproblematic extension of the modernisation process (Frenkel 1993: 5–6).[2] Neo-classical economics, which is almost exclusively concerned with the operations of market forces, sees the outcome of labour struggles as largely pre-determined by the conditions of the labour market (e.g. Manning 1995). In this context, the development of labour movements, for example, is essentially presented as contingent on labour market tightening. New Institutionalism, the origins of which are in rational choice theory, tends to emphasise the workings of institutions (Freeman 1993) in solving 'collective action dilemmas' without taking into account the interests embedded in them and their place in the interplay of class and state forces.[3] Thus, the World Bank, which has incorporated New Institutionalism into its analysis since the mid-1980s, emphasises the development of industrial relations institutions in developing countries, including trade unions, that would not impede, but support, the rational, and therefore beneficial, operations of the market (World Bank 1995).

By contrast, what is employed here is an approach which, on the one hand, emphasises the configuration of class forces, the role of the state, and the timing of industrialisation in both determining the political outcomes of industrialisation, and in creating the context within which working classes and working-class movements emerge. To that extent, it has much in common with the 'structuralist' position discussed below. In this approach, however, models of accommodation between state, capital and labour are also treated as the product of struggle between active historical agencies, which suggests concerns that go beyond those of the structuralist position.

Indeed, in contrast to a rigidly 'structuralist' position, a great deal of importance is attributed in this study to the political struggles waged by historical agencies – within particular contexts. From this viewpoint, the outcome of such concrete struggles creates 'legacies' which, in turn, help to shape the later context and the terms within which the next round of struggles between historical agencies take place. Such a concern, which will inform subsequent Chapters that specifically deal with the Indonesian case, departs considerably from the structuralist orthodoxy, within which the working class in particular usually does not figure at all as an active historical agency.

State, class and the 'timing' of industrialisation: the structuralist approach

The most influential work on the political outcomes of industrialisation is arguably Barrington Moore's *The Social Origins of Dictatorship and Democracy* (1966) which discusses the respective roles of landed oligarchies and bourgeoisies in determining the paths to modernity. Moore was of course primarily concerned to explain (liberal) democracy as the outcome of particular industrialisation experiences and authoritarianism as the outcome of others. On the basis of detailed analysis of a number of historical case studies, he concludes that the bourgeoisie has invariably been the most important agent for the development of democracy, and that conversely, the presence of strong landed classes whose power is based on the exploitation of agricultural labour, has been the most serious impediment to it. Thus, Moore's famous dictum, 'No bourgeoisie, no democracy' (Moore 1966: 418). Needless to say, the working class is virtually nowhere to be seen in Moore's scheme of things.

Another pioneer in the literature is Alexander Gerschenkron (1962), who emphasised the importance of the timing of industrialisation in determining the extent of state dominance over economic development and sought to explain the differences between the European countries that industrialised earlier (Britain and France) and those that industrialised later (like Germany and Italy). He argued that the more backward a country, and delayed its industrial development, the more likely that its industrialisation would proceed under the direction of the state. This, according to Gerschenkron, explains the emergence in the later industrialisers of authoritarian governments, whose function was to mobilise capital or repress wages and consumption (Kurth 1979: 323). Thus, the development of a relatively laissez-faire state in Britain is attributed to the fact that the British capitalist class was able to spearhead the process of industrialisation with relatively little state protection and finance.

Albert Hirschman (1968) considered the even later industrialisers of Latin America. According to Hirschman, these countries showed little of the inspiring 'elan' that was characteristic of late-industrialising Germany, Russia and Japan, because their industrialisations 'started with relatively small plants administering "last touches" to a host of imported products, concentrated on consumer rather than producer goods'.[4] Importantly, he also observed that the industrialists associated with these experiences were more willing to ally themselves politically with conservative, traditional, landed interests, and thus did not pose a significant challenge to their political dominance. To Hirschman, then, the strong authoritarian impulse in Latin American societies is attributable to the timidity of its weak bourgeoisie.

Clearly, Hirschman's conclusions about the political consequences of the relationship between the landed oligarchy and the fledgling bourgeoisie of Latin America fit comfortably with those of Moore. Significantly, like Moore, neither Hirschman nor Gerschenkron considered the importance of the presence or absence of substantial working-class movements in determining the political outcomes of the industrialisation process, nor paid any attention to the models of accommodation between state, capital, and labour embodied within them.

In an important critique of Moore, Therborn (1977) distinguishes between the advent of bourgeois revolutions and the establishment of (liberal) democracy, arguing that the latter was an outcome inextricably linked to working-class struggles – represented by trade unions and socialist parties – of the nineteenth century.[5] A similar, but more detailed, argument is presented in Rueschemeyer et al. (1992), who argue that, historically, the democratic impulse has been weakest where organised labour has not been strong.[6] Importantly, 'democracy' is also presented in the latter study as essentially a class compromise, in which the interests of the contending forces within capitalism are accommodated to varying degrees (Rueschemeyer et al. 1992: 272). Such a view suggests that liberal-democratic social and political frameworks involve a particular form of accommodation between capital, labour and the state. It is on the basis of such a recognition that we may proceed to look at social and political frameworks other than that of liberal democracy, linked to models of accommodation different from those that emerged from the European industrialisation experience, and to assess the position of the working class within them.

However, if the importance of the presence or absence of substantial working-class movements in helping to shape the political outcomes of the first industrialisations in Europe has been relatively overlooked, the role of such movements in later industrialisations has tended to be even more neglected. In part, this is attributable to the relative weakness of the working class itself in these societies because the uneven nature of industrialisation in the 'Third World' has meant that for the most part, their working classes have remained small, and their working-class movements have emerged under inhospitable circumstances. The important works of O'Donnell (1973) on Latin America and Deyo (1989) on East Asia largely typify the way in which the working class has been treated within the mainstream of the structuralist literature.

O'Donnell identified two distinct phases of industrialisation in Latin America and suggested their different political consequences. The early or 'easy' phase of import substitution industrialisation (ISI) is said to have expanded the urban middle and working classes, who were then included in populist coalitions. However, as this 'easy' phase (based on the production of consumer goods) depended on revenues deriving from the export of primary products – used to import capital goods – Latin American economies were always vulnerable to the vicissitudes of demand in the world market. Thus, this phase came to an end when a balance of payments crisis arose as the result of declining demand for such primary products.

In O'Donnell's analysis, the resolution of the crisis appeared in the form of industrial deepening through the development of a capital goods sector. This required the reduction of popular consumption in order to raise the level of domestic investment. A larger role for foreign, multinational corporations was also required. In order to ensure the success of this development strategy and to stave off opposition from the popular sector, including the labour movement, authoritarian forms of control had to be imposed by the state. To O'Donnell, the 'bureaucratic authoritarian' regimes of Latin America which emerged as an outcome of the latter phase of ISI, propped up by a coalition of civilian technocrats, the military and the big bourgeoisie, were essentially geared to curb the power of organised labour (Rueschemeyer *et al.* 1992: 22).

Following on the structuralist orthodoxy, the notion of the increasing centrality of the state's role in progressively later industrialisation experiences has greatly influenced the literature on the still-later industrialisation of the East Asian NICs. Deyo for example suggests that

> Strong, developmentalist states have been important in guiding and orchestrating rapid industrialisation in Singapore, South Korea, and Taiwan, especially during the economic restructuring of the 1970s. These states ... have been sufficiently insulated from the political forces that typically compromise technocratic 'rationality' in other Third World countries.
>
> (Deyo 1987: 182)

Significantly, Deyo also suggests that, 'this state autonomy from social forces has been rooted in the political subordination of organised labour'.

He argues that '[d]isciplined and low-cost labour, in East Asia even more than elsewhere, has been a prerequisite for development' (Deyo 1987: 182). Deyo contrasts this situation with that of Latin America, where industrialisation oriented toward the domestic market minimised the need to maintain internationally competitive labour costs as a basis for growth. Suggesting that ISI in Latin America 'encouraged stimulation of domestic purchasing power to support industrial development', he concludes that this 'fostered the growth of broad, developmental coalitions of the urban middle classes, industrialists, state bureaucrats, and unionised workers' and 'partially muted the contrary pressure from employers to restrict labour costs and justified government efforts to increase welfare expenditures by firms and the state for workers' (Deyo 1987: 183).

Structuralist accounts do go a considerable way in explaining the options available to states and other political actors in particular historical contexts. In relation to labour, they suggest useful explanations in dealing with the specific environments that emerging working-class movements have to contend with. They fail, however, to take adequately into account the strategies that the working class adopts to cope with these environments. Furthermore, they fail to give due recognition to the way these strategies, in turn, can also impact on the policies pursued by state and capital and therefore help to influence how these environments are shaped.

In O'Donnell's analysis of Latin America, for example, the degree of political inclusion attained by the working class is, in effect, attributed simply to the designs of state elites.[7] The ability of the working class to organise and partly to deter attempts to subordinate it politically at crucial points in history is largely overlooked. Significantly, the crux of Deyo's most important work (1989) is devoted to elaborating the sources of the continuing weakness of organised labour in the East Asian NICs, an endeavour not wholly suited to deal with the great wave of labour unrest in South Korea beginning in the late 1980s, as well as the significant, though much less conspicuous, upsurge in Taiwan (Frenkel 1993: 12).

Bringing historical agency 'back in'?

According to Munck, various strategies of labour protest and resistance are rooted in the very process of proletarianisation associated with industrialisation and urbanisation. This process, he argues, 'concentrated workers in a locality, facilitated communications and the organisation of collective action'. Furthermore, just as capital follows various strategies to assure the process of accumulation, he argues that 'the working class constantly devises counter-strategies, which in turn, modify capital's approach'. His position, in essence, is one which presents the working class as a distinctly more active political actor than is conceded in analyses that treat it as mere recipients of the strategies adopted by state and capital (Munck 1988a: 141).

Implied in Munck's position is an assertion of the centrality of the notion of struggles between historical agencies – including those involving the working class – in helping to shape the very contexts within which further struggles take place. Unfortunately, the way in which this assertion can be usefully incorporated into concrete analysis is largely left unsatisfactorily treated by Munck.

Several issues need to be raised in order to 'bring back' into the analysis the role of struggles between historical agencies. With reference to the working class, one of these involves the conditions that affect the strategies adopted by different working-class movements in different environments. The experiences of diverse working-class movements show that these strategies are in part accounted for by the specific, nationally defined, political and economic terrain which they encounter. This in itself would not entail any serious departure from the structuralist position mentioned earlier. As structuralists would contend, the strategies of state and dominant classes toward labour are crucial in shaping the responses, ideologies and strategies of the working class.

Conversely, however, another point which needs to be explored is the impact of working-class movements on state policy and on the strategies of dominant classes. For example, some Latin American states of the 1930s and 1940s clearly had to consider the presence of fairly well-developed organised labour movements before selecting industrial policy options, certainly to a greater degree than the states of the East Asian NICs have had to do more recently. A political strategy of partial incorporation of the interests of organised labour within the framework of ISI strategy was more plausible in the Latin American circumstance, as Deyo indeed suggests. To give another example, state and capital in Bismarckian Germany adopted a much more reactionary strategy in dealing with organised labour than their contemporaries in Britain partly because they confronted a labour movement that was ideologically more radical. Such a situation made the development of a social-democratic accommodation between state, capital and labour a much more turbulent process in Germany than in Britain, and also hindered the establishment of a liberal-democratic social and political framework.

In presenting the working class as an active historical agency, a crucial point of discussion is the organisational capacity of the working class. This relates to such factors as the size and type of working class that emerges in the industrialisation process, though some care needs to be taken when pre-determining the 'preparedness' of particular working classes to organise. For example, it is readily apparent that substantial, more urbanised working classes, concentrated in sizeable industrial areas, are more inclined toward organisation, particularly if industrialisation entails the development of relatively homogeneous working-class areas of residence, usually conducive to the emergence of class identity and solidarity. Indeed, it is precisely when urban residence is perceived as being more or less permanent (Hanagan 1986), and when participation in capitalist relations of production becomes intensified, as within the modern factory, that a better social base for working-class organisation emerges (e.g. Rueschemeyer *et al.* 1992: 271).[8]

At the same time, however, it should be recognised that under particular historical circumstances, agrarian industry-based workers have also mobilised effectively in the absence of a substantial urban proletariat. An example is the largely plantation worker-based labour movement of the first decades of the twentieth century that was part of the early stage of the anti-colonial struggle in Indonesia, though the fragility of the movement – rooted in the limited extent of industrialisation and proletarianisation – was ultimately exposed in the face of state repression. Similar working-class movements developed earlier this century across Southeast and East Asia, primarily linked with anti-colonial political movements.

Some (e.g. Deyo 1989) have argued that higher skill, capital and technology-based, and male-dominated industries, provide a better setting for workers' organisations in the NICs of East Asia. The assertion fits nicely with the experience of the first industrialisers of Europe insofar as the first workers who organised and participated in strike action regularly were usually from among the better-skilled and more secure ranks of workers (Geary 1981: 17), rather than those most impoverished or powerless. Significantly, however, workers employed in relatively smaller light industries, such as textiles, and those employed in heavier industry alike seemed to have been involved in the European labour struggles of the nineteenth century, the latter being more predominant in Britain and the former in such later industrialisers as Germany, given their respective industrial structures. In the European experience, there is some evidence which suggests that workers employed in heavier, larger-scale industry tended to be radicalised more easily (Geary 1981: 17), presumably because they were pitted against powerful employers, often backed by the might of the state, and because they encountered particularly stifling structures of authority within firms.

At the same time, however, it is clear that what organising is occurring among workers in contemporary Indonesia is largely concentrated in female-dominated, low-skill, labour-intensive industries so central to the success of the export-led industrialisation strategy, as is the case across Southeast Asia. It appears that the tendency toward militancy and radicalisation may also be enhanced if the labour struggle entails frequent direct confrontation with the state's repressive apparatus, as was probably the case in South Korea in the 1980s, some Latin American countries at particular times, and more so in late nineteenth-century Germany than in Britain. Even in the latter case, writers like E.P. Thompson have emphasised how the experience of engaging in concrete confrontation with state and employer, combined with the conditions of life and work, helped to shape the social and political sensibilities of the working class of late eighteenth- and early nineteenth-century England (Thompson 1968).

Importantly, the working classes of the much later industrialisers of Asia are pitted against capital which is much more highly mobile than that faced by workers in Europe during the formative period of its working-class movements. This greatly impacts on the options currently available to the working classes in later industrialising Asia. On the one hand, such a situation may stifle organisation among workers – as the threat of capital relocation always looms large – or conversely, help to radicalise whatever organisation takes place, precisely because of the experience of having to wage a struggle within particularly inhospitable terrains. Working-class movements emerging in currently industrialising countries that are characterised by chronic excess labour supply seem to be particularly badly placed, given the ease with which the militant worker can be replaced by someone more compliant from the long unemployment line. Nevertheless, the relationship between high unemployment and low labour militancy seems to be more complex than the one suggested by neo-classical economists, given that, for example, Luddism and Chartism occurred in Britain in the context of acute unemployment, that economic insecurity provided 'the mainstay of support for the German Communist Party (KPD) between the wars' (Geary 1981: 16), and the experiences of some Latin American countries.

An additional important issue that requires exploration concerns the political legacies bequeathed to working-class movements and the political ideologies that are available to them. Latin American working-class movements clearly inherited the legacy of European (particularly Southern European) labour struggles through large-scale immigration, which gave rise to strong socialist as well as anarcho-syndicalist tendencies. The German working-class movement emerged along with the rise of socialist ideology, a fact which must have contributed to its greater politicisation compared to the British movement which was already on its way to an accommodation with state and capital before some of the great upheavals in Europe of the second half of the nineteenth century. It has been suggested that the political development of the working class in France in the nineteenth century is inexplicable without consideration of the legacy of the French Revolution (Katznelson 1986: 33). In such post-colonial societies as Indonesia, where the labour movement initially emerged in conjunction with the rise of a militantly anti-colonial nationalism, radical political ideologies have figured into its chequered history and provide an important legacy.

PATHS TO ACCOMMODATION: THE POLITICS OF LABOUR

This section presents an exploration of the different historical experiences that have given rise to a variety of models of accommodation between state, capital and labour. Throughout, the emphasis is on understanding the specific contexts within which different working classes and their movements have emerged, as well as the impact of the political struggles waged by them within these contexts. It is through such an understanding that we may be able to appreciate more fully the structural and historical contexts within which contemporary working-class struggles are taking place in Indonesia as well as the significance of these struggles.

The first industrialisers and the 'social-democratic' model of accommodation

Industrialisation began at different times in the various European countries, within which the social-democratic accommodation historically emerged, and in the context of a different balance of class forces. Thus, the working class and its organisations appeared in a variety of political environments, and confronted states and capitalist classes with quite different characteristics. As is argued by the structuralists, this affected some of the strategies that emerging working-class movements adopted in the various countries. Significantly, the later industrialisation took place, and the more central the state's directing role, the more difficult the terrain appeared to have been for the working class.

The labour historian Geary asks why the British working class tended to eschew radical political strategies in comparison to its counterparts on the Continent. In answer to his own question, he suggests that

> The relative liberalism and non-interventionism of the British state, the willingness of many British employers to deal with trade unions, the continuing strength of liberal-constitutionalist values among sections of the British population *outside* of the working class – all of these go a long way in explaining the relative moderation of British workers, the dominance of trade union, rather than radical political strategies, and the relatively small support achieved by explicitly socialist organisations. Where a bourgeoisie is weak or tied to an existing authoritarian state, as in Russia before the First World War, or in countries where the middle class increasingly abandons liberal values and comes to support semi-authoritarian political systems, as was the case of Imperial Germany . . . , the prospects for working-class liberalism appear to be weaker, whilst political radicalism on the part of labour becomes more marked. Conversely, the Republican traditions of at least sections of the French bourgeoisie and the buoyant liberalism of the British middle class enable a fair proportion of workers to remain in the liberal camp.
>
> (Geary 1989a: 2–3)

He also observes that

> a repressive state apparatus can transform economic into revolutionary struggles through direct military intervention . . . .The prohibition of legal channels of protest could lead protest over wages and working conditions into violent insurrection . . . .On the other hand, the relatively liberal institutions of late nineteenth century Britain obviously bear some responsibility for working class reformism.
>
> (Geary 1981: 20)

The experience of the first industrialisers of Europe also demonstrates, however, that the struggles waged by the working class may, in turn, influence the strategies adopted by states and bourgeoisies. Threatened by radical working-class movements – which emerged precisely because of the difficult terrain – both of these may be encouraged to adopt increasingly authoritarian and repressive strategies. Such a situation conceivably made the emergence of the social-democratic accommodation between state, capital, and labour a more turbulent process than in cases where they encountered working-class reformism.

The driving force behind the first industrialisation experience, that of Britain, was a bourgeoisie that presided over a process that was largely propelled by the light consumer goods sector, in particular textiles. Kurth (1979) argues that this was attributable to the fact that the production of such goods required relatively small amounts of capital, so dependence on state protection and finance was avoided. This experience was, it may be said, replicated in the next industrialiser, France, although bourgeois ascendance took place here less smoothly. In the case of later industrialising Germany, however, the development of a capital goods sector encouraged the authoritarian alliance between the bourgeoisie and the landed interests which dominated the state, as the large amounts of capital required for industrial deepening could only be obtained through state finance (Geary 1981: 26).[9]

By 1848 – the year of revolutionary upheaval in continental Europe – the scope and extent of industrialisation in the major European countries varied quite widely, as did the extent to which their respective working classes had developed (Geary 1981: 25–26). By this time Britain had had a century of rapid industrial development and many forms of working-class movements had appeared and made their impact, the most prominent of which were Luddism and Chartism, as well as trade unionism. Even by the early nineteenth century, Britain possessed a comparatively large industrial sector.[10] When workers in France, Germany and, later, Russia were developing strategies to deal with state repression, working-class organisations in Britain were already operating within a relatively relaxed political environment.[11]

In France the bourgeoisie was engaged in a protracted battle with the old aristocracy for control of the state, often with the support of the growing working class.[12] The latter, however, subsequently experienced the consequences of 'betrayal' by the bourgeoisie when its troops fiercely repressed an insurrection by workers in the so-called June Days of 1848 (Geary 1981: 41; Magraw 1989: 54). This left a legacy which made cooperation and peaceful accommodation somewhat difficult and helped to ensure that French organised labour would tend to espouse more radical ideologies – anarchism and socialism, fused with the political language of rights inherited from the French Revolution (Katznelson 1986: 34) – than their British counterparts (Geary 1981: 60–61). In the German states, significantly, the working-class movement developed at a time when Marxism and socialist ideologies were rapidly gaining influence (Katznelson 1986: 40).[13] Here, the bourgeoisie had found an ally in the conservative German states dominated by the landed oligarchy. In contrast to Britain, German employers, especially the larger ones in heavy industry, refused to deal with labour unions (Geary 1989a: 4). Nevertheless, the Wilhelmine state wavered from time to time between an authoritarianism and semi-liberalism which, in part, accounts for the fact that the German working-class movement itself wavered between reformism and radicalism (Geary 1981: 20).[14]

However, a vicious circle begins to emerge from an explanation that concentrates exclusively on the influence of actions taken by state and bourgeoisie on the political character of nascent working-class movements, because at the same time, working-class radicalism seemed to have caused states and bourgeoisies to adopt more conservative, if not reactionary, strategies. The German state and bourgeoisie were certainly more wary of a working-class movement which more enthusiastically embraced revolutionary Marxism than were their British counterparts of one based on reformist trade unionism (Geary 1981: 68). Perhaps much the same may be said for those in Russia who later confronted the threat of Bolshevism, which in part accounts for the failure of the social-democratic accommodation to emerge there.

Moreover, the Luddite and Chartist experiences suggest that the contrast between Britain and the European Continent in the latter half of the nineteenth century was as stark as the contrast between Britain in the first and Britain in the second half of that same century. In this sense the relative tolerance that the British bourgeoisie and state displayed toward organised labour by the mid-nineteenth century could be interpreted as the result of long experience of unsuccessfully quelling working-class action through brute force. From this point of view, the liberalism of the British bourgeoisie and state can be seen, in part, as the product of experience in dealing with earlier workers' struggles.

Thus, European revolutionaries of the nineteenth century lamented that the British working-class movement was too politically reformist, in spite of its strength (Kelly 1988: 11). While French working-class organisations continued to embrace revolutionary ideologies well into the twentieth century, they too were eventually accommodated in a manner that was, though more tumultuous than in Britain, less turbulent than in the later industrialisers. In the case of Germany, the process of establishing the social-democratic accommodation was so protracted that it was only firmly in place following the country's defeat in World War II (after having led a precarious existence during the Weimar government).[15]

Notwithstanding the differences in the way the social-democratic model of accommodation was achieved in the different cases discussed, it was clearly always the eventual outcome of a long struggle on the part of the working class. As mentioned earlier, the development of this model of accommodation is linked to the establishment of wider liberal democratic social and political frameworks insofar as the latter, as argued by Therborn and Rueschemeyer *et al.*, are predicated upon the exertion of the same working-class pressure. Such frameworks are characterised by popular political participation through representative parliaments (and sometimes directly elected executives), free elections and – particularly important to the working class – freedom of association.[16]

A major characteristic of the social-democratic model of accommodation which emerged from some European experiences is the maintenance of the autonomy of working-class organisations from the state, insofar as they confine themselves to activities in the immediate social-economic field. Workers are also guaranteed relatively high standards of living, including through the assurance of welfare benefits (hence, the 'welfare state'), in exchange for forfeiting the highly political, socialist project. Thus, the survival of the basic framework of capitalism and the dominance of the bourgeoisie is assured.

Throughout most of the twentieth century the social-democratic model of accommodation has proved to be the most resilient of the models discussed here, though in recent decades, as noted earlier, new tensions are arising in advanced capitalist countries that may force radical readjustments.[17]

The Latin American experience and the 'populist' model of accommodation

Different models of accommodation between state, capital and labour have been the product of later industrialisation experiences. The position of the working class in these later models of accommodation became progressively weaker, as working-class movements confronted increasingly hostile social and political environments.

In the later industrialisations of Latin America, the working class encountered bourgeoisies that were politically dependent and closely aligned with traditional, landed oligarchies whose interests were intertwined with that of the state. Significantly, however, the states encountered were in no way as consolidated and capable of playing the directing role in the industrialisation process as the German Bismarckian state, for example, was able to. Indeed, unlike the main European cases discussed earlier, foreign capital played an exceedingly central role in the industrialisation process of Latin America, which further reflected the weakness of its bourgeoisie. Such a situation, however, provided the opportunity for working-class movements to develop in spite of concerted state repression, which seemed to succeed only in encouraging their radical tendencies.

Indeed, from the European experience, Latin American labour movements had a ready-made set of tactics, strategies, ideologies and forms of organisation to choose from, in part made available by large-scale immigration of working people from Europe in the nineteenth and early twentieth centuries (Spalding 1977: 37). Prominent among them were those associated with various forms of socialism and communism, and the anarcho-syndicalism particularly prominent in Southern Europe, from where most of these immigrants originated. The success of the Bolshevik Revolution was also a major influence on the labour movement (Collier and Collier 1991: 62). It was only with the consolidation of state power with the later emergence of regimes such as that of Vargas in Brazil and Perón in Argentina that a model of accommodation between state, capital and labour – the 'populist' – was successfully developed.

Initially, the influence of radical ideologies on many Latin American working-class movements seemed to have encouraged authoritarian tendencies within the fragmented, but repressive states. These tendencies were of course mainly directed at the working class. While middle-class employees, the urban petty bourgeoisie and professionals could organise themselves quite early on into interest groups and political parties, the organisations of the working class continued to be restricted (Rueschemeyer *et al.* 1992: 185–186) and were subject to acts of suppression by the police or the army (Collier and Collier 1991: 6). Here, however, the vicious circle alluded to earlier emerges again: state repression, in turn, seemed to have discouraged the development of a reformist stream in the working-class movement. Thus, as in Europe, there appears to have been a relationship between the experience of repression and the attractiveness of radical strategies and ideologies.

In spite of this hostile political environment, workers' organisations continued to grow in many Latin American countries. If in the nineteenth century they commonly took the form of mutual-aid societies, by the time of World War I, the predominant vehicles of workers' organisation were labour unions, federations and confederations (Spalding 1977: 2). While the course of development of working-class movements in the different Latin American countries varied considerably (again as in Europe), there was a similarity across the countries in that by the 1920s – which brought about relative prosperity, urban expansion and further growth of the working-class – rural workers still constituted an important element of this class. Indeed, a large section of the working class by this time was still employed in huge agricultural enterprises that produced primarily for export, spurred on particularly by foreign capital, especially American and British. Other wage labourers were employed in foreign-owned mines, oil fields and on cattle ranches (Spalding 1977: 64–66). However, as industrialisation continued to a more significant degree with the growth of the manufacturing sector, a more numerous urban-based industrial working class also began to develop, although the pace of industrialisation was slow compared to the European experiences already discussed.[18] Its especially prominent development in Argentina contributed to the comparatively greater strength of that country's labour movement, which was, for example, able to mobilise large numbers of workers in huge general strikes.

As the problems of industrialisation became more complex, states had to set out a more sophisticated policy for dealing with the presence of the growing working classes and of their movements. Again state elites must have learned in this latter stage from later European experiences which demonstrated that organised labour could, somehow, be accommodated and therefore, did not necessarily constitute a revolutionary threat (Rueschemeyer *et al.* 1992: 283). Indeed, Kurth suggests the populist brand of politics that developed in Latin America was the political response of elites to the growth of a local working class and their interpretation of the European experience. Its essence was the preemptive organisation and cooptation of the working class from above (Kurth 1979: 357–358).

The culmination of this process of cooptation took place in Brazil under Vargas in the 1930s and in Argentina under Perón in the 1940s (Collier and Collier 1991: 7). Vargas' 'New State' provided the framework for the control of the labour movement by establishing unions for every group of workers, as well as employers and professionals. Existing trade unions had to submit themselves to stringent supervision by the Ministry of Industry, Commerce and Labour. Significantly, however, they also functioned as the agency through which the state distributed social welfare programs (Collier and Collier 1991: 746). Such state patronage effectively meant that trade unions became tied to the government financially in an unprecedented manner (Alexander 1963 :156–157). In Perón's Argentina the emphasis of the incorporation was on the mobilisation of working class support for the state (Collier and Collier 1991: 746).[19] In fact, Perónism developed into a political movement that was more or less consciously based on trade unions (Alexander 1963: 164). As a result, however, the autonomy of the working-class movement from the state was severely compromised as a more centralised industrial relations system was established to ensure greater state control.[20]

Notwithstanding their differences, the Latin American experiences discussed above demonstrate an alternative way in which an accommodation was struck between state, capital and labour. Its essence was the partial political inclusion of organised labour in return for support of the state's political and economic agenda. The basis for the accommodation was the existence of working-class movements too weak to push for a significant opening of the political system through the extension of democratic institutions, but too strong to be stamped out by force. The relative weakness of the working-class movement was in turn rooted in the lateness and unevenness of industrialisation, which ensured that large sections of the population remained outside of the constituency of organised labour.[21] The populist model was inextricably linked to the wider development of a social and political framework which may be described as being 'inclusionary-corporatist', characterised by the prevalence of state-legitimated, monolithic, non-competitive institutions, which at the same time had significant representational and mobilisational roles. It is in relation to such roles that the populist model of accommodation also rests on the improvement of workers' welfare levels – particularly of the more privileged, unionised, minority in the formal sector of the economy.

A source of tension and contradiction, however, was always present in the model because populist ideology and rhetoric ensured that the demands of the popular sector would always grow. Since a revolutionary transformation of society was never the real aim of the regimes of Vargas or Perón, the disjuncture between rhetoric and reality grew as the ISI strategy based on consumer goods could not be maintained (Spalding 1977: 196–197), as mentioned earlier, because of balance of payment problems. These disjunctures came to reach more serious proportions in the 1950s and 1960s, as Latin American states turned to an ISI strategy of industrial deepening that was more dependent on foreign capital. In Brazil this disjuncture was finally resolved by the seizure of power by an anti-labour military regime in 1964. In Argentina, where organised labour was gradually peripheralised politically after the fall of Perón in 1955, successive governments came to power with which workers' organisations had to struggle to maintain their privileged position. After the brief return to power of Perónism in 1973–76, a military government took over which was bent on breaking the back of organised labour (Munck 1988b).

The tenuous nature of the populist accommodation, however, also meant that the legacy of radical political ideologies would continue to help shape the political character of working-class movements in many Latin American countries. This was especially because under the terms of the accommodation, organised labour remained politicised, not being so strictly confined to the social-economic realm. Such is certainly the case in Argentina, where the legacy of Perónism continues to imbue the working-class movement with a radical populism that remains influential, and arguably, is of considerable importance in reactivating the democratic impulse in society following the fall from power of the military regime in the early 1980s. Radical unionism also re-emerged in Brazil in the late 1970s (Collier and Collier 1991: 756–757). Here the labour movement also played an important part in the strengthening of the democratic impulse in society following the fall of the military regime (Keck 1989: 282–289).

The East Asian Experience and the 'exclusionary' model of accommodation I

Emerging working classes and labour movements in the East Asian NICs (South Korea, Taiwan, Singapore and Hong Kong) have had to confront states which play a more central role in the industrialisation process than in the countries of Latin America or the first industrialisers of Europe.[22] They have also had to participate in a model of accommodation in which the interests of labour are considerably more subordinated than in the previously discussed models. Under this 'exclusionary' model of accommodation, the political marginalisation of the working class is more complete, and its demobilisation as a social force likewise, although as we shall see, in some cases the very progress of industrialisation may be creating some conditions that are more amenable to the development of more substantial working-class organisation. The model of accommodation is usually linked to social and political frameworks which may be described as exclusionary corporatist. Such frameworks are characterised by the arrangement of state–society relations on the basis of state-controlled and established, monolithic and non-competitive institutions, geared to facilitate the control and demobilisation of society-based organisations and movements, including those of the working class.

In contrast to the Latin American cases, the states of the East Asian NICs were free to embark on policy choices with little consideration of the interests of an organised working class either because the latter was not historically present or had been demolished during earlier struggles. Indeed, the exclusionary model of accommodation in East Asia has usually been rooted in struggles between historical agencies particular to periods which preceded the advent of export-led industrialisation itself (Deyo 1987: 183–186; Deyo *et al.* 1987: 43–48). These struggles were the product of a drive to curb the influence of important left-wing or radical streams in the existing labour movements prior to EOI. Significantly, the export-led strategy was largely based, particularly in the crucial early period, on the maintenance of an abundant, cheap and politically docile labour force. Thus, spearheading the industrialisation of South Korea, Taiwan, Singapore and Hong Kong were such labour-intensive and low-technology industries as textiles, garments and footwear.[23]

In South Korea, efforts to curtail the growth of militant unionism were made by the dictator Syngman Rhee well before the early 1960s reorientation to EOI. In the context of the Cold War, concerns about the possibility of the rise of communist influence brought the government to suppress the labour movement with the support of the United States. In fact, it was during the period of American occupation that a communist-led labour grouping was crushed and replaced by a right-wing organisation which eventually evolved into the state-sponsored, and staunchly anti-communist, Federation of Korean Trade Unions (FKTU) (Deyo *et al.* 1987: 44; Kim 1993: 135–136). Authoritarian controls over labour were then reinforced and intensified during the EOI period.

Similar developments can be discerned in the cases of Singapore and Taiwan. In Singapore, left-wing elements in the labour movement, which had been active during the anti-colonial struggle, were eradicated by Lee Kuan Yew in the early years of his rule. Indeed, the National Trade Union Congress (NTUC) was created by the state largely to curb the influence of left-wing trade unionists (Deyo *et al.* 1987: 45–46). As in the case of South Korea, increasingly stringent controls were imposed upon the labour movement following the advent of the export-led industrialisation strategy. In part, controls over labour were intensified, though not initiated, to make Singapore more attractive to foreign capital (Leggett 1993a: 118–119).

In Taiwan, the political exclusion of labour was part and parcel of the political system that operated after the promulgation of martial law in 1949, and was only lifted in 1987. Under the system of one-party rule there was little room for independent unionism as the leaders of the Kuomintang realised at an early stage the importance of pre-empting the development of autonomous working-class organisations (Deyo *et al.* 1987: 44; Frenkel *et al.* 1993: 163). In addition, geopolitical considerations were likely to have been as prominent in Taiwan in influencing the direction of state policy toward labour as they were in South Korea: if the latter faced the threat of communist insurgency from the North, the Kuomintang rulers of Taiwan were wary of mainland communist invasion.

Of the four original NICs, Hong Kong represents a deviation. Here, a colonial administration influenced by laissez-faire ideas encouraged the development of Western-style trade unionism. But even in this colony the threat of the incursion of communist influence from mainland China would have constituted a factor that considerably influenced state policy toward labour organisations. Thus, when a distinctly political, anti-colonial orientation began to influence organised labour in the 1950s, the state responded by arresting and deporting militant workers and union leaders. Reinforcing the point about the need to stamp out left-wing influence, it is notable that the government again clamped down on the activities of trade unions after a series of disturbances took place in 1967 which involved radical unionists (Levin and Chiu 1993: 187).

The cases discussed above demonstrate that the exclusionary model of accommodation in the East Asian NICs is a legacy of struggles prior to the advent of the EOI strategy. Notably, however, the specific form it takes has varied significantly from country to country. For example, variations in its implementation may allow for a larger role for control mechanisms at the enterprise level and a less directly repressive state role. In South Korea the state has played a much more direct role in labour affairs than in Taiwan, where labour discipline is more rooted in employment relations at the level of the firm. Here, a kind of company welfarism has been promoted to develop worker loyalty. A change in that direction has also subsequently taken place in Singapore (Deyo *et al.* 1987: 48). In spite of some shift to enterprise level controls in South Korea more recently, state repression continues to be a feature of labour relations, which may partly explain the continuing greater attractiveness of radical strategies to Korean workers (see Ogle 1990).

One issue which arises from the industrialisation experience of the East Asian NICs is whether rapid, successful industrialisation provides some of the conditions that favour the development of more significant working-class movements. Deyo suggests that the very characteristics of the industries which have underpinned the successful industrialisation of the East Asian NICs provide structural obstacles to the development of a working-class movement. In fact, he attributes what he sees as the relative political docility of workers in the East Asian NICs to the nature of employment in the industries which have been crucial to this EOI strategy. These industries are defined by the predominance of young, low-skilled, often female workers whose employment is characterised by low pay and lack of job security or career mobility. This in turn encourages low job commitment, high levels of turnover and a low degree of attachment to work groups or firms. According to Deyo, all of this constrains the development of working-class solidarity, independent organising and militancy (Deyo 1989: 8, 168–195). He also argues that the counterparts of such workers in the generally higher-skilled, male-dominated, heavy industries sector – where the workforce tends to be less transient – have been more successful in developing high levels of organisation and in winning their demands (Deyo 1989: 194–195).

Nevertheless, the structural impediments Deyo describes may not be as insurmountable as he suggests. This is indicated by the political resurgence of labour in South Korea in the late 1980s (Ogle 1990; Kim 1993; Koo 1993) which not only involved male-dominated industries such as automobiles and shipping, but also workers of low-wage and low-skilled industries, with predominantly female workforces. Indeed, militant labour, together with some politicised sections of the middle class, particularly the NGO and radicalised student movements, emerged as a potent political combination (AMRC 1987; Ogle 1990) that undermined the monopoly of the FKTU as the sole state-sponsored workers' peak organisation. In 1990, an alternative peak trade union organisation emerged, though it has subsequently been on the receiving end of government suppression (Kim 1993: 145–147). Wage increases were utilised in an attempt to slow down the extraordinary growth of labour unrest, which contrasts sharply with the employment of sheer force that would have been the preferred option of the state in earlier times (Cumings 1989: 30). Significantly, the resurgence of the labour movement has had a substantial role in activating the democratic impulse in South Korean society (Potter 1993). In spite of these advances, the extent to which these considerable achievements can be safeguarded in the near future is unclear, as a new wave of anti-unionism has emerged even more recently (Kim 1993: 159–160).

In Taiwan, working-class activism began in the early 1980s, in the context of the inhospitable political conditions of martial law. Following the demise of martial law in 1987, new-style unions began to emerge that have demonstrated 'their independence . . . and a willingness to engage in industrial action to assert their members' legal rights'. According to Frenkel *et al.*, such organisations are in the vanguard of the workers' movement. Furthermore, their presence indicates how the process of democratisation has been interconnected with the emergence of opposition political parties with an interest in securing working-class support (Frenkel *et al.* 1993: 184). Indeed, working-class activism has been significant enough for newly formed opposition political parties to try quickly to establish significant working-class constituencies in the post-martial law period (Chu 1993).

In Singapore, rapid industrialisation has not produced many signs of working-class unrest. State controls and welfarism at the enterprise level have been much more successful in containing independent labour organising and unrest, although, with some 'demoralising' effects to the rank and file. This is reflected in the difficulty the NTUC has found in continuing to attract younger workers (Leggett 1993b: 242–243). In the case of Hong Kong – where Levin and Chiu generally agree with the conclusions of Deyo regarding the innate organisational problems of labour forces emerging out of export-led industrialisation – the independent-wing of the union movement has, nevertheless, 'become more outspoken and involved politically'. Indeed, even here there have been 'signs of renewed workplace militancy'. Still, the uncertain political future of the colony complicates the prospects of the already traditionally fragmented workers' movement in Hong Kong (Levin and Chiu 1993: 220–222).[24]

Whatever its limitations, the resurgence in working-class organisation in some of the East Asian NICs seems to be attributable to rapid industrialisation, which in turn, has resulted in the growth and maturation of an industrial working class.[25] In general, this rapid pace has also provided the milieu in which a greater level of working-class identity and organisational capacity has developed. Thus, as the potential for working-class organisation increases, strains also tend to appear in the exclusionary model that, in the first place, was an integral part of the successful pursuit of an export-led industrialisation strategy in the 1960s and 1970s. Such is the fundamental source of tension and contradiction in the exclusionary model of accommodation. Significantly, where pressures for the partial unravelling of the exclusionary model have been present, pressures for democratisation of the social and political framework have also been stronger.[26]

Sustained industrialisation, however, has ensured that the living conditions of workers have gradually improved as real wages levels increase substantially from the levels that existed at the beginning of EOI. Still, wage level increases, for the most part, continued to lag behind rises in productivity, demonstrating how industrialisation in these countries continue to be based partly on the effective deployment of cheap labour (Deyo *et al.* 1987: 52). In spite of this fact, rising wage levels have encouraged the shift in orientation to higher added value production, in which labour-cost competitiveness is a less important consideration. The recipient of the benefits of such a shift should be the workers and labour organisations entrenched in heavier industry, whose bargaining position would be enhanced (Petras and Engbarth 1988: 93). Continuing labour unrest in such industries in the case of South Korea in the 1990s, however, appears to show that the contradiction inherent in the exclusionary model is difficult to resolve, probably because of its implications for the maintenance of the wider exclusionary corporatist social and political framework. Importantly, the wage levels of industrial workers in the East Asian NICs also continue to lag behind those of their counterparts in some Latin American countries, and welfare outlays by the state – historically a concession made to rising working-class demands – remain disproportionately small compared to countries with a similar level of industrialisation (Deyo *et al.* 1987: 52).

Southeast Asia: The aspiring NICs and the 'exclusionary' model of accommodation II

The emergence of an exclusionary model of accommodation between state, capital and labour is also a characteristic of the industrialisation experiences of Southeast Asia, where many countries are emulating the success of the EOI path of the four original East Asian NICs. As in the earlier cases, this was considerably assisted by the fact that in many of the aspiring NICs of Southeast Asia, organised labour was demolished in previous political struggles before it was able to develop into a significant social force.

Indeed, in Thailand, Malaysia, the Philippines and Indonesia (the aspiring NICs), the political exclusion of labour is also a legacy of political struggles prior to the advent of the EOI strategy. In all of these countries the first period of sustained industrialisation within the framework of an ISI strategy occurred simultaneously with state efforts to suppress organised labour. In all these cases, like many of the original East Asian NICs, the process was intertwined with struggles to eradicate thriving left-wing political movements.

In Thailand, a comparatively independent labour movement has long existed whose constituency has grown in conjunction with industrial progress.[27] From time to time, organised labour has had a significant role to play in the national political arena (for example, in the 1973 popular uprising against the military government), even in the face of often violent repression. However, the resumption of military rule in the late 1970s signalled the beginning of a period of setbacks for organised labour, as it did for the Left. The advent of EOI also saw more stringent state controls over labour being imposed, at the same time that economic liberalism and parliamentary-style politics have been gaining ground (Hewison and Brown 1992).

In colonial Malaya, both Chinese nationalists and the Malayan Communist Party were able to mobilise workers, mostly based in the plantation sector, into a significant source of resistance to colonial rule (Todd 1992). By the early post-war period the strength of the communist-backed labour movement was strong enough to elicit reprisals from the colonial government aimed at curbing its further growth (Arudsothy and Littler 1993: 112). A state-sponsored anti-communist trade union organisation, the Malayan Trade Union Council (MTUC), was established in the early 1950s, signalling labour's long decline into domestication. Following independence, the state was insulated from any significant working-class pressure as a result of this colonial legacy.

In the Philippines, in spite of the concerted efforts of colonial and post-colonial states, a tradition of labour militancy that began with the establishment of communist-led unions in the first decades of the twentieth century (Ofreneo 1993: 98–128) has continued to be influential in significant sections of the labour movement. In part, this has been due to the fragmented nature of state power and the weakness of the bourgeoisie. Thus, some of the features of the 'populist' model mainly associated with some Latin American countries may be discerned in the case of the Philippines. Significantly, here the Left was never successfully crushed completely as a force.

Indonesian working-class organisations – mainly based on transport and plantation workers – also played a part in the independence struggle (Ingleson 1986; Shiraishi 1990; Tedjasukmana 1958). (The Indonesian case is discussed in Chapter 3.) After being crushed by the Dutch colonial government in the aftermath of a failed uprising driven by the Communist Party in 1926, organised labour resurfaced in the 1940s revolutionary war for independence. In the 1950s and early 1960s the communist-backed SOBSI (*Sentral Organisasi Buruh Seluruh Indonesia*; All-Indonesia Central Workers' Organisation) was the most active labour organisation, and initially spearheaded the nationalisation of Dutch companies operating in Indonesia. However, martial law and managerial control over these enterprises placed the army in a position in which it was directly pitted against militant, organised labour (Hawkins 1963a and b). The demolition of the Communist Party by the army after 1965 brought an abrupt end to the tradition of militant labour unions.

Notwithstanding its common roots, the way in which the model of accommodation characterised by the political exclusion of labour has operated in the aspiring NICs of Southeast Asia has varied. Thailand, for example, stands out as a case in which state intervention into labour affairs is now far less direct and in which controls over labour have mostly been left to the enterprise level (Limqueco *et al.* 1989: 33). In this there are similarities with Malaysia, where in recent times the development of enterprise-level controls with greater encouragement of in-house unionism has also been pronounced (Arudsothy and Littler 1993: 128–129; also Wad 1988). Thailand also stands out as the example in which the labour movement is comparatively free because of the absence of state-imposed peak union organisations, and of rigid, monolithic, corporatist institutions in general. On the other hand, Indonesia stands out because state control over organised labour is most direct and pervasive, and because the development of an independent working-class movement is severely constrained by the imposition of a state-sponsored peak union organisation.

It is also clear that working-class movements in the aspiring NICs face an even more inhospitable milieu than their counterparts in the first generation NICs. Deyo, for example, paints an even gloomier picture for them than he did for those of South Korea, Taiwan, Hong Kong and Singapore. Writing on Thailand, Malaysia and the Philippines, he suggests that the innate impediments to working-class organisation in low-wage, export-oriented industries are compounded by other unfavourable factors at this particular historical conjuncture. These he identifies as international pressure to open up domestic markets and the development of management strategies to cut labour costs as some industrial deepening occurs. According to Deyo, the first trend compromises the strength of Southeast Asian labour movements because the associated privatisation process leads to employment cutbacks in more unionised sectors of the economy.[28] Growing trade pressure and reduced state protection have also produced greater incentives for employers to cut labour costs and to challenge unions. It is here that he identifies the crux of the problem for working-class movements in the new batch of aspiring NICs. According to Deyo, the resultant institution of enterprise flexible production systems has assumed an

> autocratic form, with little real participation by workers or unions in enterprise or production governance. By consequence, flexibility-enhancing organisational reforms are overwhelmingly attentive to managerial agendas driven by competitive economic pressures, to the exclusion of the social agendas of workers and unions . . . .The temporal coincidence of light EOI strategies on the one hand, and post-Fordist industrial models on the other, pushes flexibility in a non-participatory direction.[29]
>
> (Deyo 1995: 11–12, 13–14)

It could be added that, as the current suppliers of global cheap labour, more so than in any of the previous cases, the working classes of the aspiring Southeast Asian NICs have to suffer the burden of operating within an international context characterised by the increasing mobility of capital. As was noted before, this inevitably results in the reduction of the bargaining position of relatively immobile working classes.

A further countervailing factor to the development of significant labour movements remains the presence of high levels of unemployment and underemployment in the context of economies with a chronic labour surplus. This applies particularly to Philippines and Indonesia. In both countries it is doubtful whether industrialisation will result in the rapid tightening of labour markets, unlike in the case of the original East Asian NICs.[30] While the market-determinism of neo-classical economists is excessive in that it ignores the interplay of a broad range of social, historical and political factors, it is clear that labour movements emerging in the context of surplus labour markets face real structural impediments to their success.

It is notable, however, that even under the inhospitable circumstances of the aspiring NICs of Southeast Asia, some of the tensions and contradictions in the exclusionary model have recently surfaced in some cases. This can only be attributed to the fact that sustained industrialisation, first in the context of ISI, and then EOI, has resulted in the growth of an industrial working class with potentially greater organisational capacities (Limqueco *et al.* 1988: 169).[31]

In Thailand, for example, workers played an important part in the events of 1992 which brought about the downfall of the military government (Hewison and Brown 1992: 25). In Indonesia, a fledgling independent labour movement has recently developed which has undermined the legitimacy of state-sponsored institutional arrangements which were initially established to prohibit the re-emergence of labour militancy. In both countries, such labour struggles take place in conjunction with some growth in the pressure for democratisation. In the Philippines, in spite of a less dynamic industrialisation process,[32] the legacy of relatively uninterrupted (compared to Indonesia, for instance) radical working-class politics, by most accounts, keeps organised labour vibrant (e.g. Ofreneo 1993),[33] as true up to a point in Thailand (Ungpakorn 1995: 366). The former case, in particular, suggests the plausibility of a scenario of permanent, or at least, long-term tension between labour and its adversaries, in the absence of real working-class power, or conversely, state and bourgeois capacity to put an end to working-class militancy once and for all. It is only in tight labour market Malaysia (ironically?), that organised labour has not exhibited a significant increase in dynamism with the greater development of its working class (O'Brien 1988). Still, even here electronics workers have made limited inroads on the way to more autonomous organisation in the face of state resistance (Arudsothy and Littler 1993: 116, 123–124).

SUMMARY

Liberal democratic social and political frameworks have been underpinned by a particular form of accommodation between state, capital and labour, which in this Chapter has been referred to as the social-democratic model. The latter has been the product of the presence of strong working-class movements able to force significant concessions from state and capital, in return for forfeiting the highly political, socialist project. The way in which this accommodation was established varied widely from country to country. In the cases discussed in this Chapter, the accommodation was reached fairly smoothly in Britain, while in Germany, and to a lesser extent in France, the accommodation was arrived at through a protracted struggle that involved a number of near-revolutionary situations.

In the Latin American cases discussed, the populist model of accommodation between state, capital and labour was established in the context of a process of late industrialisation in which state and foreign capital played a central role, the domestic bourgeoisie was more dependent, and the working class, though already beginning to organise early on, was never quite strong enough to force the kinds of concessions that their European counterparts achieved. However, they were strong enough to deter attempts at subjugation through sheer coercion. Thus, they were eventually coopted into supporting populist regimes in return for tangible economic and welfare benefits for a small, core section of the working class.

The model of accommodation associated with the experience of the later industrialisations of the East Asian NICs has been based on the more complete subordination of labour as a social force. The legacy of the early suppression of radical working-class movements, and the imposition of stringent controls over organised labour, has provided the setting for the development of a model of accommodation based on the political exclusion of labour and its demobilisation as a social force. It is in this context that an export-led industrialisation strategy underpinned by the maintenance of a cheap and politically docile labour force became a viable policy option for states in this part of the world.

Finally, the EOI route is being emulated by a number of very late industrialisers – the aspiring NICs of Southeast Asia, including Indonesia. In these cases, the political exclusion of labour is also rooted in the struggles prior to the advent of EOI which had to do with the eradication of 'threatening' left-wing movements. The development of a more substantial industrial working class has provided, however, a more solid social base for working-class movements that may create some strain in the exclusionary model which also operates in these countries. Nevertheless, it has also been noted that the environment that working-class movements face in this new batch of aspiring NICs is, for a number of reasons, even more inhospitable than that facing the original NICs.

A point which recurs throughout the discussion is that the working class should be treated as an active historical agency, rather than a passive object of the designs and strategies of state elites or bourgeoisie. This has been argued even where the working-class movement has emerged in extremely hostile environments, which is generally the case the later that industrialisation proceeds. Indeed, many of the examples discussed in this Chapter have demonstrated that it is not only the politics and strategies of the working class that are shaped by the environment it encounters, but that these environments are also affected by the politics and strategies adopted by the working class. This is because the active responses of a working class with developed organisational capacities can influence the politics and strategies adopted by states and bourgeoisie.

Thus, the models of accommodation outlined in this Chapter may be seen as the outcome of struggles between historical agencies, including the working class, within specific historical and structural contexts. The outcomes of such struggles are not pre-determined, but neither are the options and possibilities available to such agencies infinite. This may be discerned from the Indonesian case where the establishment of the exclusionary model only took place following the events of 1965, when the radical stream of the labour movement was annihilated along with the Communist Party by an anti-revolutionary coalition of army-led forces. Had the army failed to wrest political power at the time, it is highly likely

Table 2.1 Historical Models of Accommodation Between State, Capital and Labour

Model of Accommodation	Social Democratic	Populist	Exclusionary
Historical Emergence	I. Britain; II. Later European industrialisers	Late—late Latin American industrialisers	I. Very late industrialisers of East Asia; and of, II. Southeast Asia
Associated Social and Political Framework	Liberal Democracies	Inclusionary Corporatism	Usually Exclusionary Corporatism
Environment	I. Laissez-faire state; independent bourgeoisie, and; II. More authoritarian and directing states and weaker bourgeoisie	Weak or consolidating state, usually linked to landed oligarchies, but with directing role; weaker bourgeoisie, also often linked to landed oligarchies	Strong states insulated from class forces and with directing role; initially weak bourgeoisie
Characteristics of Accommodation	Strong, independent trade union movement with representational and some mobilisational roles, but largely confined to economic realm; welfare state	Relatively strong trade union movement, medium to high level of subordination to state; representational— and mobilisational roles; politicised; improving welfare primarily for urban, higher-skilled workers	Very high level of trade union subordination to state; demobilisation and control of organised labour; labour movement confined to economic realm; exploitation of cheap labour; in original NICs, subsequent improvement of welfare levels of industrial workers
Major Sources of Contradiction	Fiscal crisis of the state; dismantling of welfare state; peripheralisation of trade unions; higher unemployment levels; flexible production system; capital mobility	Initial industrial deepening; increasing state repressive tendency versus strong tradition of labour militancy	Working class maturation; in some cases, emerging independent workers' movement versus state repression, surplus labour market, capital mobility, and some flexible production system

that a more fluid, and tenuous, form of accommodation, resembling that of the populist arrangements which emerged from some Latin American experiences, would have eventually developed in Indonesia.

This Chapter has outlined the principal features of the approach that is to be utilised in the remainder of this study to consider in detail the Indonesian case. It is an approach which, on the one hand, emphasises the historical and structural context within which the working class and its organisations emerge, and on the other, recognises workers' capacity actively to actively influence these contexts through political struggle. It is on the basis of such an approach that we shall examine the historical development, operations of, and strains within the exclusionary model of accommodation between state, capital and labour, as they have manifested themselves in Indonesia.

3 Historical legacies
Working-class politics in pre-New Order Indonesia

POLITICS AND HISTORY

In contemporary official interpretations of the pre-New Order labour movement, the 1950s and early 1960s are invariably depicted as a period during which anarchy prevailed, or during which senseless confrontation ensued between workers and employers. Though the 'liberal' and 'Guided Democracy' periods of Indonesian politics are often conflated in these interpretations, their aim, of course, is to suggest an unflattering contrast with the 'harmony' between capital, labour and state which, it is said, predominates in the New Order (Moertopo 1975: 13–17).[1]

A major target of criticism by this official orthodoxy is the fragmentation of the trade-union movement of the pre-New Order period as the result of the different political affiliations of the scores of unions then in existence. One New Order trade-union leader, for example, argues that the current institutional framework of organised labour represents a successful severing of 'ties' to particular 'politics and ideologies', which allows the trade-union movement to get down to the business of improving the economic welfare of its constituency (Sukarno 1980: xvii–xviii, 10–13).

In opposition to this official orthodoxy, others have celebrated early post-colonial Indonesia for providing an arena within which a militant workers' movement could thrive and flourish (Razif 1994a). This 'militancy' is contrasted unfavourably with the heavily state-controlled, official, working-class movement of contemporary times.

Both interpretations are inadequate because they fail to take into account the context, or milieu, in which trade unions operated at that time. The official New Order orthodoxy conveniently does this in an attempt to repudiate the significance, in principle, of politically oriented workers' movements. Thus, it is only with great difficulty that the role of highly politicised labour organisations of the early twentieth century in the collective political awakening of the nation (Ingleson 1986) is acknowledged at all.[2] The opposite position does virtually the same thing in order to highlight the contemporary domestication of organised labour. In the latter case, the outcome is an uncritical glorification of 'militancy' in pre-New Order Indonesia, with little acknowledgement of the structural constraints with which the radical stream of the labour movement was confronted in pursuing its agenda.

This Chapter provides an overview of the struggles of the working-class movement of pre-New Order Indonesia. The purpose is to explain the way in which struggles between historical agencies set the stage for the eradication of a tradition of labour militancy, which in turn, was the basis for the later development of an exclusionary model of accommodation between state, capital and labour.

The legacy of the first workers' organisations of the 1910s and 1920s greatly influenced the politics and ideologies that predominated in the trade-union movement of the early post-colonial period, and contributed to the ascendance of a radical stream. However, there was a relationship between fluctuations in the power and influence of the trade-union movement and the gradual consolidation of state power in the early post-colonial period. When state power was dispersed and diffuse, as was the case in the first years of independence, the labour movement, particularly its most radical stream, was able to thrive, in spite of the relative underdevelopment of labour as a class. The fortunes of organised labour became rather uncertain, however, as soon as the process of consolidation of state power began to accelerate. In fact, the tide distinctly turned against the radical stream of the labour movement after a section of the state, the military, began to cooperate with urban and rural petty bourgeois forces predisposed against radical unionism. The outcome of the struggle between these forces was the elimination of the possibility of radical unionism throughout most of the New Order.

In spite of its radical rhetoric, the trade-union movement of the 1950s and 1960s was constrained by the fact that it operated in a social and economic environment that was largely unaltered from the late colonial period. That environment was characterised by the dominance of enclave export-commodity production – though this too was in quite severe trouble by the early 1960s (Robison 1990: 39–40) – and only a limited degree of industrialisation and proletarianisation. Such a context conceivably posed problems for the section of the labour movement that was ideologically inclined toward a proletarian-led, radical restructuring of economic and political power, in spite of its superior organisational capacities in relation to some of its foes within the movement.

A large part of the power and influence of organised labour in the 1950s and early 1960s was actually attributable to the links, whether formal or semi-formal, between workers' organisations and the various existing political parties. Though there were exceptions to the rule, it was no coincidence that it was those labour organisations that were linked to the more powerful of the political parties that were also the most influential. This was as much the case for SOBSI, linked to the PKI, as it was for the other organisations, in spite of the Communist union's highly vaunted organisational capacities (Hawkins 1963b: 95). However, SOBSI possessed an advantage *vis à vis* its rivals, in that it was linked to a party that had more or less a 'natural' working-class constituency.

Clearly, only less 'natural' links with the working class could be said to exist with regard to SOBSI's main rivals within the trade-union movement. These included the more moderate SBII/GASBIINDO (*Serikat Buruh Islam Indonesia/Gabungan Serikat Buruh Islam Indonesia*; Indonesian Islamic Trade Union/Amalgamated Islamic Trade Unions of Indonesia), linked to the urban, petty bourgeois-based MASYUMI (*Majelis Syuro Muslimin Indonesia*; Consultative Council of Indonesian Muslims), the party of the 'modernist' wing of Islam; the SARBUMUSI (*Serikat Buruh Muslimin Indonesia*; Indonesian Muslim Trade Union), linked to the rural constituency of the NU (*Nahdlatul Ulama*; Islamic Scholars Association), regarded as representing the 'traditionalist' wing of the Islamic movement; the KBKI (*Kesatuan Buruh Kerakyatan Indonesia*; Populist Workers' Union of Indonesia), rooted in the PNI (*Partai Nasional Indonesia*; Indonesian National Party), the party of the Javanese *priyayi* and the state bureaucracy;[3] and the KBSI (*Kongres Buruh Seluruh Indonesia*; All Indonesia Workers' Congress), associated with the urban intelligentsia-based PSI (*Partai Sosialis Indonesia*; Indonesian Socialist Party), which represented the social-democratic stream of the nationalist movement (see Table 3.1, p. 51).[4]

Such close association with political parties was a mixed blessing. Obviously, the parties provided valuable political direction and patronage to the union organisations, some of which automatically benefited from the rise in fortune of their associated parties (Hasibuan 1968: 4). However, as we shall see, it also meant that union policy and strategy was often dictated by the party leadership. This was not only conceivably problematic for union organisations associated with political parties whose main constituency was not working class, but also to the PKI, whose SOBSI often acted as a springboard and training ground for apparatchik whose main loyalty was to the party.

THE EMERGENCE OF THE TRADE-UNION MOVEMENT IN COLONIAL INDONESIA

The trade-union movement was born in Indonesia in the context of the emergence of a nationalist, anti-colonial struggle. This considerably shaped the political character of the movement. Significantly, the ideologies adopted by many of the first union organisations were distinctly anti-capitalist, albeit to varying degrees. Though the early labour movement was quickly crushed, as mentioned earlier, it left a long-standing legacy in that its politics and ideologies were inherited by a number of the working-class organisations that later operated in the early post-colonial period.

An important period of social change was heralded in Indonesia (or the Dutch East Indies, as it was then known) in the 1870s, with the liberal agrarian reforms instituted by the colonial government to replace the archaic *Culturstelsel*, or cultivation system. As a result of these reforms, private enterprise was provided with opportunities to develop sugar estates, mills and refineries, mines, factories and railroads. It was at this point in history that Indonesians became engaged for the first time in significant numbers in non-traditional agricultural activities, and employed as wage-labour.

By the early twentieth century, there were clear signs that socio-economic changes set in motion by these agrarian reforms had proceeded to a significant level, especially in Java, the centre of the colonial administration and economy. For example, while the first railway was inaugurated in Java in 1870 (to transport sugar produced by private plantations to the port of Semarang) by 1894, a whole railway system had linked all the major cities in the island (Shiraishi 1990: 8). At the same time, these cities themselves began to grow considerably. According to Ingleson, 'from the 1870s the rate of urban growth in Java probably outstripped the rate of general growth for the first time, a process which accelerated from the early 1900s' (Ingleson 1981a: 485). In 1905 only Batavia, Surabaya and Surakarta had populations of over 100,000. By 1930, Semarang, Yogyakarta and Bandung had joined their ranks (Ingleson 1986: 14).

Writing on the first decades of the twentieth century, Ingleson argues that urbanisation 'paved the way for new forms of social and political organisation' which endeavoured to 'reintegrate people and communities' and gave them 'a sense of common identity and purpose' (Ingleson 1981a: 485). To Ingleson, this contributed to the development of a new kind of political consciousness among part of the Indonesian population, which stimulated not only the growth of trade unions, but also the wider nationalist movement that was developing simultaneously.

The processes that Ingleson refers to were undoubtedly significant, but it is important to keep in mind the relatively limited scale of social transformation involved, owing to the comparatively limited level of industrialisation that had taken place. Furnivall, for example, notes in his classic study that almost all experiments in promoting manufacturing industry in the Indies had been stopped by the end of World War I, having made only limited progress. There were important developments in extractive resource-based industries (tin, coal and oil) (Furnivall 1944: 325–329; 333–334). On the whole, however, the economy remained firmly based on cash-crop production. Thus, Ingleson's cities largely served as administrative and commercial centres facilitating Java's economic function as a producer of cash crops for the world market.[5]

Reflective of the importance of enclave export-commodity production, the 1930 census classified over 1.3 million people as deriving most of their income from the plantation sector (Mansvelt and Creutzberg 1979: 96).[6] By contrast, even as late as 1939, it is estimated that there were just over 5,000 manufacturing establishments in the Indies that used 'considerable mechanical installations, electrical or steam power', and which employed '50 or more workers'. Usually 'run by Europeans and Foreign Asiatics', they comprised 'machine shops, electric works, rice mills, shoe factories, textile mills, and many others', which altogether, employed an estimated 300,000 people (Mansvelt and Creutzberg 1979: 46–47).[7]

Furthermore, the urbanisation that Ingleson describes was clearly at an early stage: in 1930 only 8.7 per cent of the population of Java lived in towns of more than 5,000 people (Ingleson 1986: 14). Significantly, most of these people were not permanent urban-dwellers. Indeed, the development of a working-class identity must have been severely hampered by the fact that circular migrants made up as much as 40 per cent of the adult Indonesian population in the cities. 'As transient residents, their hearts as well as their families remained in the villages' (Ingleson 1986: 6). Thus, the first trade-union organisations established in the initial decades of this century grew in the context of an economy characterised by the dominance of enclave export-commodity production, an undeveloped manufacturing sector, and a society in which the urbanisation process had just begun.

The transport sector had a particularly strategic role in the plantation-based economy.[8] Indeed, it was railway and tram workers who formed the first union open to all races in the East Indies – the now legendary *Vereeniging voor Spoor- en Tramwegpersoneel* (VSTP)[9] – established in 1908. Those most responsible for transforming the VSTP into one of the most important of the trade unions of the early twentieth century were the Dutch revolutionary, Sneevliet, and his young Indonesian protégé, Semaoen, both of whom played prominent parts in the introduction and propagation of communism in the colony and in the nationalist cause (Tedjasukmana 1958: 4–6; Ingleson 1981b: 53–55; Shiraishi 1990: 98–99). Thus, from its earliest years the trade-union movement in Indonesia had some distinctly political concerns.

Other unions were soon established by workers employed in government services and enterprises, including those of customs service workers, teachers, and employees of the public works office. Among the more prominent was the union of pawnshop workers, the PPPB (*Perserikatan Pegawai Pegadaian Bumiputera*), founded in 1916 by Sosrokardono, a member of *Sarekat Islam* (SI). The latter was an organisation originally formed in 1911 by the indigenous Islamic petty bourgeoisie, as a vehicle to oppose the domination of the ethnic Chinese in trade.[10] Though initiated by small traders, the SI became the first mass-based organisation in the colony, garnering a following among the peasantry and workers. By 1919 this following was significant enough that members who were simultaneously linked to the socialist ISDV (*Indische Sociaal Democratische Vereeniging*) – effectively the precursor of the PKI – asserted that the task of the SI was the creation of 'the organisation through which the proletariat of the Indies will liberate itself' (McVey 1965: 44).[11]

After World War I, private enterprise unions, both white and blue collar, also began to be formed, the most notable of which was that of sugar-refinery workers, organised by *Sarekat Islam* activist Surjopranoto. Other unions established at about the same time were those of dockworkers and seamen, mineworkers, metalworkers, printers and electrical workers (Tedjasukmana 1958: 6–8; also King 1982: 32). The actual membership of the unions at the time is almost impossible to establish, although claimed membership totalled a relatively modest 60,000–150,000 in 1920. All of these organisations, not surprisingly, had their headquarters in Java, from where they drew most of their membership (King 1982: 33).[12]

The growth of trade unionism in the Indies was assisted by the pervasive political atmosphere during the last years of World War I when the colonial government tended to espouse a policy that emphasised the need for appeasement of growing nationalist sentiment in the colony (Shiraishi 1990: 94–98). Significantly, politics in the Netherlands itself was increasingly being influenced by advocates of socialism or social democracy who adopted a more sympathetic attitude toward nascent nationalisms in colonial societies. Thus, until the early 1920s, the official position taken by the colonial government toward trade unionism in the Indies was one of 'benevolent neutrality', characterised by a role confined mainly to maintaining order (Shiraishi 1990: 109).

Writers like Shiraishi have emphasised the way in which trade unionism, and the wider nationalist movement, was spurred on by the growing awareness of many Indonesians of the radical changes that were then transforming the world stage, and the way they imagined these changes to affect their own country. Strongly linked to this sense of connection with the unfolding of world history was the growing influence of socialist and Marxist ideas – though to varying degrees, and with different manifestations – among a wide spectrum of nationalists and trade unionists.[13]

Indeed, Indonesians began to freely adapt Marxist and socialist ideas to 'fit' their situation as well as to develop strategies of political action. It was not only the communist-oriented trade-union leaders that undertook this, but also such anti-communists as the *Sarekat Islam* leader, Agus Salim. According to McVey, at one time he announced that Islam contained, 'in addition to spiritual values, all the major economic and social principles embraced by Marxism', and at another, that 'everything stated by Marx was already contained in the Koran, even the principle of dialectical materialism' (McVey 1965: 100, 104). Indeed such influential figures might have discovered an affinity between the egalitarian ethos of socialism and the values of Islam,[14] as was reflected in the popularity of the idea of 'sinful' capitalism (McVey 1965: 14; Soewarsono 1991: 16). Capitalism itself tended to be identified by communists and Muslims alike as the source of the poverty of native Indonesians (Soewarsono 1991: 14). Importantly, however, some of the latter tended also to be alarmed by notions of class struggle employed by more straightforward communists (McVey 1965: 104). This is not surprising, for such notions potentially constituted as much a threat to the interests and sensibilities of the petty bourgeois traders that initially founded the SI as they did to the colonial social order.

The process of adapting Marxism, as it affected thinking within the trade-union movement, was perhaps best exemplified in the ideas of Semaoen, the VSTP leader and communist propagandist. In contradiction to the Leninist orthodoxy of the time, he essentially argued that a proletarian revolution could occur in the East Indies independent of developments in the West (Cribb 1985: 254). To be sure, Semaoen could not have failed to recognise that the unevenness of capitalist development in Indonesia had led to the existence, side by side, of more primitive forms of production alongside capitalism. Still, he maintained that because colonialism oppressed all Indonesians in the same way, cooperation between classes in the anti-colonial struggle was based on a long-term identity of interest. Furthermore, he reasoned that since colonialism was the prime proletarianising force in Indonesia, a nationalist revolution against it would be a vehicle for proletarian victory (Cribb 1985: 256).

Arguably, however, the social transformation engendered by colonial capitalism was still quite limited, even by the early twentieth century, to sustain a proletarian revolutionary struggle. As noted earlier, this capitalism took a form in which enclave export-commodity production predominated. Notwithstanding the important social changes occurring at the village level noted with care by such scholars as Breman (1982) and White (1983), this type of colonial capitalism could not assure the rapid and more pervasive spread of capitalist relations of production in the countryside. Thus, the proletarianised can be said to have existed in a vast sea of non-proletarians. Such a social base was clearly problematic for revolutionary political movements (Robison 1990: 83) that were supposed to be proletarian-led.

To make things worse, the labour movement was plagued by chronic disunity. Such disunity was in turn associated with rivalries within the nationalist movement, particularly between the ISDV/PKI and the SI. In spite of various attempts at amalgamation, the labour movement remained highly fragmented.[15]

Not surprisingly, the vulnerability of the labour movement was revealed as soon as the colonial authorities abandoned their position of 'benevolent neutrality' in favour of a more repressive stance. Indeed, the government had become increasingly alarmed at the agitation and propaganda activities of trade unions during the period that Shiraishi aptly calls the 'Age of Strikes' (Shiraishi 1990: 109–116). The turning point came in the government's response to a general strike organised in 1922 by sugar factory workers led by Surjopranoto (Shiraishi 1990: 113). The strike in fact failed dismally in the face of government repression, resulting in the effective crippling of the PFB itself (Shiraishi 1990: 220–224). In rapid succession, the PPPB and the VSTP were also smashed by colonial authorities following other failed attempts to organise general strikes.[16] In the crackdown that ensued, Semaoen himself was banished to Europe, while other trade-union leaders were arrested (Ingleson 1981b: 87). Thus, the PFB, the PPPB and the VSTP, the three most important unions of the nationalist, anti-colonial struggle, had already been eliminated from the political scene as early as 1923 (SOBSI 1958: 52).

The final blow to labour militancy came in the aftermath of the failed mass uprising against the Dutch in late 1926 and early 1927, initiated by the PKI leadership. After crushing the uprising, the colonial government retaliated by arresting and exiling the party's leaders, many of whom were also leading trade unionists (Tedjasukmana 1958: 14; Sandra 1961: 42).[17] With the destruction of the PKI, and the earlier abandonment by the SI of the labour cause – following the demise of the PFB and the PPPB – organised labour appeared to be permanently crippled. Although unions continued to exist into the 1930s, their political role in the nationalist movement was largely negligible.

Ingleson suggests that the most important legacy of the early labour movement was to the next phase of the nationalist movement, in that the latter benefited from the political experiences and organisational skills gained by Indonesians in trade unions (Ingleson 1981a: 500–501). However, it should also be remembered that the nationalist movement of post-1927 – in which figures like Soekarno became pre-eminent – was largely dominated by *priyayi* and urban intelligentsia-led political parties and organisations that did not have a distinctly mass-based character.

More significantly for our purposes, the legacy of the struggle of the 1910s and the 1920s, was in defining the political ideologies that were to be taken up by workers' organisations in post-independence Indonesia. The experiences of the period helped to form a tradition of militant unionism which was to be carried over into post-colonial times by important sections of the movement. The radical politics espoused by the VSTP, for example, continued to inform the activities of labour unions in the 1950s and early 1960s, particularly those affiliated to SOBSI. There was, however, another long-lasting legacy of the 1910–1920 period: that of internal rivalries and schisms. To an extent, the major lines of political division within the movement established earlier in the century were replicated during the first decades of formal independence insofar as the main rivalry that developed was between communist- and Islamic party-linked organisations.

Clearly though, the political context had changed by this time. Unions were operating within a newly independent republic. But as the more radical unions in particular were to find out, the requirements of running the inherited colonial economy would present governments of the new republic with a strong incentive to curb the growth and political power of trade unions.

WORKERS' ORGANISATIONS AND THE POST-COLONIAL STATE

Union politics and ideologies

It took two decades for the trade-union movement to resurface in the national political arena following the débâcle of the 1920s. Its re-emergence took place in the midst of the nationalist revolution of 1945–49, the egalitarian ethos of which greatly encouraged the growth of a highly politically oriented labour movement. But unions flourished even after the euphoria of revolution had subsided. The labour movement – particularly its radical stream – was able to continue to thrive in the following decade largely because of the slowness with which state power was consolidating and the absence of substantial class adversaries. It also benefited from the ready availability of political ideologies inherited from earlier working-class struggles.

Not long after the proclamation of independence in August 1945 and, with government encouragement, the BBI (*Barisan Buruh Indonesia*; Indonesian Workers' Front) was established in Jakarta as the first federation of workers' organisations in 'independent' Indonesia (Tedjasukmana 1958: 18).[18] In spite of overt Republican government support, there were, however, already tensions between the authorities and organised labour as early as 1946. Even at this time there was considerable alarm in government circles about the lack of control that could be exerted on organised labour.

Specifically, the government disapproved of the frequency of cases of workers taking over foreign-owned workplaces without authorisation. Its response was to bring in a regulation requiring all labour (and peasant) organisations to register with the government. A requirement was also imposed on workers to hand over control of seized workplaces to the government (King 1982: 95).[19]

Such tensions notwithstanding, the overall political environment was highly favourable for organised labour. In accordance with the revolutionary mood of the times, an upsurge of labour organising soon took place after the establishment of unions in the sugar industry, railways, plantations, and of dockworkers' and seamen's unions. Importantly, many of the leaders of these new unions were activists whom the Dutch had incarcerated or exiled in the 1920s (Tedjasukmana 1958: 18–21), whose vision and political sensibilities had been shaped by the struggles of that period.

In 1946, SOBSI was formed – initially by non-PKI socialists – to reunite workers' organisations which had temporarily split up when the initial supporters of the BBI divided into the *Gabungan Serikat Buruh Indonesia* (GASBI; Amalgamated Trade Unions of Indonesia), a proponent of 'craft' unions, and the *Gabungan Serikat Buruh Vertikal Indonesia* (GSBVI; Amalgamated Vertical Trade Unions of Indonesia), a proponent of 'industrial' unions.[20] It soon came to be dominated, however, by veteran PKI figures, many of whom had just returned after years of exile.[21]

Organised along industrial lines, but in which craft unions were also prominent (King 1982: 90), SOBSI effectively functioned as the sole workers' federation in Indonesia for a short time, until rival federations began to be formed. One of these was the SBII, which later became GASBI-INDO, established by the MASYUMI party.[22] Significantly, in a clear reference to the communists, one of the stated reasons for the establishment of the SBII was to 'prevent workers from undertaking such un-nationalist actions as taking part in wildcat strikes, which are detrimental to the State economy'. Even less obliquely, another stated reason for its establishment was to develop trade unionism based on Islam, given the predominance of those that base their struggles on 'the teachings and aims of Marxism–Leninism' (GASBIINDO 1967: 41–42).[23]

SOBSI's influence, however, was temporarily eroded when many of its leaders were implicated in the Madiun Affair of 1948, in which the PKI leadership under Musso challenged the authority of President Soekarno and Vice-President Hatta, and was decisively crushed by an armed forces loyal to the central government. Numerous SOBSI leaders were imprisoned and executed in its aftermath. Thereafter, 16 of SOBSI's member unions, with about half of its membership, seceded, some of them even joining the rival SBII (King 1982: 91). The main legacy of the Madiun Affair for the trade-union movement, however, was to establish the armed forces' animosity and distrust of the communists, whom they regarded as having betrayed the fledgling republic (Anderson 1994: 132). Such a distrust would very much colour the way in which the military would deal with SOBSI's brand of radical unionism once it was pitted in a directly confrontational relationship with the organisation.

The years immediately following the transfer of sovereignty to republican hands saw another upsurge of labour strikes (Feith 1962: 84). Meek sees the times as being characterised by exorbitant wage demands, the non-existence of collective bargaining, virtually automatic strikes, frequent violence and low labour productivity (Meek 1956: 153). According to King, more working hours were lost through strikes in 1950, just after formal independence, than in any of the subsequent eleven years. Notably, the largest strike involved 700,000 plantation workers affiliated with SOBSI (King 1982: 114). Indeed, in the meantime, SOBSI had quickly been revived and rehabilitated, as was the PKI itself, whose membership grew at an astounding rate under a new generation of communists led by D.N. Aidit.

Though initially pro-labour in its outlook, the governments of the newly sovereign republic gradually came to develop stronger anti-labour tendencies, as strikes became increasingly perceived as posing an obstacle to the running of the economy. In 1951, Emergency Law no. 16 was announced.[24] While falling short of actually banning strikes, it imposed limitations on the exercise of that right. For example, it carefully regulated the handling of disputes and in reality established a system of compulsory arbitration to determine wages, hours and working conditions in place of a free system of collective bargaining (Hawkins 1963a: 264). The institutions created by this law for the adjudication of labour disputes were regional and central disputes committees respectively called P4D and P4P. The promulgation of the emergency law was the first clear indication of the gradually changing mood of the political elite and of the times, as the euphoria of revolution was replaced by the new, more pragmatic business of running the government and economy.

Organised labour found that it had to operate within an enclave export-production economy little changed from that of the late colonial period. This was a context that continued to impose some constraints on the development of a strong trade-union movement. Out of the 25,000 registered firms that operated in 1953, only 575 had over 500 employees, while 1,500 had 100–500 employees. More than one-third of the plantation establishments had more than 500 employees, but most industrial firms had fewer than 20. The vast bulk of these were both small and family-oriented. Not surprisingly, the great majority of industrial workers were at the stage of handicraft rather than factory production at this time (Hawkins 1963b: 85–86). Therefore, while the PKI claimed that there were 20 million 'workers' and their families in Indonesia in the 1950s, it also conceded that the modern industrial proletariat was comprised of barely 500,000 workers (Aidit 1958: 61).

Moreover, like the colonial economy, the modern sector was largely in foreign, mainly Dutch hands. To an extent, this helped radical organisations like SOBSI to mobilise support among workers as they were able to exploit highly nationalistic sentiments that still prevailed at the time (Hawkins 1963b: 114). However, though debate about economic development was to continue until the conditions for Soekarno's Guided Democracy began to develop in the late 1950s, most government leaders took the position that only a very gradual disengagement from the neo-colonial economy was possible and, moreover, that a domestic capacity for accumulation had to be developed before a meaningful national economy could be constructed (Robison 1990: 83).[25] The prevalence of this cautious, pragmatic line would have some implications on the government's dealings with organised labour.

Another important law was enacted in 1957 (Law no. 22 on the Settlement of Labour Disputes), which demonstrated continuing government concern about the activities of labour's militant stream. Aside from changing the composition of the P4D and P4P to include worker representatives and employers – in addition to state officials – it stipulated more rigorous conditions and procedures for the undertaking of legal industrial action by workers (Hawkins 1963b: 131–133). A further stipulation was that the Minister of Labour had veto power over decisions of the national-level committee, thus ensuring central government jurisdiction over industrial relations matters. By that same year, moreover, undertaking strike action became increasingly difficult in the context of martial law. In 1963, Presidential Instruction no. 7 was announced which banned strike action in 'vital' state institutions.

Though the government's stance toward labour gradually toughened, the political atmosphere of the earlier part of the 1950s was still favourable enough to provide the opportunity for trade unions to flourish. Thus, most unions were established during the high-spirited early years of the republic. As was the case in the 1920s, it is virtually impossible to accurately estimate the strength of the respective trade unions as exorbitant claims were often made. Hawkins considers the 1955 combined claim by trade unions of membership amounting to 5,694,000 workers to be a gross exaggeration (Hawkins 1963a: 260-261).

What is clear is that the fragmentation of organised labour reached astounding levels. Tedjasukmana observed that workers in the late 1950s were grouped in as many as 150 national unions and hundreds of unaffiliated local ones. They ranged from the *Sarekat Buruh Perkebunan Republik Indonesia* (SARBUPRI; Plantation Workers' Union of the Indonesian Republic), an organisation that claimed a membership of 600,000, to one that claimed no more than 680 members (Tedjasukmana 1958: 25–26). In 1955, the Ministry of Labour listed a grand total of 1,501 national, regional and local unions, nearly half of which were unaffiliated (King 1982: 114). Interestingly, the majority (56 per cent) of the national unions in 1955 were without affiliation. By 1958, when the number of national unions had grown to 261, 62 per cent were unaffiliated (King 1982: 116).

Another feature of the 1950s was the re-assertion of the organic links between labour and political organisations. As mentioned earlier, all the major unions and union federations were somehow associated, if not affiliated, to political parties, and thus to a large extent, served to further the interests of the latter, including in the important matter of mobilising votes during elections. This was not unusual, because during this time, most of the major political parties also operated women's, farmers' and youth divisions (Hawkins 1963b: 94).

Therefore, although the PKI and SOBSI, for example, were formally independent entities,[26] there was no question of their organic links to one another. This was even expressed physically, in the number of individuals holding important positions in both organisations. According to Hasibuan, at least six out of the thirty-two individuals elected to the national parliament in the 1955 elections, under the PKI ticket, held leadership positions in SOBSI or one of its constituent unions. The most important was Nyono, chairman of SOBSI and member of the PKI's Central Committee (Hasibuan 1968: 84).[27]

However, the organic link between party-union federation was not one that was confined to the PKI/SOBSI. Hasibuan, for example, also notes, in reference to the PNI-linked KBKI and the NU-linked SARBUMUSI, the reality that the leaders of the federations were more closely intertwined with the respective party leaderships than their constituent vertical unions. Giving examples of how decisions were often made with regard to applying pressure on specific enterprises, Hasibuan concludes that unions in fact had very little independence from the political parties. Among the examples given: KBKI unions unenthusiastically demanding pay rises for workers if the head of an enterprise contributed funds to the PNI; SARBUMUSI unwillingness to go along with other unions to make demands on a state plantation that had officers of NU background. The relative ease with which the SOBSI/PKI appeared to develop a working-class constituency was also emphasised by Hasibuan, who suggests that 'SOBSI in general was in a better position to apparently fight for the interest of workers because there were not many PKI members in control positions of the state enterprises' (Hasibuan 1968: 85–86).

None the less, the effects of party supremacy over union affiliates were demonstrated just as clearly in the case of SOBSI. This was so particularly in the early 1960s when the PKI increasingly found it politically expedient to seek an ally in President Soekarno. (Recall that the latter was then heavily pushing his NASAKOM concept (Reeve 1985: 210–213) under which the country would be guided by a progressive National Front which included 'nationalist', 'religious' and 'communist' elements.) To the apparent displeasure of some of the constituent unions of SOBSI, the federation was increasingly geared to adopt a less confrontational stance by the central leadership of the PKI.[28] To bring unions into line, Aidit reportedly endeavoured to force SOBSI's acceptance of a formal position as a mass organisation of the PKI, while warning against the federation's degeneration into mere European 'trade unionism'. He failed, however, probably in part because many trade-union leaders opted for the 'relative freedom' from the party apparatus that was still afforded under the prevailing arrangement (Anonymous 1994: 2–3).[29]

Table 3.1 provides data on the claimed membership level of individual

Table 3.1 Membership and Affiliations of Labour Organisations[30]

Organisation	Affiliation/orientation	Members
SOBSI	PKI (Communist)	2,733,000
KBSI	PSI (Socialist)	376,000
SBII/GASBIINDO	MASYUMI (Muslim)	600,000
KBKI	PNI (Nationalist)	1,002,000
HISSBI[31]	Partai Buruh (Labour Party)	261,000
SOBRI[32]	Murba (National—Communist)	281,000
SARBUMUSI	NU (Muslim)	12,000
GOBSII[33]	PSII (Muslim)	1,000
GSBI[34]	PNI (Nationalist)	145,000
KBIM[35]	MASYUMI (Muslim)	42,000
SOB Pantjasila	Partai Katolik (Catholic)	61,000
SBKI[36]	PARKINDO (Protestant)	n.a.
Regional		n.a.
Non-federated		180,000
Total		5,694,000

trade-union federations in the late 1950s and establishes their respective political affiliations. It is clear that the largest union federation was by far the PKI-linked SOBSI. Table 3.2 shows the membership of registered unions in Indonesia in 1955 by industry. Significantly, there is a huge disjuncture between the figures for total membership presented in the two tables, likely the result of the exaggerated claims of the union organisations. Table 3.2 also indicates the predominance of the non-industrial sectors of the economy. Importantly, of the 596,000-odd unionised workers employed in manufacturing, 530,000 were members of SOBSI (Hawkins 1963b: 106). According to Hawkins, government employees were among the most highly organised, 'perhaps more strongly than in private industry'. He estimates that about a quarter of industrial and government workers were trade-union members (1963b: 107) .

Table 3.2 Union Membership by industry[37]

Classification	Membership
Agriculture	1,009, 962
Mining	27, 356
Industry	596, 115
Building	1, 377
Public Utilities	13, 496
Trade	22, 108
Communication	122, 834
Services	275, 047
Unclassified	381, 427
Total	2,449, 722

SOBSI was apparently also more successful in securing leadership from the rank and file of workers than the other trade-union federations. Moreover, it tended to represent the more numerous less skilled workers,[38] in contrast to the non-communist ones, who tended to attract the fewer, more highly skilled, white-collar workers.[39]

As mentioned earlier, the major rivalry within the trade-union movement in the 1950s and 1960s was between SOBSI and various non-communist unions, but particularly those affiliated with Islamic political parties. As was the case in the 1920s, the main area of dispute related to the notion of 'class struggle'.[40] Hawkins observed that

The difference in ideology between the Communists, who stress the class struggle, and the Muslims, who talk about the principle of sharing wealth with the poor, is significant in labour relations in Indonesia. Since some of the Muslim unions tend to talk in terms of the Islamic faith instead of the class struggle, they sometimes refuse to join in certain strikes and are considered more moderate.[41]

(Hawkins 1963b: 96)

SARBUMUSI, linked to the rural-based NU, was apparently particularly affronted by the atheism implied in the communist ideology of the SOBSI/PKI.[42] Indeed, one short history of the federation stresses that it was established in 1955 as a vehicle for Muslim workers, to countervail the influence of the 'atheistic' SOBSI/PKI, and credits *ulama*, or religious scholars, for taking part in the process (Widjaja 1969).

Opposition to the idea of class struggle was clearly not only confined to the Islamic-based unions. The Catholic Party-linked SOB Pantjasila, for example, adhered to the papal encyclicals *Rerum Novarum* (1891) and *Quadrogesimo Anno* (1931), which encouraged cooperation between workers and employers to overcome class divisions and conflict, in pursuit of the common good. The teachings of the church on labour relations were presented by the union as an alternative to those embodied in the doctrines of liberalism, communism and (Western) socialism (see SOB Pantjasila 1960: 27–57; also see Bourchier 1996: 205–206).

However, what was in question was not simply a matter of differences of industrial relations philosophy, nor for that matter, theology. As many actors involved in the labour struggles of the 1950s and 1960s now readily admit, the aim of improving the welfare of workers often took second place to wider political objectives that were set by political parties, themselves embroiled in a struggle to contain the PKI. In the 1955 general elections, the PKI took fourth place, behind the PNI, MASYUMI and NU (Feith 1962: 434–435). In the 1957 local elections, it won first place in Java. Thus to many of the non-SOBSI unions, curbing the influence of the communists became of overriding importance.[43] Fortunately for SOBSI's rivals, an ally soon came in the form of the armed forces, particularly the army. The latter was to become a more significant foe to SOBSI as it took the lead in coordinating the other trade unions against it.[44] It is to the important role of the army in labour politics after 1957 that we must now shift our attention.

The roots of military involvement in labour affairs

Military involvement in labour affairs began to be pervasive in the late 1950s. During this time the military increasingly became the site of state administration, as the result of the promulgation of martial law in response to regional rebellions in Sumatra and Sulawesi, as well as Soekarno's campaign to establish Indonesian sovereignty over West Irian. The gradual consolidation of state power that took place following these developments in fact largely centred on the military (Kahin 1994: 207–208). Moreover, as mentioned earlier, it was at this time that military personnel took up management positions in newly nationalised state firms, thus directly pitting these enterprises against the militant stream of the labour movement. It was as state administrators and enterprise managers that the military became embroiled in an increasingly bitter conflict with the radical stream of the labour movement.

Many changes occurred in the political arena during the first fifteen years following the proclamation of independence.[45] Although the 1945 Constitution stipulated a presidential system of government, by November that year a prime minister, the socialist Sjahrir, was for the first time put in charge of the daily affairs of government. Following the transfer of sovereignty, a liberal parliamentary system operated in the infant republic during which many governments came and went. Cabinets during that time were usually dominated by four parties: the MASYUMI; the PNI, which President Soekarno himself was originally linked with; the NU; and the Sjahrir-led PSI. The PKI itself was for the most part confined to a place outside of direct government.

However, the liberal political system was eventually abolished by President Soekarno, largely because, under its rules, he did not have a strong enough formal foothold on power. In 1959, he replaced it with Guided Democracy. Under this system powers were concentrated on the President while political parties were supplanted by a method of representation that emphasised the role of 'functional groups'.[46] An important part of the call to dismantle the liberal system was the charge that its workings had divided society into mutually antagonistic groups represented by the parties. What Soekarno envisaged instead was a system in which the interests of society as an organic, holistic body would be upheld (see Reeve 1985: 108–149).

Of the major political parties of the 1950s, the PKI was the only one to survive this change without serious damage, as it was able to capitalise on Soekarno's passionate opposition to capitalism and imperialism. Importantly, the only other major force that could rival the power of the PKI during Guided Democracy was the armed forces, which had supported Soekarno's abolition of liberal democracy, in which it also had no formal basis of power (King 1982: 123–124).

As the military took on wider economic, political and administrative roles than ever before under martial law, it also began to intervene pervasively in labour affairs, the main result of which was further restrictions on the right to strike. Initially, that involvement was represented by the establishment of the BKS-BUMIL (*Badan Kerjasama Buruh-Militer*; Labour-Military Cooperation Body), in December 1957, as part of a wider mobilisation of society in support of the West Irian campaign. Fourteen labour unions were drawn into the organisation, including SOBSI. Notably, military involvement in the resolution of industrial disputes took place via this institution, as some unions began to appeal labour disputes to it rather than to the formal labour disputes committees (King 1982: 128). According to Hawkins (1963b: 134), many of the smaller unions attempted to enhance their prestige through participation in the BKS-BUMIL, which of course, meant maintaining good relations with the military.

Hostility between the army and SOBSI, in the meantime, was on the rise as a result of the assumption of the former of managerial positions in newly nationalised foreign-owned enterprises. These had been seized in 1957 in a retaliatory measure against Dutch unwillingness to transfer control of West Irian. Ironically, their seizure was initially spearheaded by unions, particularly SOBSI, which demanded that workers be given a much larger role in the actual running and management of enterprises through the establishment of workers' councils. The idea was quickly rejected, however, by the government, which instead placed the enterprises under the control of military personnel.[47] The consequence of this action was that the army, now performing managerial functions, was placed in a structural position which would make opposition to militant unionism more directly in its interests.

However, the BKS-BUMIL did not prove an adequate force to deal with SOBSI. This led to the establishment of an organisation called *Sentral Organisasi Karyawan Sosialis Indonesia* (SOKSI; Central Organisation of Socialist *Karyawan* of Indonesia), in which direct military involvement in labour affairs was primarily represented in the early 1960s. Founded by Soehardiman, an army officer who had earlier served as secretary of the *Badan Nasionalisasi* (Nationalisation Board) – the institution responsible for the management of the nationalisation of foreign-owned firms – SOKSI soon established a base of power in state-owned enterprises which the army now controlled. Significantly, the organisation appeared to have garnered much of its support among white-collar workers (Hawkins 1963a: 269).[48]

The establishment of SOKSI had a significance that went beyond day-to-day political struggles and extended into the realm of the ideological. In fact it became the focus of army attempts to challenge SOBSI, ideologically, by countervailing notions of class struggle. SOKSI promoted an ideology of harmonious relations between workers and employers (Boileau 1983: 41), which of course, better served the army's interest in preserving industrial peace in the enterprises it controlled. In this connection, it is important to note the significance of the term *karyawan*, which SOKSI developed and juxtaposed to the term *buruh*, which had political connotations as it had been used by the militant labour unions of the 1910s and 1920s. *Karyawan*, roughly translating as 'employee', was a much softer, neutral, word, and did not conjure up images of struggles in the political realm.[49]

Aware of the reasons for its establishment, the PKI leadership responded very critically to SOKSI. In 1963, Aidit, chairman of the party, suggested that

> Certain elements wish to eliminate the word *buruh*, a word inseparably bound to the most militant traditions of our national liberation movement, in order to substitute it for the word *karyawan*. In this way they intend to completely blot out the dividing line between the roles of production and management. More than that, with the word *karyawan*, with what they call *karyawan* unions or organisations, these elements are evidently trying to break the trade unions as militant working class organisations.
>
> (cited in Capizzi 1974: 41; and Leclerc 1972: 77)

Another PKI leader quipped:

> the capitalist-bureaucrats are trying to concoct for use one of those reactionary theories, with regard to *karyawan*, according to which there will no longer be (referring to nationalised industries) '*l'exploitation de l'homme par l'homme*', but the collaboration of associates. One tacks on to the worker the high sounding title of *karyawan*, the bureaucrat boss acquires *karyawan* in his turn and the trick is played: they are both equals. But who is then going to tell us why the former gets 31 rupiahs a day and the other, 130,000 a month.
>
> (Capizzi 1974: 42; Leclerc 1972: 78)

The PKI leadership was wary of SOKSI for good reason, for it quickly became the spearhead of the army's effort to thwart the influence of the party on all fronts. Undertaking a massive organisation-building program, SOKSI trained 1,800 cadres in 1963, and incorporated 60 national and 48 local mass organisations. By the end of that year it had established branches in 24 regions and claimed to have trained 100,000 cadres. Its membership also rose spectacularly: in January 1963 the organisation claimed 1,615,800 members; in November of the same year, 7,500,000 members (Reeve 1985: 220; Boileau 1983: 41). Whatever truth there was in these claims was most likely due to the organisation's establishment of mass organisations of youth, women, farmers and intellectuals (Soehardiman 1993: 122).[50] In response to SOBSI attacks that it was not a proper trade union, SOKSI also formed the KONGKARBU (*Konsentrasi Golongan Karya Buruh*; Workers' Functional Group Concentration), under the leadership of Adolf Rachman, a former member of SARBUMUSI.[51]

Still other attempts were made by the army to exercise greater control over the labour movement. One was represented in the 1960 call to amalgamate labour unions in a single state-sponsored organisation, the OPPI (*Organisasi Persatuan Pekerja Indonesia*; Organisation of Indonesian Workers' Associations), promoted by the Minister of Labour at the time, Ahem Erningpradja, who was president of the KBKI, and significantly, closely associated with the army leadership. However, OPPI was opposed by SOBSI because the communists knew that it would not be able to dominate an organisation that the army had designs for. Support for OPPI, nevertheless, was forthcoming from the BKS-BUMIL,[52] as well as such federations as the KBSI, Erningpradja's own KBKI, and SARBUMUSI (KBSI 1961: 25–27; Reeve 1985: 170).

Although various regional bodies were then formed by non-communist unions toward the establishment of OPPI, the organisation did not take off as planned (Hawkins 1963a: 268–269). Thus, there were to be subsequent schemes to form labour coordinating entities over which the army would exercise influence. One such scheme was the Joint Secretariat of Labour Federations, set up in 1962 in the context of mobilising further support for the West Irian campaign. Also initiated by Erningpradja, it was comprised of the six labour organisations represented in parliament (Hawkins 1963a: 269) – then already dominated by 'functional groups'.

Another notable development was the establishment of the *Dewan Perusahaan* or enterprise councils, geared to give labour a voice in the setting of enterprise policy, while maintaining management authority at the same time (Hawkins 1963a: 269–270). First put into place in 1962, these councils were planned for all levels of management in each state enterprise, down to company, factory and estate (Reeve 1985: 217). Although in theory labour representatives were included in these councils, they were in fact carefully screened by the government (King 1982: 129).

According to SOKSI leader Soehardiman, the enterprise councils were probably President Soekarno's own idea, inspired by his observations of the running of firms in East European countries. However, he also suggests that the army was able to persuade Soekarno that these councils should play a more limited advisory role, rather than the kind of semi-executive role that the President might have envisaged.[53] Equally important, the army itself was to have a major presence in the enterprise councils, through SOKSI and mass organisations affiliated to it.

By the end of 1963 there were reportedly 656 enterprise councils in existence as well as 21 central industrial councils. Most of the enterprise councils were in plantations (Reeve 1985: 220; King 1982: 129). In spite of the efforts of SOKSI, SOBSI was able to gain a strong foothold in them. Reeve notes that of the enterprise councils' combined membership of 2,737, a total of 677 or 24.7 per cent were affiliated to SOBSI, much more than any of the other party-linked union federations. Those affiliated to SOKSI itself only numbered 406 or 15 per cent of the membership. However these numbers were bolstered by the fact that managers also nominated representatives. These representatives numbered 656, giving SOKSI and management a total of 1,062 seats (Reeve 1985: 221). Although the councils' role was limited to a largely advisory one, that did not mean that they were unimportant. In fact, these enterprise councils came to take over the arbitration of labour disputes in state enterprises from the regular machinery (King 1982: 129).

It is clear, then, that the main aim of army involvement in labour affairs after 1957 was to maintain industrial peace, particularly in the state enterprises over which the military came to have managerial control. Foreshadowing future developments in the New Order, the army began to propagate the idea that conflict between employer and worker was a 'historical remnant of liberalism', and unsuited to Pancasila (BKS-BUMIL 1961a).[54] An integral part of the effort was to encourage some degree of unification of the highly fragmented trade-union movement, thereby facilitating its control by the army. SOBSI constituted the main obstacle to the army's plans.

As revealed in Table 3.3, increased army intervention into labour affairs after 1957, together with the pervasiveness of NASAKOM politics, all resulted in a marked reduction in the number of strike actions. Virtually total industrial peace had been achieved by the early 1960s.

Table 3.3 Labour Strikes 1950–1963[55]

Year	Number of Strikes	Workers Involved
1950	184	491,000
1951	541	319,000
1952	349	133,000
1953	280	420,000
1954	347	158,000
1955	469	239,000
1956	505	340,000
1957	151	62,000
1958	55	14,000
1959	70	27,000
1960	64	15,000
1961	86	63,000
1962	0	
1963	0	

SUMMARY

The foregoing discussion shows that a tradition of labour militancy in Indonesia was established by a trade-union movement that emerged in the context of a nationalist, anti-colonial struggle in the early part of the twentieth century. However, there were serious structural obstacles to the realisation of any agenda of proletarian-led revolution, owing mainly to the limited level of industrialisation. While the trade-union movement underwent a relatively early collapse in the face of colonial government repression, an important segment of its early post-colonial successor inherited the legacy of its militant politics. Nevertheless, a consolidated and unified trade-union movement did not emerge in the 1950s and early 1960s, partly because of the entanglement of organised labour in the rivalries between political parties.

An important development was the widespread involvement of the army in labour affairs, particularly after the promulgation of martial law and the nationalisation of foreign companies in 1957. The emergence of the army as a major actor in the labour area also signified the beginnings of a growing tide that would eventually result in the all-out demolition of the militant stream of the labour movement. Indeed, at the same time, a coalition of social forces – including the urban and rural petty bourgeoisie – was crystallising around the army, whose interests were diametrically opposed to the kind of radical social transformation to which organisations such as SOBSI and the PKI were ideologically predisposed.

What power and influence the radical stream of the labour movement had developed in the 1950s was partly due to the absence of formidable foes. State power, for example, was extremely diffuse and fragmented in the immediate post-colonial period until the push toward centralisation initiated by Soekarno in the form of Guided Democracy. The propertied classes were still struggling to find a niche for themselves in the post-colonial economy. Importantly, the centralisation process also provided a platform for the concentration of a significant degree of power in the hands of the army, an institution which had a historical basis for animosity toward militant labour. Much of the actual power of the state apparatus had been appropriated by the army by the early 1960s. As state managers, it was also in the army's interests to try to circumvent the influence of radical unionism.

As the army began to develop concrete interests in the maintenance of industrial peace, it also began to develop its own labour institutions to curb the PKI-linked SOBSI. The eventual result of this was the quelling of militant labour and the establishment of the tradition of military involvement in labour affairs which would become ever more ubiquitous in the New Order. Initial army involvement in labour affairs also saw the spawning of the idea of an army-controlled corporatist labour federation, the discouragement of strike action, and the development of an ideology of harmonious relations between capital, state and labour, all of which continue to be features of the workings of the exclusionary model of accommodation between state, capital and labour in New Order Indonesia. As we shall see, the demolition of the radical stream of the labour movement in Indonesia paved the way for the establishment of that model.

4 Reconstituting organised labour
The genesis of New Order labour policy

POLITICS AND ECONOMICS IN THE EARLY NEW ORDER

The position of the working class in the balance of class forces after 1965 was weaker than it had ever been. In the aftermath of the abduction and murder of six leading army generals late that year, dramatic events occurred which permanently changed the constellation of political power, and profoundly impacted on the fortunes of organised labour. The PKI was accused of being the instigator of these murders – as part of a wider attempt to wrest political power – and became the target of a violent, army-directed campaign of reprisal. The party was crushed as hundreds of thousands of its members and sympathisers were either killed or imprisoned. President Soekarno, who was regarded as being too close and sympathetic to the PKI, was gradually forced to relinquish his own power under pressure from a number of political groups which included students, secular intellectuals, religious organisations and most importantly, the corps of army officers now led by General Soeharto. The latter himself took hold of formal political power in March 1966 although he was only named full President in 1968.

The array of mass organisations linked with the PKI – some 26 of them – including its labour-arm, SOBSI (with its 62 affiliated unions), were crushed, along with the party (Capizzi 1974: 37). The non-SOBSI labour unions and federations joined with the army in the campaign and were subsequently directed to participate in the new forms of institutional arrangements which were to govern state–capital–labour relations, in terms which were unilaterally determined by the new holders of bureaucratic power. However, establishing an appropriate format which would ensure the ability of the state to supervise and control organised labour was not an easy task, given the confusing array of labour unions and federations that existed, each with its own political histories and party orientations. Thus, it took no less than seven years before the matter was more or less resolved and a viable post-SOBSI institutional vehicle for organised labour was developed.

The development of this vehicle ultimately took place at the same time as the gradual entrenchment of a wider exclusionary corporatist, social and political framework. The latter was characterised by the establishment of monolithic, non-competitive, and state-dominated institutions, geared to ensure control over society-based organisations and movements. Among such institutions were the KNPI, which 'represented' youth, the HKTI, which 'represented' the peasantry, and the HNSI, which 'represented' fishermen. Organised labour would have little if any real power within the framework that was constructed. Thus, the development in Indonesia of the 'exclusionary' model of accommodation between state, capital and labour was inextricably linked to the wider development of such a social and political framework.

One of the principal tasks that Soeharto's 'New Order' set for itself in the mid-1960s was to revitalise Indonesia's floundering economy. In view of this, King (1979) has proposed that labour policy in the early New Order was primarily shaped by the narrow goals of economic development. Indeed, these goals served to distinguish the new regime from the old, accused as it was of causing the economy to deteriorate through neglect and mismanagement. As King points out, these goals, in turn, required industrial peace. He writes that

> The economic stabilisation program launched in 1966 required wage restraint and the contraction of credit which inhibited the expansion of domestic business and curtailed the creation of new employment. In addition, the government policy of rationalisation of the bureaucracy, which called for steady across the board salary increases for civil servants, assumed smaller increments in the private sector, which caused wage 'pressures' there. Finally the door had been reopened to foreign investors further adding the potential for labour unrest. No doubt each of these factors contributed to the government sense that a controlled labour force was more important than ever.
>
> (King 1979 : 187)

Thus, for King, corporatist controls over organised labour in the New Order – in formal terms, initiated with the establishment of the *Federasi Buruh Seluruh Indonesia* (FBSI; All-Indonesia Labour Federation) in 1973 – was part of a wider strategy of 'defensive modernisation', by which regimes attempt to manage change and control the consequences of organised labour. This term he borrows from early theorists of corporatism.[1] The strategy itself, according to King, is related to a particular historical configuration, namely that of delayed, dependent, capitalist development (King 1979: 185).

Although King is certainly not incorrect to relate New Order labour policy to the requirements of its economic development agenda, this interpretation overlooks the equally important, and more distinctly political considerations which helped to shape early New Order labour policy. Thus, a somewhat different interpretation is presented here which is particularly concerned with the way that the evolution of early New Order labour policy was specifically geared toward the eventual establishment of an exclusionary model of accommodation between state, capital and labour.

The importance of these political considerations can be appreciated when one takes into account the legacy of the political struggles of the late 1950s and early 1960s, discussed in the previous Chapter, in which the PKI and the army emerged as the principal protagonists. Newly victorious over the Left, the army-dominated New Order coalition's main political agenda was to prohibit the reemergence of radically inclined mass-based movements, such as that of organised labour. Ultimately, the leitmotif of the early New Order was the control of all kinds of organisations which by their very nature were mass-based, whether political parties, trade unions or peasant associations.

Therefore, rather than being a necessary outcome of 'delayed, dependent, capitalist development', the subjection of organised labour to a state-dominated corporatist strategy should be seen instead as a political response by a newly consolidating political coalition – representing the interests of the army, the upper strata of politico-bureaucrats, and the urban as well as rural petty bourgeoisie – to the possibility of the reemergence of a left-wing dominated, militant, labour movement. It is significant that labour in particular, as discussed in the previous Chapter, had always largely been dominated by the Left since its early constitution as a political force during the early nationalist struggle. While some members of the New Order coalition – e.g. sections of the urban petty bourgeoisie that comprised the constituency, for example, of the old MASYUMI party – might have had some qualms about the gradual stifling of *all* political parties, the members of the coalition would have been in agreement about the desirability of a controllable, and ideologically moderate organised labour movement.

There is also another problem with the somewhat functionalist presentation of the correspondence of this strategy of labour control and that of 'delayed, dependent, capitalism', which gives the impression of the existence in Indonesia of a capitalism which somehow deviates from a kind of 'norm'. In fact, as was discussed in Chapter 2, the way in which the process of capitalist industrialisation has proceeded in different societies – and the relative strength of the social forces engendered by that process – has varied greatly over time, and thus the historical models of accommodation that have been struck by state, capital and labour have also differed. A crucial factor has been the relative strength of the working class: earlier industrialisations have provided a more favourable milieu for working-class movements to develop and then press for some degree of political inclusion. During later industrialisations, the political context in which working-class movements have emerged has usually been less than favourable, and the prospects for a successful struggle for political inclusion considerably more limited.

Therefore, insofar as the Indonesian corporatism referred to by King is related to 'a particular historical configuration', it is to one that is characterised by a balance of class forces in which the working class is relatively underdeveloped, in terms of size, power and organisational capacity. The imposition on organised labour, by the state, of the kind of corporatist framework that would ensure the demobilisation of labour as a social force is undoubtedly more possible in the absence of a significant working-class movement.

It was seen in the previous Chapter that the working-class movement in Indonesia did exhibit a high degree of political activism and militancy during the early part of the twentieth century. This, however, was primarily due to the fact that working-class organisations emerged within the context of a nationalist movement which was heavily influenced by revolutionary and socialist ideas. In the 1950s organised labour – particularly its radical stream – was helped by the fact that it operated in a milieu characterised by the unconsolidated nature of the state and the negligible existence of a bourgeoisie. The limited level of industrialisation at the time, nevertheless, imposed real constraints on the pursuit of a revolutionary proletarian agenda.

None the less, particularly during these early years, New Order state planners were concerned about pre-empting the re-emergence of left-wing influence over organised labour. This is indicated by the number of times its spectre was invoked by state officials, undoubtedly in an attempt to exorcise the spirit of militant unionism from the body, as well as the collective memory, of organised labour. Thus, in 1967, Minister of Manpower Awaloeddin Djamin warned the 'Indonesian nation and people' that for as long as the PKI was not completely smashed, labour would always present a problem (*Angkatan Bersendjata* 3 March 1967). In October 1968, GOLKAR Chairman General Sukowati warned that strike action could be exploited by PKI remnants (*Antara* 19 October 1968).

However, having highlighted the importance of the more strictly political dimension, it is also quite evident that there was a relationship between the labour and wider economic policies of the early New Order. Clearly, the reemergence of independent, and potentially radical trade-union organisations in these years of concerted efforts to attract badly needed foreign capital was something that New Order state planners had to take care to prevent.

Indeed, the primary concern was to reconnect Indonesia's economy with the international one, in such a way as to facilitate the infusion of foreign capital and investment. During the late Soekarno years, Indonesia was growing increasingly estranged from major Western industrial countries, as the result of the President's deeply anti-foreign capital and imperialist rhetoric, as well as his ideological commitment to an Indonesia which would be strong and industrialised through taking a largely autochthonous development path. Such a commitment, which gained impetus after the adoption of Guided Democracy, ultimately led to economic disaster. The fall of export earnings of primary commodities resulted in a balance-of-payment crisis as well as a serious inability to pay off foreign debt. Meanwhile, vital state-owned plantations were allowed to degenerate through neglect. By the 1960s rampant inflation – reaching up to 600 per cent per annum – plunged the national economy into a state of utter chaos (Robison 1990: 39–40).[2]

Within the first years of the New Order, a group of Western-trained liberal technocrats at the University of Indonesia's Faculty of Economics was given the task of directing economic policy. While opening up Indonesia to foreign aid and investment, they concentrated on the development of an ISI strategy primarily based on consumer goods such as textiles. In 1967 a law on foreign investment was introduced which provided tax concessions and exemption from import duty on raw materials and spare parts. It also provided safeguards for the repatriation of profits and against nationalisation (Robison 1982: 54; 1990: 103).

The technocrats' policies have been described by Robison as being counter-revolutionary, as they were made possible by the disappearance from the political scene of forces whose ideological predispositions favoured the radical redistribution of wealth and resources. These policies were embraced because they were ideologically acceptable to foreign investors and donors and because the vision of economic development that they offered allowed for the maintenance of the existing social order. Importantly, within the confines of this vision, economic growth was not seen to be the outcome of radical social reform or redistribution of wealth but of increased investment, technological development and the concentration of economic and political power. In Rostowian fashion, it was assumed that the fruits of economic growth would be diffused through a trickle-down process. The promise of such economic development – without great social upheaval – was naturally most attractive to such sections of society as the urban salaried and state officials, whose income and living standards had been hit hard by the rampant inflation of the last years of Soekarno's rule (Robison 1990: 44), and who were wary of the excesses of radical mass-based action.

Significantly, the remnants of organised labour were seen to have a part to play in the cultivation of Indonesia's new image. With this in mind it was given the task of convincing potential foreign donors and investors that Indonesian labour could now be counted on to be supportive of the new government's economic agenda.[3] This task was an important one, given the anti-foreign capital actions and rhetoric of the SOBSI-affiliated unions of the 1950s and early 1960s which had helped to estrange Indonesia from the West.

In June and July 1969, a trade-union delegation consisting of senior trade-union leaders Agus Sudono of GASBIINDO, Adolf Rachman of KONGKARBU-SOKSI, Darius Marpaung of KESPEKRI (a small Protestant-oriented union), P.D.F. Manuputty of SOB Pantjasila, A. Dahlan Siregar of SARBUMUSI and M.O. Tambunan of the KBM, embarked on a government-sponsored mission to various European countries. As Siregar explained to the Indonesian press when the group returned, one of its aims was to convince potential European investors that the political climate in Indonesia, and specifically the attitude of workers, did not pose a threat to the security and interests of foreign capital.

Statements to the press made by members of the delegation upon their return were indicative of the extent to which leaders of organised labour were actively supporting the implementation of economic policy. For example, when questioned in Europe about the imposition of restrictions on the right to strike in Indonesia, Siregar reported that the mission explained how workers were 'patriots bound to national interests', and that they realised that such restrictions were tied up with considerations of national interest. Pressed about why workers would not pose a threat to the security of foreign investment, the mission replied that 'workers were conscious of the fact that the struggle of the Indonesian nation had entered upon a phase of development that badly needed capital' (*Nusantara* 30 July 1969). Revealingly, it has been reported that the trade-union mission did not attempt to contact European labour organisations during the visit (INDOC 1981: 78).

The remarks made by Siregar indicate that by that time organised labour had recognised that its own fate was now determined by the new holders of state power. Presiding over relatively weak labour organisations, labour leaders came to recognise that their organisations' continuing existence could only be defended if they could present themselves as playing a constructive role in the New Order's economic development plans.

The compliance of organised labour sent a clear, favourable message to foreign investors – that organised labour no longer posed a threat, and that the new government ensured that workers at the enterprise level adopted a totally new attitude toward employers, particularly foreign employers. These included those who were returning to Indonesia having had their properties seized in the 1950s. Thus, one American guide to doing business in early New Order Indonesia told its US readers that

> Since the communist party was banned in 1966 . . . the major source of militancy and strike making in the labour movement has gone. Strikes are not now a problem and do not appear to be a potential danger for the next few years . . . . [T]he government has stressed the importance of maintaining harmonious relations with their work forces. This was clearly considered a sensitive matter in some regions and some plants and plantations. The reason is probably that the Government was concerned over the attitude to foreign investors among some sections of the labor force, who had been subjected to years of anti-foreign and anti-capitalist propaganda during the Soekarno period. In practice, however, most workers were apparently happy to see the foreign owners return.
>
> (*Business International Corporation* 1968: 74–75)

At the same time, the economic development aims of the New Order provided added legitimacy to the practice of imposing stringent state controls over organised labour. The imposition of these controls was clearly supported by the influential notions of 'developmentalism' – in part inspired by the Huntingtonian version of modernisation theory – which strongly linked economic success to the maintenance of social and political stability. Such notions were primarily, though not exclusively, expressed by state officials associated with the army-linked, quasi-clandestine and highly influential political intelligence group, OPSUS, led by General Ali Moertopo (Moertopo 1975: 5–6).

Significantly, such 'developmentalist' ideas served to underscore the potential 'threat' to stability – and hence to 'development' – that organised labour would pose. Thus the search for an acceptable institutional format for organised labour was presented as being part and parcel of the development of institutions in 'society' that would be supportive of the process of development. Ideologically, this meant the hegemony of corporatist ideas of partnership between state, capital and labour and the exclusion of any notions of class conflict. Hence, Ali Moertopo was to exclaim in 1971 that 'workers and employers must go; only one class will remain, that of the *karyawan*' (cited in Capizzi 1974: 42).

Moertopo was not alone in voicing such ideas. The late 1960s saw a rash of statements by state figures on the virtues of a non-confrontational philosophy of industrial relations. As Mursalin, Minister of Manpower during the late 1960s, was reported to have declared 'interpretations of labour relations based on class conflict and free fight liberalism must be immediately wiped out and replaced by interpretations of labour relations based on Pancasila' (*El Bahar* 18 March 1969).

Pancasila, the state ideology, was itself increasingly presented as being opposed to any kind of intra-society conflict, and as being exclusively in favour of the consultative process in the resolution of disputes between groups (*El Bahar* 18 March 1969). Significantly, Pancasila was also being interpreted and elaborated in such a way as to enable the government to wield extensive power over every part of life. As Ali Moertopo (1972: 55–56) wrote: '[Modernisation] requires the clarification of the model of the Pancasila state and the application of the principles of Pancasila in every field of life, every organ and body of the state and at all levels of society, both in the towns and in villages.'

The ideology of harmonious relations between employer and employee was eventually codified as the doctrine of *Hubungan Perburuhan Pancasila* (HPP; Pancasila Labour Relations) in 1974, later renamed *Hubungan Industrial Pancasila* (HIP; Pancasila Industrial Relations) (see Chapter 5). HPP or HIP defined industrial relations essentially as being similar to those that existed within the family – with the state playing the role of benevolent father to both capital and labour. Importantly, this doctrine does not recognise the right of workers to strike, viewing such a right as 'liberal' and thus contravening the family-like principles which govern Pancasila.

Furthermore, the official propaganda increasingly saddled workers and worker organisations with responsibilities in ensuring the success of the development process. As one Minister of Manpower of the 1960s, Mursalin, put it:

Apart from having rights as an organisation of workers to fight for the lot of their members by means customarily used by labour organisations in other countries, . . . labour organisations also have responsibilities for national economic development in general and production together with productivity in particular (sic).

(El Bahar 18 March 1969)

Thus, the official philosophy of industrial relations was one of partnership between capital, labour and the state in the pursuit of common development goals. By the same logic, organised labour's activities were more strictly limited to the social-economic realm. This clearly contrasted with the highly politicised labour movement of the Old Order.

The real significance of political considerations in the search for an appropriate institutional format for organised labour is also indicated by the fact that it went hand in hand with the process of depoliticising labour – synonymous with the elimination of left-wing figures and sympathisers from the labour scene. This was not a process that impacted only on labour organisations affiliated with SOBSI but also one that extended to the state bureaucracy. Thus, besides PKI and SOBSI figures, state officials regarded as being sympathetic to the Left were targeted for elimination. *Ad hoc* organisations such as the so-called *karyawan–buruh* arm of the KAP-GESTAPU, a grouping formed to crush the 'September 30 Movement' , as the episode of the abduction of the six generals was now called, played a leading role in this effort. This organisation, in which many trade unionist foes of SOBSI participated, called for the removal of three cabinet ministers, including Minister of Labour Soetomo of the left-leaning party, the PARTINDO. In 1963 Soetomo had replaced Ahem Erningpradja, a close ally of the army leadership. Regarded as being hostile to SOKSI, he was replaced by Awaloeddin Djamin, a high-ranking police officer and a SEKBER GOLKAR executive (Reeve 1985: 284). Notably, the latter institution was originally established in 1964 as a vehicle which presided over mass organisations directed by the army, particularly those cultivated by SOKSI, to oppose the PKI (Soehardiman 1993: 164; Boileau 1983: 45–47).

In this regard, one act of significance, cited by both Capizzi and INDOC, was the renaming of the title of *Menteri Perburuhan* (Minister of Labour) as *Menteri Tenaga Kerja* (Minister of Manpower). As INDOC observes, the change of name 'expresses the passage of workers from a condition of (sic) active subject to one of passive object in the governmental scheme of things' (INDOC 1981: 78). Indeed, the act was an apt symbol of the aim being pursued at the time of transforming a historically militant labour movement into one that was ideologically moderate and controllable. Again the word *buruh*, rich as it was in political connotations, particularly because of its employment by the labour organisations of the nationalist struggle, was deemed to be less amenable to the goal of developing a labour movement with a strictly limited social and economic agenda. Thus the employment of the term *tenaga kerja* in the early New Order was based on similar reasoning as the employment of the term *karyawan* by the army in the early 1960s. In fact, according to Reeve (1985: 284), like *karyawan*, the term *tenaga kerja* was also a SOKSI proposal.

The task of those newly saddled with responsibility over labour affairs was obvious. Awaloeddin Djamin, the New Order's first 'Minister of Manpower', describes succinctly how early New Order state planners saw the labour situation:[4]

> The antagonistic contradiction between labour and capital is the doctrine of the PKI . . . In this doctrine capital must lose. Bung Karno was influenced by the doctrine as well. This (doctrine) of course would have taken us to a dictatorship of the proletariat.
>
> . . . My job was to clean up the communist doctrine, the communist labour doctrine.

Significantly, the Ministry of Manpower portfolio was to be taken up by individuals who had either made a career within the security or military apparatus or who would be predisposed to ensure the maintenance of industrial peace for the sake of economic development objectives. In 1968, Awaloeddin was replaced by Mursalin, an air force officer who had also been active in the establishment of the armed forces-sponsored SEKBER GOLKAR, later to be developed into the state's formal electoral vehicle (Reeve 1985: 284). Later still, in 1971, Mohammad Sadli, a leading economic technocrat, replaced Mursalin as Minister of Manpower, before he in turn was replaced in 1973 by yet another technocrat, Subroto. Although all of these figures were formally responsible for labour affairs, it was Ali Moertopo and his OPSUS that ultimately played the most significant role in the establishment of a corporatist strategy of labour control in the early New Order.

The late 1960s and early 1970s saw several efforts to develop a single, corporatist, state-dominated institution of labour representation. These efforts naturally involved the participation of the non-SOBSI unions and union federations of the 1950s. It should be remembered that many of these organisations had cultivated close relations with the army in their own struggle for supremacy on the labour front with SOBSI. Understandably, many non-SOBSI labour leaders attempted to build on the links that they had earlier established with the army leadership – now the unchallenged centre of political power. Apparently, there was a significant degree of expectation that maintaining such links would not automatically preclude the possibility of developing a relatively independent labour movement.[5]

To be fair, the political mood of the first years of the New Order was conducive to the emergence of such expectations, for many believed at the time that the New Order would usher in a process of increasing democratisation. Moreover, these expectations were clearly not exclusively held by labour leaders. For example, there were indications that civilians would come to take up an important role in political life in partnership with the army. There were also expectations regarding an enhanced role for parliament and the rehabilitation of banned political parties. The involvement of economic technocrats in policy-making was also seen as a positive signal to those hoping for greater freedoms. Young intellectuals and student activists also shared the high hopes regarding the prospects of greater freedom of thought and expression, of human rights, rule of law, and democracy, all 'in the cause of modernisation and development' (Reeve 1985: 267).

This was the context in which, in 1968, GASBIINDO's Agus Sudono demanded that the right to strike be restored to workers, in 'harmony with the aspirations of the New Order to establish a democratic and constitutional way of life' (*Antara* 3 October 1968). He was of course referring to restrictions on the exercise of the right to strike which had been implemented since the 1950s, particularly after the promulgation of martial law. At about the same time, the NU's SARBUMUSI urged the government to rescind the 1963 Presidential Instruction which prohibited strikes in vital state institutions and projects (SARBUMUSI 1968: 10).

However, it soon became clear that such expectations were ill-founded. Parliament continued to be largely powerless, while the government took an increasingly active role in the internal affairs of political parties and mass organisations. By the early 1970s, the government electoral vehicle, GOLKAR, had won an overwhelming victory in a heavily controlled election contest, at the expense of the Old Order political parties. In the meantime, members of the civil service were coerced into practising 'monoloyalty' to the government, while rescinding their trade-union affiliations. The reconstitution of organised labour itself was soon to be undertaken clearly on the initiative of state officials rather than of trade-union leaders. Some of the major actors involved in the process included General Ali Moertopo of OPSUS, Minister of Manpower Mursalin, and labour leaders Agus Sudono (GASBIINDO) and Adolf Rachman (KONGKARBU-SOKSI).

THE STATE-LED RECONSTITUTION OF ORGANISED LABOUR

The weakness of organised labour

As stated earlier, it soon became apparent that the New Order government was intent on playing a dominant and directing role in labour affairs. It also gradually became evident that the government was not willing to risk the development of an independent labour movement, not even one that was for the time being 'cleansed' of left-wing elements.

However, even when hopes of developing a labour movement that was relatively independent of the state started to diminish, labour leaders continued to be supportive of New Order labour policy. Of course they had little choice, given that there was no viable alternative political force to the power of the army-dominated state. As Sutanto of the SARBUMUSI succinctly described his assessment of the prospects for labour by the early 1970s: 'We knew that there was little hope left for independence, but we had no choice . . . but to cooperate.'[6]

In fact trade unions were gradually pushed into taking up a supporting, rather than leading role in the labour picture. As noted earlier, many of the remaining labour unions were weak and thus had little bargaining power with the government. Even the larger ones had always been dependent on party directives for political and strategic orientation – parties which were now increasingly crippled themselves. Equally significantly, none of the political parties, with the possible exception of the MURBA, constituted 'natural' allies of the working class, as their main constituencies were comprised of other interests.

Thus, labour unions could do little when the first years of the New Order saw a marked increase in retrenchments, for efficiency reasons, of civil employees, particularly of state-owned companies. Even though the labour disputes that arose in many state enterprises (*Indonesia Raya* 14 December 1968), including the state airline (*Suara Merdeka* 15 October 1968) , and the state-owned Hotel Indonesia (*Angkatan Bersendjata* 11 October 1968), were widely reported, labour unions were generally powerless to assist the workers involved.

In this context, it was significant that the NU-linked SARBUMUSI was the only trade union in the early New Order period regularly to voice criticism of the government's labour policy, in particular regarding its growing penchant for control. Most importantly, the union attacked the government's policy of separating trade unions from their civil service constituency by introducing compulsory associations of civil servants called *Korps Karyawan* (KOKAR) – which eventually led to *Korps Pegawai Republik Indonesia* (KORPRI; Civil Servants' Corps of the Republic of Indonesia). It also criticised cases of the forced dismantling of various labour union branches at the level of the firm (SARBUMUSI 1971: 1). The union was able to take a relatively critical stance because it was linked to a party that was still a considerable political force, albeit one that mainly catered to the interests of the rural petty bourgeoisie.

Of the four parties that emerged victorious in the 1955 elections, the NU was the only one that was more or less intact by the early 1970s. The PKI, as well as its labour arm, SOBSI, was of course crushed and eliminated from the political scene by that time, while the MASYUMI had been banned by Soekarno in 1960. Perhaps for lack of political protection, the latter's labour arm, the GASBIINDO, while continuing to exist, increasingly moved into a position of compromise and cooperation with the army. The PNI, traditionally the party of the state bureaucracy, but also the bastion of Soekarnoism, was only a shadow of its former self. Weakened by the expulsion of those regarded to be left-wing or too-avid Soekarnoists, the party also lost hold over its traditional constituency, as the government sought to increase control over the civil bureaucracy. Moreover, the PNI's labour arm was already weakened by an internal rift in the early 1960s (Hawkins 1963b: 96). Besides, one section of the 'nationalist' labour stream, led by former Minister of Labour Ahem Erningpradja, had already demonstrated in the past its willingness to cooperate with the army.[7]

Smaller trade unions, such as the Protestant KESPEKRI or the Catholic SOB Pantjasila never had much of a constituency. The political parties with which they were linked were also weak and small. Thus, it was more or less natural that they were easily placed in a position of compromise and cooperation, which meant a greater degree of identification with the government's SEKBER GOLKAR, then promoting itself as the umbrella for all 'functional groups' in society. As Sutanto of the SARBUMUSI complained, few of his fellow trade unionists supported with equal vigour his attack on the government policy of separating state employees from trade unions, even though it was of direct relevance to the very principle of freedom of association.[8]

The early 1970s in particular was the period that saw the rapid demise of the influence of political parties in the face of systematic government efforts to undermine them. The success of the government's efforts was underscored by the poor performance of the nine political parties that participated in the 1971 general elections – all virtually demolished by the government-backed SEKBER GOLKAR.[9] The final blow to political parties came in the form of a state-engineered fusion in which the nine then in existence were amalgamated into just two parties. One of these hybrid new entities was the 'Islamic' United Development Party (PPP), which included the historically competing 'traditionalist' and 'modernist' wings of Islam, respectively represented by the NU and MASYUMI. The other was the 'nationalist' Indonesian Democratic Party (PDI), whose most important component was the Indonesian National Party (PNI), but which included an amalgam of Christian, Catholic and socialist groups (see Moertopo 1974: 66–68). There was no way that either of the two newly created parties, constructed out of elements which were in many ways mutually antagonistic, could stand as a viable opponent of the state-backed GOLKAR. With this final act, what Soekarno had attempted to do in the late 1950s – reduce the role and influence of the political parties – with the support of the central army leadership, was actually more fully achieved by the army without Soekarno himself.

The impact of the decline of political parties is difficult to overstate. In essence, because all the 'Old Order' parties were being gradually sidelined, the existing trade unions and trade-union federations which were traditionally linked to them were bereft of their source of political orientation and power. The weakening of political parties encouraged organised labour to support the establishment of a single, unified organisational entity with close links to the army-dominated state (Sukarno 1980: 9), in a fashion similar to the one envisaged in the failed attempt to create OPPI in 1960.

There were of course other reasons for the lack of significant voices of opposition to increasingly blatant acts of state intervention into labour affairs. This support stemmed from the labour unions' own past experiences, particularly during the 1950s, when there was incessant bickering among competing unions, often in the same enterprise. As one labour leader of the 1960s put it in recalling the situation that existed in the 1950s: 'Negotiations among labour unions were usually more protracted than negotiations with employers.'[10]

Labour leaders also favoured the establishment of a unified workers' entity because they probably thought it would institutionalise links with the state and thereby afford organised labour some measure of political support and protection – while simultaneously hoping that its structural form would allow individual labour organisations to continue to exist. It is worth reiterating that few perhaps envisaged until later the extent to which the state would play a role in directing the life of such an organisation.[11] In essence, what labour leaders were expecting was the development of a kind of state-supported trade unionism, in which labour organisations would back the state's economic policy agenda in return for a significant degree of inclusion within the political process as well as some degree of autonomy.

Indonesian labour leaders had in mind something similar to what emerged in some Latin American countries in the 1940s, where trade unions were an important constituency of populist regimes. What the labour leaders eventually got, however, was a form of exclusionary corporatism, by which organised labour, 'represented' in a state-controlled corporatist institution, was essentially peripheralised, if not excluded from the political process. Essentially, what remained of organised labour in Indonesia in the late 1960s constituted too negligible a social force to be able to negotiate a more favourable form of accommodation. Notably, similar arrangements emerged in the experiences of very late industrialising countries like South Korea – where the reason for their emergence also had to do with the concerns to pre-empt a leftist political challenge.

In search of a format

As mentioned earlier, concerted efforts to push organised labour toward the development of a simplified, unified organisational entity – much in the manner of the army-supported OPPI – had in fact begun since the first years of the New Order. Early on, several vehicles were created to link closely what was left of organised labour after the demise of SOBSI to the institutions of the state. For example, SEKBER GOLKAR, which was gradually being developed into the party of the state, set up a labour coordinating body, and brought under its wings such organisations as the KBKI, the SOB Pancasila, SOKSI, the PGRI (a teachers' union), the PSPN (a civil servants' union) and the MURBA-linked SOBRI (Reeve 1985: 284). Labour organisations combined in the SEKBER Buruh established an action front, the *Kesatuan Aksi Buruh Indonesia* (KABI; Indonesian Workers' United Action) (SPSI 1990a: 3) which counted among its members anti-communist labour leaders, including Darius Marpaung, Adolf Rachman and Agus Sudono. Though the aim of KABI was also to cleanse organised labour of communist sympathisers,[12] it had a more active 'political' role to play, in that it was directly organising mass demonstrations in support of the New Order. According to Agus Sudono, the three-pronged aims of KABI were to eliminate communism in Indonesia and eradicate the influence of SOBSI, strengthen the New Order, and gradually improve the welfare of workers.[13]

Playing a leading role among the labour organisations which comprised KABI were the GASBIINDO and KONGKARBU-SOKSI. These organisations were of course the two most serious foes of SOBSI within the trade-union movement in the early 1960s. With its inclusion in KABI, KONGKARBU-SOKSI finally won recognition as a legitimate trade union. Earlier, it had been barred from membership in the SEKBER Buruh created largely because of SOBSI criticism that it was not a true workers' organisation.

Labour figures associated with the army-created political vehicle SEKBER GOLKAR (later shortened to GOLKAR) – among them Adolf Rachman – were prominent in KABI. In fact, SEKBER GOLKAR itself, as an organisation, was playing an increasingly interventionist role in labour affairs. The interventions of SEKBER GOLKAR in these early years were so extensive that it effectively promoted itself as 'the sole link for workers associations with overseas institutions', monopolising relations with the ILO (International Labour Organisation), ICFTU (International Confederation of Free Trade Unions), and the AFL-CIO (American Federation of Labor-Congress of International Organizations). As a result, some labour organisations, notably SARBUMUSI, started to express their disgruntlement. This led to attempts at the creation of a single organisational entity, representing labour, closely linked, but theoretically separate from SEKBER GOLKAR (Reeve 1985: 284–285).

Such a move was given greater impetus by pressures from international organisations such as the ICFTU, FES (Friedrich Ebert *Stiftung*) of West Germany and the AFL-CIO. These institutions in fact played an important role in the period of searching for an appropriate format for organised labour in the early New Order. They found more room to manoeuvre in Indonesia with the demise of the communist bloc-oriented SOBSI, gained a greater degree of political clout because of the new importance of Western governments as a source of aid funds, and lobbied for the creation of some kind of an independent workers' organisation. Both the ICFTU and FES, for example, are reported to have played an important role in the two early attempts to form loose associations of labour organisations in Indonesia, the *Badan Koordinasi Proyek Buruh Indonesia* (BAKERPROBI; Indonesian Labour Project Coordination Body) (INDOC 1981: 79) and the *Majelis Permusyawaratan Buruh Indonesia* (MPBI; Indonesian Labour Consultative Council).

Initially the involvement of these institutions met with some domestic criticism. Again it was the SARBUMUSI that expressed concern about the role of foreign organisations. At one point, the NU-linked union refused to attend a conference of Indonesian trade unions organised by the ICFTU because 'as a matter of principle' it rejected the idea of such conferences being initiated by foreign organisations (*El Bahar* 18 October 1968). SARBUMUSI was also probably concerned that the initiative was taken outside of KABI (*Berkala SARBUMUSI* no. 4/October 1968: 11), the action front in which all the anti-communist unions were represented, thus allowing SEKBER GOLKAR to play the dominant role again. Interestingly, Adolf Rachman, who as well as heading KONGKARBU-SOKSI was a member of SEKBER GOLKAR, also attacked the idea of the ICFTU conference, although in the end, he was pressured by senior GOLKAR figures into supporting it. Importantly, Rachman was opposed to the conference for a different reason – he was concerned that it would merely serve the interests of trade unions affiliated to the ICFTU,[14] a clear reference to Agus Sudono's GASBIINDO.

Such criticism, however, did not stop the issuing of a joint statement by trade unions, following the conference, which expressed their preparedness 'to accept international aid with gratitude and with a full sense of responsibility' (*Angkatan Bersendjata* 21 October 1968). SARBUMUSI itself eventually joined the ICFTU.

While international organisations began to play an increasingly important role in Indonesian labour affairs following the demise of SOBSI, they did in fact have a longer historical presence in Indonesia. For example, the ICFTU had been active in the country for many years, establishing close links with the MASYUMI-affiliated SBII/GASBIINDO.[15] Following the ban on the MASYUMI party in 1960, the ICFTU was subsequently forced to reduce its role in Indonesia, although the labour arm of the MASYUMI continued to operate (INDOC 1981: 80). Notably, Agus Sudono, secretary general and then chairman of the GASBIINDO, had been a vice-president of the ICFTU for the Asia and Pacific region since 1958, and in 1966, was elected to the organisation's governing body (Sudono 1985: 63).[16]

The AFL-CIO also had a representative to Indonesia as early as 1966. This representative – one Harry Goldberg – had made many visits to Indonesia since the 1950s and was well acquainted with the labour and political scene. He was known as a critic of Soekarno and for being virulently opposed to the communists (INDOC 1981: 80).[17] Thus, he knew members of the army leadership as well as the anti-SOBSI trade-union leaders, many of whom had had training experience in the United States.[18] It must be remembered that the AFL-CIO's early involvement in Indonesia took place in the context of the Cold War, hence the operations of people like Goldberg were decidedly geared to strengthening the non-communist elements of the labour movement.

The relative newcomer was FES, a foundation linked to the Social

Democratic Party of West Germany. This organisation had only begun to have a presence in Indonesia in the last years of the Old Order, but was already prepared to train Indonesian labour activists, reportedly numbering in the hundreds, in Germany. It has been reported that before the upheaval of 1965, FES had engaged in talks with Agus Sudono and offered to help the Indonesian trade-union movement through GASBIINDO. This was of course at a time when the latter was regarded as one of the stronger alternatives to the Communist SOBSI.[19] FES, in fact, played an important supporting role in the reorganisation of the Department of Manpower. With its full financial support, the Department set up the *Yayasan Tenaga Kerja Indonesia* (YTKI; Indonesian Manpower Foundation), a human resources development centre, on the basis of an agreement signed by Minister of Manpower Mursalin in Bonn in 1969 (*Abadi* 26 June 1969), and negotiations which were initiated by Awaloeddin.[20] This project included the erection of a high-rise building in Jakarta to house its offices.

Initially fuelled by hopes that the New Order would usher in a period of relative democratisation, international labour organisations apparently expected labour unions to fare well. Thus, hopes that an independent labour movement would develop in the New Order were not confined to domestic quarters, because they were shared by the international organisations that were aiding, and in fact partly financing, the process of reconstituting organised labour.[21] Indeed it was probably to a degree because of the strength of such hopes that Indonesia was given a seat on the governing body of the ILO in 1969 (*Antara* 25 June 1969), lending the New Order considerable credibility in the arena of international labour affairs.

In reality, however, the government was in no way loosening its hold over domestic labour affairs. As Awaloeddin explained, the Indonesian government could not accept the ideas of such organisations as the ICFTU and AFL-CIO because they reflected 'free fight liberalism' in which workers and companies were always engaged in a contest of strength. Unwittingly providing a fairly accurate class-based analysis, Awaloeddin rejected the compatibility of these ideas with the Indonesian situation in the mid-1960s, in which both labour and capital were weak and disorganised, which meant that the government had to step in to play a major directing role.[22] Thus, the unifying of labour organisations in Indonesia would be a process that would inevitably depend to a larger extent on the direction and dictates of the state apparatus than on the volition of the organisations themselves.

The first attempt to create such a 'unified' labour entity in the New Order was the loosely defined BAKERPROBI, established in October 1968, as the product of the internationally sponsored conference of Indonesian trade unions mentioned above. Its establishment was initiated by the government, through SEKBER GOLKAR, rather than by labour leaders, as is reflected in the fact that its president was a high-ranking military officer, General Sukowati. Sukowati was also at that time General Chairman of SEKBER GOLKAR, demonstrating again that organisation's intent of promoting itself as the ultimate umbrella of organised labour. However, the word 'project' in BAKERPROBI's name signified that it was regarded primarily as a means toward the proper amalgamation of organised labour rather than as an end-product in itself. Thus, the main initial purpose of the organisation appeared to be to channel international aid for Indonesian trade unions (*Angkatan Bersendjata* 21 October 1968). SEKBER GOLKAR's control of such funds would have undoubtedly enhanced its powers of control over individual unions. BAKERPROBI, however, never took off and was promptly forgotten when other institutions bypassed it as the search for an appropriate format for organised labour continued.

Demonstrating the fact that the government did not as yet have a very clear idea about the kind of institutional format that it sought for organised labour, Minister of Manpower Mursalin soon proposed the amalgamation of existing trade unions in yet another entity, the *Majelis Buruh Indonesia* (MBI; Indonesian Workers' Council). This idea was well received by the trade unions. The usually sceptical SARBUMUSI, for example, agreed to its establishment and suggested that it could be a non-governmental and democratic body of representatives of worker organisations that 'would reflect the real potential of Indonesian workers' (*Nusantara* 14 December 1968). More promising than the BAKERPROBI, it was inaugurated with a slight name change – MPBI – by President Soeharto at the State Palace on 11 November 1969.[23]

According to King, Soeharto heralded the organisation as 'the one and only receptacle' for workers and urged the council to deal with matters that had to do directly with the interests of workers and not to serve those of outside groups. Echoing the themes that were being repeated in official circles with regard to labour, the President called on the council to create a good working climate for management and labour, to arouse the worker's spirit, and thus facilitate the implementation of the First Five Year Development Plan (King 1979: 187). Providing encouragement for those who hoped for labour freedoms, he also asserted that the establishment of any organisation by force was of no use because it would not develop 'naturally' and 'effectively' (SARBUMUSI 1971: 2).

In spite of its initial promise the MPBI too did not function well due to intense competition between the political-party linked labour unions which comprised it (INDOC 1981: 83). In fact the structure of the organisation was much too loose and the individual member organisations too autonomous to allow the organisation to function effectively. For example, the MPBI could not make binding decisions without the consent of its member organisations. In practice, it never amounted to more than a discussion forum (Sukarno 1980: 8), because each of the individual trade unions was jealously guarding its own autonomy. It was only by February 1970 that the MPBI even produced a constitution for itself (INDOC 1981: 84). Not surprisingly, though it fared better than the still-born BAKERPROBI, the MPBI was to have a short and dismal history.

According to Reeve, the relative independence of the member organisations of the MPBI was a victory for the trade unions because Mursalin had intended the organisation to be much more regimented (Reeve 1985: 285). If this was indeed a victory, it did not last long. The formation of the KOKAR and eventually KORPRI by the government in 1971 – which prohibited trade unions from contacting state employees – further weakened the already fragile MPBI. More importantly, it exposed the inability of the MPBI's member organisations to challenge effectively state policy which directly impinged on the interests of the union movement.[24]

Although other unions also pointed out that the government, by forming the KOKAR, was using tactics of coercion and intimidation, it was SARBU-MUSI in particular that criticised the KOKAR vehemently, probably because it lost an important base of power within the traditionally NU-dominated Department of Religion. The organisation even lodged a formal complaint with the ILO, instigating one of the first cases in which the New Order government had to confront international criticism for its labour policy. Such criticism, however, did not achieve more to change government policy than had the limited domestic challenge (Capizzi 1974: 43).

Initiatives taken by Ali Moertopo's OPSUS, notably with the cooperation of labour leader Agus Sudono, was to ensure the MPBI's final demise in early 1973, marked by the establishment of the FBSI.[25] The latter was designed to be a much more internally cohesive and centrally directed organisation, largely owing to the experience of the MPBI, which was no more than a loose and ineffective association, and thus, less reliable as a government instrument. Therefore, throughout its existence there was continuing discussion among trade unionists as well as state officials of how a yet-to-be attained ideal union movement structure should be organised.

Establishing the FBSI

The move to create a more cohesive trade-union federation was first apparent in an MPBI seminar which took place on 21–28 October 1971, in which Agus Sudono played an important role.[26] Here labour leaders agreed to the idea of developing a structurally more cohesive organisation, though notably no mention was made at the time about the formation of a new one. Presumably, it was thought that the MPBI itself could be transformed into such an organisation, and thus no mention was made of its possible dissolution.

It was during this seminar, organised in conjunction with Awaloeddin's YTKI and the West German FES, that Agus Sudono (1981: 26) put forward ideas that

1 The labour movement must be independent of all political forces, and that it had to be a 'pure' trade-union movement;
2 the labour movement must not be financially dependent on outside

sources, and thus, a system of collecting dues at the workplace must be developed;
3 the activities of organised labour must emphasise the social and economic fields;
4 the restructuring and unification of the existing trade unions was desirable. 'Social engineering' by the government, in the form of a Trade Union Act would be useful because the 1955 act which has governed the establishment of trade unions was too liberal;
5 Industrial-based trade unions ought to be developed.

The fact that the restructuring of organised labour was conceived as being reliant on the production of a law by the government or on 'social engineering' from above was indicative of how labour leaders at the time became increasingly dependent on initiatives from the state. Trade unions were unable to resolve problems among themselves, partly because their leaders were formally of equal standing and stature, and represented organisations that were traditionally linked to mutually competing political parties.[27] Thus, even from the point of view of many organised labour leaders, state intervention was required to determine who would be the 'first among equals'. Revealingly, even the initial meetings that led to the establishment of the FBSI were held at the office of the state intelligence agency, the *Badan Koordinasi Intelejen* (BAKIN; Intelligence Coordinating Body), one of General Moertopo's bases of power.[28]

The mention of industry-based unions signalled that the end was near for the existing trade-union federations, because it meant that there would be no place for the old types of affiliations. Moreover, the desirability of a 'pure' trade-union movement in this context meant that the links between members of the old federations and their respective political parties would have to be more or less severed. Finally, confining the labour movement to activities in the social and economic fields effectively meant that it was expected to refrain from the more overtly political activities that trade unions of the past had been engaged in. Given his relationship with OPSUS, it is likely that Sudono was not only expressing his own ideas, but also the preferences of Ali Moertopo and the OPSUS group.

The follow-up to this seminar was a plenary session of the MPBI, held on 24–26 May 1972. This led to the declaration of the *Ikrar Bersama*, or Common Resolve, which reiterated the intention to reconstitute the labour movement so that it may have a socio-economic function and a development orientation. The aim of simplifying labour organisation was also expressed in this session of the MPBI (Sukarno 1980: 118–119; SPSI 1990a: 4–5). Notably, however, the declaration again does not mention the need to form a new organisation, but instead states that the MPBI itself should reform in order to establish more strongly its identity as the sole workers' organisation in Indonesia. The document was signed by Adolf Rachman and Rasyid Sutan Rajamas, of the nationalist KBM, respectively as chairman and deputy chairman.

Adolf Rachman was pushing for a kind of united, but still fairly loose, organisation that would not automatically entail the termination of all the old labour organisations, as it would within the framework of the FBSI. According to Rachman, he was arguing for a kind of 'confederation' in which the major labour organisations would survive, more or less by a process of natural selection. In his scheme of things, only one union, with the largest membership within an enterprise, would be able to operate within that enterprise. Thus, only unions with real membership strength at the enterprise-level would be admitted to this confederation. Those smaller unions who could not win over the majority of workers in a significant enough number of companies would either be eliminated or forced to join with larger ones. This, he claims, was the direction in which he was pushing the MPBI, but which Ali Moertopo rejected as being too protracted.[29]

Events which followed determined that a more centrally directed and cohesive labour organisation would finally emerge, but that organisation would not be some revamped MPBI. This position was to be taken up instead by a newly established organisation – the FBSI.

The latter organisation's establishment was marked by a Declaration of Unity that 'announced' the fusion of all existing labour organisations into one single entity. The declaration itself was the culmination of a series of meetings between labour leaders in the offices of BAKIN and therefore, presumably involved the participation of security officials. Notably, this declaration was only signed by nine individuals. Among the signatories was none other than Agus Sudono of the GASBIINDO. The others were Rasjid Sutan Radjamas of the PNI's KBM; Oetojo Oesman, a SOKSI functionary; Sukarno, an official of the Department of Agriculture, and according to Capizzi, an OPSUS associate (Capizzi 1974: 44); Sukijat, of the Department of the Interior; Sutanto Martoprasono, of the NU's SARBUMUSI; Thaheransjah Karim, also of the SARBUMUSI; Sjofjan Hamdani, of GASBIINDO; and Radjudin Jusuf of the KBM. Reportedly, it was Ali Moertopo himself who personally selected and approached the individuals who would sign this document.[30] Excluded from the process was Adolf Rachman, who chaired the plenary session of the MPBI which produced what was considered to be the historic *Ikrar Bersama*, and who was a prominent figure in KABI and KONGKARBU-SOKSI.[31]

Interestingly, the document showed the extent to which leading representatives of organised labour had by that time taken up the developmentalist rhetoric of the New Order, which subordinated the struggle of workers to the interests of 'development' as defined by the government. For example, the declaration contained the idea that

> The essence of the struggle of Indonesian workers, taking place in the midst of developing Society and Country, is not only to protect the social and economic interest of workers, but also to enhance its participation in that process of development.[32]

Furthermore, clearly in reference to the now defamed tradition of labour militancy, it argued that the 'mental attitudes and ways of thinking' of organised labour had to be revamped so that workers might better participate in development.

The declaration also stipulated that a committee consisting of six individuals would henceforth be given the task of taking measures to ensure the establishment of a unified labour organisation. These six individuals were all among the signatories of the Declaration of Unity, but only three of them had particularly strong trade-union credentials. The three union leaders within the committee were Agus Sudono (GASBIINDO), Sutanto (SARBU-MUSI) and Rasyid Sutan Radjamas (KBM). The other three committee members, who could be described as government bureaucrats, represented the implantation of GOLKAR into the body of organised labour. These were Sukijat, Sukarno and Oetojo Oesman (INDOC 1981: 85).

It is significant that the SARBUMUSI was approached to participate in this endeavour given the fact that it had been critical over some aspects of New Order labour policy. The acquiescence of SARBUMUSI to Moertopo's designs on organised labour was probably the clearest reflection of how labour leaders by that time had given up on the idea that organised labour would be able to maintain somehow a degree of autonomy within the New Order framework.

The official date of the founding of the FBSI is now regarded as 20 February 1973, marked by the Declaration of Unity, signed by these nine individuals, at least three of whom were not even trade unionists. In quick fashion, the new 'organisation' was able to brush aside the MPBI. One week later a meeting took place between the signatories of the Declaration of Unity and members of the plenary session of the MPBI to discuss how the latter stood in view of the Declaration. On 8 March 1973, the *Badan Pimpinan Harian Sementara* (BPHS; Provisional Executive Board) of the MPBI announced a declaration of support for the new FBSI. This included the expression of support for the idea that the Committee of Six would be entrusted with the task of formulating a new constitution for the organisation; that all the members of the MPBI's provisional executive board should be included in the new central board of the FBSI; and that one of the Committee of Six should be elected as chairman of the new organisation (Sudono 1981: 35).

On 11 March 1973, the composition of the board of the FBSI was announced.33 On 20 March a constitution and work program was produced while the MPBI formally submerged itself within the FBSI by virtue of a declaration signed at a plenary session, which was now chaired by Rasyid Sutan Radjamas. Significantly, he was the only member of the plenary session that produced the Ikrar Bersama who was also a member of the Committee of Six and a signatory of the 20 February Declaration of Unity. If the meetings that led to the establishment of the FBSI took place in the offices of BAKIN, the 20 March 1973 plenary session of the MPBI took place in the 'Operations Room' of the Department of Manpower. On 26 March of that year, the MPBI ceased to exist (INDOC 1981: 86; SPSI 1990a: 5) as a 'transfer of power' from the MPBI to the FBSI officially took place – in a ceremony attended by Minister of Manpower Mohammad Sadli (Pedoman 27 March 1973).34 Representing the MPBI was Rasyid Sutan Radjamas. The FBSI itself was represented by its new general chairman, Agus Sudono (see Table 4.1).

Having resolved the way in which power would be transferred from the MPBI to the FBSI, some legal technicalities still had to be dealt with before the new organisation received full official recognition from the state. On 11 March 1974, a decision was signed by one of the director-generals of the Department of Manpower, Transmigration and Cooperatives, as it was known at the time, which registered the FBSI (Sukarno 1980: 15). This decision enabled the new organisation to establish horizontal as well as vertical 'organs' and to negotiate collective labour agreements. Also by virtue of this decision, the old trade-union federations were regarded as having ceased to

Table 4.1 Initial FBSI Central Board Composition and Original Affiliation of Members[35]

Position	Name	Organisation
General Chairman	Agus Sudono	GASBIINDO
Chairman	Sukijat	Dept. of Interior
	Rasjid St. Radjamas	KBM
	Sutanto M.	SARBUMUSI
	Adolf Rachman	SOKSI
Secretary-General	Sukarno	Dept. of Agriculture
Deputy Secretary-General	Thaheransjah K.	SARBUMUSI
	P. Muljadi	SOB Pantjasila
	DM Sihite	PERKABI
	Radjuddin Jusuf	KBM
	Ch Tanjung	MKGR
Member	Sjaiful DP	GASBIINDO
	Daud Badaruddin	KBIM
	S. Idris	KUBU Pantjasila
	M. Hatta	PGRI
	T. Tjokroaminoto	GOBSII
	Saralen Purba	KESPEKRI
	Koeswari	KBSI
	Soekirman	SOBRI
	Kamil P.	KBKI
	Mc. Anas	FBII
	A. Rachman TA	IKM
	M. Djaelani	SOKSI
	Ichsanuddin Ilyas	PORBISI
	TR Siagian	GERBUMI
	Imam Soedarwo	KBKI
	B. Messakh	SOKSI
	A. Wartono	SOB Pantjasila
	Suharno	SOB Pantjasila

exist, although there was never an official act which specifically stipulated their disbandment, nor did they formally disband themselves. Further strengthening the legal position of the FBSI, a 1975 Minister of Manpower, Transmigration and Cooperatives Regulation (no. 1/MEN/1975) annulled a 1955 Minister of Labour decision which had made the establishment of trade unions an easy task – only ten people were required to establish one – and which Agus Sudono had called too 'liberal' (Soekarno 1980: 28–29; Sudono 1981: 18–19). According to the new decision, a trade-union federation could only be recognised if it had at least branches in twenty provinces and comprised of fifteen sectoral unions, effectively making it almost impossible for an 'upstart' rival union federation to emerge.

Thus the corporatist vision of societal 'representation' that was encouraged by Ali Moertopo was finally realised for organised labour. Technically independent, the FBSI was to become heavily reliant on the government for resources as well as direction. Increasingly, its leadership was to become more closely linked to GOLKAR, as figures more clearly associated with that organisation became dominant. Agus Sudono himself, an old MASYUMI figure who joined its revitalised New Order version, the PARMUSI, eventually crossed over to GOLKAR, and by 1978, was registered as a deputy chairman of the latter's KOSGORO component.[36]

Therefore, the idea of OPPI, first hatched in 1960, was finally realised under the direction of the OPSUS group led by Ali Moertopo.[37] As mentioned earlier, Moertopo himself not only engineered the reconstitution of organised labour, but also of political parties and mass organisations in general. The FBSI was to survive until 1985, when newer requirements resulted in its transformation into the SPSI (see Chapter 5).

One last point needs to be made regarding the process which led to the establishment of the FBSI in 1973. The demise of the MPBI and its replacement by the FBSI was attributable to the internal incohesion of the former organisation, but this development was also related to wider political dynamics, specifically those related to elite power struggles. The fact that it was Agus Sudono and not Adolf Rachman who was selected to become the first general chairman of the newly formed FBSI gave some indication of the way in which these power struggles were developing. This point is an important one, but has been largely overlooked. INDOC (1981:86), for example, suggests that the selection of Sudono may have simply been a concession to the ICFTU, given that he, as well as his erstwhile colleague and rival, had strong army links. Conferring one of the deputy-chairmanships of the central board on Adolf Rachman was, according to INDOC, also designed to placate a rival international labour organisation, the World Council on Labour (WCL) (INDOC 1981: 88). It was Rachman who had earlier affiliated SOKSI to the WCL, while GASBIINDO had long been attached to the ICFTU.

Such an interpretation, however, fails to take into account the importance of the domestic political affiliations of Sudono and Rachman. While

Sudono had clearly established considerable links with the army leadership of the 1950s, intent on curbing the influence of SOBSI on labour, it is apparent that he subsequently widened his contacts within the army in the first few years of the New Order. By his own account, his main role in KABI was to cultivate organised labour's links with the officials at the helm of the New Order, including the new army leadership, the new officials at the Department of Manpower, and those technocrats linked with the University of Indonesia's Faculty of Economics.[38] An astute politician, he later aligned himself more closely with the army's ascendant OPSUS group. Having played a role in the establishment of PARMUSI – a less intimidating version of the old MASYUMI – and facilitating army intervention into that party in 1970 (Reeve 1985: 329), he would have established himself then, if not earlier, as a trusted associate of Ali Moertopo.[39] It was more or less natural, therefore, that his own fortunes would rise as the OPSUS group became increasingly dominant.

In contrast to Agus Sudono, Adolf Rachman's star was hitched to a group within the army whose fortunes were on the decline. As the leader of the KONGKARBU, the labour arm of SOKSI, Rachman's political prospects were waning due to the gradual erosion of SOKSI's power, and of its maverick chairman, General Soehardiman. By Soehardiman's own account, SOKSI's influence, within GOLKAR, for example, was at its height between 1964 and 1967, although it began to decline after the general election of 1971, concurrent with the rise of the group under the leadership of Ali Moertopo (Soehardiman 1993: 176). This was not surprising considering that SOKSI's basic reason for existence was to combat the PKI's mass organisations in more or less open war. Once its foe was crushed, SOKSI had largely outlived its usefulness. Moertopo, on the other hand, was demonstrating his own political value by the initiatives he took to domesticate and control a number of political parties and mass organisations. The decline of SOKSI was so marked that Soehardiman was later to lament that his organisation was not even consulted about the establishment of the FBSI (Soehardiman 1993: 176), even though it was the GOLKAR component that was supposed to be responsible for overseeing labour affairs. In the end, SOKSI's inability to maintain its early 1960s position as, in effect, the army's main instrument in dealing with labour, was attributable to the fact that by the early 1970s it had by and large become obsolete.

SUMMARY

The reconstitution of organised labour in the early New Order was the result of a complex interplay of economic and political considerations. There was no simple correspondence between the economic aims pursued by the New Order and its labour agenda, although the maintenance of a politically moderate labour movement was certainly in the interest of the pursuit of these aims. Equally significant, though, were political considerations, specifically those related to the pre-empting of the re-emergence of independent, militant tendencies within organised labour. In this sense, the political constraints imposed upon organised labour had little direct relevance, for example, to any specific requirement of the ISI-led industrialisation strategy, based primarily on the production of consumer goods – except in the wider sense that such stability was needed for any kind of economic development to take place. In that regard, their imposition was more immediately attributable to the need to wipe out any lingering influence of the Left from the labour as well as the wider political arena.

The process of establishing an acceptable new institutional framework for organised labour took a rather protracted seven years, in which at least two failed attempts at 'unifying' organised labour were made, largely on the initiative of state officials such as Awaloeddin, Mursalin, Sadli and Ali Moertopo, rather than trade-union leaders themselves. This reflected the degree to which the organised labour movement was weak and incoherent, and therefore unable to bargain effectively with the new holders of state power.

Again, some of the reasons for the inability of organised labour to bargain effectively for some independence and a limited degree of political inclusion were structural in nature. In essence, labour unions were presiding over a labour constituency that was as yet underdeveloped. Arguably the most developed sector of organised labour – represented in the communist SOBSI – had been smashed in the aftermath of the 1965 upheaval.

As mentioned earlier, the tide turned against SOBSI's brand of radical unionism as a counter-revolutionary coalition led by the army consolidated in the late 1950s and early 1960s. After this coalition struck back at the Left in 1965–66, it was clear that there would be no place for radical unionism in Indonesia because its presence would contradict the logic that underlay the processes of economic and political restructuring that were taking place up to the early 1970s.

The developments discussed here have essentially led to the establishment of an exclusionary model of accommodation between state, capital and labour, intertwined with the development of a wider exclusionary corporatist social and political framework. The primary feature of this model of accommodation is stringent state controls over organised labour and the continued demobilisation of the working class as a social force.

5 Politics and ideology

Exclusionary corporatism at work

DEVELOPMENT STRATEGY AND POLITICAL EXCLUSION

One of the major theoretical issues in the literature on industrialisation in East Asia is the relationship between the political exclusion of labour – represented in large part by state policies of labour repression – and the success of the export-led industrialisation strategy. Neo-classical economists, almost exclusively concerned with the presence or absence of market forces, have tended to ignore the political and social underpinnings of the much vaunted 'success stories' of the region (e.g. Krueger 1982), and therefore have paid little attention to the issue of labour repression. In the meantime, those influenced by the New Institutionalism, while displaying sensitivity to different political environments (Freeman 1993), have demonstrated a continuing lack of concern with the structural and historical contexts within which state and class forces emerge. Because the focus is on the operations of institutions, rather than the interests embedded in them, or their position within the matrix of state and class relations, they continue to theorise inadequately the social and political basis of state repressive policy. Equally inadequate, however, is a dependency style analysis which mechanistically posits a direct correlation between policies of labour repression and economic success, or alternately, maintains the superficiality of that success (e.g. Bello and Rosenfeld 1992).

The most thoughtful consideration of the relationship between labour repression and economic development in East Asia is perhaps represented in the work of Deyo (1987; 1989), who retreats considerably from the suggestion that mechanisms of control over labour were in place specifically because of the distinct requirements of the export-led development strategy. He and others (Deyo et al. 1987) have demonstrated that the initial development of such controls clearly pre-dates the onset of export-led industrialisation and was more directly attributable to political considerations on the part of the state, especially with regard to the pre-empting of radical, left-wing, social and political movements.[1] For all that, a less direct link between export-led industrialisation and the political exclusion of labour, still emerges: the presence of stringent mechanisms of control and the absence of strong working-class movements able to mitigate against them, made export-led industrialisation, based on the maintenance of a cheap and politically docile labour force, a viable policy option for East Asian state planners. In this sense, the model of accommodation between state, capital and labour which has emerged from the East Asian industrialisation experience – referred to in this book as the 'exclusionary' – became integrated with the needs of the export-led development strategy.

The nature of the controls over labour, however, has varied markedly from case to case. Thus, the literature on labour and the industrialisation process in East Asia has had to be sufficiently complex to accommodate variations associated with specific cases. As mentioned earlier, in South Korea, the state (and its institutions of repression) has played a much more central role in containing organised labour than its counterpart in Taiwan, where the model appears to provide a greater role for enterprise-level mechanisms of control. Moreover, corporatist institutions in the form of a single, state-sanctioned and controlled trade-union organisation appears to have been more prominent in some cases (e.g. South Korea) and much less in others (e.g. Thailand, where it is notable for its absence). Notwithstanding such important differences, the maintenance of the political exclusion of labour, as suggested in Chapter 2, gains importance as the very success of the industrialisation process gives rise to a more sizeable and mature industrial working class.

At another level, controls over labour are legitimised in various countries by ideologies of industrial relations which stress cooperation and harmony, as well as a rejection of class-based notions of conflicting interests between workers and capital. Typically, such ideologies refer to what is claimed to be indigenously rooted cultural traits, predisposed toward harmony, such as those expressed within Confucianism, or Pancasila (see pp. 64–65). Taking their cue in part from these official ideologies, the maintenance of industrial peace in East Asian societies is explained by some authors by reference to this cultural dimension (e.g. Hofheinz and Calder 1982). In the process, 'Asian Culture' is reified as some kind of innate, immutable factor, unperturbed by changing social and economic conditions. State policies curbing freedoms such as that of association and organisation, historically won during the struggles of working-class movements of earlier industrialisers, are either ignored or justified in the process.

Earlier Chapters revealed that stringent state controls over labour in Indonesia also preceded the advent of export-led industrialisation, which only occurred in the mid-1980s. Largely through the efforts of Ali Moertopo's OPSUS, a wider exclusionary corporatist social and political framework had been substantially put in place by 1974 – one that not only precluded the emergence of radical politics, but also prohibited the independent development of society-based political movements in general. Included in this strategy was the establishment of the FBSI in 1973 as the sole, state-sponsored corporatist institution of labour 'representation'. At the same time, the New Order policy of excluding the 'masses' from the political process became neatly encapsulated in the officially coined term 'floating mass politics' made popular by such figures as Moertopo in the early and mid-1970s. This policy, which impacted greatly on organised labour, was to a large degree justified in Huntingtonian fashion, by the assertion that 'political participation is an unaffordable luxury, given the far more pressing problem of achieving economic development' (Boileau 1983: 68). Thus, the establishment in Indonesia of an exclusionary model of accommodation between state, capital and labour, defined by stringent state controls over organised labour and the demobilisation of the working class as a social force, was intertwined with this whole process.

Importantly, the New Order also developed to even greater lengths throughout the 1970s and 1980s the integralist notion of social and political organisation which had previously attracted Soekarno. Integralism embodies within the state the interests of society as a whole, and imbues the state with the power to define the exact nature of that common interest. Such a notion was claimed to be rooted in the indigenous values from which the Pancasila and 1945 Constitution emerged, and which the New Order has sworn to uphold.[2] As mentioned earlier, besides the FBSI, which 'represented' workers, peak organisations 'representing' the peasantry, women, youth and other groups were created to preserve the harmony and maintain the balance of state and society within this integralist scheme of things.

I pointed out in Chapter 4, however, that the concrete interests which underlay arguments for an exclusionary socio-political format were in fact related to the army's abhorrence of mass-based politics, which was in large part attributable to the success of the Left in pre-New Order Indonesia. At the same time the army did not want a return to the civilian-dominated liberal democracy of the 1950s, in which it had virtually no place in the official workings of politics. It is therefore not surprising that the New Order pushed further the centralising tendencies of Guided Democracy by imposing even stricter controls on mass organisations and political parties throughout the 1970s and 1980s. A high point came in 1985, when legislation was introduced that determined clear and constraining guidelines for the establishment and operations of mass-based organisations as well as political parties. Moreover, all such organisations were to profess adherence to Pancasila as the *azas tunggal* or single ideology (Robison 1993: 44). The significance of this was a formal acceptance of integralism: the surrender of claims to representative democracy and to the very notion of oppositional politics.

Ironically, important as it was to the New Order's wider social and political strategy, the political exclusion of labour had little direct relevance to the specific requirements of its economic development program, well into the 1980s. I noted earlier that the reconstitution of Indonesia's economy on the basis of foreign investment and loans in the late 1960s, and the development of an ISI (Import Substitution Industrialisation) strategy founded on light consumer goods, did not necessarily entail the outright pacification of organised labour except in the very general sense that a measure of industrial peace was necessary for the success of any kind of development and in order to help regain investor confidence. This situation did not change during the next phase of economic development: the oil boom period which began in the mid-1970s and ended in the early 1980s. Windfall oil revenues, which greatly enhanced the state's independence from external sources of aid and investment,[3] brought about a significant shift of emphasis to an ISI format which prioritised higher technology and more capital-intensive projects involving steel, petrochemicals, cement, paper and automobiles (Robison and Hadiz 1993: 19). The state was also able to act as a catalyst to the development of a new class of domestic bourgeoisie, whose formation was inextricably linked to state protection in the form of the provision of monopolies, credit and subsidies (see Robison 1986). The imposition of strict controls over a large and predominantly unskilled labour force had even less relevance to the success of that particular economic development strategy. Thus the concern remained predominantly political – wariness of the potentially destabilising effect of an independent labour movement.

An important development occurred, however, in the mid-1980s, with the reorientation of industrial strategy to one that was more significantly export-led, and necessarily underpinned by low-wage and -technology industries, such as garments, textiles and footwear. This change of industrialisation policy, which was brought about because the fall of international oil prices had caused serious balance- of-payment problems, would have considerable impact on labour. State controls appeared to acquire greater economic, as opposed to mere political, significance, given that part of Indonesia's economic competitiveness was seen to lie in its abundant, cheap and politically docile labour force.

The remainder of this Chapter deals with the ideological and institutional underpinnings of the political exclusion of labour in Indonesia through the 1970s and 1980s. In essence, it looks at the workings of the exclusionary model of accommodation between state, capital and labour as it has been manifested in Indonesia. There are two main concerns throughout: the ideological and political significance of the enforcement of Pancasila Industrial Relations (HIP); and the operations of the actual institutions which directly maintain the political exclusion of labour. Specifically the focus is on the role of the state-sponsored FBSI, and its successor, the SPSI,[4] as well as the role of the security apparatus, represented by KOPKAMTIB, and later BAKORSTRANAS,[5] in addition to local-level military and police commands. Significantly, it is the latter type of institution rather than the former that has played the most crucial role in the maintenance of order in the labour area.

THE IDEOLOGY OF EXCLUSION

HIP has been enshrined as the official doctrine governing state–capital–labour relations in Indonesia since 1974. As mentioned earlier, the fundamental tenets of HIP have been defended by state officials in largely cultural terms: on the grounds that they draw on the specific Indonesian cultural context, as opposed to an alien 'Western' one from which 'liberal', as well as 'Marxist', concepts of industrial relations arise. Thus, HIP has been presented as a manifestation of the values embodied in the five principles of the Pancasila and in the 1945 Constitution, both of which are said to have developed in accordance with the 'National Character' and 'National Culture'.[6] As one document argues, in contrasting industrial relations in the New Order with that of the Old:

> The consequences of the labour relations systems of the past, unsuited to the Pancasila evironment and the National Character, brought the people to an anxious situation and created disharmony between Worker and Entrepreneur, thus reducing work peace and constraining the achievement of the social and economic stability required for development.[7]

Obviously referring to the influence of the PKI-linked SOBSI in the 1950s, Moertopo asserts that the dominant concept of industrial relations in the Old Order was one that emphasised the class struggle. He counterposes this to a concept which emphasised harmony between capital and labour, presenting the latter as more suited to the Pancasila way of life which stresses cooperation and the family spirit. While the doctrine of class conflict exacerbates the differences between capital and labour, according to Moertopo, in Pancasila Labour Relations the two are 'synchronised, harmonised and attuned' (Moertopo 1975: 20).[8]

Prominent state or state-connected figures such as Ministers of Manpower Awaloeddin Djamin and Mursalin, as well as labour leader Agus Sudono, had repeatedly made references as early as the late 1960s to industrial relations based on Pancasila.[9] As an actual doctrine, however, HIP (or HPP as it was originally known) was only codified in 1974 when the institutional arrangements of state–society relations under the New Order had been more or less firmly established. Presented as embodying a 'national consensus', this codification was the direct outcome of a seminar which took place in Jakarta in December of that year, held under the auspices of the Department of Manpower, Cooperatives and Transmigration. It involved the participation of FBSI leaders, government officials, representatives of business, as well as a number of university-based intellectuals (Sukarno 1980: ix). Perhaps inevitably, General Ali Moertopo, then at the height of influence, came to cast his long shadow on the proceedings, contributing a speech on Pancasila Labour Relations which effectively set the agenda for the seminar. Indeed, it was the elaboration contained in his contribution that was most indicative of the direction that the state's labour policy was taking at the time.[10]

For Moertopo, workers, like any other group in society, must contribute to the pursuit of the goals of economic development set by the state. In terms which have become an integral part of the New Order's ideological armoury, the ultimate goal of development is defined as the achievement of a 'just and prosperous' society based on Pancasila. Accordingly, it was important to ensure that capital and labour effectively subordinate their own interests to the wider state-defined national interest (Moertopo 1975: 10).

Moertopo's scheme of things would obviously be facilitated by the establishment of an organised labour movement that was easily controlled and supervised by the state, and that would eschew confrontational methods. He was not alone, however, in envisaging the development of such a labour movement. In a 1974 Presidential speech quoted at length by Moertopo, Soeharto states that

> The nurturing of organised labour must continue to be seen in the framework of national development in the wider sense. Together we have to soon think about the relationship between worker and employer or company in the Pancasila environment. There must be mutual respect, understanding of each other's position and role. In the Pancasila environment there is no place for confrontation or exploitation by the strong of the weak. If each of these foundations can be established, then strikes by workers and lock-outs by companies or employers because of conflict between the two can be avoided.
>
> (Moertopo 1975: 15)

The imprint of Moertopo's ideas was evident in the actual document elaborating on HPP, produced by the December 1974 seminar, which stated that 'HPP is also grounded on government policies aimed at creating national security, national stability, ensuring social participation and continuity in national development.'[11]

The fact that this 'developmentalist' view remains influential today may be seen in the following summary of the role of the government contained in a more recent official manual on the implementation of Pancasila Industrial Relations (Department of Manpower 1985: 12), which is even more explicit about the all-important role of the state:

> In respect to Pancasila Industrial Relations, the Government adopts a role as protector, guide and arbitrator – in brief, the protector of the community at large and a partner in the process of production.[12]

Because of the developmentalist emphasis on harmony and leadership of a benevolent state, one of the main outcomes of the practice of HIP has been the effective elimination of the right to strike, even though several unrepealed pieces of legislation still formally guarantee its exercise. Indeed labour laws of 1957 and 1969 explicitly mention the right to strike (Soepomo 1989: 1–8, 290–306). As early as 1971, Agus Sudono also declared that 'strike action, which is usually regarded as a lethal weapon by workers in their struggle to improve their lot, is not only unrequired, but also seems unsuited to Pancasila Labour Relations' (Sudono 1981: 55).[13]

An integral part of attempts to dissuade workers from exercising the right to strike has been the eradication of vestiges of a militant labour tradition from the collective memory. Apart from the codification of HIP or HPP in 1974, such attempts were raised to their greatest heights in the mid-1980s when the Department of Manpower – with former KOPKAMTIB chief Sudomo at the helm – officially institutionalised the use of the word *pekerja* to replace *buruh* (both meaning 'worker') in the very name of the FBSI, as well as the word *industrial* to replace *perburuhan* in HPP. Thus the FBSI officially became the SPSI (*Serikat Pekerja Seluruh Indonesia*; All-Indonesia Workers' Union) while HPP became HIP. According to Sudomo, the term *buruh* was objectionable because it was used in the colonial period and conjured up the image of a worker who is exploited by his employer (*Pelita* 17 July 1985).

Given such a rationale, it is difficult to ignore close parallels between Sudomo's initiative and SOKSI's efforts in the early 1960s to supplant *buruh* with *karyawan* (employee). SOKSI's attempts were undertaken while in the midst of a crusade against militant labour organisations undermining army authority over newly nationalised foreign firms. Sudomo's took place in the face of fresh requirements regarding the effectiveness of state controls over labour given the shift in industrialisation strategy mentioned above. Notably, Sudomo's initiative also took place after some degree of industrial strife had occurred in the late 1970s and early 1980s – the result of currency devaluations which raised prices (INDOC 1984: 5) and recessionary trends that discouraged wage increases and led to mass-dismissals. The fairly vigorous strike action that occurred in spite of the domestication of the formal organised labour movement clearly heightened the level of wariness among state planners of the potential destabilising effect posed by labour, especially in the light of the change of policy emphasis.

In such a context, Sudomo's brief in the mid-1980s was not merely to reinforce existing mechanisms of control but also to prohibit the development of crisis situations.[14] Earlier, as chief of KOPKAMTIB, he had gained much experience in dealing with labour matters. It is also noteworthy that Sudomo was a state official who, even by New Order standards, was particularly fixed on the maintenance of political stability as a buffer against the revival of leftist ideologies.[15] The KOPKAMTIB methods which he employed as Minister,[16] would have a lasting legacy as the operations of the security apparatus in the maintenance of industrial peace would continue largely to overshadow that of more 'legal–formal' institutions.

THE 'LEGAL–FORMAL' INSTITUTIONS

Tripartism

Putting the principles of HIP into practice has been a fairly elaborate industrial relations framework, replete with a number of 'legal–formal' and, theoretically, regularised institutions. Their presence has helped to lend some credibility to the claim that a degree of 'legal–formal' rationality operates in the industrial relations area, in spite of the pervasiveness of the interventions of security-related institutions in the resolution of labour problems. These interventions, however, underscore the fact that 'legal–formal' institutions of industrial relations, by themselves, have not been an adequate safeguard against the emergence of industrial unrest, or more recently, against the development of independent organising outside of the official state-dominated system.

Among the more prominent of the 'legal–formal' institutions have been the regional and central labour disputes resolution committees (respectively P4D and P4P) whose existence harks back to the 1950s.[17] Theoretically, their function is to adjudicate cases of labour disputes that cannot be resolved at the enterprise-level, and only after unsuccessful mediation by a Minister of Manpower officer. According to Law no. 22 of 1957, these committees operate on a tripartite basis, as each comprises five representatives of government departments,[18] five representatives of workers (which in the New Order has meant FBSI/SPSI officials) and five representatives of the employer's association, APINDO. The latter is the recipient of a mandate from KADIN (the Chamber of Commerce and Industry), to represent the interests of business in various industrial relations bodies.[19]

Independent labour activists, not surprisingly, make the claim that the P4P/P4D have not been impartial, making decisions which generally favour the interests of employers (Lubis *et al.* 1981: 56).[20] Notwithstanding the truth of such claims, it is clear that the committees are not equipped with sufficiently strong punitive powers seriously to intimidate employers, a fact that in itself conceivably works against the interests of workers. As late as 1990, one reference book on Indonesian labour laws stated that they could only impose penalties of 'bodily incarceration up to a period of 3 months' and 'a fine of up to Rp 10.000, or approximately US$5, to parties found guilty of infringing labour laws' (Manulang 1990: 96).[21]

Among the 'legal–formal' institutions are the tripartite bodies of cooperation between government, employers and workers, which exist at central as well as regional levels. These have an important position in the promotion of the image of tripartite harmony and cooperation within the HIP framework. As Manning points out, projecting the image of tripartism has helped in the New Order's dealings with such international organisations as the ILO (Manning 1993: 69). Admiral Sudomo, for example, is quick to recount how he dispelled foreign criticism of his policies as Minister of Manpower by citing that they were the result of prior tripartite discussions.[22]

In reality, the role of the tripartite bodies is strictly advisory, as they are geared to be no more than 'a forum for consultation and communication'. Furthermore, their brief is 'to assist in the development of a single concept, attitude, and plan to deal with current labour issues or to take *preventive*[23] measures in facing future problems' (Department of Manpower 1985: 14). At the central level, the National Body for Tripartite Cooperation is chaired by the Minister of Manpower, although the institution is formally 'independent and autonomous', and as such, 'does not have any organisational link with any government agency or other councils' (Department of Manpower 1985: 31). At the regional level, they are chaired by provincial governors. Again, workers and employers are respectively represented at the central and regional levels by the FBSI/SPSI and APINDO. Of critical importance to this system of industrial relations is the FBSI/SPSI, as the sole 'representative' of workers, and it is to this organisation that we now direct our attention.

The FBSI/SPSI

The FBSI/SPSI takes part in a number of bodies which form an integral part of the industrial relations system of the New Order. Besides those already mentioned, its representatives take part in bodies, invariably organised on a tripartite basis, which, at least theoretically, have a role in establishing the minimum wage (the National and Regional Wage Appraisement Councils), monitoring productivity levels (the National and Regional Productivity Councils), and in setting health and safety standards (the National and Regional Health and Safety Councils) (SPSI 1990a: 56). It also encourages the formation of company-level agreements between workers and employers, and promotes workers' education programs (Sudono 1981: 20–21; SPSI 1990a: 73–82, 97). Since its establishment, however, the organisation has been the object of widespread domestic, as well as overseas, criticism and ridicule (e.g. INDOC 1981; 1982; 1983; 1984). The focus of such attacks has usually been on its inability to act as a genuine vehicle of labour representation or to promote the interests of workers.

It may be argued, however, that many critics of the FBSI/SPSI have missed an essential point: it makes little sense to criticise the organisation's failings as a trade union given that the underlying logic to its establishment had determined that it would primarily serve as a vehicle for the maintenance of the political exclusion, rather than inclusion, of organised labour.[24] The organisation's function was not so much to mobilise working-class acceptance and support of the goals set by the state; rather, it was to act as a safeguard against the emergence of potentially destabilising independent organisational activities from within the ranks of labour. In effect, the FBSI was created to demobilise, rather than to mobilise labour, on behalf of the state.

Given this demobilisation task, there has been little reason for the state to provide the level of patronage or to allocate resources which would enhance the institution's organisational capacities beyond what is required to prohibit labour organising outside of its reach.[25] In other words, there has been little incentive to develop the FBSI/SPSI as an effective instrument of cooptation, in contrast to a mere instrument of preemption. It may be argued that the underdevelopment of labour as a class had ensured that a strategy of repression toward the working class would be more attractive to the state than one of cooptation, which would have better guaranteed an interest in the cultivation of the FBSI/SPSI's organisational capacities.

Thus, it is precisely because repression has continued to be a viable option that the state's security apparatus has had a large role to play in labour affairs, while such 'legal–formal' institutions as the FBSI/SPSI have played a largely supplementary role. The implications of this are of overriding importance: only if there is a significant shift to a strategy of cooptation, and away from one of repression and coercion, can these 'legal–formal' institutions be expected to gain greater importance relative to more strictly security-oriented organisations. However, this is only possible when the political costs of repressing labour through brute force and coercion become too high.

It is in this context that there is an essential difference between the FBSI/SPSI in Indonesia and other corporatist labour organisations which have emerged in the experiences of earlier industrialisers, particularly in Latin America. Unlike their Indonesian counterpart, the labour movements of Perón's Argentina and Vargas' Brazil were, as suggested in Chapter 2, sufficiently strong *vis à vis* state and capital to ensure a relatively favourable form of cooptation. Essentially, they were able to do this because the political costs of repressing labour were high. It was for this reason that for long periods of time labour enjoyed the state patronage that allowed their organisations to flourish considerably. In turn, the labour movement provided an important pillar to the power of the populist and authoritarian regimes of such figures as Perón and Vargas.

Organisational development of the FBSI/SPSI

The FBSI was officially established as a federation of *Serikat Buruh Lapangan Pekerjaan* (SBLP; Industrial Sector Unions) rather than as a federation of the numerous non-Communist Party-related trade unions that existed at the beginning of the New Order. The fact that the SBLPs had to be 'created', however, *after* the establishment of the FBSI, demonstrated a conscious attempt to ensure that the old party-related federations did not somehow continue to survive.[26] The initial establishment of the SBLPs was indicative of the continuing depoliticisation of organised labour, a trend already set in motion during the first few years of the New Order.

The SBLPs which comprised the original FBSI were 'founded' according to a provisional list drawn up by Sukijat and Sukarno, both government 'representatives' in the FBSI (see Chapter 4). These SBLPs covered the following categories:

1 Agriculture and Estates Workers (SBPP)
2 Oil, Natural Gas and General Mining Workers (SBMGPU)
3 Cigarette and Tobacco Workers (SBRT)

4 Food and Beverages Workers (SBMM)
5 Textile and Garments Workers (SBTS)
6 Wood Products Workers (SBP)
7 Printing and Publishing Workers (SB PERPEN)
8 Pharmaceuticals and Chemicals Workers(SBFK)
9 Metallurgy and Ceramics Workers (SBLK)
10 Machine Assembling Workers (SBAMP)
11 Rubber and Leather Workers (SBKK)
12 Electronics Workers (SBE)
13 Building and Public Works Workers (SBBPU)
14 Commercial, Banking and Insurance Workers (SBNIBA)
15 Tourism Workers (SB PAR)
16 Maritime Workers (SBM)
17 Seafarers (SPI)
18 Transport Workers (SBT)
19 Health Industry Workers (SB KES)
20 Teachers (PGRI)

However, the above composition was to change as the teachers' union, the PGRI, announced that it was a professional organisation and not a labour union. Still, the number of SBLPs increased to twenty-one when the Transport Workers Union divided into three separate ones,[27] and thus, the FBSI was to consist of twenty-one SBLPs until its transformation into the SPSI in 1985.

Although it was clear that the SBLPs were artificially created, the original structure of the FBSI was notable for the fairly high level of autonomy that the former enjoyed from the latter's central executive board. Each SBLP had its own central board, and provincial as well as district level branches, which existed parallel to those of the FBSI-proper. Actual enterprise-level units, called the *basis* (and later, *Perwakilan Unit Kerja* or PUK) were also affiliated to one of the SBLPs rather than to the central executive body of the FBSI.

By 1978 the FBSI claimed that the SBLPs had provincial level branches numbering 144, and district level branches numbering 247. At the same time the FBSI proper claimed 26 branches at the provincial level and 276 branches at the district level. The rank-and-file *basis* under the SBLPs supposedly numbered 8,081 in 1978, the combined membership of which totalled 2 million by 1978 (Sudono 1981: 20).

For its first few years, the FBSI's statistics indicate a steady growth in its membership, although there is no way of corroborating the figures presented. In 1981 the FBSI claimed a membership level of nearly 2.8 million, with 9,760 enterprise-level *basis* linked to the SBLPs (Sudono 1981: 47). There is something wrong with these figures, as indicated by the fact that in 1990, the organisation which had by then become the SPSI, claimed a membership of just over 900,000 workers, and enterprise-level units numbering 8,846 (SPSI 1990a: 55).[28] To my knowledge, at no time has the

SPSI attempted to explain the apparent tremendous drop in membership levels. In 1993, the SPSI reported another substantial rise in membership: it now claimed nearly 2 million members, spread over more than 11,000 enterprise-level units. In addition, it claimed 268 district-level branches (SPSI 1993b: 20, 25), and branches in all twenty-seven provinces (including East Timor) (Lambert 1993: 9).

It was in fact the fairly high level of autonomy that the SBLPs had within the FBSI that prompted the transformation of the organisation into the SPSI in 1985. This change took place under the direction of Minister of Manpower Sudomo,[29] who was particularly critical of the FBSI's 'dualistic' structure (*Pelita* 17 July 1985; *Merdeka* 17 July 1985), which he saw as being in contradiction to the aim of maintaining tight controls over organised labour. Commenting on the FBSI's structure, Sudomo suggested that 'people become confused about which one they have to obey, the FBSI or the SBLP. This has to be made clear' (*Merdeka* 17 July 1985).

Thus, the 'dualistic' structure – dubbed by Sudomo as 'liberal' (*Sinar Harapan* 27 November 1985) – was replaced by one that was more centralised, hierarchical, and military command-like. Clearly such a tighter and centralised organisation was more amenable to direct control and supervision from above and therefore more suitable to Sudomo's security considerations.

Sudomo arrived at his conclusions regarding the SBLPs on the basis of his experience in dealing with the wave of strikes that occurred in the late 1970s and early 1980s. Many of these strikes took place in factories that had FBSI workplace-level units or were sparked off as a result of employer non-compliance with worker demands for the establishment of such units in enterprises.[30] Thus, in Sudomo's view it was the autonomy of these *basis* from the central leadership of the state-controlled FBSI which was largely responsible for this growing industrial unrest,[31] in spite of the labour union's formal eschewal of strike action.[32] For Sudomo, the solution was to undercut enterprise-level independence by making units more directly accountable to a central structure that was more easily controllable by the Department of Manpower.[33]

In accordance with Sudomo's plan, the twenty-one SBLPs of the FBSI were eliminated and replaced by ten 'departments' which were directly under the control of the central executive body of the newly created SPSI. These were: Health and Pharmaceuticals; Chemicals, Energy and Mining; Metals, Electronic and Machinery; Trade, Banking and Insurance; Tourism, Cigarettes, and Food and Beverages; Public Works and Wood Products; Agriculture and Plantations; Textiles, Garments and Footwear; Transport; and Seafarers (SPSI 1990a: 192–229). Importantly, enterprise-level units were formally tied through district and regional branches of the SPSI to the central executive body, rather than the individual 'departments'. Thus, unlike the SBLPs of the old FBSI, these 'departments' had far less autonomy.

Such important changes were officially approved at the Second FBSI Congress, which took place in November 1985. This was a congress which was particularly noteworthy for the open and fierce competition that took place over the position of general chairman. Press reports indicate that the congress was characterised by a high degree of confusion that veered toward chaos and the prevalence of backroom intrigue (*Kompas* 29 November 1985; *Merdeka* 29 November 1985). Such intrigue was probably due to indications that Agus Sudono would not keep his job at the helm of the FBSI, particularly as Minister Sudomo had expressed his desire that a process of 'regeneration' take place (*Suara Karya* 11 September 1985).

It was also during this Congress that Sudomo orchestrated the rise of the man who would replace Agus Sudono – Imam Soedarwo, who, in spite of his high formal standing within the FBSI[34] – had essentially been a businessman in the garments industry. Despite claims to the contrary (*Sinar Harapan* 5 November 1985; *Pelita* 5 November 1985; *Jakarta Post* 2 December 1985), Soedarwo's rise was widely perceived as being a result of Sudomo's interventions as he had not originally been considered as a contender for Agus Sudono's position, and clearly lacked the credibility to establish a real base of support from the organisation's activists. Indeed, Sudomo took an active part in the Congress proceedings, not only by delivering the customary opening address, but also to the extent of holding private meetings with key participants of the Congress (*Merdeka* 28 November 1985). One such meeting was allegedly with the team of 'formateurs', or electors, which took place at his private home just before the final process of selecting individuals which would comprise the SPSI's new leadership.[35]

Prior to the Congress, the main challenge to Agus Sudono was expected from his old rival, Adolf Rachman. Shortly before, Rachman had stated his objection to the unwillingness of the FBSI leadership to differ with Sudomo on any matter (*Suara Karya* 20 September 1985). He also expressed the hope that a process of regeneration would occur in the FBSI without outside manipulations (*Kompas* 20 September 1985). It was also notable that Sudono, as general chairman, and Rachman, as secretary-general (since 1980), had given contradictory assessments of the condition of the FBSI in a parliamentary hearing. Sudono had testified that all was well with the organisation, while Rachman characterised it as being 'sick' (*Suara Karya* 21 September 1985).

However, Adolf Rachman's chances of succeeding Agus Sudono were virtually nil as Sudomo dismissed him as a 'radical' and clearly disapproved of him.[36] Agus Sudono himself, who had been entrenched long enough to develop a substantial base of support within the FBSI, was unable to oppose Sudomo, given that his old political protector, Ali Moertopo, was no longer on the scene.[37] It was notable, however, that his support particularly came from the regional branches of the FBSI proper rather than from the SBLPs, the majority of which voiced opposition to his reappointment (*Sinar Harapan* 29 November 1985), a fact which may have indicated an inability to cultivate support from grassroots-level activists.

The legacy of open conflict during the 1985 Congress, and the rather blatant interventions from above that took place, dealt a severe blow to the credibility of the new SPSI. For several years, Adolf Rachman led a group of dissenters who favoured the preservation of the SBLPs and a looser, federation-style, organisation. He organised a SEKBER-SBLP (SBLP Joint Secretariat) to challenge the authority of the SPSI, and continued to argue against the elimination of the industrial unions (*Berita Buana* 30 April 1986). Although it lacked the muscle – and perhaps real political intent – to serve as an effective focus of opposition, the SEKBER-SBLP came to symbolise the presence of a strong dissenting view within the official labour movement to increasing centralising tendencies set in motion by state labour policy. It was only after the 1990 Congress that Rachman rejoined the fold and dismantled his organisation, in return for one of the positions of 'chairman' of the SPSI (see SPSI 1990b).

Meanwhile Agus Sudono set up a new organisation called *Induk Koperasi Pekerja Indonesia* (INKOPERINDO; Central Indonesian Workers' Cooperative) which was initially viewed with some suspicion by the government as another attempt to undermine the SPSI (*Kompas* 26 March 1986; 2 April 1986). However, whatever problem existed was quickly resolved as Sudono's organisation, later called INKOPKAR,[38] agreed to work in conjunction with the SPSI (*Kompas* 12 May 1986; *Suara Karya* 12 May 1986; *Berita Buana* 12 May 1986).

Although the rift in the SPSI had been bridged, the Sudomo-created structure was still the target of domestic as well as international criticism. As we shall see in later Chapters, it was later left to Sudomo's successors as Minister, Cosmas Batubara and Abdul Latief, to revive the old SBLPs in still another form in the 1990s, in a bid to gain greater credibility for the SPSI.

It was in this connection that in 1990, during Batubara's tenure as Minister, the SPSI adopted a new constitution which stipulated the creation of thirteen industrial-based unions which resembled the old SBLPs. It also determined mechanisms that would ensure, at least on paper, a greater level of central accountability to lower levels of the organisation. Lambert described these mechanisms thus:

> The new constitution affords each of these unions the opportunity to fully represent the interest of their members at national level. Each union is able to elect representatives to the National Congress which is the supreme policy making body. The Congress also has the power to elect members to the National Executive Board of Industrial Sectors. A National Executive Committee of some 43 leaders is also elected to meet between Congresses to 'discuss and evaluate' programs. The majority on this Executive comprises two elected representatives from each of the thirteen industrial unions.
>
> (Lambert 1993: 9)

Subsequent chapters show that it took three years following the adoption of the constitution before any real move was made in the direction of the realisation of such a structure. By that time the revival was geared toward thwarting a growing challenge from a number of labour organisations that operated outside of the official state-created institutions and threatened to undermine the SPSI's corporatist monopoly, as well as to counter growing international criticism.

Problems of funding a trade union

As noted earlier, one of the implications of the way in which the FBSI/SPSI was conceived by state officials as having a primarily demobilising role is that it never quite enjoyed the benefits that would accrue from a substantial degree of state patronage. Insofar as its existence, in principle, pre-empted the possibility of alternative, independent, organisations developing, or unsupervised grassroots organising, there was not much concern about raising its organisational capacities. In the past, whenever the union has been inadequate to the task of preempting independent organisational activities, the state has merely responded by increasing the level of intervention of the security apparatus, rather than developing the capability of the FBSI/SPSI to act as a more credible workers' organisation. It is only very recently that the idea has been expressed that the legitimacy of the SPSI among workers needed to be enhanced, as a means of countering the attractiveness of alternative organisations.[39]

Thus, in spite of periodic proclamations of the intent to secure financial self-reliance, acquiring adequate sources of funding became a continuing problem for the FBSI, and its successor, the SPSI. One attempt to achieve a greater level of self-reliance was the introduction of a check-off system at the firm level in 1977, as a means of collecting workers' dues. In order to ensure employer cooperation, this system was instituted via a Ministerial Decree (FBSI 1981: 148).

In a clear demonstration of its lack of credibility and influence, the FBSI /SPSI even required government assistance in the actual operation of the check-off system.[40] Thus, the Department of Manpower, via its local and regional offices, at one time had the responsibility of managing the collection and 'storing' of these dues before they were actually transferred to the FBSI/SPSI. As a result of this practice, the FBSI, and later, the SPSI, appears to have had very little authority over these funds. Quite astonishingly, a 1984 Minister of Manpower Decree unambiguously stipulates that FBSI/SPSI branches were accountable to the Department of Manpower with regard to the use of funds collected from members (SPSI 1990a: 68).

Still, the amount of funds involved in the collection of dues through the check-off system has always been rather limited, and therefore the ability of the FBSI/SPSI to fund itself has been seriously constrained. It was only in 1985 that the system was actively promoted, at a time when the FBSI made public its difficulties in funding that year's Congress (*Kompas* 23 November 1985). According to 1981 FBSI figures, the organisation received an average of just Rp 4 million per month in members' dues. In accordance with the organisation's constitution, only 2.5 per cent or Rp 100.000 of this amount went to the central executive board of the FBSI, the remainder being divided among provincial and district branches and enterprise-level *basis*. In 1985, Agus Sudono claimed that workers' dues amounted to Rp 60 million per month, of which Rp 1.5 million were received by the central executive board (*Kompas* 23 November 1985). By 1990, the SPSI reported that membership dues amounted to Rp 13.3 million per month, although only 1,333 units of a claimed 8,700 units were actually involved in collecting them (SPSI 1990a: 55). It also reported that it had collected dues, from 1977 to 1989, totalling Rp 4.2 billion (roughly US$2.1 million) (SPSI 1990a: 70). In 1993, the SPSI claimed that a total of nearly Rp 2.7 billion or roughly US$1.35 million had been collected (SPSI 1993c). Even so, the total sum was not enormous for a nationwide trade-union organisation with more than two dozen regional and hundreds of district branches with numerous functionaries.

Thus, not surprisingly, the FBSI/SPSI has always been dependent on additional state subsidies for its operations, thereby exacerbating its vulnerability to state domination. The actual value of this subsidy is unclear, though it appears to be limited. That being the case is clearly reflective of the lack of real intention to develop the organisation as an effective vehicle of representation and of a contentment to allow the organisation simply to remain as a barrier to the development of independent organising. On two separate occasions in 1985 it was reported that government aid to the FBSI amounted to just Rp 2 million per month (*Jakarta Post* 25 February 1985) and Rp 5 million per month (*Kompas* 20 September 1985) respectively. SPSI records specifically cite contributions made regularly by the Department of Manpower, although how much is involved is not divulged (SPSI 1990a: 75). In 1985, however, Agus Sudono reported the amount to be Rp 1 million per month (*Antara* 20 September 1985). Presidential funds also appear to have been allocated to the trade union, at least in the past: again in 1985, Agus Sudono stated that the FBSI central executive received Rp 4 million per month in presidential aid. At the same time he estimated that he required Rp 600 million per month to run the organisation (*Suara Karya* 21 September 1985). Another form of subsidy, which has been provided more recently, derives from the State Secretariat. This subsidy currently enables the SPSI central executive board to maintain offices in a building on one of central Jakarta's busiest streets – which also houses the offices of KADIN[41] – and to move out from the small, rundown building that it formerly occupied in a nearby area.

Given the limited amount of state resources at its disposal, still another important source of funding for the FBSI/SPSI are cooperation schemes with external organisations – such as the American AAFLI, the German

FES, the ILO, and the ICFTU (SPSI 1990a: 75). The amount of assistance provided by these external organisations has rarely been made public, although the cumulative amount up to 1985 was estimated by Agus Sudono to be approximately Rp 10 billion (*Antara* 20 September 1985). Notably, the allegations of misuse of funds deriving from such external sources has been a thorny internal issue (*Merdeka* 16 April 1985).[42]

These cooperation schemes generally cover workers' education and welfare programs, as well as publication and surveying activities (*Kompas* 23 November 1985). Both the FES and the AAFLI have been particularly prominent in this regard. For a number of years the FES supported SPSI programs run in conjunction with the YTKI. The AAFLI most recently ran a program, in conjunction with the SPSI's Women's Institute, which aimed to 'disseminate information about trade unions and workers' rights, collect survey data about wages and working conditions, and provide legal assistance to workers'.[43] Another recent example is a workers' education program run with Australian government funding, in conjunction with the ILO. A former official of the ACTU has been involved in this program, reinforcing the suggestion that the Australian trade-union movement might become 'a new actor in the field' (Etty 1994: 8).[44]

Notwithstanding such schemes, the fact that the FBSI/SPSI's credibility as a genuine union has been widely questioned abroad has resulted in particular limits to the organisation's international linkages. For example, its application for membership in the ICFTU has been repeatedly rejected, although programs run with the latter's funding have taken place and its Asian arm, APRO, has lobbied in favour of the SPSI. Still, the only international trade-union grouping that the SPSI is currently a member of is the ASEAN Trade Union Council (ATUC) (SPSI 1990a: 148). However, the SPSI, and the FBSI before it, has undoubtedly benefited from state-imposed arrangements which greatly prohibit external organisations operating in Indonesia from engaging in open cooperation schemes with non-government approved institutions.[45]

Considering the FBSI/SPSI's lack of resources, it is not surprising that it is unable to provide its numerous functionaries with adequate salaries. Thus, many of them, from the top level down, have been occupied in various activities outside of their strictly trade union-related ones, perhaps further ensuring the inability of the organisation to act as an effective trade-union organisation. As mentioned earlier, before Imam Soedarwo replaced Agus Sudono, he was better known as the owner of a garments factory in Jakarta – although he had been in an FBSI central executive board member since the organisation's inception in 1973 (by virtue of his association with PNI labour organisations).[46] Nurbaiti writes that FBSI functionaries, particularly those senior enough to have built personal reputations, have been known to open law or consultancy firms, specialising in labour affairs, to teach in universities, or to take up management-level positions in domestic or multinational enterprises. She reports that they see no contradiction between their role as functionaries of a trade-union organisation and other jobs that they may have, even as a board-member of a business association (Nurbaiti 1986: 56). Notably, one senior SPSI leader recently criticised his colleagues for spending more time cultivating relations with businesspeople than with workers (*Jakarta Post* 11 November 1995).

Political affiliations

I have indicated already that one of the aims of the establishment of the FBSI in 1973 was to sever the links that organised labour had with its pre-New Order political past. This was achieved by the effective disbanding of the old party-oriented trade-union federations, following the creation of the FBSI as a federation of SBLPs. However, for at least the first decade of the life of the FBSI, old trade-union connections continued to play an important, though unofficial, role within the organisation (*Merdeka* 1 November 1985). As late as the mid-1980s, individuals were identified as being 'GASBIINDO, SOKSI or KOSGORO' (Nurbaiti 1986: 55). Veteran trade-union leaders are often quick to point out that there was never an official order for the old federations to disband and none had ever formally announced its dissolution.[47] The past decade, however, has seen the distinct 'GOLKARisation' of the organisation, thereby cementing at the level of individuals the function of the organisation as an instrument of state control.[48]

It was inevitable in any case that because the old trade-union organisations lacked any formal means of leadership renewal and regeneration, by about the mid-1980s most FBSI activists had ceased to identify with any of them.[49] In contrast, GOLKAR affiliations, through SOKSI, KOSGORO or MKGR, have remained prominent as the latter organisations have formal executive bodies, congresses and cadre-forming mechanisms, even though their own importance within GOLKAR itself has diminished over the years. This has been more so the case, as old party-related senior figures themselves have crossed over to the state's electoral vehicle. As mentioned earlier, Agus Sudono himself, MASYUMI activist and a founder of its revived, tamer, New Order version, the PARMUSI, officially crossed over to GOLKAR in the late 1970s, although 'Islamic' parties had been amalgamated into the PPP in 1973.

Thus, eventually, identification of the political affiliations of individuals would be made more on the basis of the categories of GOLKAR and non-GOLKAR, with the former being overwhelmingly predominant. The extent of the 'GOLKARisation' process was already clear by the time the first SPSI central executive board had been formed in 1985. Fourteen of the seventeen positions in that board were held by GOLKAR members, while PPP and PDI members held two and one seats respectively (Government of Indonesia 1989: 19). Besides the position of general chairman, held by KOSGORO member Imam Soedarwo, four of the six positions of 'chairman' in the board were held by GOLKAR figures as well. In addition, the important positions of secretary-general and treasurer were also in the hands of GOLKAR members. These developments are significant because they demonstrate that the SPSI has increasingly become a clear appendage of GOLKAR, itself an appendage of state power.

One implication of these developments is that the control and domestication of organised labour by the state has been further reinforced by the linking of trade-union careers with that of political careers within the state apparatus. However, the way in which this has taken place has also been influenced by the fact that the SPSI has continued to function as a vehicle for the maintenance of the political exclusion of labour, with little representational or mobilisational role.

Because of this, the organisation has remained, essentially, a politically peripheral institution within the wider framework of the New Order. Thus, ambitious individuals would find that long-term involvement in the FBSI/SPSI has been, for the most part, a political dead-end. The lack of state-endowed resources meant that the organisation was not a very good base for the development of extensive networks of patronage and influence, or for that matter for simply securing economic well-being. Therefore, involvement in the FBSI/SPSI was only a stepping stone to higher political office for some individuals. Oetojo Oesman, a founder of the FBSI, is, at the time of writing, Minister of Justice. Earlier, he had served as a director in the Department of Manpower. It was probably his pre-FBSI, SOKSI/GOLKAR background, however, that was crucial to his success. Significantly, when the FBSI was established in 1973, he was already closely identified enough with state power to be named to the organisation's advisory board, along with other prominent figures, rather than to its executive body. For the most part, however, occupiers of the very top echelons of the FBSI/SPSI have found a seat in the DPR, usually representing GOLKAR, the highest reward for their involvement with the organisation. Examples include Imam Soedarwo, and Bomer Pasaribu, his secretary-general. In 1988, Agus Sudono was appointed to the *Dewan Pertimbangan Agung* (DPA; Supreme Advisory Council), a largely powerless advisory body widely regarded as being reserved for political has-beens. Later he found his way onto one of the boards of the Chamber of Commerce and Industry, KADIN.

The FBSI/SPSI and the military

While the 'GOLKARisation' of the FBSI/SPSI has been an object of scrutiny among observers of the Indonesian labour scene, links between the FBSI/SPSI and the military have long been an even more contentious issue (e.g. INDOC 1981). Perhaps the most blatant evidence of its existence is the open involvement of the FBSI in the 1980s in supporting the operations of security-oriented organisations geared to detect, prevent and suppress industrial action, which will be discussed in greater detail later in this Chapter. Though this was in complete accordance with the basic logic of the organisation's establishment, such an involvement created much controversy. In an unusual emotional outburst, one FBSI founding figure, Sutanto Martoprasono, publicly decried the organisation's implication in such teams, and openly accused it of not promoting the interests of workers (INDOC 1982: 4).

Such an arrangement, however, was not the only link that the FBSI/SPSI has had with the security apparatus. As many observers have pointed out, the FBSI/SPSI itself is internally 'colonised' by the security apparatus as a number of the organisation's local-level functionaries have in fact been individuals with military backgrounds. In 1983, INDOC identified the FBSI regional branch in East Kalimantan as being headed by an active military officer, as was the transport workers' SBLP branch in Solo, Central Java (INDOC 1983: 9). The level of military 'colonisation' apparently increased following the transformation of the FBSI into the SPSI in 1985, which is indeed conceivable given the security considerations described above which prompted the change (Etty 1990: 11).

Not surprisingly, the response of the Indonesian government to such criticism has highlighted the principle of *dwifungsi* – the military's dual function – which harks back to the 1950s (Lev 1994: 40). Indeed, *dwifungsi* has been the basis for the assignment of active and retired military officers to various government departments and bodies. Moreover, the response has stressed that there is nothing inherently wrong with ex-military officers taking up trade-union positions. It argues that 'retired military officers have the same right as others to participate in the private sector; once they have retired they have all the rights and privileges of a private individual' (Government of Indonesia 1989: 25).[50] In the same vein, the SPSI central leadership responded to AFL-CIO criticism of military presence in trade-union boards by suggesting that

> We do not believe in political restraints, discrimination in religion, sex, race or cultural background. We keep an open equal opportunity (sic) to become a member or leader of the SPSI whether or not one is retired from government or military service.[51]

The extent of the military 'colonisation' of the FBSI/SPSI continues to be a point of controversy, particularly because there is little dependable data on this matter. Some clues, however, are provided by the Indonesian government itself. From the same official response to AFL-CIO criticism, it is possible to establish that there were at least three regional branches of the SPSI that were chaired by ex-military officers in 1989 and that, at the district level, at least 10 per cent of such positions were held by ex-military officers (Government of Indonesia 1989: 26).[52] A picture which is not very different is provided by external observers. The AFL-CIO suggested in 1989 that retired military men chaired SPSI branches in West Java, West Kalimantan,

Bandung, Surabaya, and Solo (AFL-CIO 1989: 22). More recently, Lambert pointed to South Sumatra, East Kalimantan, West Java, and Jakarta, as areas where SPSI regional branches are chaired by individuals with military backgrounds (Lambert 1993: 16).

Furthermore, there have been suggestions that persons of military background have even taken up positions as heads of SPSI branches at the level of the enterprise. The SPSI, however, disavows knowledge of such cases, claiming that 'officers of SPSI company unions are the workers of the company concerned and have been elected democratically by other workers' (Government of Indonesia 1990: 31).

Nevertheless, military 'colonisation' has indeed taken place at the level of the firm, as men with military backgrounds have taken up managerial positions (e.g. in personnel departments) in private companies which involve active engagement with the workforce.[53] Here lies another parallel with the South Korean case, as firms in that country were known to have employed military officers to maintain industrial peace at the enterprise level, even in their overseas operations (Katz 1994: 161). Lambert (1993: 15–16), cites a suppressed official publication that explained the presence of retired army officers in the personnel departments of private companies as being the result of demand for a particular skill – the need on the part of factory owners for individuals of proven managerial abilities who can assert their authority and impose discipline on the workforce.

Whatever the real extent of military colonisation of the SPSI (or for that matter, personnel departments of individual private enterprises), the fact remains that military involvement in labour affairs has a long history, and thus, is not exclusively a New Order phenomenon. Chapter 3 indicated that such an involvement could be traced back to at least 1957, with the advent of martial law and the assumption by the military of managerial control of newly created state firms.

However, even in consideration of this historical background, a clear high point in military intervention can still be identified to have occurred in the early 1980s, when KOPKAMTIB, under Admiral Sudomo, came to be blatantly involved in the resolution of industrial disputes. The course was thus set for the policies which Sudomo would continue to pursue as Minister of Manpower between 1983 and 1988, a period which also coincided with the early stage of Indonesia's embarkation on a more export-led development strategy. Because of the obvious importance of the security apparatus in the maintenance of state control over labour, its role needs to be further examined.

THE SECURITY APPARATUS AND LABOUR

In a 1990 article, Tanter described the workings of security and intelligence institutions in the political supervision of urban labour over the previous decade. He suggested that these organisations would continue to operate in the industrial relations area given the increasing importance of manufacturing sector exports to the economy as a whole (Tanter 1990: 253). Subsequent developments have largely proved this prediction to be correct.

As Tanter demonstrates, the capacity of security-oriented institutions to monitor, prevent and suppress independent worker activities was greatly enhanced during the important period in which Admiral Sudomo, as chief of KOPKAMTIB, and later Minister of Manpower, was the most outstanding state official overseeing labour affairs. While at KOPKAMTIB, he effectively overshadowed the civilian Minister of Manpower, Professor Harun Zein, who had no jurisdiction over the operations of security organisations. As Minister himself, he adopted a hands-on approach[54] and a profile that was much higher than that of any of his predecessors. As we shall see, it was during this time that the aims of what has been popularly dubbed 'the security approach' to industrial relations (Nurbaiti n.d.) was most clearly articulated.

It was also no coincidence that while Sudomo was Minister of Manpower, General Sutopo Yuwono, once head of the state intelligence body, BAKIN, served as secretary-general of the department (INDOC 1984: 7). The significance of the fact that the two most important positions in the Department of Manpower were held by such luminaries of the security and intelligence forces has not been lost on observers (Tanter 1990: 255).

As mentioned earlier, the level of strike action began to rise sharply following a devaluation of the Rupiah in 1978, which raised prices of consumer goods and undermined the already weak buying power of workers. It worsened as recessionary trends in the economy constrained the ability of employers to fulfil worker demands for wage increases, and in fact, spurred a wave of massive dismissals (INDOC 1984: 5, 22–23) This, in turn, encouraged more industrial strife as workers went on strike in solidarity with dismissed colleagues. Workers who took part in action demanding pay increases were often the subject of dismissal without due process (*Merdeka* 20 July 1982 and 8 September 1982; *Berita Buana* 8 September 1982; *Sinar Harapan* 2 October 1982). It was estimated in 1982 by the Department of Manpower that a total of 62,000 workers had been dismissed in various industries, not counting those who had been dismissed in the textile industry (*Sinar Harapan* 29 December 1982; *Kompas* 30 December 1982).[55] Such trends were to continue for several years. In 1985, nearly 12,000 workers lost their jobs (*Pelita* 14 March 1986).

Although estimates of the frequency of strike action during this period differ wildly, they do indicate that a fairly serious problem had emerged by the early 1980s. Rudiono suggests that there were 455 strikes altogether between 1976 and 1980 (Rudiono 1992: 62). Manning's estimate is much lower: he suggests that between 1976 and 1980 there were 66 strikes; and between 1981 and 1985, 112 strikes altogether – which would still indicate a sharp rise from the five cases of strike action he calculates to have occurred between 1971 and 1975 (Manning 1993: 70).

The areas in which most of the strikes took place were the more significantly industrialised areas of Jakarta, West Java and East Java. In terms of sectors, those which were most affected were: textiles, assembling, pharmaceuticals and metals and ceramics (*Suara Karya* 16 January 1982; *Sinar Harapan* 16 January 1982). Many of these had been the bulwark of the ISI strategy that emphasised the production of consumer goods. Apparently, domestic investment firms were the site of an overwhelming number of these strikes, although a number of important foreign investment firms were also hit.[56] Numerous newspaper accounts of the period also refer, although rather obliquely, to the role played by security forces in the resolution of individual disputes (*Sinar Harapan* 23 April 1982; *Suara Karya* 17 June 1982; *Merdeka* 15 July 1982).

In fact, by the early 1980s, concerns about the possible destabilising effect of the wave of strikes had increased within state circles. In 1981, as head of KOPKAMTIB, Sudomo argued that the institution 'has the duty to step in if the problem gets out of hand and results in negative excesses endangering state security' (INDOC 1982: 2). It was at this time that, a message was 'sent to all regional commanders in their capacity as regional executive officers' of KOPKAMTIB, which 'ordered direct military intervention in labour disputes' (INDOC 1982: 2). It is notable, however, that prior to KOPKAMTIB's formal involvement in labour matters, military units from local KORAMIL (Komando Rayon Militer; military sub-district commands) had already been involved in suppressing the labour unrest which followed the 1978 currency devaluation (INDOC 1984: 5).

Under Sudomo, the operations of KOPKAMTIB and the Department of Manpower became 'intertwined through the establishment of *Tim Bantuan Masalah Perburuhan* (Labour Assistance Teams) to prevent and detect industrial disputes (Tanter 1990: 254). These teams comprised representatives of KOPKAMTIB, the Department of Manpower, KADIN/PUSPI (later APINDO), the FBSI, as well as representatives of the Departments of Information, Trade and Industries. They were chaired by a Department of Manpower official from the Directorate General of Guidance and Protection, *Binalindung* (INDOC 1982: 3; INDOC 1983: 4; Tanter 1990: 254).

Sudomo described the task of the teams thus:

> If information is received about the possibility of a problem in an enterprise, the task of the team is to resolve it as soon as possible, by bringing together the leaders of the workers and the industrialists, pushing them into discussion, and convincing the workers that there is no use in striking.

He suggested that the teams were designed to pre-empt strikes, lockouts and disturbances that would pose a threat to national stability and stressed that they were designed to complement, rather than override, the P4D/P4P. They would, he said, only intervene if problems got out of hand (quoted in Tanter 1990: 254).

Notably, another of the team's tasks, according to Sudomo (INDOC 1982: 7) was to 'prevent the defence of workers' disputes from being handled by individuals or organisations outside of the channels of the [FBSI] law team or other official law agencies'.[57] With these aims in mind, Sudomo created national- and local-level teams. The former coordinated the operations of the latter, whose job, in particular, was to 'monitor the situation and . . . to act at the first signs of trouble'. They were particularly geared to supervise areas that were identified as potential troublespots, which included Jakarta, West Java, Riau, North Sumatra and East Java (INDOC 1983: 4).

However, the wave of strike action continued largely unabated. This drove Sudomo to take more drastic action: in mid-1982 he announced that all labour disputes would be directly handled by KOPKAMTIB at the central level (INDOC 1983: 6), a decision which constituted a very public mockery of the position of the P4D/P4P.

In March 1983 Sudomo took up his new position as Minister of Manpower. In the same month a second devaluation of the Rupiah occurred which opened up fresh possibilities for increased working-class unrest. Shortly afterwards, the early detection and prevention teams were scrapped altogether and replaced by a *Pusat Pelaksana Pencegah Konflik* (Conflict Prevention Executive Centre), which this time was chaired by a KOPKAMTIB representative. The organisation's other representatives comprised of personnel from various sections of the Department of Manpower, KADIN/PUSPI, the local government, 'technical' departments, as well as the KOPKAMTIB area executive (LAKSUSDA), or the local police (Tanter 1990: 255–256).

According to Sudomo, the task of the new centre was 'to resolve a conflict of interests between management and labour before the conflict turns into a crisis; to localise the conflict and encourage both sides to go to the negotiation table' (INDOC 1984: 11). Like its predecessor, the centre also operated at two levels, for it contained a so-called policy-making centre as well as *Kelompok Aksi Lapangan*, or Field Action Groups. It was particularly the task of the latter to 'prevent a dispute from spreading and to cope with the dispute on the spot' (INDOC 1984: 11). Henceforth, the involvement of KOPKAMTIB officials in the resolution of labour disputes became increasingly unconcealed. Furthermore, barely disguised intelligence methods began to be applied to deal with the labour unrest. For example, questionnaires were regularly given to workers involved in strike action, containing questions which were geared toward identifying how workers were being organised and by whom (Tanter 1990: 262–263).

Thus, by the end of 1983, Sudomo's *ad hoc* organisations had clearly superseded the 'legal–formal' institutions of the industrial-relations system. Moreover, as Minister he was prone to making decisions which were often portrayed in the press as contradicting existing laws (*Tempo* 9 July 1983: 24). In January 1984, Sudomo announced an agreement with KADIN, PUSPI and the FBSI to ban all strike action and slow-downs. According to

Sudomo, although strike action was allowed by law, its exercise required his permission, and he would never provide it because strikes were against the principles of Pancasila Industrial Relations (INDOC 1984: 4–5).[58] Another step toward superseding legally established convention came as Sudomo declared that collective labour agreements in the workplace – the slow development in numbers of which the FBSI/SPSI has been particularly proud (see Sudono 1981; SPSI 1990a) – were 'liberal' and thus contravened principles of Pancasila Industrial Relations (INDOC 1984: 13–14).[59] Notably, this was a sentiment that was similarly expressed by some business figures (*Merdeka* 14 October 1983).

During this time, the involvement of security organisations in labour matters continued to be legitimised by the characterisation of industrial disputes as a threat to national stability. The culmination of this took place in 1986, when Sudomo officially pronounced Ministerial Decree no. 342/1986, which provided a legal basis for military intervention into labour disputes on the basis of national stability considerations (YLBHI 1994a: 3). In fact, by this stage there appeared to have been increasing efforts to provide a legal basis for what had been largely extra-legal common practices. For example, in justifying the quelling of strike action by security personnel, Sudomo often referred to the 1963 Presidential Instruction which prohibited strikes and lock-outs in 'vital' institutions and projects (*Kompas* 4 June 1987). This reached almost comical proportions when a strike at a beverage producer was pronounced illegal by Sudomo on the basis of that particular instruction, thereby deeming the enterprise a 'vital' national institution.[60]

The efforts undertaken by Sudomo to re-establish industrial peace appear to have produced clear results: in 1988 and 1989, there were, according to government statistics, respectively just thirty-nine and nineteen cases of strike action in all of Indonesia (Thamrin n.d.). Manning's data supports this observation, as they also show a downward slide to just forty-six cases of strike action between 1986 and 1990 (Manning 1993: 70).

However, Sudomo was appointed Minister for Politics and Security in 1988, and replaced as Minister of Manpower by the civilian Cosmas Batubara. As we shall see, from such a position Sudomo was to continue to exert some influence over labour policy. In spite of this, it appeared that his *ad hoc* teams had ceased to operate. In the same year, KOPKAMTIB was dissolved and replaced by a new coordinating security agency, BAKOR-STRANAS.

These changes did not signal the end of the security and military forces' involvement in labour matters. Within more contemporary arrangements, the emphasis of the 'security' approach seems to lie in coordinating the activities of district and sub-district military commands, respectively the KODIM (*Komando Distrik Militer*) and KORAMIL, with those of the local police and government apparatus, in bodies called *Musyawarah Pimpinan Daerah* (MUSPIDA; Regional Consultative Leadership), and *Musyawarah Pimpinan Kecamatan* (MUSPIKA; Sub-district Consultative Leadership)

(YLBHI 1994a: 3–6). Furthermore, BAKORSTRANAS came to take up essentially the same role as its predecessor. In 1990, this agency was given the right to intervene in labour affairs, again in the interest of maintaining national stability, by virtue of a decree signed by its head – who was simultaneously commander-in-chief of the Indonesian Armed Forces (BAKORSTRANAS 1990). This would indicate continuing high-level interest in maintaining stringent controls over organised labour.

SUMMARY

Similar to the other cases of East Asian industrialisation, the development of an exclusionary model of accommodation between state, capital and labour in Indonesia initially occurred under the impetus to pre-empt the re-emergence of grassroots, left-wing political movements. Likewise, the pre-established mechanisms of control were later integrated into the requirements of an export-led development strategy which was underpinned by low-wage, labour-intensive industries. Notably, immediately prior to and during the early years of embarking on this development strategy, the state's capacities of control over labour were greatly enhanced.

Moreover, as in the other East Asian cases, a doctrine of industrial relations that places emphasis on industrial harmony and cooperation between state, capital and labour, has been very prominent. This doctrine is formulated in reference to what is claimed to be culturally rooted, intrinsic traits, which value harmony and cooperation, and eschew conflict and confrontation. In the case of Indonesia, the doctrine has been that of Pancasila Industrial Relations.

Among Asian late industrialisers, Indonesia's is a case which displays a clear emphasis on the development of state-sponsored corporatist institutions as well as the development of the capacities of security-oriented institutions to handle industrial unrest. In this regard, there are close parallels between the institutions of exclusion and control that operate in Indonesia and those that operated in South Korea, particularly before 1987. In Indonesia, these security-oriented institutions came to override 'legal–formal' ones as the latter have been incapable of preempting the development of grassroots labour organising.

It has been argued that the attractiveness of a 'security approach' toward industrial relations in Indonesia has been related to the underdevelopment of an industrial working class. Such a situation has made a strategy of cooptation, which would involve a qualitatively higher degree of labour's political inclusion, unnecessary, as the political cost of repression and coercion has remained relatively low. In turn, because of attractiveness of a strategy of repression, the capacities of security-oriented organisations to deal with labour unrest were greatly developed. This was particularly so throughout the 1970s and 1980s, the period which has been the focus of most of this Chapter.

However, the 1990s has seen a new expression of working-class unrest, and the growth of new, independent working-class organisations which have been challenging the monopoly of state-created institutions. These trends are in themselves inextricably related to the gradual development and maturation of the industrial working class, a by-product of decades of relatively successful industrialisation under the New Order. Whether such developments are increasing pressures toward the dismantling of corporatist arrangements of control and demobilisation as they concern the working class is the central concern of the remainder of this study.

6 A class in the making
The new urban proletariat

INDUSTRIALISATION AND INDONESIA'S WORKING CLASS

Sustained industrialisation under the New Order has brought about vast changes which are transforming Indonesia's social landscape, as new social classes, associated with the maturation of capitalism, gradually appear and develop. The industrial working class, slowly emerging within the new sprawling industrial areas which now surround many major cities in Java, and some areas beyond, constitutes one of these classes.

This new industrial working class is largely the product of Indonesia's increasingly important manufacturing sector. In the mid-1960s, at the onset of the New Order, manufacturing accounted for a mere 8 per cent of Indonesia's GDP (Hill, H. 1994: 57). However, this share changed quite dramatically, especially after the fall of international oil prices in the early 1980s, which prompted the adoption of a development strategy that was based more on the export of manufactured products than on oil revenue. Although manufacturing only contributed 12.2 per cent of Indonesia's GDP in 1981, by 1992 it contributed a quite impressive 21 per cent (World Bank 1994: 203), rising again to 24 per cent in 1995 (World Bank 1996: 139). In 1993, the export of manufactured products accounted for over half the country's total exports (World Bank 1995: 190), and could account for as much as 65 per cent of total exports by 2000 (World Bank 1993a: 13).[1]

In the meantime, employment in Indonesia's manufacturing sector has also grown gradually. In 1971 there was a total of a mere 2.7 million people employed in the sector, which constituted 6.5 per cent of the labour force. In 1980, the number of workers in manufacturing had grown to 4.4 million, representing 8.5 per cent of the total workforce. By 1990, however, there were 8.2 million people working in the manufacturing sector, representing 11.6 per cent of Indonesia's labour force (World Bank 1994: 197), indicating a slow, but fairly steady growth. In 1991, 3 million of these were employed in approximately 16,500 establishments classified as medium and large-scale (BPS 1993: 307).

Given that this industrial working class has largely developed within the kind of low-wage and labour-intensive industries which also underpinned the early export-led success of the first group of East Asian NICs, it is not surprising that a large number of those employed in the manufacturing sector have been young females. The feminisation of the workforces of low-skill, labour-intensive industries has been related to the view, common among employers, that the wages of female workers are more easily repressed and that women are by nature more docile and controllable. As will be discussed below, however, such stereotyping is not necessarily supported by reality.[2] In accordance with trends toward feminisation, though, Hull (1994: 5) reports that 3.6 million women were employed in manufacturing in 1990, compared to 4.6 million men (to give the figure in context, 25 million women and 46 million men made up the total workforce in that year).

An important feature of the growth of manufacturing employment is that it has thus far been concentrated in only a few industrial centres. In 1990, according to White (1993: 131), 'the two regions of Jabotabek (Jakarta, Bogor, Tangerang and Bekasi) in West Java, together with Surabaya-Malang-Mojokerto-Gresik in East Java, accounted for almost two-fifths of all Indonesian manufacturing employment and more than half of manufacturing employment in Java.' The experience of earlier industrialisers has shown that heavy concentrations of a growing urban proletariat in increasingly strategic industrial centres will have implications for the ability of the working class to organise (Deyo *et al.* 1987). Significantly, the growth of newer industrial centres, particularly in Java, also appears to be taking place in tandem with increasingly strong trends toward urbanisation. White points out that throughout the 1980s, the urban population of Java grew from 23 to 38 million, in contrast to the vastly more limited growth of its rural population from 68 to 69 million. This suggests a large-scale movement of people to the cities during that decade. The most important growth, furthermore, did not occur in Jakarta, but in Java's provincial urban centres, suggesting the gradual process of the geographical spread of urban centres as industrialisation proceeds (White 1993: 129).

Obviously, these figures, as important as they are, do not by themselves reveal the complete picture. What lies behind these figures is no less the complex processes which are involved in the gradual, subjective, as well as objective, development of an industrial working class. This development not only involves an increase in terms of the absolute and relative size of the industrial workforce, but also entails the very creation of a more peculiarly working-class identity. Such an identity is one which emerges from the experiences and struggles of everyday life and work within a new urban and industrial milieu, and, arguably, one that will increasingly distinguish the industrial proletariat from the larger masses of urban poor and migrants who have to toil and persevere in an increasingly hostile urban environment.

One theoretical issue which is pursued throughout this study concerns the political significance, if any, of the emergence of working classes and fledgling working-class movements in very late industrialising countries like

Indonesia. This raises the question of whether it has had any effect on the model of accommodation between state, capital and labour which in this study has been called 'exclusionary'. After decades of neglect, some attention has been given to the Indonesian working class with the appearance of some signs of strain in long-established, state-constructed, institutional arrangements, primarily geared to hinder the development of independent labour organisations and to maintain labour's political exclusion.3 This has involved a marked rise in industrial unrest, accompanied by the increasing activity of alternative labour-based organisations, over which the state has had very little direct control.

Not surprisingly, a large proportion of this unrest has taken place in the industrial areas of the so-called Jabotabek area, the site of the greatest concentration of export-oriented factories and of the proliferation of new, more distinctly working-class neighbourhoods and areas.4 However, as there has been a gradual spread of export-oriented production to new locations, lately there has also been a correspondingly wider geographical spread of industrial unrest. Most notably, East Java and North Sumatra, which have sizeable industrial production zones, have also witnessed a significant surge in industrial action. Predictably, a large number of these strikes have occurred in textiles-, garments- and footwear-producing establishments.5 Moreover, labour struggles in East Java have received much recent attention because of the widely publicised 'Marsinah' case, which involved the brutal kidnapping, torture and murder of a female labour leader.6 North Sumatran labour struggles have also received much attention because of the Medan riots of April 1994, which involved mass action by an estimated 20,000–30,000 workers.

In spite of such developments, some commentators, like Manning, have pointed to the structural constraint posed by Indonesia's labour-surplus economy to the growth of a significant working-class movement (Manning 1995), although some tightening of the labour market appears to be taking place (Manning and Jayasuriya 1996). Indeed, this constraint is formidable, as estimates suggest that well over a third of the Indonesian labour force is unemployed or underemployed (*Asian Wall Street Journal* 11 July 1990; *Australian* 30 August 1995). Furthermore, Deyo (1989) suggests that for various reasons (which are discussed below) the characteristics of the proletariat emerging from those industries that have underpinned the export-led development strategy have in fact been an impediment to the growth of strong working class-based movements.7 Given such arguments, this Chapter focuses on whether the growth of a new, more defined, industrial

Table 6.1 Industrial Action, 1988–1994[8]

Year	1988	1989	1990	1991	1992	1993	1994
Number of Strikes	39	19	61	114	250	180	367[9]

working class, in the Indonesian context, has provided a social base more conducive to the development of greater working-class organisational capacities.

A range of primary sources of material has been utilised for the analysis presented in this Chapter. Some of the information on the new industrial working class given below derives from studies and surveys undertaken by labour activist groups in Indonesia, which up to now have surfaced very rarely in academic work on Indonesian labour. The bulk of the information, however, is based on a series of interviews and discussions, of varying degrees of formality, with numerous individual workers and groups of workers during the course of fieldwork from late 1993 to mid-1994. The majority of such sessions took place in working-class communities in Tangerang and some of the industrial areas between Jakarta and the town of Bogor, although others took place in other parts of the Jabotabek area. Most of these sessions were necessarily highly unstructured and often spontaneous. However, throughout the sessions, the concern was to delve into questions which relate to the issue of working-class identity and the way it is linked to the changing experience, and material conditions, of life and work in the new urban centres of industrial production.

PROLETARIAN POLITICS AND IDENTITY: SOME CONCEPTUAL ISSUES

Discussions on the politics of the working class have traditionally been linked to debates regarding the 'objective' interests of that class – particularly identified in the Marxist tradition as the overthrow of capitalism and its replacement by socialism. Thus, many writers, especially those working from within that tradition, have expected the rank-and-file worker to be endowed with a revolutionary temper and frame of mind. If he or she were not, something had to be wrong, most likely with existing working-class organisations and their leadership. Indeed, 'the worker as revolutionary' is an exceptionally attractive concept to writers, especially if the actual act of writing about the working class is consciously regarded as a means of contributing to the practice of its struggle (Lloyd 1982: 12).

Interestingly, the English worker of the nineteenth century is sometimes invoked as a model for the 'worker as revolutionary' concept, although this is ironic given the findings of Geary's comparative study of European working-class movements of the latter part of that century, and given Engels' famous lament about the distinct political moderateness of England's active working-class movement of that time. Lloyd, for example, cites Goldthorpe as an advocate of the idea that the Victorian-age toiler was the 'traditional' worker who was both 'poor and radical'. No less an observer than Giddens is cited as one writer who cannot find the existence of the 'traditional' worker in the contemporary world but who accepts that he (and presumably, to an extent, she) once existed in an earlier time (Lloyd 1982: 22–23).

Obviously, the discussion of 'objective' working-class interests and of revolutionary consciousness is itself inextricably linked to the debates about the 'failure' of the working class of the first industrialisers to undertake its 'historical mission', which within the classical Marxist framework, was to act as the 'gravediggers of capitalism'. Some, like Burawoy, argue that the failure to fulfil this perceived mission, to 'emancipate itself' and 'the whole of humanity', has resulted in a strong intellectual tendency to dismiss the significance of labour in analyses of contemporary capitalist society. Thus, he argues, the working class 'as saviour of humanity' has been replaced by the working class 'incapable of shaping its own destiny' (Burawoy 1985: 5–7). As discussed in Chapter 1, it is the new non-proletarian social movements, – 'environmentalism', 'feminism', etc. – which have taken the place of the working-class movement as the focus of challenge to capitalist society in the academic discourse. Indeed, writers like Gorz (1982) have bid 'farewell to the working class'.

Clearly the main problem is that the working class in the developed world is seen to be bereft of the 'revolutionary temper' that was expected of it within classical Marxism. However, as pointed out at the outset of this study, some scholars have come to look for the re-emergence of that almost mythical 'traditional', poor *and* radical proletarian in the later industrialisers of the 'Third World'.

To some extent it may be said that such a position is found in Burawoy, who argues that 'Just as revolutionary impulses are not innate characteristics of the working class, so resignation to the status quo is neither natural nor inevitable but is produced by specific conditions'. It is also significant that he optimistically points to the 'international recomposition of the industrial working class', which 'entails that the conditions for the renewal of working class radicalism are to be found in the industrially advancing areas of Latin America, Africa and Eastern Europe' (Burawoy 1985: 7). Echoing more or less the same sentiment, Thompson writes that 'Causes lost in England might, in Asia or Africa, yet be won' (Thompson 1968: 12), suggesting that processes that are strikingly similar to many of those that occurred in Europe in earlier centuries are still taking place with unforeseeable results.

The question of the 'revolutionary-or-not' temperament of the working classes of later industrialisers has particularly permeated the literature on Latin American working-class movements (Munck 1988a: 11), which as may be expected, is much more sizeable than the literature on East Asian working classes. Significantly, some Latin American states espousing particular brands of populism (such as Perónism) have demonstrated the political importance of local working-class movements by partly embracing and accommodating them in the structures of power. By contrast, in East Asia, states have mostly been concerned with maintaining the political peripheralisation and exclusion of labour.

Perhaps in part because of such an accommodation – falling considerably short of the objective of founding socialism – the debate on the political character of the labour movement in Latin America has echoed in some respects its European counterpart. One particularly important issue which emerged in European cases had to do with the development of an increasingly privileged and decidedly un-revolutionary 'labour aristocracy'. Latin American debates have also more than touched upon this subject. Echoing Engels' lament that English trade unions concentrated too much on narrow economic objectives and lacked a wider political agenda, some authors writing on Latin America argue that the pursuit of 'bread and butter' issues by trade unions supports the cause of imperialism (as cited in Munck 1988a: 11). Recall that Lenin too had given warning about the dangers of 'bread and butter' trade unionism to wider revolutionary aims.[10]

However, the intention to find in the worker, say in Tangerang, the revolutionary temperament that the worker in Manchester lost or arguably, never really developed, may be unfruitful for two reasons. First, even if the working-class movements of the nineteenth and early twentieth centuries in Europe were to be labelled as 'reformist' and 'un-revolutionary', it is indisputable that they played an important role in influencing the direction of political struggles of the period, not to mention in improving the general welfare and bargaining power of workers. Thus, the presence of a strong working-class movement was a crucial factor in the very gradual democratisation of European polities from about the mid-nineteenth century, resulting in, among other things, universal suffrage, often in the face of bourgeois resistance, as argued by Therborn (1977) and more recently by Rueschemeyer *et al.* (1992). The social-democratic form of accommodation of state, capital and labour mostly associated with the European experience, and whose central feature is the welfare state, is an unimaginable outcome without the presence of strong working-class movements.

Furthermore, against those who suggest the overriding importance of a revolutionary, proletarian outlook, Scott argues that there is no compelling evidence on the relationship between revolutionary consciousness and working-class action. In sharp contrast to many Marxist writers, his position is to maintain the unwarrantedness of expectations that the rank-and-file worker will necessarily espouse revolutionary ideals in the first place (Scott 1985: 340–341). Not surprisingly, therefore, he rejects Gramsci's proposition that the working class has been limited to a reformist, trade unionist consciousness as a result of its intellectual subordination by dominant classes. Scott suggests, to the contrary, that

> Rather than being motivated by a vision of a radically new social order, the ordinary worker has generally been motivated by the wish to obtain things which in principle – though often not in practice – can reasonably be accommodated within the existing social system. Thus, revolutionary situations, partly occur when these simple demands are thwarted.
>
> (Scott 1985: 341)

Scott's position is supported, among others, by the work of Barrington Moore who raises the cases of working-class action in Germany at the end of World War I and in Russia in 1917, regarded as good examples of political spontaneity. Moore points out that workers were essentially struggling for 'trade unionist' or 'bread and butter' issues, often easily dismissed as irrelevant from the Leninist perspective. However, the political impact of the actions taken by workers in each case was not insignificant (Moore 1978: 351–352; 369–370).

In spite of contributing such important observations, Scott and Moore may have, in the process, been guilty of throwing out the baby with the bathwater. Even if it is accepted that working-class revolutionary consciousness has seldom emerged in history and, if it ever did, has rarely been sustained, the process of the formation of a proletarian class identity remains of great importance. Thus what is more relevant to an understanding of the emergence of working-class action is the development of a working-class self-identity, which should not necessarily be confused with the notion of a revolutionary consciousness.

Thompson has given the best illustration of how class identity emerges. He writes that

> class happens when men,[11] as a result of common experiences (inherited or shared), feel and articulate the identity of their interests as between themselves, and as against other men whose interests are different (and usually opposed to) theirs . . . . Class consciousness is the way in which these experiences are handled in cultural terms . . . . If the experience appears to be determined, class-consciousness does not. We can see a *logic* in the responses of similar occupational groups undergoing similar experiences, but we cannot predicate any *law*. Consciousness of class arises in the same way in different times and places, but never in just the same way.
>
> (Thompson 1968: 9)

It is clear that Thompson rejects the view that the working class mechanistically arises out of a set of 'objective conditions'. In his seminal study of the 'making of the English working class' in the late eighteenth and early nineteenth centuries, Thompson argues that workers' growing understanding of the social and political order in which they found themselves was due to their own participation in concrete struggles and a process of education that included involvement in study groups, political meetings, cultural activities and workers' associations (Morris 1992: 353–354). In his well-known formulation: 'the working class made itself as much as it was made' (Thompson 1968: 213). Undoubtedly, Thompson would have been supported in this by Lukacs, who proposed that in history, there was nothing less automatic than proletarian class consciousness (cited in Lebowitz 1991: 133).

Thompson's detailed study showed the complex processes through which the class consciousness of English workers emerged out of the body of fragmented worker thoughts, feelings, shared knowledge, experiences, values and suffering – rooted in a network of worker organisations and institutions.[12] According to Thompson, this enabled workers to form a picture of the organisation of society out of their own experience and with the help of their 'hard-won' and 'erratic' education, which was above all a political picture. Thus, class consciousness emerged as 'the objective social structures' conjured up by the industrialisation process – 'working-class neighbourhoods with their myriad of institutions, along with factories and their vast numbers of embedded social relationships – became infused with highly charged debates concerning the nature of worker exploitation, worker rights, and the place of workers in the overall social order'. At the same time, 'workers were engaged in numerous confrontations with the capitalist class and the state', confrontations which were 'characterised by limited goals and initiated by segments of workers and not guided by a coherent social and political vision'. In essence, therefore, 'working-class consciousness' may be said to have 'emerged slowly through a process of concrete social and political struggle, information sharing and organisation building' (Morris 1993: 353).

The single, most innovative work thus far on East Asian industrialisation and labour is that of Deyo (1989). If Thompson was primarily concerned with the processes of class formation, Deyo's work, which takes the emergence of a proletariat in East Asian countries to be largely a 'given', focuses on how 'circumstances have inhibited and distorted the development of trade unions and labour movements' in the region which 'elsewhere has enfranchised and empowered workers'. The main question that Deyo asked was why organised labour has remained such a weak political entity in East Asia in spite of the clear growth of working classes as a result of rapid industrialisation. Notwithstanding Potter's (1993) more recent analysis of the political significance of the working-class movement in South Korea, which to an extent contradicts Deyo, many of his findings are still pertinent and require careful attention.

Among these is the assertion that the establishment of authoritarian controls over labour in many East Asian countries – prior to the adoption of export-led industrialisation – had significantly constrained the organisation of the working class which had emerged as a result of rapid industrialisation. According to Deyo, these controls were established for political reasons. In earlier parts of this study it was demonstrated that the same observation may be applied to Indonesia, where strict controls over labour significantly pre-dated the adoption of EOI in the mid-1980s. Other assertions that Deyo makes also warrant some consideration.

As mentioned earlier, for Deyo, another fundamental constraint to the growth of strong working-class movements in East Asian countries is related to the *kind* of working class that export-oriented, labour intensive, industries engendered. He writes that

The attraction of young, low-skilled, often female workers to employment characterised by low pay, tedium, minimal job security, and lack of career mobility encourages low job commitment, high levels of turnover, and lack of attachment to work groups or firms. These circumstances impede independent unionisation efforts among workers in light export industries.

(Deyo 1989: 8)

A further source of weakness of East Asian working classes is traced by Deyo to their communities. He proposes that, in contrast to Latin America, where 'working class communities provide an essential foundation for labour protest', similar communities in East Asian countries 'fail to play a supportive role for worker organisation and political action' (Deyo 1989: 8–9).

Yet another of Deyo's assertions that may be considered relates to the significance of patriarchical values to strategies of inhibiting working-class movements. Indeed, despite adopting a clearly structuralist position, and being critical of primarily culturalist arguments, Deyo identifies a distinctly more cultural reason for the weakness of organised labour in East Asian countries. Thus, he writes about the 'continued vitality, and indeed the expansion, of employment relations based on patriarchical, paternalistic, and patrimonial systems of labour control. Within these systems, economic conflict rarely assumes the form of collective organisation and protest in public places' (Deyo 1989: 8).

Given that the four examples that constituted Deyo's case studies were South Korea, Taiwan, Hong Kong and Singapore, this patriarchical system, not surprisingly, was viewed by Deyo as arising from Confucian values which emphasise authority and hierarchy.

Many of Deyo's observations are very useful as a point of comparison for studies on more recent examples of other industrialising Asian countries. This applies even though there might be reasons to debate the validity of these very observations as they relate to Deyo's own case studies. Potter's analysis of the South Korean case appears to contradict Deyo's findings to quite an extent. Moreover, even Deyo admits that the feminised workforces of export-oriented, labour-intensive industries in South Korea have been quite militant, albeit less successful, compared to the workforces of higher-skill, more male-dominated industries, in achieving favourable results from their demands. It is also questionable, again taking the example of South Korea, but also increasingly of Indonesia, that 'economic conflict rarely assumes the form of collective action or protest in public places' in East Asian countries, supposedly because of the influence of patriarchical values. Given these considerations, any transposition of Deyo's observations to other cases, say Indonesia, should be made with great care.

It is Deyo's observation of the impediment to organising caused by the often transient nature of employment in low-skill, low-wage industries that most squarely hits the mark with regard to the case of Indonesia. Indeed, one common lament of Indonesian labour organisers relates to the difficulty of sustaining bases of influence, after painstaking efforts to establish them, in particular factories because of the often sudden disbandment of local worker groups. Echoing Deyo, they suggest that this has been partly due to the fact that the workers, often young women, employed in such industries, have had a very high tendency to change places of employment for little reason.[13] The relative ease of moving from factory to factory, as Deyo recognised, has obvious ramifications for the development of a more sustainable working-class movement, because stable leadership and membership of workers' groups within particular factories cannot be guaranteed as workers come and go too quickly.[14] The problem has been compounded in Indonesia, of course, by the tendency of employers, sometimes with the help of local police or military commands, to dismiss, or somehow get rid of, 'troublesome' workers, even after employer/employee disputes have been settled.[15] Such practices often leave worker groups bereft of experienced and respected rank-and-file leaders.

However, other of Deyo's assertions require greater care in their extrapolation to the case of Indonesia. Particular attention, it seems, needs to be given to the assertion of the influence of patriarchical values in maintaining the subordination of feminised workforces.

In previous Chapters it was demonstrated that the particular interpretation of Pancasila as state ideology during the New Order, which has been applied and codified in the concept of Pancasila Industrial Relations, has indeed helped to maintain the continued domestication of organised labour in Indonesia. It was shown that the emphasis given to such values as harmony, partnership, authority and responsibility in HIP has in the past hindered efforts to organise the working class, especially because conflict, and by implication, working-class action, was regarded as anathema to its principles. In this regard, Deyo's assertion seems quite valid, particularly if the propagation of patriarchical values is placed within the context of concrete economic and political interests, as Deyo himself suggests.

More serious problems arise, however, when culturalist explanations of labour subordination, undoubtedly those that would also emphasise the significance of patriarchical values, take on a life of their own, as they so easily do. Mather (1983), for example, writing about female factory workers in Tangerang in the early 1980s, identified the influence of religion-derived patriarchical values as a factor in her explanation of the relatively mild surges of labour unrest in that area at the time. Presumably, as industrialisation in the area then had been sufficiently limited that demand for low wage labour could be largely fulfilled by the local populace, she suggested that patriarchical forms of domination in the family were reproduced, or at least reinforced, in the factory, and thus served to ensure the continued docility of the local labour force. Hence, the female employees of factories operating at that time in Tangerang (local males, claims Mather, looked down on factory work) simply moved from one milieu of subordination to another, as they played the roles of mother, wife or daughter at home, and then of worker in the factory, where male authority figures supervised their work (Mather 1983: 157). This subordination, according to Mather, is rooted in the low esteem given to women in Islam. Thus, for example, low wages paid to women were legitimised, she says, by religion-derived patriarchical values which regarded a woman's contribution to the income of a household as of minor importance, even if this was contradicted by reality.

However, this seems to be an oversimplified explanation of how cultural values intermingle with strategies of labour subordination. It may be argued, for example, that the same source of patriarchical values may also produce results that contradict the interests that had caused their propagation in the first place. For example, Pancasila itself simultaneously acts as a source of legitimacy both to extensive state intervention in everyday life, including industrial relations (see Moertopo (1972) and the discussion in Chapter 4), and to expectations that the state's own propaganda regarding harmony and common interests translate into policies that protect the interests of the weak, including workers. Thus, the same patriarchical values that legitimise the authority of the state – as benevolent father-figure – may simultaneously contribute to the disillusionment of workers, and therefore to industrial unrest, when the state has demonstrably not used that authority for the common good, but only to serve particular individual interests.[16]

The same may be said about the patriarchical values that Mather argues derive from religious belief. It is notable that Mather only fleetingly mentions workers in the industrial areas to the south of Jakarta, which she says were more militant than Tangerang workers (Mather 1983: 149). Presumably, as West Javans, like the Tangerang local population, workers in those southern areas would be significantly influenced by the same patriarchical values of Islam. There is no doubt that Mather's sympathetic work provides useful information that is so sparsely available on the everyday life of workers in Tangerang in the early 1980s. Its importance, unfortunately, is somewhat reduced because of an absence of any real effort to compare Tangerang workers to that of other areas, thereby bringing into question some of her conclusions.

Even if Mather's analysis is accepted for the time and place in which she carried out her fieldwork, there is good reason to question its applicability to the contemporary situation. One of the most outstanding features of contemporary cases of labour unrest – including in the far more industrialised present-day Tangerang, where young migrant workers predominate – is the militancy, and leading role taken by many female workers. Undoubtedly, any fieldwork done today in Tangerang or any other industrial area, which included an observation of the activities of the many small workers' groups that are now spread across innumerable working-class communities, could not fail to register the leading role that a large number of young women have played in them. Even some of the more formal gatherings of workers, aimed at discussing and publicising macro-level labour issues in the offices of such NGOs as YLBHI – often together with middle-class intellectuals and activists – are outstanding for the fact that many of the female workers in attendance tend to be more active and outspoken than their male counterparts.[17]

There is also a problem with Mather's (rather than Deyo's) specific identification of Islamic-derived patriarchical values as a prohibiting factor for working-class organisation. In spite of the propagation of such values, an argument could be made for the simultaneous contribution of religious belief to the emergence of some cases of labour unrest. In fact, because the religious belief of the majority of factory workers is different from those of their supervisors and employers, who are often foreign, or Indonesian Chinese, it may be argued that it has acted as a mediating factor in the emergence of working-class solidarity. Perhaps some useful comparisons can be made here with the proposed idea that adherence to Islam plays a role in the development of class consciousness among workers in northern Nigeria, where 'Capitalism, its technology and language, and the very social relations it introduced were associated with Christianity, and thus inimical to the Muslim community' (Munck 1988a: 102).

Indeed, employers in Indonesia have been known to complain about the time that is lost as workers demand the right to observe the Muslim requirement of daily prayers at set times, two (out of five) of which would take place during regular work hours.[18] It is not inconceivable that some workers who have made this demand have not done so exclusively for reasons of piety, but as a small gesture of resistance to the grinding routine of factory work. Moreover, it is also significant that one demand that has often appeared on the lists that workers present during cases of strike action is for the provision of adequate places of worship in the factory compound, again suggesting an ironic role of religion in helping to cement working-class solidarity – in spite of its simultaneous role as a legitimiser of patriarchical domination.

Thus, value systems, including those that directly relate to patriarchy, could fruitfully be viewed as simultaneously carrying out mutually contradictory functions. Therefore, there is also ample evidence to support the view that patriarchical values do indeed have a role in inhibiting the organisation of substantially femininised workforces. For example, some (male as well as female) labour organisers claim that they have experienced some difficulty in developing young, female, 'cadres'. This they often attribute to the fact that many such young women entertain the thought of escaping work, and thus being 'saved' from present circumstances, by an eventual marriage.[19] It is maintained that these young women do so in spite of the remoteness of the possibility of marrying a male worker who is not similarly poverty-ridden. Some organisers have also cited the effectiveness of the reprimands of local neighbourhood (usually male) notables, such as the head of an administrative district (RT or RW)[20] in preventing females from participating in organising activities on the basis of some normative code of appropriate behaviour for young women – ostensibly rooted in religious values.[21] As such male authority figures point out, many of these organisation-related meetings take place during evening hours, involve some travel by young women in the dark of night, and then huddling in cramped quarters with male counterparts.

The leading role that male NGO activists have tended to play in the organisational efforts of feminised workforces also provides good cause to suspect that patriarchical values not only inhibit organising but also helps to shape the way in which any organising takes place.[22] Even so, the role of such male activists should be seen to be mitigated to some degree by the increasingly important role that has been played by women-oriented labour groups, often initiated by female middle-class NGO activists, influenced to varying degrees by strands of liberal or radical feminism. Furthermore, unlike the usually male-dominated NGO leadership, leaders who have emerged from the rank and file of the working class itself have been more likely to be female. This is perhaps best exemplified by the East Java worker Marsinah, who was killed in 1993 in connection with her role in organising a strike, and who has since, without much exaggeration, been regarded as a kind of working-class martyr by workers from Medan to Surabaya.

It should be clear from this discussion that I am not suggesting here that Deyo's identification of a more culturally rooted explanation of labour's weakness in East Asia is unwarranted. Likewise there is no suggestion that patriarchical values do not have a role in shaping the nature of working-class struggles in Indonesia. However, if Deyo's idea that patriarchical values have impeded the growth of labour movements in East Asian societies is accepted, the fact that value systems as obviously divergent as Confucianism and Islam can have the same effect in terms of labour subordination suggests that a more complex culturally rooted explanation still needs to be found.

There is also good reason, in reference to the Indonesian case, to qualify Deyo's observations about the lack of a role of working-class communities in East Asian countries in advancing the cause of organised labour. Contrary to this suggestion, the labour-organising activity that has taken place recently in Indonesia has often been initiated at the community level, instead of the factory, because of the immense difficulty and danger involved in organising in the latter context. Community-based organisational activities have done much to lift the quality of the working-class struggle to a higher level in recent years, although it is less certain whether they are adequate to sustain a longer-term and demonstrably more effective labour movement in the near future. These activities are briefly considered here, and more thoroughly in Chapter 7.

URBANISATION AND CLASS FORMATION

The conditions for the development of a more mature working class have been developing in Indonesia, albeit at a slow pace, as industrialisation proceeds. At the same time, the subjective development of a more distinctly working-class identity is being facilitated by the experience of everyday life in a growing urban and industrial milieu. Also as already mentioned, the number of people involved in the manufacturing sector has been rising steadily. Perhaps more significantly, by now a new generation of workers, growing up or maybe even born in urban or peri-urban areas, especially in Java, has come of age. For an increasing number of such workers, life in the city and work in the factory is not conceived of as being temporary, as it was by their predecessors. Because the factory is the main source of livelihood, as the city is the major source of living experience, contemporary workers have more or less naturally come to feel that they have a greater stake in the struggles that take place in this urban milieu. This is especially so in comparison to members of generations of urban workers that preceded them, and who might not have stayed in the urban context. In essence, it is in part because of these developments that the 1990s have seen the emergence of a fledgling working-class movement in Indonesia, even in the face of an elaborate, repressive, system of control.[23]

Indeed, the numerous interviews, conversations and discussions I conducted with individual and groups of industrial workers showed a strong predisposition among them to stay and fight it out in the cities. Virtually all workers I encountered uniformly saw, with little hesitation, their futures to lie in the city, for better or for worse, as the village no longer represented a viable place of refuge or retreat. Furthermore, with the exception of only a few individuals, all workers rejected the possibility, or even the desirability, of permanently resettling, sometime later, in his or her home village. It was clear that to them, at least, there was nothing temporary about their urban situation.[24]

It is not being suggested here, however, that ties between today's urban workers and their home villages have been totally severed; they definitely have not and it would take a longer, sustained period of industrialisation for this to happen. If anything, the yearly return of workers to their places of origin, usually undertaken during the Muslim annual *idul fitri*, and involving an often physically taxing trip – due to the sheer numbers of people sharing in this tradition – is evidence of the continuing importance of these links to individual workers in the definition of their self-identity.[25] The 'de-linking' of urban workers from their rural origins will gradually happen, however, perhaps as early as in the case of second generation urban proletarians, and almost certainly in the case of the third, as new families begin to take root in the cities and remaining close relatives die out in the villages.[26] Even today's first-generation proletarians are quite clearly more urbanised than first-generation factory workers of previous periods, who would have tended to see their time in the city as a temporary, rough, stint – which had to be made before eventually returning to the village – hopefully with some savings. Compared to past urban workers, today's workers, as Hull (1994: 5) puts it, 'have an increasing realisation of their role in the urban and urbane world'.

Importantly, working-class formation in the cities is not unrelated to the great transformations which are also affecting rural areas as a consequence of the very same industrialisation process which has given rise to harsh, congested, urban and industrial centres. Specifically, the development of what Young calls the 'urbanisation of the rural' (Young 1994), which has taken place especially in Java, but also to some degree in parts of other islands, has had a crucial, though perhaps, indirect, influence on class formation in the cities.

Echoing a suggestion made by Hull (1994: 8), Young argues that the distinction between 'rural' and 'urban' is not as clear-cut as it is usually presented in contemporary census results. According to Young, areas in Java usually regarded as 'rural' have gradually taken up many of the characteristics of those considered 'urban' and many 'rural' areas now have population densities and access to facilities, such as education, transport and communications, which would be regarded as 'urban' under current definitions. Thus, for many contemporary workers, the transition from a 'rural' lifestyle and world outlook to one that is more clearly associated with an 'urban' existence may not involve such a great cultural, or for that matter physical, leap at all: many of the industrial sites are located 'outside' the cities in peri-urban areas, or along major highways, while the workforce for these factories are drawn in from 'rural' villages around the cities and highways so that areas well beyond the administrative boundaries of the cities are changed along with the city itself (Young 1994: 252).[27]

Thus, according to Young, the lifestyles and outlook of much of the population classified as 'rural' in census results are in some ways qualitatively similar to those of proper 'urban' dwellers.[28] In this sense, it may be said that the more urban outlook of today's industrial workers has in part been facilitated by the great changes that are simultaneously reshaping the landscape of much of what is known as the 'rural' in contemporary Indonesia, especially in Java, as these have better 'prepared' them for the struggles of life and work in the cities. Even so, there are particular experiences (discussed below) which can only be gained from living and working in a more properly urban and industrial milieu, which help to define the self-identity of members of the contemporary working class and, in turn, help to give shape to working-class struggles.

An important characteristic of workers employed in the export-oriented manufacturing sector is their youth. Researchers have consistently found that the ages of contemporary urban industrial workers usually range from mid-teens to late twenties (e.g. White 1993: 133; Roesli 1992: 34), although longer established factories in Java (and not necessarily export-oriented ones – e.g. in batik and cigarette manufacturing) have workforces of a more varied age. They have also consistently found that the education level of such workers has been quite high in comparison to that of previous generations of urban workers.[29] In contrast to the less sizeable urban, industrial workforce of fifteen or twenty years ago, it is more common today for graduates of secondary schools, and even those with some tertiary education, to be employed in low-wage and low-skill manufacturing jobs (White 1993: 133; Roesli 1992: 34).[30] Thus, today's urban worker is also typically more literate than that of the past.[31] One worker, in describing the importance to his class of recent repressive state policy toward the press, argues that newspapers and newsmagazines have had a considerable role in raising worker awareness of social issues and their situation in society. He suggests that such Jakarta-based publications as *Harian Terbit*, and *Pos Kota*, as well as the Surabaya-based *Jawa Pos*, have been particularly significant, because they 'always publish pictures of workers who are undertaking strike action. News of workers' strike action is a means of communication and education among workers. They can see that the workers' struggle has spread everywhere.'[32]

It is suggested here that both of these factors – youth and education – have been important with regard to an understanding of the inner dynamics of the wave of industrial unrest that has occurred in the industrial centres of Indonesia in the 1990s. Arguably, young and relatively more educated urban workers would tend to have greater aspirations in terms of their future and would be more inclined to make demands than an older, uneducated and less urbanised workforce. These characteristics (which I discuss in due course) have also made labour organising today, in a sense, a little easier than before. This is especially so with regard to facilitating the interaction of workers with similarly young, middle-class activists in many of the new labour-based organisations that have proliferated since the late 1980s.

The social setting encountered in Tangerang, located just to the west of Jakarta, and one of the most important manufacturing centres of Indonesia, provides a good illustration of some of the social changes ushered in by the process of industrialisation and the way they have impacted on the formation of a new, more urbanised, industrial working class. Up to the early 1970s, the regency of Tangerang was no more than a widely spread network of small villages or *kampung* which dotted an unremarkable, dry, expanse of 423 square kilometres (Roesli 1992: 32). In spite of the relative dryness of the land here, locals used to subsist primarily on agricultural activities, although many were also involved in small trading and craft-related work. In most ways, therefore, Tangerang was quite indistinct from other outlying areas which were quite a distance from the still largely condensed metropolitan centre which constituted Jakarta-proper at the time. As Jakarta spread out, however, Tangerang, along with Bekasi in the east, and large, much greener areas to the south, between the capital and the town of Bogor, became subsumed and integrated into the life and economy of Jakarta. Although politically a part of the province of West

Java, modern Tangerang has become an organic and integral part of the national capital. Nothing underscores this fact as much as the network of roads and highways which now links Tangerang to Jakarta, traversed by innumerable people each day as they commute to and from the now not-so-remote Tangerang.

Not surprisingly, industrialisation has not only altered the physical appearance of Tangerang, but also irrevocably changed the nature of life itself in the regency. As late as 1980, the population of Tangerang stood at a mere 228,000, compared to over 1.5 million in 1990 (Hancock 1994: 54). Initially, the process of change which followed the identification of Tangerang as an area of industrial expansion occurred quite gradually. Nurbaiti (1986: 70), for example, cites an official reference which, quite remarkably, only noted the existence of 115 factories of varying sizes operating in the regency area as late as 1985. Indeed, in the late 1970s Tangerang still seemed less an industrial area than a collection of quite ordinary rural or semi-rural communities into which mostly small and medium-scale industry had made limited incursions. Today, however, there is no doubt that a much larger number of factories operate in Tangerang than was noted by Nurbaiti. Any casual inspection of the area today will no doubt register the seemingly endless rows of foreboding high factory walls, and closed factory gates, through which countless workers – mostly migrants from other parts of Java as well as other islands – routinely stream in and out twice daily.

Indeed, by the late 1980s, no fewer than 900, mostly export-oriented, factories were in operation in Tangerang (Roesli 1992: 32). As a result, once an ordinary, quiet, rural setting, Tangerang is now a crowded, noisy, polluted, and dusty urban formation. In other words, in many ways it is no different from large parts of the increasingly inhospitable (and uninhabitable) capital of Jakarta – only worse. Recently, because of its astounding rate of development, President Soeharto officially closed Tangerang as a site for new manufacturing operations, in order to encourage investment in other areas (*Kompas* 16 February 1995).

It was the shift to an export-led industrialisation strategy in the mid-1980s which accounted for the greater pace of change in the last decade or so. Industrial development was still sufficiently limited in the late 1970s and early 1980s for Mather (1983) to note that a large proportion of the industrial workforce consisted of locals. Then as now, a large proportion of the factory workforce consisted of women, though in the earlier period the female employees were more diverse age groups. Even as late as 1986 a quite sizeable 13.3 per cent of Nurbaiti's (1986: 78) respondents came from Tangerang itself. However, as more factories were built, further waves of (predominantly young female) migrants who have come to call Tangerang home have transformed it into a multicultural hub of Sundanese, Javanese, Sumatrans and Sulawesians.[33] Furthermore, because of the relatively recent rise in demand for factory workers, it is unsurprising that the current workforce basically constitutes a first-generation urban proletariat, though the social milieu from which many of them originated could, as Young (1994) has argued, be classified as semi- or peri-urban, according to a wide range of criteria.

Most of the members of this new proletariat live near their places of employment or occupy dormitories made available by employers nearby.[34] This has created areas which are distinct for their heavy concentration of factories surrounded by sprawling communities of workers – essentially a new form of urban slum. Indeed, having found employment, a newly arrived worker would typically rent a small 'house', or *bedeng* (barrack), virtually the size of a room, in the environs of his or her place of employment, together with as many as three or four co-workers at a time. The point, of course, is to share the burden of rent and to limit as much as possible the cost of transport. As Roesli (1992: 34) notes, these 'houses' are often no more than 2 by 2.5 metres in size, and are rented from local residents (the native Tangerang population), especially more well-to-do ones who have recently invested in housing for the area's growing population of migrant workers. Such 'houses' or barracks in Tangerang, which are usually no more than makeshift attachments to the main homes of these Tangerang locals, conform to the description that White has given with regard to workers' accommodation in general:

> crowded and cramped rooms, poorly lit and ventilated, often with damp earthen floors and with minimal facilities for cooking, personal hygiene, etc. Furniture is minimal (no beds or chairs) and even basic items like soap and toothpaste are likely to be shared.
>
> (White 1993: 155)

Indeed, 'houses' in these working-class *kampung* usually do not have bathrooms or running water, so common bathrooms must be shared with the residents of a group of other 'houses', with water usually being drawn from nearby communal wells.

Such details, while appearing to be mundane, have actually a part to play in explaining the inner dynamics of working-class unrest. Clearly, the intensive, regular interaction taking place among fellow workers in densely populated communities – where the nature of everyday life necessitates the sharing of such basic amenities as sources of water – not only helps to enforce a culture of sharing, but also to create a sense of solidarity. The development of such solidarity undoubtedly in turn facilitates the undertaking of collective action by workers when it has been necessary. One labour organiser has pointed out that the regular morning and late afternoon congregations of workers at communal wells are a good opportunity for them to exchange gossip, experiences and information. Not surprisingly, sometimes discussions that begin in these situations give rise to plans of staging collective actions of protest.[35]

An alternative mode of accommodation for workers, especially in the case of young, unmarried women, is to live in spartan, company-owned dormitories that effectively separate them from their immediate environment and hinder interaction and exchange of information with other groups of workers. Some companies make it a requirement that young unmarried female workers reside in such dormitories. In reference to this practice, another labour activist has suggested that the dormitories have effectively acted as an instrument of employer control over workers as they have strict, regimented rules of behaviour – even with regard to simple comings and goings outside of work hours. Such a regimen may be predicated on more than just the pre-emption of social interaction. As this labour activist observed, workers living in company dormitories are easier to mobilise for overtime work (Djajusman 1992: 55–57).[36]

Descriptions of the miserable conditions of life and work that contemporary industrial labourers have to endure are available in abundance and need not be replicated.[37] The point to be made here is only that large concentrations of impoverished, young, and relatively educated workers provide a good social setting for the emergence of better coordinated, local, informal and sometimes semi-clandestine efforts at organising. Given the restrictions on formal organising in the factories, and the conditions of everyday life outside of work hours, it is not surprising that the site for the independent organising of the working class has largely been the sprawling, congested working-class communities rather than actual workplaces. As will be discussed more thoroughly in the next Chapter, it is here in the working-class *kampung* that new labour-based organisations have been most active. It is for this reason also that, especially since the rise of working-class action in the past few years, the state's security apparatus has recently extended its supervision to include these communities – though with only mixed success – on the basis of cooperation from local neighbourhood chiefs (RTs and RWs) and *Lurahs* (village or *kampung* headman). Such local 'notables' have frequently acted as virtual government spies.[38]

It was stated earlier that in spite of the harsh conditions of life and work which workers uniformly describe, it is telling that, during discussions and interviews I conducted, few workers compared 'rural' life favourably to 'urban' life. Formulated negatively, the conclusion that one may draw is that, no matter how bad life and work are in the cities and factories, and how difficult it is for workers to make ends meet, life in the home village is even worse. From this point of view, such an assessment may only reflect the even more dire circumstances and prospects of life outside the already daunting urban and industrial centres. Formulated positively, however, the conclusion is that, no matter how much urban workers complain about being exploited and deprived, in truth industrialisation and modernisation is providing a qualitatively better life for the vast majority of workers than they could possibly aspire for in the villages.

However, whether life in the city and work in the factory represent a qualitative improvement in an individual's personal welfare, or provide a greater degree of happiness for today's young worker, is not really a point with which we are immediately concerned. The fact is that few workers already in the cities have any other choice but to stay, and many young people who are not yet there, may make the gamble and choose to migrate for some of the same reasons as their predecessors: the search for employment opportunities, visions of the excitement of life in the cities, the hope of escaping perennial poverty – even though many of these ambitions may ultimately be frustrated in the cities as well.[39] Ironically, given the above discussion of the role of patriarchical values in supporting labour subordination, in the case of young women in particular, migration to the city is in part seen as a way of escaping the restrictions imposed on young females who remain in their parents' household.[40] To such households, the departure of children to the cities only makes immense economic sense in that it helps to alleviate the burden of poverty.

What needs to be emphasised here, however, given the wider theoretical concerns of this study, is that life and work in the city and factory cast the rank-and-file worker in the midst of a social setting that considerably helps them to shape and form new sensibilities, aspirations and world-views even if he or she originates from the relatively 'urbanised rural areas' that Young speaks of. Along with new hopes and aspirations, however, inevitably come new pains and frustrations. For example, the worker who expresses some joy in a conversation one day at being in an environment in which he or she is in greater physical proximity to a department store or cinema, is likely to be the same worker who, in a conversation on the following day, is frustrated that the daily minimum wage – which may not even be fulfilled by his or her employer – allows little room for buying clothes or watching films. In this context the observation that the great majority of strike action that has taken place recently has primarily been triggered by the issue of wages (Wibowo 1992) acquires importance. This is especially so given that, as late as 1991, state officials were admitting that the officially stipulated minimum wage only covered 60 per cent of a worker's minimum physical needs. It is also significant that one way in which the government has tried to placate recent working-class unrest is by raising the minimum wage, while at the same time continuing to exercise stringent controls over labour organising.

Another important consequence of life in the cities is that workers are daily exposed to evidence of glaring social disparities, because their own poor living conditions contrast starkly with better ones close by or readily accessible by public transport. Given the heavy concentration of wealth in a few major cities, especially Jakarta, such stark contrasts are not generally seen or directly experienced by the rural or even semi-urban population. While it is difficult to say exactly how urban workers experience and make sense of such a situation, it is not hard to imagine the ease with which a sense of injustice can arise, especially when compounded with the daily experience of subordination and humiliation associated with factory work.[41] Some workers, in conformity with largely middle-class stereotyping, have passively attributed these disparities to fate. However, the deep impact of the consequent sense of injustice on the pysche of a growing number of young, urbanised, relatively highly educated men and women, forced to consider their own bleak futures in the context of a society clearly growing in affluence – should not be underestimated.

A further consequence of life in the cities and work in the factory, alluded to earlier, is the presentation of a greater potential for organisational activities and for the undertaking of collective actions of protest. Speaking of the English working class of the late eighteenth and early nineteenth centuries, Thompson emphasised the importance of the concrete experience of confrontation with employers and the state in the shaping of a working-class self-identity. The experience of a growing number of young, contemporary, Indonesian workers in confrontations of basically the same nature will no doubt also influence the way in which the self-identity of Indonesia's new industrial working class is defined.[42] Experience in taking part in such confrontations, as well as involvement in an array of new working-class based organisations that have challenged state-imposed restrictions on organising, have had a crucial role in reinforcing the sense of solidarity among contemporary workers. This point is discussed in the next chapter.

Indeed, this point is the main reason why Marxist-inspired perspectives have given so much weight to the expansion of capitalist relations of production in creating the conditions for the development of the organisational capacity of subordinate classes, while at the same time recognising that this capacity will be geared toward transcending at least some of these very same conditions. It is also the reason why in the Marxist tradition the industrial working-class is set apart from the remainder of the masses of urban and rural poor, who, although they may be as disadvantaged within the existing framework of distribution of economic and political power, are theoretically less empowered to stage an effective struggle to amend it. Such a view is well-summarised by Rueschemeyer *et al.*, who propose that the contradictory nature of capitalist development itself creates a working class with the capacity for self-organisation; and that

> Capitalism brings the subordinate class or classes together in factories and cities where members of those classes can associate and organise more easily; it improves the means of communication and transportation facilitating nationwide organisation; in these and other ways it strengthens civil society and facilitates subordinate class organisation. Though the working class has not proved to be the gravedigger of capitalism, it has frequently been capable of successfully demanding its own political incorporation and an accommodation of at least a part of its substantive interests. No other subordinate class in history has been able to do so on anywhere near the same scale.
>
> (Rueschemeyer *et al.* 1992: 271–272)

Clearly, the potential they describe has historically been better fulfilled in the case of the first industrialisers of Western Europe, in spite of the abandonment of the socialist revolutionary project by their working classes. What is more, progressively later industrialisations have provided a social, political and economic context which has been increasingly less favourable to movements of the working class, geared toward securing a greater degree of political inclusion of labour. In this regard, the findings of this study thus far do not seem to indicate the Indonesian case to be an isolated one.

However, it is also clear that a more sizeable and mature working class is developing in Indonesia as the process of industrialisation proceeds. Moreover, a more distinctive working-class identity is being formed as a result of the everyday experiences of life, work and struggle in the new, urban industrial centres of production which have quickly proliferated since the mid-1980s. Thus, in spite of the particularly inhospitable context associated with very late industrialisations, the emergence of this new industrial working class has been inextricably linked to the recent resurgence of working-class action. Unlike previous outbreaks of unrest, this resurgence has brought into question the continuing viability of institutional arrangements that have governed the relationship between state, capital and labour for more than twenty years. Notwithstanding Deyo's dismissal of the possibility of collective forms of action emerging from working classes focused on export-oriented industries in East Asia, there appears to be a definite link between the process of class formation and the rise of working-class action in contemporary Indonesia.

SUMMARY

Even in the face of an elaborate and long-established system of stringent labour control, and in the absence of properly functioning independent unions, the 1990s are seeing the escalation of working-class unrest in Indonesia. This is in sharp contrast with the relative calm that has characterised the labour front in the country since the ascendance of the New Order, the only exception being the period in the late 1970s and early 1980s, which saw some growth of labour unrest in response to the impact of economic recession on the livelihood of workers. As was seen in Chapter 5, this surge of unrest was quelled by the intensification of the role of security-oriented institutions in labour affairs, under the direction of security chief, and later Minister of Manpower, Admiral Sudomo. Since then, a remarkable atmosphere of industrial peace has accompanied Indonesia's reorientation to an export-led strategy of industrialisation in the mid-1980s – that is – until the recent, more serious, resurgence of labour unrest.

In this chapter, a relationship has been proposed between the escalation of such unrest and the processes of social change brought about by capitalist industrialisation. In addition, in contrast to earlier, less sizeable and more temporary generations of urban workers, today's workers are far more culturally and physically urbanised. This is an important distinction because contemporary workers have naturally tended to view their future to be more unambivalently linked to the success of their struggle in the cities and factories than did their predecessors. As a result, they have more keenly responded to opportunities to organise, albeit sometimes semi-clandestinely, and to undertake collective action, even if these have not entailed the adoption of any kind of revolutionary outlook that some analysts of the working class tend to expect from a class-conscious proletariat.

Deyo's presentation of factors that prohibit the development of strong working-class movements in East Asian countries was found to be partly applicable to the case of Indonesia. Earlier chapters in this book showed that stringent state controls over labour in Indonesia, as in Deyo's four case studies, were initially developed on the basis of political considerations, and therefore, were less directly attributable to the specific requirements of an export-led development strategy. Moreover, as Deyo also suggested, the often transient nature of employment in export-oriented factories was shown to be a factor which clearly impeded the development of a more effective and successful working-class movement. Other factors identified by Deyo, involving patriarchical values and the inadequate support base provided by working-class communities to working-class movements, were found to be only partly valid.

Finally, this chapter has indicated that some characteristics of today's industrial working class, for example, its youth and comparatively high level of education, have facilitated the development of informal and semi-clandestine forms of organisation by workers, which have had some recent success in superseding state-imposed restrictions. As discussed in Chapter 7, many of these forms of organisation are mediated by distinctly non-political activities: participation in cultural or musical groupings, prayer meetings, or mutual-aid and cooperative schemes. Much of this 'alternative' organising is taking place at the community level and has involved the participation of labour-based NGOs. It is to such organising and the work of some of these NGOs that we now turn our attention.

7 Disturbing the peace
Organisation and struggle

EMERGING WORKING-CLASS MOVEMENTS AND THE POLITICAL TERRAIN

Emerging working-class movements have had to adopt various strategies to cope with constraints on organising imposed by state and capital. Notwithstanding the differences in the specific contexts (discussed in Chapter 2), 'creative' strategies have had to be employed particularly during the early, formative period of their development – that is – before the establishment of trade unions became a distinct political possibility. At such a time, workers were typically forced to adopt and develop a variety of informal vehicles, often in semi-clandestine fashion, to overcome the political constraints to organising. Although such forms of organisation are usually associated with a very early industrial social context, they often served as the basis for the later development of trade unionism when more favourable political circumstances arise.

The initial form of working-class organisation in nineteenth-century Europe was the mutual-aid or friendly society whose main concern, ostensibly, was with the provision of insurance for workers. However, before trade unionism became politically feasible in Britain, France and Germany, these and similar organisations were often suppressed because they effectively served as the training ground for the development of working-class organisational capacities (Geary 1981: 42–43). Latin American working classes were also mainly organised through similar groupings before trade unionism became politically possible (Spalding 1977: 2), and often suffered from intense repression as well, although the role of radical mass-based parties in mobilising the working class was considerable (Rueschemeyer *et al.* 1992: 167; also Collier and Collier 1991). As in Europe, the substitution of some of the more repressive strategies of containment of working-class movements with 'softer' ones only occurred after labour had developed sufficiently strong organisational capacities, thus making its all-out repression politically costly.

Importantly, working-class movements in the later industrialisers of East and Southeast Asia have usually emerged within even more inhospitable political terrains. In some of these countries, non-trade union forms of organisation have served as a major vehicle of working-class struggle well past the very early period of industrialisation. This is because of the presence of particularly strong constraints to establishing free trade unions. Even where trade unions have had a fairly long and virtually uninterrupted existence – in the Philippines, for instance – they have not been vehicles that have successfully pressed for a significant degree of political inclusion of organised labour, although their adversaries have also lacked the capacity to demobilise them to the same extent as in Indonesia.

The case of South Korea provides an example of the role played by non-trade union vehicles in very late industrialisers in preparing the way for the development of independent trade unionism. Here, organised labour was particularly constrained by its identification by the state as a potential avenue of communist (North Korean) incursion. Moreover, at its emergence, the working-class movement had to deal with state-controlled institutions which were specifically developed to hinder the independent organisation of the working class and to ensure its political demobilisation.[1]

In confronting an exclusionary, corporatist, form of labour control, Korean workers eventually established an array of semi-formal vehicles that prepared the conditions for the subsequent establishment of an independent trade union movement. Notably, this was achieved in tandem with disenchanted sections of the middle class – including a student movement that grew to be increasingly radicalised in the 1980s. Though unrecognised by the state, and severely repressed, the working class later achieved some success in challenging the corporatist monopoly of the state-sanctioned FKTU, with the flourishing of what became known as the *minju no-jo* (free labour movement). Significantly, NGOs, likely to be run by middle-class activists, also played an important role in the development of this independent working-class movement (AMRC 1987: 35–37).[2]

Something of a similar nature seems to be developing in contemporary Indonesia, although it is much less clear whether its non-trade union forms of organisation will provide the basis for the development of an effective independent trade union movement. It is important to note that although the Indonesian working-class movement has had a long history (see Chapter 3), the upheavals of 1965–66, and the subsequent formation of a system of exclusionary, corporatist, controls over labour, have conspired to ensure that contemporary workers would not be the direct heirs to the legacy of past struggles. The implication is that workers now have to start again from the beginning, as the ideologies, organisational capacities and skills that were developed during earlier periods have largely been lost to them. Significantly, these workers have been re-learning the skills of organising largely through non-trade union vehicles, based in the local community, frequently operating in conjunction with NGOs.

The NGOs include the SBM *Setiakawan* (*Serikat Buruh Merdeka Setiakawan*; the Solidarity Free Trade Union), formed in 1990, and the SBSI

(*Serikat Buruh Sejahtera Indonesia;* the Indonesian Prosperous Workers' Union) formed in 1992. Both organisations are attempts to form trade unions independent of the state. There is also a wide range of smaller organisations which ostensibly carry out activities as diverse as promoting workers' education and cooperatives, and organising training programs and discussion groups. Many of these have assisted workers in undertaking strike action and thus have had a considerable role in the recent surge in industrial unrest. Most of them have involved a large number of middle-class activists, thereby suggesting the potentially stronger alliance between workers and disaffected members of the middle class in pressing for a variety of social and political reforms. The more recent (1994) establishment of a third self-proclaimed union, the PPBI (*Pusat Perjuangan Buruh Indonesia*; Centre for Indonesian Working Class Struggle) demonstrates the existence of links between student and worker groups in Indonesia that suggests parallels with those that existed in South Korea.

As indicated in Chapter 6, organising efforts have mainly been concentrated in the increasingly distinct working-class communities spread within the sprawling new industrial centres which surround many large cities today, especially in Java. Organisational activities have not taken place at the factory, primarily due to the enormous obstacles to organising openly through vehicles that have no formal place in the official industrial relations system, not to mention the grave personal danger to which individuals involved in such activities would be subject.[3] Thus, even aspiring unions like *Setiakawan* and the SBSI have had to confine most of their direct contact with rank-and-file workers to the community rather than work directly at the enterprise level.[4] Therefore, the essential nature of their activities, in spite of aspirations to trade union status, have not been significantly different to that of other organisations, except in the sense that they have constituted a wider network of grassroots organising vehicles.

The aim of this Chapter is to assess the 'alternative' labour organising that has taken place at the community level largely independent of state-controlled institutions. Special attention is given to the role of labour-based NGOs that operate in the Jabotabek area, which was the focus of fieldwork. For the sake of convenience, organisations within which middle-class activists and workers have collaborated are henceforth referred to as labour-based NGOs, unless there is a specific need to refer to the distinctiveness of such organisations as *Setiakawan*, the SBSI or the PPBI, as aspiring trade unions. Many of these organisations' activists are former factory workers dismissed for participating in previous strike action and are for that reason held in high esteem by their colleagues. Previously, stringent state controls over labour made it difficult for such leaders to emerge from the working class itself. Now such former workers play a crucial role in the efforts of labour-based NGOs to support and help organise strike action, provide legal and strategic advice and assistance to workers, as well as in their promotion of educational, cultural, and welfare-related schemes which often lead to better organisation.

COMMUNITIES, ORGANISATIONS AND MILITANCY

Bypassing controls

The process of organising at the community level, and thereby by-passing stringent controls over organising activities within the official industrial relations system, involves a long, protracted and often frustrating effort. Sometimes labour-based NGOs have actively initiated such organising. In other instances, already formed and active informal groupings of workers have made contact with such NGOs – usually, initially on the basis of personal relationships – and requested assistance in undertaking a range of possible activities geared to develop organisational capacities.[5]

Former workers who had been dismissed because of their identification by employers as instigators of industrial unrest often play a crucial *liaison* role between labour-based NGOs and groupings of workers at the community level. Some of them, many of whom are young females, have even acquired reputations as 'troublemakers' in particular industrial areas, and are well-known across a range of factories.[6] The options that such workers have is either to move and seek employment in other industrial areas, or to become full-time labour organisers. It is usually via the latter option that experienced and respected leaders emerge from the working class itself.[7]

What are essentially semi-formal and semi-clandestine forms of organising typically begin by the formation of a core group of workers on the basis of a long-term involvement in a variety of ostensibly welfare, educational, cultural or even religious-oriented (as in the case of prayer meetings) activities. Members of this group will participate in regular activities which usually take place in the homes of the workers or at a small house that has been rented for that purpose. Although meetings could take place without the participation of NGO personnel, many others will deliberately be conducted with them.[8] Frequently, members would have come together because of an interest in gaining an alternative source of knowledge and education or because of the practical benefits of participating in some cooperative scheme or mutual-aid society, sometimes established in conjunction with a labour-oriented NGO. When discussions take place among these groups, a favourite topic, not surprisingly, is labour laws and regulations.[9] At other times workers would have simply been motivated by a desire to find an inexpensive means of recreation through involvement in theatre and music groups which are often also developed in association with an NGO.

That fact that labour-based NGOs have played such an important role in recent organising efforts is down to a number of reasons. First, they are able to provide some of the resources necessary to begin organisational work, because of their access to sources of financial support through the international community of NGOs. Such support may enable the renting of a venue where regular organisational meetings can take place, or assist in the photocopying of materials essential to the discussion of, for example, labour laws and regulations. Second, because labour-based NGOs are not constrained by the tight regulations on the establishment of unions, they have been well-suited to bypass the mechanisms of state control by carrying out community-oriented activities. Indeed, as these organisations are small, generally flexible, and relatively un-bureaucratised, they have been especially appropriate to the task of evading the long arm of the state.

For the time being, it is likely that the participation of workers in the kinds of groups described above will continue to be crucial to the development of working-class organisational capacities in the absence of fully functioning independent unions. As suggested in Chapter 6, the potential for the greater development of a distinctly working-class identity is already present because of the way in which the processes of social change impact on the way that life and work are experienced by the contemporary urban worker. The realisation of this potential, however, is undoubtedly facilitated by these workers' active participation in the kinds of organising efforts described above. It is also undoubtedly facilitated by experiences of direct confrontation with employers and the state apparatus, especially in cases of strike action. Importantly, though many such actions are spontaneous and take place locally, they appear to involve an increasing level of planning and preparation, and therefore contribute directly to the maturation of organisational capacities. There also appears to be a gradually increasing level of coordination between workers in different factories, sometimes in different areas, often through the mediating role of NGO personnel, so that planned simultaneous strikes now commonly occur.[10]

It is perhaps important to note at this stage that because such activities as the running of discussion groups have been mainly predicated on the everyday, immediate needs of workers, they have mainly addressed conventional 'bread and butter' issues. It was noted earlier that workers are particularly keen to improve their awareness of the labour laws and regulations and how they affect their lives. They are also keen to discuss and exchange experiences in dealing with employers when disputes arise, as well as in dealing with the dreaded security forces of the state when they intervene in industrial disputes. Typically, much time would also be spent on discussing the minutiae of problems or complaints that individuals or groups of workers may have, in relation to pay, overtime, safety and health conditions at work, or abuse by foremen, managers and employers – often of foreign nationality[11] – in the workplace.

While such discussions may appear mundane, they do in fact, when conducted consistently over a long period of time, help to develop a kind of 'Us' and 'Them' mentality among workers, which arguably lies at the very heart of any sense of class identity. When they exist, cultural groups – theatre and music, for instance – also conceivably stimulate the development of class identity for they will invariably focus on such themes as the daily suffering and humiliation that urban workers have to endure ('Us'), while linking the source of their troubles to the greed of businessmen or corrupt officials, backed up by security forces ('Them').[12]

Significantly, however, some of the more radical of the NGOs have tended to encourage the study by workers of broader contemporary social and political issues, as well as the political history of Indonesia's working-class movement. Middle-class agents of such organisations, usually with a background in the radical stream of the student movement, have recognised the potential value of the presentation of a heroic model from the past in providing 'encouragement' to workers.[13] That other NGOs are less interested, or less equipped, or even ideologically opposed, to pursue broader political and historical matters has in fact been the subject of criticism by the more radically inclined.

A transitional form of organisation?

The previous Chapter discussed the potential relevance to Indonesia of Deyo's assessment of the impediments to organising posed by low-wage, export-oriented industries. Emphasis was placed on Deyo's observation regarding the unfavourable implications of the high mobility of workers in these industries in terms of the development of organisational capacities. Indeed, it was suggested in that discussion that as workers regularly change employment, either by choice or because of dismissal, workers' groups can simply fold because of the departure of energetic and respected leaders. Thus, hard-won, important bases of influence in particular factories or communities could be lost in a relatively short time.

This situation reinforces the most serious shortcoming of the current form of organising, well-suited as it is to bypassing tight controls, but evidently inadequate to guarantee longer-term continuity and leadership. It also suggests that, ultimately, the growth and future prospects of an independent labour movement would lie in the successful establishment of organisations that take the form of a more regularised trade union. The establishment of such organisations, however, continues to be problematic, not only because of constraints imposed by the state, but also because of the internal problems of the contemporary, fledgling, working-class movement, which are considered next.

The issue identified is of course closely related to the question of the longer-term sustainability of an independent working-class movement in contemporary Indonesia. On the one hand, recent developments show that the formation and gradual maturation of a new industrial working class is itself providing a stronger social base for the development of a working-class movement independent of the state. On the other, hopes for the success of such a movement must be tempered by the recognition of the persistence of state repression, due primarily to a continuing wariness of the potentially destabilising effect of an independent workers' movement. Indeed, as state power is currently constituted, there are few formal avenues for an independent labour movement. They must also be tempered by a recognition of the constraining effects of operating in a chronically labour-surplus economy, as well as an international context that poses pressure on governments of very late industrialising countries like Indonesia to compete with each other in creating the kind of social, economic and political conditions that would attract foreign investment.

Still, it is undoubtedly the case that labour organising is much more likely to be successful now than in the 1970s. The inroads that have been made recently in organising as well as the rise of strike action in the face of state repression probably testified to this fact. Thus, the issue mainly concerns the relationship between structure and agency: while the possibility for the development of a more significant working-class movement is better now than it was before, it does not follow that the actors involved in building such a movement will necessarily be capable of exploiting it to the fullest extent. In turn, the inability to exploit current possibilities obviously reduces the likelihood of further possibilities arising in the future. This point is particularly pertinent in the context of the following discussion regarding the inability, thus far, of those now posing the challenge to official industrial relations system, to form a cohesive, common front.[14]

The development of such a front probably acquires greater importance given that, ultimately, whatever success the working class movement achieves will be directly related to its ability to take a part in, and make an impact on, wider political struggles involving state elites. Though these struggles pertain to a subject that lies outside of the immediate concerns of the current study – the reconstitution of the New Order in the post-Soeharto period – they are a factor that needs to be considered in assessing the prospects of the independent labour movement in Indonesia.

The inability to form a common front is in part attributable to the absence of a common, basic, political orientation among the influential labour-based NGOs. These differences have in turn exacerbated disagreements on questions of strategy.[15] Given the important role that these NGOs have played in the labour movement, the nature of the internal rifts among them now requires a more thorough analysis.

POLITICS AND STRATEGIES

Three clusters of labour-based NGOs are identified in the following analysis. These are, respectively, the 'corporatist reformist', the 'liberal/social democratic reformist', and the 'radical'. The first cluster is primarily defined by a firmer attachment to the stated ideals of Pancasila Industrial Relations, though this is usually accompanied by a critical awareness of the shortcomings of their workings.[16] The second cluster is largely defined by an attraction to liberal ideals of human rights and social democratic notions of freedom to organise, and therefore implies a commitment to a more or less thorough reorganisation of the institutional arrangements of industrial relations. This would at least involve the recognition of the right to form independent trade unions. The third cluster of organisations is chiefly identified by an attachment to notions of the inter-relatedness of labour struggles with the more fundamental restructuring of economic and political power in society, and thus involves the presentation of these struggles as being primarily political in nature.

Clearly, the classification presented here is somewhat stylised, as inevitably, there is considerable overlap between the three clusters. Moreover, differences exist among labour-based NGOs within the same cluster, especially in the one termed 'liberal/social democratic reformist', if only because of the large number of groups included in it. Significantly, groups of similar orientations could still be unfriendly to each other, although this is sometimes the result of rather banal petty rivalries, rather than real differences in strategy, for example. The difficulty of categorising some of these groups also means that this clusterisation is somewhat stylised. For example, it is particularly difficult to categorise several specifically women-oriented organisations which entertain varying notions of liberal or radical feminism, mixed with generous doses of social democratic or more radical ideas. Among these are such organisations as *Yayasan Perempuan Mardhika* (YPM), operating in the Jabotabek area, or *Yayasan Anisa Swasti* (YASANTI), operating in Central Java. This is undoubtedly a problem in itself as the work of such groups is of potentially greater importance given the large numbers of women employed in the labour-intensive sector.

Thus, rather than neat, mutually exclusive compartmentalisations of 'orientations' it is perhaps more useful to conceive of a kind of continuum with endpoints that are respectively occupied by distinctly 'corporatist-reformist' NGOs and distinctly 'radical' ones. This would allow for a conception of a larger, middle ground, occupied by various 'liberal/social democratic reformists' who may occupy points in the continuum of greater relative proximity to either endpoint (see Figure 7.1).

Differences between the clusters of organisations may also be fruitfully conceptualised in table form, with particular attention to their position on several basic issues to be discussed below (see Table 7.1).

Figure 7.1 Clusters of Labour-Based Organisations

Corporatist Reformist	Liberal/Social Democratic Reformist	Radical

Table 7.1 Labour–Oriented NGO Position on Some Basic Issues

Cluster/Issue	HIP Principles	Independent/ Alternative Trade Union	Military Intervention in Labour Matters	Labour Struggle as Political Struggle
Corporatist Reformist	Yes	No	No	No
Liberal/Social Democratic Reformist	Ambivalent	Yes	No	Ambivalent
Radical	No	Yes	No	Yes

The 'corporatist reformists'

Organisations within this cluster are less likely to be confrontational toward the state and employers, and tend to see their role as simply providing essential services to workers that the SPSI inadequately provides. Though they can be very critical of state policy, they will also tend to view their activities as guided by sincere social concern, rather than the intention to take a part in the longer process of developing a militant, independent workers' movement. Thus, distinctly humanist sentiments, and charitable intentions, have been the main source of motivation behind the operations of these labour-based NGOs.

A distinctive feature of this type of NGO is that they tend to discourage workers from taking up strike action, and instead emphasise the technical enhancement of workers' negotiating skills, and the raising of their awareness of labour laws and regulations. They are also likely to encourage workers to make use of existing formal channels by establishing SPSI PUKs in their factories or taking over existing ones. Notably, some workers' groups have been successful in assuming control of official SPSI workplace units because they have been able to mobilise the majority of their co-workers, in spite of attempts by employers to hinder them – as well as the monitoring efforts of higher branch levels of the SPSI.

They also tend to be dismissive of attempts to establish alternative trade unions, pointing to the immense technical, as well as political, difficulties of running a proper trade union organisation without the blessings of the state. Thus, such organisations are likely to resign themselves to the hope of eventual reform within the SPSI. Importantly, this type of labour-oriented NGO would tend to have less fundamental problems about Pancasila Industrial Relations as an instrument of control. The issue for them is how to ensure the proper practice of its ideals in reality. The single distinct characteristic they would share with organisations of other clusters is a critical stance toward widespread military intervention in labour affairs. However, because of the essential acceptance of the ideals of HIP, another distinctive feature of 'corporatist reformist' NGOs is that they will be more unreserved about distinguishing working-class struggles from political ones.

One such labour-based NGO is the YBM (*Yayasan Buruh Membangun*; Foundation of Workers in Development), an organisation set up in part by disenchanted SPSI activists who have developed an extensive network of local-level organisers and workers' groups in Jakarta and its environs.[17]

Notably, a particularly strong link exists between the YBM and the LEM (*Logam, Elektronik dan Mesin*; Metals, Electronics and Machine industries) department of the SPSI, which includes individuals who were most opposed to the elimination of the SBLPs in 1985.[18] This means that YBM is essentially steered by those within the SPSI who have been critical of that organisation's performance, and find it necessary to work simultaneously through an NGO in order to fulfil roles they are not able to within the state-sponsored union. In spite of its strong links with LEM, the work of YBM is directed more widely to workers of a variety of sectors, including that of the export-oriented textiles and garments sectors.

The essential absence of a confrontational outlook in YBM is basically expressed by the organisation's modestly stated aim of 'assisting workers during an industrial dispute by appealing to the conscience of those directly involved ... without having to depart from existing legal norms at all' (YBM 1994).

Thus, it is YBM policy to discourage workers from taking strike action. Moreover, YBM personnel tend to see labour organisers who actively encourage workers to take strike action as irresponsible and self-serving.[19] This relative moderation however, has not ensured that YBM is immune to state repression – in early 1995, its bulletin, *Problema*, was banned by the government, in the midst of a general clampdown on organisations that produce critical, semi-clandestine, publications.[20] Later that year, the head of LEM, closely linked to YBM, was arrested for organising a seminar without a permit, in which a radical Japanese trade unionist spoke (*Republika* 16 October 1995).

The moderation of YBM can be traced to two factors. First, some of its key personnel have a background in one of the anti-communist labour organisations of the pre-New Order period, namely the Catholic SOB Pantjasila. Thus, some of its key individuals were already labour organisers around the time of the creation of the FBSI in 1973 and the promulgation of HIP in 1974, and therefore were politically socialised in an atmosphere in which the de-politicisation of labour unions was regarded as almost unambivalently progressive. Second, the YBM has a close association with some figures formerly linked with the similarly anti-communist, intelligentsia-based party, the PSI,[21] as well as its workers' organisation, the KBSI.[22] Recall that in spite of their own links to the PSI, KBSI leaders were critical of the practice, in the 1950s and early 1960s, of trade union affiliation to political parties,[23] a stance which is more or less replicated in YBM's clear-cut distinction between narrow trade unionist and political struggles.

Still another example of the reformist cluster is the unique case of the LWR (*Lembaga Wanita dan Remaja*; Women's and Children's Institute of the SPSI). Though it is clearly not an NGO, it is perhaps the only effectively semi-autonomous body within the SPSI. In spite of its organic links to the SPSI, the LWR has played a role which has not been much different to that of NGOs, with whom its personnel have been closely involved. Notably, the LWR has undertaken workers' education and training programs which stand out from others conducted by the SPSI for the seriousness of its endeavours to raise workers' awareness of their legal rights under the law. However, as it is closely and formally linked to the SPSI, the LWR could not conceivably encourage the use of strike action as a weapon by workers,[24] and maintain the existence of opportunities that workers can take advantage of within the official system of industrial relations. Thus, the official philosophy of LWR organisers is one of reform from within the existing corporatist system rather than radical change from without.

The 'liberal/social democratic reformists'

Other clusters of labour-oriented NGOs are inclined to adopt a more confrontational stance and are dismissive of the prospects for reforming the SPSI. They would also tend to argue that the improvement of the lot of workers is more directly dependent on their ability to win back the right to organise and the right to strike. Two distinct clusters may be described as being of such an inclination. The first consists of 'liberal/social democratic reformists' that emphasise the virtues of democratic pluralism, while displaying a somewhat ambivalent view of the relationship between working-class and political struggles.[25] The mainstream of the labour-based NGOs can be placed in this category.

A distinguishing characteristic of this type of labour-based NGO is that they are primarily inspired by the example of contemporary Western trade unionism, one of whose features is the separation of political from purely trade unionist objectives. This is so even though they recognise that the advancement of the workers' cause is a part of the wider struggle for democracy and human rights, and therefore is intertwined with reform in the political system. Moreover, their aims are primarily couched in terms of securing internationally accepted principles and standards. While this would entail a considerable degree of scepticism about the virtues of the ideals and practice of HIP, it does not necessarily involve an outright rejection of them as an instrument of control. Notably, the less radical vision of Western trade unionism and the 'tripartism' of such organisations as the ILO allow 'liberal/social democratic reformists' to speak sometimes in the language of HIP without ostensibly contravening their stated commitment to workers' rights. Their major concerns include reform in the legal area (Pakpahan 1993), guaranteed safeguarding of labour standards, and the elimination of military intervention in labour affairs.

Significantly, the two most well-known attempts to develop alternative trade unions, respectively the *Setiakawan* and SBSI experiments, have been inspired the 'liberal/social democratic' notions of trade unionism.

SBM Setiakawan: pioneering independent trade unionism

SBM *Setiakawan*, the first attempt to challenge the corporatist monopoly of the SPSI as a trade union, began as an uneasy coalition of human-rights activists, NGO leaders, labour organisers and rank-and-file workers. Among the labour organisers involved were former SPSI activists who had become disenchanted. The union, officially established on 20 September 1990,[26] played a leading role in helping workers organise strike action and demonstrations throughout 1991 (Bourchier 1994a: 59). The name *Setiakawan*, meaning 'Solidarity', itself was obviously inspired by the famous Polish trade union (*Jakarta Post* 19 December 1990).[27] The organisation's key figures included H.J.C. Princen, a long-time human-rights activist and founder of the Institute for the Defence of Human Rights (LPHAM), whose high profile and strong international connections were especially valuable to the organisation's efforts to cultivate support from the international community.[28]

Because Princen lacked a strong background as a labour organiser, responsibility for building grassroots support for the aspiring union largely fell on its secretary-general, the much younger Saut Aritonang. The son of a retired low-level military officer, and a former worker at the West Java factory of Indocement, the country's largest cement producer, Aritonang had originally been an FBSI activist who rose through the ranks as a key officer of the Chemicals and Pharmaceuticals SBLP (Bourchier 1994a: 6).[29]

The establishment of *Setiakawan*, surprisingly, did not elicit an overt act of suppression from state authorities. Initially, some attributed this leniency to the advent of a new period of political 'openness', signalled by President Soeharto's Independence Day speech in August of that year, which stressed the importance of divergent views in a dynamic society (Soeharto: 1990). More realistically, however, others have related this to power struggles which were then taking place at the elite level, and which indirectly impacted on the labour movement. Bourchier (1994a: 58), for example, suggests that a combination of two factors accounted for the relative leniency of the state toward *Setiakawan*: a concern to maintain a benevolent image abroad, especially given the sustained overseas criticism of labour policy at the time,[30] and the indirect 'protection' provided to *Setiakawan* by an armed forces group loyal to General Benny Moerdani, then Minister of Defence, and one time ABRI commander-in-chief/intelligence tsar. The latter had recently emerged as President Soeharto's greatest political foe within the ruling elite.[31] According to this explanation, the 'protection' given was motivated by the desire to embarrass the GOLKAR-dominated SPSI, by exposing its inability to constrain working-class unrest, and by implication, hit at Soeharto himself.[32]

Setiakawan's aim of gaining government recognition was in fact primarily frustrated legalistically, rather than repressively. One ministerial regulation specified at the time that official recognition could only be granted to labour unions that had no fewer than 20 branches in 20 provinces, with 100 sub-branches at district level, and 1,000 factory-based chapters. Meanwhile, *Setiakawan*, which could not claim to have a membership of more than a modest 5,000–10,000 workers, only had branches in 16 regions, and certainly could not prove that it had union chapters in 1,000 companies (Bourchier 1994a: 56).[33]

In spite of the absence of overt measures of suppression, the attitude of state officials toward *Setiakawan* was clearly unfavourable. This could be gleaned from the reported reactions of various state officials, up to and including the President, to *Setiakawan's* efforts to win government recognition.[34] Ominously, but not surprisingly, it was Coordinating Minister of Politics and Security Sudomo who bluntly suggested that *Setiakawan* would be left alone by the government, 'until it commits a mistake' (*Pelita* 28 November 1990).

However, *Setiakawan* was able to organise its first congress near the end of 1990, attended by sixty-two delegates from fifteen of Indonesia's provinces (*Jakarta Post* 19 December 1990). The delegates who attended were mainly workers and labour activists who had organised small NGOs in various parts of Indonesia well before the formation of *Setiakawan* (Bourchier 1994a: 57). This is significant because it provides a clue to the way the union quickly boosted its grassroots support levels, given the constraints to open recruitment efforts at the factory level. The key was in fact its ability to tap into an already considerable network of existing grassroots organisations that constituted a rich pool of experience and influence in the labour area. Thus, rather than a union in the usual sense, *Setiakawan* was more a coalition of labour groups that operated at the local community-level.

But *Setiakawan* quickly faltered. It is sometimes suggested that its disintegration was in part due to infiltration by state agents, indicating that the strategy taken by the government was in fact to engineer the organisation's disintegration by fermenting internal strife. Such conspiratorial theories aside, what is clear is that *Setiakawan's* demise involved a bitter conflict between key players in the organisation, which to a considerable degree was reflective of the ambiguity of *Setiakawan's* attitude toward the link between trade unionist struggles and wider political ones. Besides Aritonang and Princen, the conflict also involved Indro Cahyono – a former student activist who was also the leader of a radical environmentalist group – and who had been appointed *Setiakawan's* First Deputy President.[35] It was Cahyono, significantly, who accused Aritonang of being a government spy and of misusing organisational funds, after failing to expel him from the union.[36]

Aritonang's account, however, sheds more light onto the underlying reasons for the break-up of *Setiakawan*, which from his point of view, was due to a basic disagreement on whether the organisation's trade-unionist aims should be subordinated to broader political ones. Indeed, his main objection to Princen, Cahyono and others was that they were using the organisation as a mere political tool, a bargaining chip in the context of their broader objective of reforming the political system. He is particularly derisive of the fact that he was undermined by individuals whom he did not regard as genuine labour leaders.[37] If Princen could be judged by Aritonang to have harboured ulterior motives in joining the working class struggle, then Cahyono, whose politics were considerably more radical than either Princen's or Aritonang's, would have certainly been perceived as being less agreeable. That said, Aritonang's control of the day-to-day operations of *Setiakawan* would have appeared to Cahyono as a major stumbling block to the organisation's radicalisation.

It is important to note that unlike Cahyono, who was a product of the student movement, Aritonang's political sensibilities were the product of socialisation in the distinctly depoliticised FBSI. This is reflected, for example, in the fact that he has continued to embrace the virtues of HIP as an ideal, while simultaneously being very critical of its practice. Unlike the more radically inclined, Aritonang does not consider HIP an integral part of state attempts to maintain labour's political domestication.[38] Reflecting a concern for the independence of trade unions from the dictates of political forces (which ironically is found in both the philosophy of HIP and to a lesser extent in Western-style trade unionism), Aritonang is adamant that a trade union must not serve as an instrument of political groups. He emphasises this in spite of the fact that *Setiakawan*'s own Work Program for 1990–95 was developed on the basis of a recognition that 'economic, social, cultural, political and moral struggles could not be separated from each other'. Moreover, this work program even had a distinct 'socialist' flavour about it, in that its 'economic aspect' explicitly stated the aim of establishing 'socially functional forms of ownership', as well as to win for workers the right to participate in the management and planning of firms, and to share in part of the profits (SBM *Setiakawan* 1990: 1–2).

It is highly unlikely that the leaders of *Setiakawan* did not appreciate that such aims could only be achievable in the context of a rather fundamental restructuring of economic and political power, thereby legitimising the union's involvement in broader political struggles. Still, considerable tension evidently developed regarding the specific nature of that involvement. Thus, the ambiguity suggested above with regard to the relationship between broader political and labour struggles embodied in 'liberal/social democratic reformist' NGOs is reflected in the experience of *Setiakawan*, and in fact, featured prominently in its disintegration.[39]

The SBSI: resurgence and débâcle

The vacuum created by the collapse of *Setiakawan* was later filled by the SBSI, in which some figures previously involved with the former organisation took a major part. The SBSI was established in April 1992, under the leadership of Muchtar Pakpahan, a North Sumatran lawyer and activist who received a doctorate in law from the University of Indonesia in 1993 (*Jakarta Post* 7 August 1993). It was in North Sumatra that Pakpahan began his advocacy of workers' rights in the late 1970s.

Later relocating to Jakarta, Pakpahan came to play a key role in an organisation called *Forum Adil Sejahtera* (FAS; Forum for Justice and Prosperity), an NGO primarily working with the urban poor. Pakpahan himself was involved in the early days of *Setiakawan*, to the extent of being named its Second Deputy President (Bourchier 1994a: 57–58).

Like *Setiakawan* before it, the SBSI became the focus of much international and domestic attention, to the point that it came more or less to symbolise the growth of an independent workers' movement in the face of continued government repression. This was the case in spite of the fact that it existed alongside an array of lower profile, smaller grassroots organisations that did not recognise the SBSI's leading role. Also like *Setiakawan*, the SBSI attempted to attain government recognition as a trade union,[40] but failed (Human Rights Watch/Asia 1994: 47).

Unlike *Setiakawan*, however, the SBSI benefited from the fact that Pakpahan was the unchallenged key personality. This appears to have been no small achievement, given the fact that the SBSI received support from a fairly wide range of groups, including Muslim-oriented student activists,[41] while Pakpahan himself had roots in a Christian-oriented student organisation.[42]

The SBSI's central leadership of eleven persons pointedly consisted of nine workers. According to Pakpahan, this showed that the SBSI was an organisation controlled by workers, unlike the SPSI, which was 'easily controlled by the government' (*Tempo* 2 May 1992: 24). Like *Setiakawan*, some of the membership of the SBSI consisted of former labour activists who had had experience working from within the SPSI, but were disenchanted by the powerlessness of that organisation.[43]

Also similar to the case of *Setiakawan*, SBSI support levels were boosted by the inclusion of already existing groups involved in labour-based NGOs, in various regions of the country, into its organisational structure. Even at its initial establishment, Pakpahan maintained that the SBSI had the support of worker representatives of eighteen provinces. Though the figures presented by the SBSI itself should be treated with caution (given the necessity to inflate membership levels for propaganda purposes) the organisation seems to have enjoyed a remarkable level of growth. Within one year, the SBSI claimed more than 30,000 members. By the end of 1993, Pakpahan was claiming 250,000 members,[44] which doubled to 500,000 at the end of 1994 (*Reuters* 26 September 1994).

It is notable that, in Pakpahan's view, *Setiakawan* could not have effectively advanced the workers' cause because it had objectives which were too blatantly political. While this view is virtually identical to that expressed by Aritonang earlier, ironically, it also mirrors those frequently expressed by government officials, not only with regard to *Setiakawan*, but also to Pakpahan's own SBSI.[45] Pakpahan, in fact, has been much stronger than Aritonang in his insistence that Indonesian trade unions should emulate the path which he sees as having been taken by those of advanced industrial societies. That path, he suggests, is not that different from one that is inspired by 'Pancasila Socialism'.[46] A trade union, Pakpahan maintains, 'should not be political, although its presence may be viewed as having political consequences. But it must not directly aim at overthrowing the government, change the constitution, etc. It is only an interest group.'[47] It could be suggested, certainly, that the undisguised expression of broader political objectives by Pakpahan would have opened up the possibility of an outright government clampdown on the SBSI. Thus, it could be argued that the neat separation between political and strictly trade union objectives that Pakpahan expressed was merely a case of displaying political tact.

However, the expression of such views may be less a matter of tact than a matter of adopting orthodoxies that have primarily been formed in the context of the contemporary situation of the labour movements of the advanced industrial societies. To Pakpahan, the form of accommodation between state, capital and labour which emerged within the European experience is one that should and could be simply transposed to the Indonesian situation by political decree. The fact that the European model evolved over a long period of often bitter class struggle, is apparently not really considered. In this context, the organisation's emphasis on raising the awareness of workers of their legal rights (SBSI 1993a: 36) – as opposed to their political awareness – has generated criticism from within labour NGO circles.

On the other hand, it must be said that the dominance, among contemporary labour-based organisations in Indonesia, of social democratic notions of the separation of narrow, trade union, interests from those that are more overtly political, is in part attributable to the great influence of such organisations as the ICFTU and the ILO. It is also attributable to the influence of trade union organisations in the United States, the Netherlands and Australia – which represent examples from within a 'social-democratic' form of accommodation between state, capital and labour. This model is attractive owing to the fact that, on the surface, it does not entail radical social change.

Nevertheless, Pakpahan clearly relished being part of the political game and was able to enlist the support of various well-known politicians to his cause. Notably, one of the most famous critics of the government, Nahdlatul Ulama-leader Abdurrachman Wahid, gave an opening address in the conference which marked the establishment of the SBSI in 1992. Pakpahan also approached such figures as Rachmawati Soekarno (daughter of the former President), Oka Mahendra, Sabam Sirait and Sukowaluyo, prominent members of the PDI, giving rise to speculation of an SBSI alliance with that party. Later, he developed links with some military leaders, most prominently, General Hendropriyono, the military commander in

Jakarta, who was associated with a group within the armed forces that appeared to favour an agenda of political reform.[48] Undoubtedly, the cultivation of such links allowed Pakpahan to entertain the notion that his organisation was afforded some degree of political protection in the framework of an alliance with reform-minded military leaders.

Later, however, it become evident that Pakpahan tragically misjudged the nature and extent of that protection. In his view, ABRI leaders had simply become genuinely progressive and enlightened about the virtues of independent trade unionism, and it was civilians in the Department of Manpower who were, in fact, being reactionary.[49] Pakpahan's faith in ABRI's enlightenment was to cost his organisation quite dearly, as we shall see in due course.[50]

To pressurise the government into recognising the SBSI, Pakpahan initiated a call to workers to engage in an hour-long nationwide strike on 11 February 1994.[51] The call was specifically a response to a Minister of Manpower Regulation which reiterated that the SPSI was the only recognised union organisation in the land. Notably, the strike was also used to promote the SBSI's idea of a Rp 7,000 (about US$3.30) a day minimum wage, which was substantially higher than the Rp 3,800 (about US$1.80) that was officially stipulated at the time. Also significantly, the hour-long strike was a test of whether the organisation could carry out a more ambitious national strike action scheduled for October of that year.[52] In that sense it constituted a dress rehearsal for future SBSI mass mobilisations of workers.

Not surprisingly, Pakpahan's call for strike action was criticised by state and SPSI officials. Deputy Secretary General of the SPSI, Wilhelmus Bhoka, for example, labelled general strikes as being 'out of fashion' (*Kompas* 1 February 1994). Nevertheless, the SBSI move was treated seriously. Department of Manpower officials, SPSI functionaries, as well as military officers, were reported to have quickly made their rounds in workplaces, prior to the 11 February date, to discourage workers from taking up the SBSI call and to discredit the organisation. Prior to the strike, Pakpahan and several SBSI activists were even placed under arrest while in Central Java (*Jakarta Post* 11 February 1994).

The SBSI's bold, if not audacious, initiative ended, however, in dismal failure. There was little demonstration of the kind of nationwide support of workers that the organisation had hoped for (*Kompas* 12 February 1994).[53] Arguably, this not only damaged the credibility of the SBSI, but also the independent labour movement as a whole, given the popular perception of the SBSI's leading role in it. Moreover, the failure did much to expose the real level of influence that the SBSI had among workers, and therefore, inevitably strengthened the government's confidence in dealing with the organisation.

Significantly, the February débâcle was partly attributable to the difficult relationship that the SBSI had with other labour-based organisations, who refused actively to support Pakpahan's call.[54] In part this difficulty stemmed from petty jealousies, but some NGO leaders had strong disagreements with

Pakpahan over the appropriateness of a strategy of openly establishing independent unions at this stage in the working-class struggle. Pakpahan himself admits to having had only mixed success in developing support from the labour-oriented NGO community for his efforts.[55] Whatever the reasons for the lack of support toward the SBSI (Etty 1994: 9), they point to one fundamental shortcoming of the contemporary labour movement in Indonesia that had already been identified: excessive fragmentation in a position of weakness and an inability to forge a cohesive, common front.

Whether the SBSI's planned October national strike action would have been more successful will never be known,[56] as preparations for it were halted as a result of an unpredicted development that took place a long way from the SBSI headquarters in Jakarta – in the city of Medan, North Sumatra. This was none other than the now-celebrated, and unprecedented, workers' riots that took place there in April 1994 (Human Rights Watch/Asia 1994: 57–76). The riots were reported to have involved 20,000–30,000 industrial workers and resulted in the death of one local Chinese businessman as well as serious damage to property, especially in the city's commercial Chinese district.

In spite of the government's scapegoating the SBSI, it is unlikely that the organisation had much to do with steering the massive act of defiance by local workers which caused the riots. Subsequent reports have in fact cited evidence that they were actually the culmination of an extended period of strike action by North Sumatran workers which began in February,[57] in which local NGOs seemed to be primarily involved. The riots were also clearly a response by workers to the mysterious death of a striking colleague in March, allegedly at the hands of police called in to restore order (*Mimbar Umum* 21 March 1994; 23 March 1994). The SBSI itself blamed the riots on the military's mishandling of the situation as well as on the work of 'gangsters' employed by factory-owners (*Jakarta Post* 6 May 1994). Nevertheless, Pakpahan, as well as several other SBSI officials, and numerous local-level activists and workers, were later tried and given substantial prison sentences.[58]

Importantly, the Medan riots ended the possibility of a more or less peaceful accommodation taking place between the SBSI and the government. Prior to the riots, and even for some time afterwards, a form of government-sponsored reconciliation between the SPSI and SBSI had been the subject of secret talks.[59] Pakpahan had even indicated his willingness to consider a compromise by suggesting that he would not be against returning to the 'spirit of 1973'. This was an exceptionally mild position given that the situation that year was characterised by the submissiveness of then-existing trade union organisations to the dictates of Ali Moertopo's OPSUS.[60] Prior to the Medan riots, Pakpahan was also talking of the attractiveness of a revamped SPSI – a government-sanctioned, new federational-structured workers' organisation – in which the SBSI would have a role.[61] The SPSI's Bhoka had publicly stated earlier that a dialogue needed to take place to improve the labour situation in Indonesia, which he said, should include the SBSI (*Media Indonesia* 22 February 1994) – thus, indicating a readiness to compromise on the government's side as well.

No such reconciliation took place, and a clampdown of the SBSI then ensued,[62] indicating that state officials later decided that the SBSI, and perhaps by implication, the wider independent workers' movement, was not as yet a sufficient enough force to be worth coopting. Indeed, the clampdown showed that the state was now more keen to utilise a strategy of outright coercion (including the use of violence) to cripple the workers' movement (e.g. Human Rights Watch/Asia 1994: 69), no doubt because it was perceived as being vulnerable to such a strategy.

Other labour-based NGOs

A wide variety of NGOs share the inclinations, described above, of *Setiakawan* and the SBSI, though they have differed with regard to the appropriateness of adopting, at this time, the strategy of openly establishing alternative trade unions. Among these are SISBIKUM, IS (*Institut Sosial*), and YAKOMA (*Yayasan Komunikasi Massa*; Mass Communications Foundation), NGOs which have assisted in the development of an extensive network of workers' groups in the Jabotabek area. Such organisations emphasise workers' knowledge of their rights under labour laws while not eschewing the development of capacities for collective protest action, though YAKOMA stands out for its interest in the cultivation of 'consciousness', perhaps in the Paolo Freireian sense of the term.

Many of these organisations' activists, like SISBIKUM leader Arist Merdeka Sirait, also emphasise how the great surge in strike action in the 1990s has helped to forge greater working-class solidarity.[63] Notably, SISBIKUM has particularly excelled in helping develop workers' organisational capacities through the promotion of cultural activities. For example, a workers' theatre group coordinated by the NGO periodically performs musical plays to an audience of thousands of workers in West Java's industrial areas. In 1994, workers associated with SISBIKUM released an album of protest songs entitled 'Marsinah', in memory of the late labour organiser. The organisation is also involved heavily in putting the issue of child labour onto the agenda of public debate.

Like SISBIKUM, IS and YAKOMA began as organisations that were oriented toward social work directed at the urban poor and the informal sector before they diverted more of their attentions to factory workers. IS, for example, used to be well-known for its work with *becak* (pedicab) drivers in Jakarta, who were forced to give up their means of livelihood by the government of the city in the 1980s.[64] It could be suggested that in both these cases there is an essential radical humanism which is as much the product of religious faith as it is the product of adherence to particular social theories: IS is predominantly Catholic while YAKOMA figures are linked with the

Protestant Church of the *Batak*, the majority native ethnic group of North Sumatra. In the case of IS, a suggested adherence to Latin American-style 'liberation theology' worked against it in the context of a government clamp-down on political opposition in 1996, when the concept was attacked by state officials for being Marxist-inspired (*Gatra* 31 August 1996: 22–30).

The main difference between organisations like SISBIKUM, IS and YAKOMA and 'radical' organisations (see below) is their disinterest in the historical legacy of the pre-New Order labour movement. This might help to explain the absence of any real effort to develop a theoretical position on the relationship between labour and broader political struggles. In this regard, they have more in common with those whose inspiration has been the Western model of trade unionism. It is notable, however, that Indera Nababan of YAKOMA, in particular, stresses that the initiative in forming independent trade unions must come from workers themselves, rather than (middle-class) NGO leaders. In doing so, he is indirectly criticising the efforts to establish independent labour unions represented by *Setiakawan* and the SBSI.[65]

One last proponent of the liberal/social democratic line is the Indonesian Legal Aid Institute (YLBHI; *Yayasan Lembaga Bantuan Hukum Indonesia*), one of the largest, oldest and most well-known NGOs in the country. Though obviously involved in various activities outside of the labour area, YLBHI has often acted as the glue that keeps together the wide array of alternative labour-based organisations. Importantly, through the work of Fauzi Abdullah, and his successor as YLBHI's labour affairs officer, Teten Masduki,[66] the organisation has been able to act as an arbiter between the different NGOs, and has served as a valuable liaison with the broader inter-national community. Clearly, YLBHI's involvement in the labour field must be seen in relation to its commitment to wider legal reform, human rights, as well as democratisation, issues. Notably, Masduki played an important role as the initial coordinator of FORSOL (*Forum Solidaritas Buruh*; Labour Solidarity Forum), a grouping of more than a dozen labour-based NGOs, which represents one of the few cooperative efforts forged by such organisa-tions to date.

The 'radicals'

NGO-type organisations that might be described as unreservedly 'radical' see the working-class struggle as essentially political. Moreover, 'radicals' tend to identify the working class as, ultimately, the prime agent of social change. Therefore, middle-class agents of such NGOs define their own role as mainly facilitating the process of consciousness-raising among workers to enable them to take up their historical role. Here, it is the past Indonesian tradition of labour militancy – essentially rooted in the experience of the nationalist struggle – that is the source of inspiration rather than the model of Western trade unionism.

Because of this source of inspiration, the 'radicals' place much importance on creating a sense of participating in a grand historical process
through heavy doses of study of the history of workers' struggles, and of the
nature of capitalism, as it has manifested itself in Indonesia. Labour repression, in their view, can only be understood in relation to the specific
workings of capitalism. Thus, they would tend to see, for example, military
intervention into labour affairs in Indonesia as a vital aspect of the capital
accumulation process. Importantly, these labour-based NGOs would tend to
have much stronger, and obviously more natural, links with the radical
strand of the contemporary student movement.

A good example of this cluster is the third organisation that has recently
adopted the mantle of trade unionism, the PPBI, established in October
1994. Proclaimed by workers from urban centres throughout Java, as well as
North Sumatra (CIWCS 1994, leaflet), the PPBI differs in many respects
from its two predecessors, *Setiakawan* and the SBSI. First of all the PPBI is
much smaller in size, partly because it is not a network of mainstream,
established labour-based NGOs across many regions. More importantly, it is
directly linked to the radical stream of Indonesia's revived student movement.[67] Because of this the PPBI has taken up a more openly
confrontational stance toward the state, by dispensing altogether with the
need for acquiring government recognition of its existence. Moreover, there
does not appear to be any ambivalence in the organisation's view of the link
between labour and wider political struggles, or about the rejection of HIP
as an instrument of state control. In July 1995, the PPBI took part in organising a highly publicised strike in Bogor and demonstrations by workers of
the brand-name garments producer, PT Great River Industries (*Kompas* 29
July 1995).

The PPBI's identification of the source of weakness of the contemporary
workers' movement as being the separation of narrow, economic struggles
from political ones, is a barely veiled attack on the mainstream of labour
NGOs. By contrast, the PPBI openly claims that its struggles take place in
tandem with existing pro-democracy forces, notably, the PRD (Democratic
People's Union, later Democratic People's Party), an umbrella organisation
that oversees such associations as SMID (Indonesian Students Solidarity for
Democracy) and STN (National Peasants' Union). While its objective of
realising workers' social and economic rights is similar to that of *Setiakawan*
and the SBSI, the PPBI also adds the distinctly 'socialist' aim of creating 'a
society without oppression'. Also somewhat uniquely, the organisation
intends to educate workers in 'political economy', in order to 'promote an
understanding of the political basis of economic exploitation and of the
inter-relatedness of narrow economic struggles with political ones' (CIWCS
1994). The reasoning seems to be that because working-class consciousness
is still at too low a level, a vanguard of middle-class radicals, who have 'a
theoretical understanding', must provide 'direction, encouragement and
education'.[68] It will never be known whether the PPBI would have acted as

the catalyst for the kind of alliance between radical students and workers that was seen in South Korea in the 1980s, or whether its radical stance would ultimately isolate it from those less radical. As discussed in Chapter 8, the PPBI has subsequently been on the receiving end of a government clamp-down on sources of opposition.

An organisation with a similar radical vision, and a similar organic link with the student movement, but which has not opted for the trade unionist path, is the YMB (*Yayasan Maju Bersama*; the Foundation for Mutual Progress). Clearly with interests that go beyond traditional 'bread and butter' issues, members of this organisation have written on themes relating to the history of capitalism and the labour movement in Indonesia. Cahyono (1992), for example, unfavourably compares the 'de-politicised' consciousness of the contemporary Indonesian proletariat to that suppos-edly possessed by workers during the nationalist struggle. In this, he is supported by another YMB organiser, Razif, who openly favours a politi-cally conscious trade union movement, while criticising labour leaders who attempt a separation between trade unionist and political struggles. At the same time he also ridicules European-style trade unionism, pointing out that, in England, capitalists created a stratum of labour aristocracy whose function was to weaken the resolve of workers to free themselves from the yoke of capitalism (Razif 1994a).

As with the PPBI, the main problem to confront the YMB is that its radi-calism may isolate it from the wider, fledgling, labour movement. Indeed, the successful pursuit of its agenda is to a large extent contingent on a funda-mental unravelling of state power as it is currently constituted. Given its relative isolation, whether the YMB can contribute to the forging of a common front among the organisations that make up the contemporary labour movement remains questionable.

SUMMARY

While the strategy adopted by alternative labour organising vehicles has been well-suited to the particular conditions present in Indonesia, it is unclear whether it can become the basis for a stronger and more effective independent movement in the future. For such a movement to come to fruition in the medium to longer-term, these vehicles would have to be able to develop a more cohesive, common front, and eschew the kind of fragmen-tation that has so far circumscribed them. Ultimately, the sustainability of this movement depends on the successful establishment of alternative trade-union organisations, which in turn, depends in large part on the ability of current vehicles of organisation to pave the way for them.

In order to reach that point, however, these would have to be able to undertake, even at this juncture, coordinated and cooperative endeavours. So far, efforts such as these have been few and far between. The most outstanding attempt is probably represented in the establishment of

FORSOL, which has been instrumental in coordinating efforts to sustain the kind of international pressure on the Indonesian government that would encourage reform in labour policy.[69] However, it has clearly not realised its full potential as a forum which could coordinate the activities of its member organisations. This is attributable to the wide gulf in political orientation of its member NGOs.

Of course, forcing the state to recognise alternative trade unions is a problem which sooner or later would have to be faced. However, there is a lesson that may perhaps be learned from the experience of South Korea, where eventually employers were forced to deal with the independent labour movement because it was an actuality at the firm level, and therefore could not just be wished away or stamped out by force – even by the state's security apparatus.

Nevertheless, there is the question of the wide gulf in the political orientations of the labour-based NGOs. There does not seem to be, in fact, any easy answer to this problem. Ultimately, bridging this gap depends on the ability of rank-and-file workers to produce more leaders in their own right, and supersede the role taken by middle-class activists, in spite of the potential importance of developing wider alliances with disaffected members of that class. Indeed, some labour activists have come to the conclusion that the present NGO format is not particularly conducive to the growth of a more effective independent labour movement. Of potential importance are developments in some areas in the Jabotabek region and in the West Java city of Bandung, where groups of workers have been organising with apparently far less coordination with labour-based NGOs. These endeavours are consciously geared toward the establishment of an effective alternative trade union, without going through a period of cooperation with existing NGO networks, as has largely been the norm up to now.[70]

8   State responses
Reform or repression?

STATE LABOUR POLICY AND THE POST-OIL 'BOOM' ECONOMY

On June 1994, the Indonesian government announced PP (*Peraturan Pemerintah*; Government Regulation) 20/1994, one in a series of measures undertaken over the previous decade designed to make Indonesia more competitive in the increasingly intense global scramble for foreign investment, particularly in low-wage industries. Under its stipulations, foreign investors are allowed to enter into 'vital' sectors previously designated off-limits, and requirements regarding Indonesian capital participation in joint-ventures were significantly relaxed.[1] Since the fall of international oil prices in the early 1980s, the attractiveness of Indonesia to foreign investors has acquired greater importance as part of the strategy of enhancing global competitiveness in the export of labour-intensive, light manufactured goods. Much of the surge in foreign investment in this sector since the mid-1980s has been driven by the relocation of production facilities from the East Asian NICs because of the rise in labour costs in those countries (Thee 1993: 434–460). Cumulative Korean foreign direct investment in Indonesia between 1988 and 1993, for example, constituted 83 per cent of its total investment in the country from 1967 to 1993 (Shin and Lee 1995: 188).

PP 20/1994 signalled a growing awareness in policy-making circles of the competition posed by countries such as China, Vietnam, Bangladesh and others which have also presented themselves as attractive production sites for labour-intensive, low technology industries. The 'threat' posed by China, for example, has been particularly worrisome.[2] Indeed, approved foreign investment was showing signs of decline at the time of the introduction of the policy. Total approved foreign investment in 1990 had increased to almost US$8.7 billion – US$4 billion more than the previous year. However, it seemed to peak at US$10.3 billion in 1992 before falling to just US$8.1 billion the following year. Meanwhile, approved foreign investment in the manufacturing sector had declined to under US$3.4 billion in 1993, from the previous year's US$5.6 billion, and a peak of over US$5.8 billion in 1990 (World Bank 1994: 240).[3]

Clearly, there is a wide range of factors that influence investment or relocation decisions when firms consider potential production sites. The most important include political stability,[4] quality of infrastructural support, tax incentives, levels of bureaucratic red-tape, natural resources, as well as access to domestic and overseas markets. Notably, Indonesia has scored low marks with regard to infrastructural support as well as the performance of its state bureaucracy.[5] One of the greatest disincentives to investment in Indonesia has been the country's reputation for high-levels of bureaucratic red-tape.[6] It is important to note that the costs incurred while dealing with an inefficient, and often corrupt bureaucracy have been presented by businesses, both foreign and domestic, as justification for maintaining low wages. The issue has acquired increasing political resonance, and has been latched onto by independent labour activists in their efforts to argue the case for improving the welfare levels of industrial workers.

In spite of the variety of considerations mentioned above, those that involve labour costs obviously figure more prominently in the case of investment decisions pertaining to labour-intensive, low-technology industries. As mentioned earlier, Indonesia has been particularly attractive to businesses attempting to escape the increasingly high cost of labour or labour unrest in their own countries of origin.[7]

However, the rise of labour unrest in Indonesia since 1990 has tarnished the image of uninterrupted industrial peace. South Korean businessmen, in particular, have been dismayed at having to deal with an increasing measure of labour unrest.[8] Indonesia is now viewed as less the haven of industrial harmony than it used to be.[9] Some Indonesian state officials have expressed concern that labour unrest could eventually deter foreign investment. This line of thinking has been expressed by economic technocrats, as well as by high-ranking armed forces officers. One officer, pointing out that the world community has its eyes on Indonesia's labour situation, and that foreign donors might want to link economic aid with human-rights improvements, emphasised the negative impact to investor confidence of the Marsinah and Medan cases (Sabarno 1994: 94).

In contrast to such a view, there is little evidence that the recent rise in industrial unrest has reached levels that would seriously deter foreign investors. At the same time, it is unlikely that Indonesia will lose its niche in the international division of labour as a production site for labour-intensive industries, solely because of escalating labour costs (Dhanani 1993). Indonesian manufacturing labour is, for example, still among the cheapest in Asia. Moreover, the growth of labour productivity in the manufacturing sector has not only exceeded the real levels of income growth of workers over the period 1970–1990, but has also far outstripped that of other ASEAN countries.[10]

It is clear, therefore, that the escalation of labour unrest in the 1990s has had more political than economic significance. Such unrest certainly sits very uncomfortably with the overriding concern with political stability and control that the New Order has displayed since its inception. With the exception of some largely isolated cases,[11] the rise of labour unrest has arguably provided the starkest challenge to the state-propagated ideology of integralism that places so much emphasis on social harmony and rejects conflict as a matter of principle.

Thus, the attention given to labour matters by state officials has been more attributable to the persistence of concerns regarding the potential political consequences of an independent labour movement, than to any real economic threat to development strategy. Such concerns are related to the continuing fixation of elements of the state apparatus upon the maintenance of a social and political framework geared to ensure the continued political demobilisation of society-based organisations and movements. More specifically, they are linked to ABRI's long-standing aversion to organised labour which is historically rooted in its experiences in the 1950s and early 1960s.

Given such a context, it is important to assess current government attempts to deal with the labour problem. There have essentially been two broadly differing strategies utilised to deal with labour unrest: the first is the limited reformism espoused by such state officials as Ministers of Manpower Cosmas Batubara and Abdul Latief; the second is the re-assertion of more outrightly repressive policies associated with the security-oriented approach, usually espoused by figures associated with ABRI.

The aim of the remainder of this Chapter is to explain the tensions and contradictions in state policy toward labour in the 1990s, while placing them in the context of the competing interests and relative strengths of state, capital and labour. A question which informs the analysis offered here relates to the impact (or conversely, lack of impact) of contemporary working-class struggles on the model of accommodation between state, capital and labour which is characterised by labour's continued political exclusion and its demobilisation as a social force. In the process, I shall examine the interplay of the two different approaches mentioned above in shaping overall state policy toward labour. Throughout, the concerns of a range of actors are considered, including the state's security apparatus, the business community and international labour organisations.

THE STRATEGY OF LIMITED REFORMISM

Cosmas Batubara

The dramatic rise in labour unrest beginning in 1990 initially strengthened those in the state apparatus that favoured limited reforms in state policy. At first, the leading exponent of such a strategy was Cosmas Batubara, Minister of Manpower (1988–1993).

Batubara's approach was two-pronged. First, he encouraged the revamping of the SPSI in a bid to improve its image and thereby shore up its legitimacy. Though clearly aimed at an international audience of labour organisations and foreign donor countries, his policy was also directed at eroding the attractiveness to workers of alternative labour organisations. Second, aware that many of the reasons for labour unrest were wage-related issues, he promoted the idea of periodic increases in the minimum wage, while at the same time side-stepping issues related to the more politically sensitive question of the rights of association and organisation. In September 1992, for example, a new regulation stipulated a rise in the minimum wage in West Java – which covers much of the strife-ridden Jabotabek area – from Rp 2,100 to Rp 2,600 a day (*Kompas* 26 December 1992) – from US$1 to $1.25.

Batubara was vehemently critical of the inadequacies of the SPSI (*Kompas* 4 May 1992).[12] Largely on his initiative, the SPSI structure was reorganised in 1990 to accommodate continued criticism of the centralism created by Sudomo in 1985,[13] although it took another three years before real steps toward the realisation of a new structure took place.

This limited reformism initially received lukewarm responses from the liberal technocrats responsible for economic portfolios, though Batubara claims that he was eventually successful in winning them over.[14] These technocrats would have conceivably been concerned about the immediate economic costs of placating labour by raising wages. More serious and continued opposition, however, was offered by Sudomo, then Coordinating Minister of Politics and Security. From this position, Sudomo was still able to wield considerable influence over labour policy, given the perceived security implications of labour unrest. Strongly critical of 'would be heroes' – a reference to NGOs (*Jakarta Post* 22 August 1991) – he often openly contradicted Batubara's usually more restrained policy statements. Sudomo, commenting in 1991 on a strike by 2,000 workers of PT Great River Industries in the Bogor area,[15] exclaimed: 'I am sure that there is no way that 2000 people can have the same opinion, so clearly someone has mobilised them. I will investigate this . . . don't even try to disrupt the peace' (*Media Indonesia* 1 July 1991).

Sudomo also warned that he would ask ABRI to 'take care' of strikes that were spreading across Tangerang, while suggesting that their instigators would be 'punished severely' (*Jakarta Post* 24 August 1991).

Nevertheless, Batubara's approach gained the upper hand. His position within any cabinet-level discussion would have clearly been strengthened while repression seemed to backfire by indirectly contributing to the militancy of some workers, increasingly hardened by the experience of direct confrontation with the state's security apparatus. Batubara himself realised that methods utilised in the past were no longer as viable in handling an increasingly aware and assertive industrial working class.[16] In this, he asserts, he was merely 'reading the sign of the times'.[17]

In the meantime, labour-based NGOs that were pushing for more fundamental reforms in labour policy were winning international support and directing world attention to the situation of Indonesian workers. At times, international pressure has played an important role in winning, temporarily, greater room for manoeuvre for independent labour-based organisations. A good example of this was seen in 1993–94, when the threat of Indonesia's expulsion from the US list of countries receiving GSP privileges loomed large.[18]

It was especially the AFL-CIO that took the lead in putting the labour situation in Indonesia on the international agenda. In the late 1980s it lodged petitions with the US Trade Representative's Office to have Indonesia removed from the list of countries receiving GSP facilities, alleging non-compliance with international labour standards (American Embassy 1994: 43; AFL-CIO 1989). These facilities played a role in raising Indonesian exports to the US, although they did not cover the import of garments or textiles. Significantly, nearly 15 per cent of Indonesia's exports to the US entered duty free under the GSP program (US$643 million of a total of US$4.3 billion) in 1992, up from just 1.5 per cent in 1987 (American Embassy 1994: 41–42).[19] Equally importantly, US investment in Indonesia might have been affected by the removal of the GSP facilities because firms would no longer be covered under the so-called OPIC (Overseas Private Investment Corporation) scheme, whereby their operations in Indonesia are insured by the US government.

As mentioned earlier, Batubara was quick to recognise the importance of salvaging the badly tarnished reputation of Indonesia's labour policy (*Jakarta Post* 20 July 1992). Batubara, noting how Indonesia's 'image must be upheld in the world forum' (*Jakarta Post* 31 August 1992), argued that:

> If [Indonesia] wants to take part in globalisation we have to respect inter-national labour standards, such as the right to organise, the right to bargain. If we do not follow international labour standards, our commodities will be blocked. We are often criticised by American workers, and then we tell them that the Indonesian government has taken action against businesses that do not pay the minimum wage.[20]
>
> (*Prisma* no. 3 1992: 67)

Batubara's efforts may have partly accounted for his success in getting elected president of the annual conference of the ILO in June 1991 (*Kompas* 5 May 1991). Though Indonesia had not formally ratified many key ILO conventions, notably Convention no. 87 on the Freedom of Association and Protection of the Right to Organise (ILO 1994: 242), Batubara claimed that his position implied that Indonesia was prepared to apply international labour standards domestically.[21]

Indonesia, however, continued to be on the receiving end of international criticism. In 1992, two American NGOs, Asiawatch and the International Labor Rights Education and Research Fund, filed separate petitions to the US Trade Representative for the elimination of Indonesia's GSP privileges (Asiawatch 1992; ILRERF 1992). Underlining the apparent seriousness of the situation at the time, the director of the Indonesian office of AAFLI, the AFL-CIO's Asia arm, audaciously warned the Indonesian government that the labour issue would be taken up more seriously by the Clinton presidency than by previous administrations (*Kompas* 14 November 1992).[22] In the next year, Indonesia's labour policies received a sharp rebuke when the USTR ordered that Indonesia's GSP status be reviewed for non-compliance with international labour standards (*Far Eastern Economic Review* 13 May 1993: 13).

In spite of his 'reformist' reputation, it was clear that the aims pursued by Batubara were limited by the boundaries of HIP (see Batubara 1991). Such limitations ensured that his criticism of the SPSI did not bring him to consider the need for an alternative labour union altogether (*Jakarta Post* 8 July 1992). Clearly, the broader political implications – in terms of a challenge to the basic exclusionary, corporatist, framework of state–society relations – that such a step represented, placed it outside of those boundaries.[23]

Summarising his position with regard to the more systemic overhaul that many NGOs demanded, Batubara suggested that 'What needs to be done is the building of a system, not its overthrow. I always emphasise improving the SPSI, while NGOs have the propensity to want to become labour unions themselves'.[24] Furthermore, speaking in metaphoric terms about the SPSI's inability to articulate the interests of workers, he argued that

If [existing] channels are blocked, there will of course be an overflow of water. Our task is to [ensure] that this water is channelled. NGOs have the tendency to aim for a constant state of overflow. . . . They should instead take on the task of guiding the water back into the system, rather than perpetuate its flow outside of it. By perpetuating such an overflow, by being against the SPSI, the government, the parliament, they are only perpetuating their own [existence].

Batubara also chastised employers for their intransigence in dealing with workers' wage-related demands. He warned them of the detrimental effects of maintaining unrealistically low wages (*Kompas* 27 January 1992), arguing that this would give rise to social instability, disrupt the economy, and thus make Indonesia unattractive to foreign investors (*Kompas* 17 December 1992). In a 1992 campaign speech for GOLKAR, he declared that the welfare of workers would be an integral part of the blueprint for development over the next twenty-five years (*Indonesian Observer* 14 May 1992). Much publicity was also given to his intent of having minimum wage levels meet the minimum physical needs of workers (*Kompas* 15 June 1992 and 16 October 1992).[25]

Importantly, Batubara's initiatives were supported by the President.[26] Echoing the minister's concerns about the SPSI, Soeharto also urged employers to refrain from interfering in the formation of the organisation's factory-level branches. Indeed, despite official support for the practice of establishing such branches, only 11,000 of the 44,000 large and medium enterprises in Indonesia were reported to have SPSI units in 1992 (*Jakarta Post* 28 April 1992). It was reported that 75 per cent of factories in Tangerang did not have functioning SPSI units (*Kompas* 22 May 1992). Soeharto also supported Batubara's call for employers to comply with minimum wage regulations (*Kompas* 14 October 1992).

Top SPSI officials also began to call more vigorously for increases in the minimum wage, clearly in a bid not to be sidelined on the issue by NGOs (*Kompas* 26 September 1991). In a rather startling departure from the norm, SPSI chairman Imam Soedarwo at one point even praised the rise of industrial action as a sign of the growing maturity and awareness of workers of their rights (*Kompas* 18 November 1992).

It would be erroneous, however, to attribute to purely altruistic motives, Batubara's greater propensity to utilise the 'carrot' while downplaying the use of the 'stick'.[27] It is important to recognise that Batubara's civilian background meant that he did not have his predecessor's institutional base in the state's security apparatus, and thus, an over-reliance on it would compromise his own authority. Hence, it was in Batubara's own interest to promote an approach that did not overly rely on the use of coercive measures, but which enhanced the stature of his Department and that of the SPSI.

As mentioned earlier, there did not appear to be a clear consensus on the virtues of Batubara's reforms. Thus, there were often developments at the local level that blatantly contradicted those at the national level. For example, several provincial tripartite bodies called for a postponement in the implementation of new minimum wage stipulations. Interestingly, the participation of local SPSI branches in this endeavour was promptly criticised by the national-level leadership (*Kompas* 20 April 1992). Furthermore, the regents of Tangerang and Bekasi attempted to impose a ban on strikes in their areas of jurisdiction (*Kompas* 15 May 1992), despite the fact that the Department of Manpower was clearly taking steps toward an acceptance of the right to strike.[28]

Abdul Latief

Cosmas Batubara was replaced in 1993 by Abdul Latief, a successful and well-connected businessman with significant interests in retail and manufacturing. The choice of Latief to replace Batubara indicated increasing recognition of the importance of persuading business to support the limited reforms aimed at containing labour unrest.[29]

As a businessmen it was important for Latief's credibility that he were not perceived as overly sympathetic toward business. He was, however, compromised very early on in his tenure by the embarrassing revelation that workers at a garments factory that he owned had gone on strike because they were not being paid in accordance with the official minimum wage (*Kompas* 23 June 1993).

Nevertheless, Latief also initiated reforms which were more or less in line with those of his predecessor. Like Batubara, he emphasised such matters as increasing the minimum wage periodically and the establishment of enterprise-level SPSI PUK, issues which could only be dealt with effectively if there were a measure of support from the business community. He also continued the effort to improve the image and performance of the hapless SPSI, which he says 'should be strong, independent and professional in fighting in the workers' interest' (*Reuters* 7 October 1994).

Unlike Batubara, Latief did not have the luxury of procrastinating on the politically charged issues of the freedom to organise and the military's continued involvement in labour affairs. Domestic as well as international pressure was building up to force quick responses from the government. The new minister was, for example, faced with a new February 1994 deadline set by the US Trade Representative for a final decision on the GSP issue.

In response to such pressure some degree of 'softening' did take place in terms of government policy toward unions. A 1987 regulation produced under Sudomo (Ministerial Regulation no. 05/MEN/87), governing the establishment of trade unions, had required that a trade union organisation have representation in 20 of Indonesia's 27 provinces (including East Timor), 100 districts and at least 1,000 workplaces, in order to be recognised. This obviously placed huge logistical and administrative obstacles on any possible upstart union outside the SPSI. By way of a new Minister of Manpower regulation, no. 03/MEN/1993, these requirements were reduced to just 5 provinces, 25 district-level branches, 100 workplace unions and 10,000 members. Even the latter requirements, however, were not easy to meet for upstart unions.[30]

Latief also formalised the Batubara-initiated commitment to re-establish industrial sector unions – attached to the SPSI – which had more than just a passing resemblance to the SBLPs that Sudomo had eliminated in 1985. In 1993, thirteen of these were registered, covering the areas of: Wood Products and Forestry; Textiles, Garments and Leathers; Trade, Banking and Insurance; Construction and Public Works; Metals, Electronics, and Machinery; Printing and Publishing; Agriculture and Plantations; Chemicals, Energy and Mining; Cigarettes, Tobacco, Foods and Beverages; Pharmaceuticals and Health; Transport; Seafarers; and Tourism (Pasaribu 1994: 24–26, SPSI 1993b: 8–9). It was significant that Latief emphasised that these 'new unions' were largely 'autonomous' of the SPSI, thus freeing the Indonesian government from the accusation that it was promoting a stifling, monolithic structure (*Kompas* 9 September 1993).[31] He continued, however, to reject the trade union status of both *Setiakawan* and the SBSI, claiming 'they were established by individuals with political interests and not by workers' (*Jakarta Post* 8 August 1993).

The revamping of the SPSI culminated in the organisation's Congress of November 1995, during which the status of these thirteen industrial unions became even more enhanced.[32] At the same time, the SPSI-proper itself began to argue that it had greater autonomy from the government than ever before. It was announced, for example, that the check-off system through which membership dues were collected would no longer be run through the Department of Manpower, but will become the full responsibility of the union.[33] As if underlining the seriousness of this change, the SPSI began presenting itself under a new name – the FSPSI, or SPSI Federation. Significantly, a new official handbook expresses the hope that the recent changes in the organisation will allow the 're-activisation' of its membership in the ICFTU (FSPSI 1996: 108). Not surprisingly, the significance of the SPSI reforms continues to be discounted by independent labour activists in Indonesia. Many pointed out that they did not alter the fact that the government-created union stood as an obstacle to freedom of association, because its existence precluded the establishment of alternative unions.[34]

There are those within the government-backed union, however, who have taken seriously the Batubara-Latief reforms. Among these is Bomer Pasaribu, secretary-general and later general chairman of the (F)SPSI. A parliamentarian and SOKSI/GOLKAR man, he has declared in somewhat grandiose fashion, the 'old paradigm' of the 'first twenty five years of development' – that 'cheap labour is a comparative advantage'- to be obsolete. Arguing that the sacrifices of workers have been responsible for Indonesia's economic successes, Pasaribu pronounced that a 'new paradigm' – that of 'democratisation, integration, and justice' – should command the next 'twenty five years of development'. The failure for this to take place, he warned, would incur 'social and political costs', the kind of which the 'Medan Tragedy' could be a harbinger (Pasaribu 1994: 113–130).

Pasaribu was elected general chairman of the (F)SPSI at the November 1995 Congress, one which he argues was far freer of government interventions than those of the past, thus making him a genuine popular choice.[35] Since then he has been aggressive about changing the image of the union. For example, he harshly criticised business commentators who suggested that raising minimum wages would hamper future investment, arguing that Indonesian wage rates were still internationally competitive (*Republika* 11 January 1996). Quite astonishingly, Pasaribu also declared that workers should go on strike if employers refused to comply with minimum wage regulations, citing the fact that they had a legal basis to do so (*Republika* 3 January 1996). Such a viewpoint contrasts starkly with the pronouncements of FBSI/SPSI leaders throughout most of the 1970s and 1980s, which often emphasised that strikes contravened the principles of harmony which underpin HIP.

In spite of the warning made by Pasaribu and others about potentially growing domestic unrest, it should be recognised that the Batubara–Latief limited reforms have been as much directed toward the US government as they have been to addressing internal grievances. Indonesian state officials have naturally recognised the importance of the USA to the Indonesian economy. They could not, for example, easily take the same stance toward the USA that they did toward the Dutch government in 1992, when they refused aid because of remarks on Indonesia's human-rights record (*Far Eastern Economic Review* 9 April 1992: 10–11). The following excerpt, from an assessment by a directorate of the Indonesian Department of Foreign Affairs, quite neatly summarises the concern of the Indonesian government to maintain good relations with the USA:

> The Indonesian attitude towards the lifting of the US GSP cannot be the same as our attitude toward Dutch aid, because the US has more leverage, for example, . . . in the form of OPIC insurance for its investment . . . We don't have the means to 'retaliate'.[36]
>
> We must therefore continue to take advantage of dialogue with the US, although the diplomatic scope has its limits. Thus, we must continue to explain to the US Team the steps that we are taking toward meeting ILO standards while considering Indonesia's situation. In addition, we should continue to improve our lobby in the US by making use of Indonesia's friends, including large US corporations that have had mutually advantageous relations with Indonesia.

(Directorate of International Trade 1993: 4)

Underscoring the seriousness with which it regarded American opinion, the Indonesian government even hired an American consultancy firm, White and Case, to help prepare its case with the US government. The firm appeared to play a key role in the formulation of Indonesian government strategy *vis à vis* the USTR.[37]

Various other limited reforms have also been undertaken by Latief to resolve tensions in the labour area. For example, in 1994 he announced Ministerial Regulation no. 01/MEN/1994, which recognised the right of workers to form enterprise-level unions unattached to the SPSI – though they were prohibited from combining to form a federation that might compete with the SPSI. In fact, these would be encouraged eventually to merge with the state-backed union, whose monopoly at the national level was upheld by the regulation.[38]

Arguably, the establishment of in-house unions has traditionally been a part of employer strategy to inhibit the growth of a unified labour movement and to create unions which they can effectively dominate.[39] Nevertheless, given the level of state control of the central, provincial and lower branches of the SPSI, it may have been argued that the regulation opened up an avenue that could have been exploited by workers, perhaps in association with NGOs, to overcome some of these controls. Indeed, this might have been the case in spite of the tendency of most independent labour activists to be dismissive of this possibility, and to shrug off the Ministerial Regulation as irrelevant to realities on the ground.[40]

One of the harshest critics of the idea of enterprise unions, not surprisingly, was the SPSI itself. Underlining the SPSI's concern, Pasaribu emphasised the need to improve the performance of the PUK to ensure that in-house unions do not become an attractive alternative to workers.[41]

The government union's fears, as it turned out, were quite unfounded as there was no immediate move to facilitate the establishment of in-house unions in any significant number. It was only in mid-1995, in another bid to demonstrate the sincerity of recent reforms to the US did the Indonesian government claim that these in-house unions had indeed been established.[42] This was further evidence that the advancement of the idea of enterprise-level unions was made more with an international audience in mind than to promote significant real reforms.[43] Like Batubara, Latief was using diplomacy to soften international criticism – in November 1993, a special ILO mission visited Indonesia to investigate labour conditions and state labour policy.[44]

Another reformist measure was presented with the announcement in the same year of Ministerial Decree no. 15A/MEN/1994, formally revoking Ministerial Decree 342/1986, which legitimised military intervention in the resolution of labour disputes. Latief's decree, however, was not as significant as it may appear to be. Independent labour activists were quick to point out that military intervention was in fact still legitimised by an unaffected decision on labour matters by the chief of BAKORSTRANAS – mentioned in Chapter 5 – in spite of the decree (*Kompas* 21 January 1994; also Nusantara 1995: 31). Indeed, they argued this as they tried to persuade visiting US officials that the extension of the GSP privileges would mean *de facto* US acceptance of repressive labour policies in Indonesia (*Republika* 4 February 1994).[45]

Other reformist measures that Latief has taken include a further campaign to ensure the enforcement of penalties for business non-compliance with minimum wage stipulations. As mentioned earlier, his predecessor Batubara had argued that part of the responsibility for the rise of labour unrest lay on the shoulders of businesses who were unwilling to pay workers the minimum wage. However, because the fine for such non-compliance was then a mere Rp 100,000 (less than US$50), Latief promoted the idea of amending the existing law. By early 1994, Latief was claiming that up to 99 per cent of firms in the Jabotabek area were cooperating with the government.[46] Still another initiative that Latief took concerned the controversial problem of annual bonuses for workers. Recognising that it has often triggered labour unrest, Latief made it mandatory for employers to provide workers with such a bonus every year (*Reuters* 22 September 1994).

Referring to official strike statistics which showed a decline in industrial action in 1993 (see Table 6.1, pp. 113), Latief suggested that business support for his reforms had helped to contain labour unrest.[47] He was referring particularly to his sanctioned minimum wage increases. Indeed, by 1995 the government was claiming that wage levels already covered 108 per cent of workers' minimum physical needs (Suwarto 1995).

However, ensuring business support for these increases was not always easy. In February 1995, the API (Association of Indonesian Textiles Producers) attacked their soundness and pleaded that 123 of its members could not afford to comply with them. Only after much public criticism of

Table 8.1 Minimum Wage in Selected Regions, 1990 and 1996 (Daily in Rupiah)[48]

Region	1990	1996
Jakarta	2100	5200
West Java	1200	4662 (average)
Central Java	780	3400
East Java	1409	3724 (average)
North Sumatra	1930	4600

its position, and after a special meeting with Suwarto, Latief's Director-General of Labour Standards, did the API leadership finally agree to support the new minimum wage stipulations (*Media Indonesia* 14 February 1995; *Republika* 18 February 1995; *Republika* 23 February 1995).

If raising the minimum wage had garnered Latief some vocal critics from within the business community, he did not win new friends among independent labour activists. The latter continued to argue that while no substantial reform had taken place with regard to the right of association and to organise, the welfare levels of workers had only been marginally improved. In Central Java, for example, they suggested that only 11 per cent of firms were complying with the minimum wage in 1994.[49] In Surabaya, Gresik, Sidoarjo and Malang, the Surabaya branch of YLBHI found that one-third of firms were contravening minimum wage regulations. Independent labour organisers also continue to emphasise that the basis for the calculation of minimum wages are too antiquated to reflect fully the realities of contemporary life. They point out that the minimum wage is at best geared to cover the minimum physical needs of unmarried male workers.[50]

But Latief remained adamant about the utility of raising minimum wage levels to curb labour unrest. He yet again announced an increase in early 1996 (through Minister of Manpower Regulation no. PER01/MEN/1996), upon which he received virtually identical reactions from businesses and labour organisers. The new regulation set the minimum wage at Rp 5,200 (about US$2.25) in the Jakarta area, up from the previous year's Rp 4,600 (about US$2.00).[51] This time, however, a furore was created in the business community because of the stipulation that workers without regular permanent employment status should be paid for thirty – rather than twenty-five – days of the month. The business community protested vehemently that this would, in real terms, result in a minimum wage in the Jakarta area of Rp 6,240, thereby creating havoc in the cost structure of labour-intensive firms (*Kompas* 15 March 1996; 25 April 1996).[52]

Some businesses responded to the latest minimum-wage regulation by applying for an official exemption. Smaller scale enterprises, in particular, pleaded that the new wage was too much of a burden to bear. Subsequently, the Department of Manpower exempted 400 enterprises, mainly in garments and footwear, from the new minumum wage regulation (Manning and Jayasuriya 1996: 36). However, business grumblings about rising wage costs were yet again greeted with cynicism in other quarters. The NGO-run *Komisi Upah* (1996), or Wages Commission, for example, argued that even the new minimum wage did not reflect the real needs of a worker as it did not take into account the rising cost of basic necessities.

The unwillingness or inability of some businesses to comply with the new minimum wage spurred a fresh round of labour unrest. In April 1996, shortly after the latest wage rise should have been implemented, a Jakarta daily reported that 'hundreds of thousands of workers' had gone on strike in such important industrial areas as Tangerang, Bekasi, Bogor and Bandung (*Bisnis Indonesia* 16 April 1996). In fact, industrial action began to rise noticeably in some industrial areas as early as March (*Economic and Business Review Indonesia* 15 May 1996: 6), no doubt in reaction to indications that employers were intending to avoid implementing the new minimum wage.

MAINTAINING THE SECURITY APPROACH

Response to the Medan riots

If the piecemeal reforms that Latief and Batubara initiated provided some basis to defend the government's recent labour record, they were not adequate significantly to curb labour unrest in the longer term. Though official statistics showed a drop in industrial unrest in 1993, the following year was to surpass 1992 as the year of the highest incidents of strike action (see Table 6.1, pp. 113). By October 1994, an unprecedented 367 strikes had been reported for the year (*Reuters* 14 October 94).[53] The number of strikes may have subsequently dropped again, but industrial unrest remains pervasive enough across a wide range of industrial areas for one major businesssman to exclaim in exasperation that 'Wherever you look their (sic) are strikes. This looks bad for foreign investors. How will they continue to invest here if workers continually cause upsets?' (*Economic and Business Review Indonesia* 15 May 1996: 7).

The fact that such a situation continues to exist arguably gives some credence to the position of those within the state apparatus who have been sceptical about the usefulness of reformist measures. Sudomo, for example, ever the proponent of tougher policies, considers the continued escalation of labour unrest to be the direct result of the 'weakness' of his two successors, Batubara and Latief.[54]

Voices which echo that of Sudomo have been heard more frequently since the middle of 1994, usually emanating from within the military leadership. These have been encouraged by the fact that the Indonesian government had largely been freed by then from the pressure represented by the threat to remove Indonesia from the US GSP list. Indeed, the GSP threat had practically become a non-issue after the US government announced, in February 1994, that it would postpone yet again a final decision until after an APEC summit to be hosted by Indonesia in November 1994. Defending this position, a top US official maintained that the Indonesian government had taken 'progressive steps' to improve the treatment of labour. The US, he said, was only responding to this by 'providing additional time for those changes to take effect' (*Jakarta Post* 4 May 1994).[55]

The US non-decision, however, was widely regarded a backflip by Indonesian state officials, who as a result, become increasingly confident, not only that the GSP threat would not materialise, but also in confronting international criticism of Indonesia's labour record in general. Coordinating Minister of Economics and Finance Saleh Affif, for example, retorted that Indonesia did not need the GSP facilities and would reject their linkage with improvement in the protection of labour rights (*Reuters* 28 October 1994). This new mood of confidence in government circles was perhaps best revealed by the tough reaction to the Medan riots of April 1994, which involved mass arrests and trials of workers and activists, partly directed at crippling the increasingly high-profile and assertive SBSI.[56]

If the reaction to the Medan riots signalled a clear turning point in government policy, the earlier, temporary, ascendance of limited reformism had not, in any case, caused the complete abandonment of the more security-oriented approach.[57] In spite of official claims to the contrary (Department of Foreign Affairs 1993: 20), in reality military personnel continued to be involved in quelling strike action right through Latief's reforms. One report noted that

> Police and military in a number of instances have been present in significant numbers during strikes, even when there has been no destruction of property or other violence. Military officials occasionally have been present during negotiations between workers and management. Their presence has been described as intimidating by plant-level union officials.
>
> (American Embassy 1994: 31)

Still, a distinctive, renewed atmosphere of repression was signalled by the government's tough reaction to the Medan riots. Significantly, this tougher line on labour was adopted at the same time that a more general step-up of repression took place against internal sources of criticism and opposition. Three mainstream publications, *Tempo*, *Detik* and *Editor*, were banned in June 1994 (Hill, D. 1994: 41). Harassment of intellectuals critical of the government also took place at about the same time.[58] Furthermore, an NGO conference in Yogyakarta, held to discuss a proposed government bill to regulate NGOs, was closed down by local security forces (*Kompas* 23 September 1994).

Of the hundreds of workers and activists arrested after the Medan riots, by mid-August, several dozen were given jail sentences of four to six months for such offences as throwing stones, while a few local NGO and SBSI officers received more serious penalties for incitement. The three most well-known figures were Muchtar Pakpahan, Amosi Telaumbanua, head of the SBSI branch in Medan, and Maiyasak Djohan, head of a local NGO. As mentioned earlier, Pakpahan originally received a sentence of three years imprisonment (*Voice of America* 7 November 1994). Perhaps underlining the Indonesian government's mood of confidence, the original sentencing of Pakpahan took place in the same month that Indonesia hosted the APEC summit, attended by such leaders as US President Clinton and Australian Prime Minister Keating. Later, Pakpahan's jail term was increased to four years on appeal.[59]

Predictably, the adoption of this tougher line eventually elicited a new round of international criticism of Indonesia's labour record. Pakpahan's trial in Medan, for example, was attended by various European and American diplomats as well as by Amnesty International observers. Latief admitted to receiving queries from various international organisations regarding the arrest and trial of Pakpahan throughout the year (*Merdeka* 17 October 1994). In addition, the General Secretary of the ICFTU urged the World Bank to apply pressure on the Indonesian government on behalf of the SBSI leader.[60] Prior to the APEC summit, 28 members of the US Congress sent a letter to Trade Representative Michael Kantor, asking for a re-examination of Indonesia's GSP status, and suggested that it was time for the USA to demonstrate its 'commitment to international workers' rights by not rewarding Indonesia with GSP status'.[61] Later, 76 members of the US Congress urged President Bill Clinton to raise the issue of 'severe labour rights violations' with President Soeharto at the APEC Summit (*Reuters* 28 October 1994). Though the US government criticised the handling of the Pakpahan case, President Clinton was not reported to have raised labour and human rights as key issues when he met Soeharto (*Reuters* 9 November 1994).[62]

Even after the APEC summit, however, and in spite of the negative reactions from the US government on the extension of Pakpahan's jail term (*Reuters* 30 January 1995), the GSP issue did not resurface very seriously. Little was changed by the visit of yet another US official to investigate labour conditions, at the end of which he restated his government's 'continuing concern'. This prompted Suwarto to lambast the US for being 'stubborn' (*Jakarta Post* 21 April 1994). In addition, in April 1995, an ILO report found increasing evidence of 'serious and worsening infringements of basic human and trade union rights' in Indonesia.[63] While neither of these developments appeared to erode the Indonesian government's new-found confidence in dealing with international criticism of its labour record, it was notable that Pakpahan was later found not guilty by the Supreme Court (*Forum Keadilan* 23 October 1995: 31). Other labour activists implicated in the Medan case had been released from prison by July 1995 (*Reuters* 28 July 1995), but not before considerable damage had been done to the SBSI.

Dwifungsi and labour

As mentioned earlier, the advocacy of a more security-oriented approach to labour problems has essentially emanated from the military leadership. Military intervention into labour matters has been defended by reference to the doctrine of *dwifungsi* (as military dual function), which originated in the 1950s (e.g. Department of Foreign Affairs 1993: 20) and has been the basis for widespread military social and political roles. Often at the heart of the hardline rhetoric has been the idea of cultural relativism, which was the foundation for the formulation in 1974 of a culturally specific 'Pancasila Industrial Relations' in the first place. Armed Forces Commander-in-Chief Feisal Tandjung, for example, has argued against the intrusion of 'liberalism' in Indonesian society (*Jakarta Post* 4 February 1994). Indeed, this rhetoric is so commonplace that it has been utilised by reformists almost as much as hardliners. According to Batubara, for example, 'foreigners' have failed to understand that in the Indonesian cultural context, asking the local military command for help to settle a labour dispute was the normal thing to do.[64]

Significantly, during an SPSI conference in late 1993, General Tanjung sharply criticised the union's performance while placing much of the blame for the rise of labour unrest on its shoulders (Tanjung 1993). This was not unusual as the hapless SPSI had by then become an easy target of criticism even from within the government. It is also possible to interpret the general's remarks, however, as a barely veiled restatement of the crucial, continuing, role played by ABRI in the maintenance of labour peace and, by implication, national stability. As we shall see, there are grounds that make such an interpretation plausible.

Following the outbreak of the Medan riots, it was also General Tanjung who spoke out most harshly against the government-identified culprits. He attacked them for threatening to ' . . . create chaos in the country, so that development does not take place the way it should'. That, he said, constituted 'subversion'. Though Tanjung stated that he was not against the idea of protests as a way of conveying aspirations in society, he stressed that those involved should not create social disruptions (*Kompas* 23 April 1994). Ominously for labour organisers, Tanjung also suggested that ABRI investigations had discovered that some SBSI personnel had PKI backgrounds. In raising again the spectre of communism, Tanjung was essentially adopting language that had begun to sound somewhat archaic since Sudomo's departure from a position of direct control over state labour policy.[65]

Tanjung was supported by some of his fellow officers. ABRI Chief of Social-Political Affairs (KASOSPOL) General Hartono castigated the 'culprits' of the Medan riots for using what he termed 'communist tactics' and raised the possibility that communists were in fact responsible for the riots (*Kompas* 23 April 1994). His assistant, General Hari Sabarno, suggested that the activities of the SBSI had caused protest incidents that it could not control, and led to brutal acts. He also accused the organisation of not only hindering the implementation of HIP, but also of posing a serious threat to national stability, and thereby to the national development effort (Sabarno 1994: 97). The Commander in Chief of the military region which includes North Sumatra, Major-General Pranowo, suggested that the 'ways and patterns' of those behind the Medan riots were 'similar to the PKI's' (*Forum Keadilan* 11 May 1994: 19). References by such generals to 'the latent dangers of communism' were clearly designed not only to mobilise public opinion against the SBSI, but also to send an unambiguous threat to other independent labour organisers – as 'communists' largely remained fair game for political persecution. But it was not only the SBSI that would be the subject of the wrath of the military. Later, as army Chief-of-Staff, Hartono also chastised NGOs in general for 'trying to expand their influence by undermining the authority of the government and ABRI', while addressing an ABRI course on social and political affairs (*Gatra* 11 March 1995).

The fact that ABRI personnel could feel comfortable enough to revert back to what was then seemingly obsolete political language is in itself not insignificant.[66] This is particularly so because of the emphasis in the previous few years of downplaying ABRI's involvement in labour matters. The Marsinah case, for example, was being successfully used by NGO activists to symbolise the pervasiveness and ruthlessness of ABRI intervention in labour affairs at the local level, in collusion with business.[67] However, ABRI figures were now on the counter-attack and spoke disparagingly of criticism of military involvement, alleging that it was 'sold to the international community as an issue which is harmful to the national interest' (Sabarno 1994: 98). Thus, the Medan riots was not only used as a pretext to cripple the SBSI, but also to undermine the credibility of labour-based NGOs in general.[68]

The basis for continued ABRI intervention into labour affairs, as has been pointed out, is a document signed in 1990 by the chief of BAKOR-STRANAS, who is simultaneously Commander-in-Chief of ABRI. This document is unaffected by Latief's annulment of Sudomo's infamous decree of 1986. Under its terms the definition of ABRI's scope of involvement in labour affairs is quite wide. According to the document, BAKOR-STRANAS, (and its regional branches, BAKORSTRANASDA) 'initiates the taking of immediate and effective measures to deal with industrial relations cases which threaten National Stability' (BAKORSTRANAS 1990: 5).

Similar to Sudomo's ad-hoc security groups, a 'special objective' of BAKORSTRANAS is to detect and monitor the conditions that might give rise to labour unrest (BAKORSTRANAS 1990: 5). Some of its 'functions' are to collect and process data and information 'on the possibilities of the occurrence of industrial relations cases', and to take 'measures against strikes/demonstrations or lockouts which are unlawful in nature' (BAKOR-STRANAS 1990: 7). Significantly, the organisation's personnel is reminded to prevent 'the possibility of abuse [of a case of unrest] by a third party' (BAKORSTRANAS 1990: 6) – an oblique reference to NGOs.

It could be suggested that BAKORSTRANAS essentially serves as the coordinating body of all state efforts, on the ground, to preserve and maintain industrial peace. Indeed, the document mentioned above also states that the 'duty' of the organisation is 'to prevent and deal with industrial relations cases at every level in the whole territory of Indonesia early on and in a thorough way' (BAKORSTRANAS 1990: 7). It is also responsible for providing 'guidance and directives' to other government institutions. Asserting the 'inadequacy' of more legal–formal institutions, the document adds that BAKORSTRANAS provides 'support to functional agencies in settling industrial relation cases which have not been dealt with effectively' (BAKORSTRANAS 1990: 8–9).

It is perhaps natural that ABRI has been the major proponent of the security-oriented approach. In the previous Chapter, however, some interpretations were presented which suggested the apparent paradox of cases in which some quiet ABRI support for the fledgling independent labour movement could be discerned. Bourchier, as it was pointed out, raised the possibility that the lack of overt moves to destroy the independent union, SBM *Setiakawan*, in 1990–92, was an outgrowth of the interests of a Benny Moerdani-led military faction to discredit the SPSI, an organisation increasingly linked to GOLKAR, itself being gradually removed from ABRI's ambit by President Soeharto. Muchtar Pakpahan, it was also pointed out, for some time entertained the notion that he was being given 'protection' by an increasingly 'enlightened' military leadership.[69] Some labour activists have observed how local military units sometimes 'encouraged' greater levels of destructiveness during strike action when some violence has been involved (Djati 1994). Indeed, similar accounts have been given about the actions of ABRI personnel during the Medan riots. For example, a YLBHI report (1994c: 12) noted how 'two middle-ranking local officers admitted to having infiltrated and incited workers' during the riots.[70] It also claimed that a worker had subsequently admitted that he was paid by ABRI to incite rioting in Medan.[71]

Can the suggestion that ABRI, or at least, some ABRI personnel, have sometimes been responsible for encouraging labour unrest, fit with the argument that the military has been the foremost proponent of a security-oriented approach? The answer is the affirmative. Bourchier's assertion that (at least one faction within) ABRI's temporary protection of *Setiakawan* was attributable to the intricacies of elite struggles is at least plausible, and indeed, an essentially similar line of argument would go quite a long way in accounting for the temporarily cordial relations between sections of ABRI (specifically the Jakarta Military Command under General Hendropriyono) and the SBSI. Such an argument makes a great deal more sense if we were to consider as well the internal logic and vested interests of security-oriented institutions like ABRI, which are primarily geared to deal with sources of instability internal to Indonesia rather than with external threats.

It is clearly in the interests of such an institution, for example, to demonstrate its continued relevance to the maintenance of stability, especially when there has not been an easily identifiable source of threat to national security. This is probably more so the case given increasing discussion in recent years about the necessity of reformulating ABRI's social and political roles (*Kompas* 24 June 1992; *Merdeka* 11 March 1995), which has prompted the suggestion of a 'return to the barracks'. Such a discussion is in itself a feature of continuing intra-elite struggles which is obviously too complex to be examined thoroughly in the present study. Suffice to say, however, that the presence of some, controlled, degree of labour unrest, would be in the interest of demonstrating the continued relevance of a pervasive social and political role for ABRI as it offers proof of the institutions's indispensability. These vested interests of ABRI have not escaped the observations of independent labour activists, who have noted that the Medan riots have served to provide the military with a new legitimacy to continue its interventions and to toughen its repression (YLBHI 1994c: 3).

Indeed, the implications of the Medan riots as presented by ABRI itself seems to support this observation. Major General Pranowo, when asked about what ABRI has concluded from the events in Medan, answered:

> The Medan incident is a lesson for other regions. The KASUM (Chief of the General Staff) of ABRI [told all the commanders] that the steps taken by BAKORSTRANAS there were justified. Then he said that the Medan problem could develop elsewhere . . . because the problem [that arose here] is universal and can be exploited by other parties. . . . Therefore, the [security] apparatus must exercise vigilance in their respective areas.
>
> (*Forum Keadilan* 11 May 1994: 19)

Furthermore, it is possible that the presence of some degree of labour unrest also serves the interest of ABRI personnel, especially, at the local level, in a more concrete, material way. Labour organisers often speak of how a degree of unrest reinforces the idea among employers of the necessity of cultivating support from local military commands to deal with their labour problems. It is suggested that the maintenance of this support involves the provision by businesses of illicit moneys, which comprise part of the infamous 'invisible costs' allocated to smooth relations with a wide variety of relevant state institutions – a highly controversial issue which is discussed further below.[72] Therefore, again in reference to the Medan case, independent labour activists have speculated that the riots – particularly because of its racial expression – would serve to reinforce 'collusion between (Chinese) business and the military . . . '.[73]

Thus, the issue of continued ABRI involvement in labour affairs clearly has many aspects. First, there is the issue of ABRI's long-held ideological hostility to an independent, militant labour movement, historically rooted in the experiences of the 1950s and 1960s. Second, there is the issue of ABRI's continuing perception of the contemporary development of such a movement as a threat to the framework of state–society relations constructed by the army-dominated early New Order, predicated on the principles of popular exclusion and demobilisation. Third, there is the issue of ABRI's interest, as the security-oriented institution *par excellence* – and in view of the nature of current elite-level struggles – continually to demonstrate the relevance of its social and political roles to contemporary times. It is suggested here that, in part, ABRI does this by stressing the threat to social order and stability that is represented by the emergence of a significant labour movement independent of state control. Last, there is also the issue of 'invisible costs' as they relate to alleged payments being made by companies to ABRI personnel to 'maintain order'.

Perhaps the most conclusive proof that the 'security approach' toward labour has not been abandoned is provided by the government's initial reaction to the 27 July 1996 riots in Jakarta, which were quickly blamed on organisations and individuals who have been prominent in Indonesia's fledgling independent labour movement. The riots themselves were not spurred by a labour-related issue but by the government's crude ouster of the popular politician, Megawati Soekarnoputri, as leader of the Indonesian Democratic Party (PDI) (The *Australian* 29 July 1996). Megawati (daughter of Indonesia's first president, Soekarno) was by then emerging as a unifying opposition leader and a symbol of political reform. She had also gained support among a wide range of NGOs, including those involved in labour struggles.

Megawati's protracted removal involved the organising of a 'rebel' PDI Congress supported by the government, the 'election' of a more pliant rival as party leader, and the storming of party headquarters by government troops, thugs and supporters of that rival. Rather than concede that the riots were the outcome of widespread anger at the blatant acts to depose Megawati, the government chose to single out the PRD as culprit, which, through its labour arm, the PPBI, had been helping to stage numerous well-publicised labour strikes for over a year.[74] The rioting was also inexplicably blamed on SBSI leader Muchtar Pakpahan, who was arrested yet again only nine months after he was released by the Supreme Court in connection with the Medan riots.[75] Both the PRD/PPBI and Pakpahan have been accused of as representing the resurgence of communism. These attacks on them may yet precipitate a more wide-ranging clampdown on sources of opposition to the government, which in turn, could affect the activities of workers organising at the grassroots level.[76]

BUSINESS: A CONSERVATIVE FORCE

Historically, the recognition by capital of its longer-term interests in the maintenance of a social and political environment conducive to production has usually served to speed up a process of accommodation between state, capital and labour in which some of the more unproblematic demands of workers are incorporated. Of course the nature of such an accommodation is dependent on the respective strengths of the three parties and their specific interests within particular historical conjunctures. However, it is suggested here that in the specific context of contemporary, very late indus- trialising Indonesia, business is an essentially conservative force that has posed more obstacles to than support for the possible incorporation of some of the demands of labour. This, it is also suggested, not only stems from the weakness of the labour movement in Indonesia, but is also the result of a deeply rooted perception of the reliability of the state's repressive apparatus to contain labour problems in the longer run.

Unlike labour, business does not inherently require collective organisation to have an impact on state policy as its influence is primarily exercised struc- turally, insofar as it has power over investment.[77] In spite of this, business associations have been increasingly important players in the struggles over state labour policy. Thus, APINDO, API and to a lesser extent KADIN have served as important outlets for the expression of collective business displeasure with government policy, particularly with regard to minimum wage increases.

Notwithstanding Abdul Latief's claims of successfully mobilising business support for government-led reforms, in reality, the business community has only grudgingly followed the state's lead. To slow down minimum wage increases they have typically argued that these have added to the cost of production almost intolerably, and therefore, have reduced the global competitiveness of Indonesia's exports (*Jakarta Post* 19 February 1995; Novo n.d.). They have emphasised that this does harm to the national interest.

KADIN, which since 1994 has been under the more dynamic leadership of Aburizal Bakrie, a politically well-connected indigenous businessman, has been at the forefront of business attempts to influence wage policy. Bakrie has repeatedly emphasised how wage increases should be tied to productivity rises,[78] even though Latief has argued that labour productivity in the manufacturing sector in the period 1984–92 has increased while real worker incomes have fallen (*Kompas* 21 October 1994). Hadi Topobroto, executive director of APINDO, emphasises the existence of an 'escape clause' in wage policy whereby, he suggests, businesses can apply for dispen- sation if they are able to prove economic difficulties,[79] as some have done in response to the most recent rounds of minimum wage increases.

As was also mentioned earlier, the issue of rising minimum wages has been linked, both by business and labour activists, to the highly charged issue of 'invisible costs' – unofficial funds which enterprises have to allocate to ensure the unhindered operations of business. Both parties have suggested that the prevalence of these 'invisible costs' – ranging from graft to money made available to ensure cooperation in security matters from local civilian and military officials – has significantly added to the total costs of doing business in Indonesia. Labour activists have emphasised the detrimental effects of the practice on labour. Employers have argued that the combination of rising minimum wages and high levels of bureaucratic costs has made Indonesia increasingly internationally uncompetitive (*Jakarta Post* 2 April 1994), especially in the production of labour-intensive goods.

The importance of the issue of 'invisible costs' is widely understood. This was underscored during interviews conducted with a number of representatives of the business community during fieldwork, the details of which are given below. For a long time, even before businesses began to raise the issue, the NGO community had argued that these costs help to keep wages low as they have significantly added to production costs. Though they have usually lacked concrete evidence to prove the point conclusively, the issue can be viewed as essentially one of exploited industrial workers subsidising corrupt government officials. The task of collecting accurate data on these clandestine practices is obviously a difficult one given the stakes involved for all parties concerned. The interviews with business representatives, however, substantiate the bulk of these allegations.

One manager of a European textiles producer calculated roughly that 'invisible' expenditures comprise only 2 or 3 per cent of total operating costs, and downplayed the amounts of money required to court government officials.[80] Other business representatives, however, estimated such costs to comprise up to 20 per cent of production costs, in contrast to direct labour costs of about 9–12 per cent. Labour groups argue that direct labour costs involved in labour-intensive production only comprise a slightly lower 5 to 8 per cent of total costs while 'bureaucracy-related' expenditures take up a seemingly fantastic 30 per cent. Sometimes they have been supported by professional economists (*Jakarta Post* 19 February 1995). Estimates that also support the trade-off argument are given by official government sources. Latief, himself an industrialist, stated that a study by his Department found that labour costs in some labour-intensive industries only comprised 9.41 per cent of total production cost – while 60 per cent, he said, went for raw materials – and the remainder to 'invisible costs' and inefficiency in financing (*Kompas* 21 October 1994). More recently, Latief indirectly confirmed, for some industries, the 30 per cent estimate given by NGOs. KADIN chairman Aburizal Bakrie, proposed the figure of 27 per cent (*Forum Keadilan* 25 March 1996: 95–99; 107). Thus, although the facts and figures given by the representatives of state, capital and labour sometimes differ in their detail, interestingly, most seem to lead to the essential trade-off argument between wages and bureaucracy-related costs.[81]

It is no wonder, therefore, that businesses have become more forthright in expressing their displeasure with corrupt bureaucratic practices. After complaining about how labour costs have risen dramatically in Indonesia, one Korean businessman admitted that bureaucracy-related expenditures tended to be regarded by employers as a cost that was far less easy to curb (and therefore had to be accepted) than the cost of labour. This, he attributed to the essential weakness of the labour movement in Indonesia and the power of the state bureaucracy.[82] An official of KOTRA in Jakarta, the South Korean government's support office for business and trade activities, suggested that Korean business would not be against minimum wages rising by up to 50 per cent if bureaucratic costs could be significantly reduced.[83] In essentially the same vein, an Indonesian garments manufacturer, and official of API, argued that if the government allowed labour costs to continue to rise, it was condemning smaller-size businesses in labour-intensive industries to bankruptcy, given their already sizeable bureaucracy-related expenditures. In such circumstances, he warned, escalating labour costs would eventually threaten the competitiveness of Indonesia's export products.[84]

The business sector's suggestions that the rise in minimum wages has caused intolerable burdens have usually been dismissed by the government. Indeed, Minister of Manpower Latief has argued that because labour costs constitute such a small portion of total production costs, the rise in minimum wages will only have a marginal effect (*Forum Keadilan* 2 February 1995: 90). In this he is supported by Dhanani, a BAPPENAS-based World Bank economist, who stresses that 'incorporated' manufacturing firms in Indonesia enjoy average profits far in excess of that of firms operating in industrialised countries, where 'returns to labour usually form two-thirds of value-added' (Dhanani 1992: 11).[85]

However, Latief did make a gesture to accommodate business grievances following his highly criticised decision to raise the minimum wage in 1996. This was done by taking the much-publicised step of reducing the levies on businesses charged by the Department of Manpower in a bid to offset the additional burden that the wage increase represented (*Warta Ekonomi* 26 February 1996: 24–26). Latief's initiative was followed by official pronouncements about the intent to undertake similar measures in other departments. Indeed, the notoriously corrupt Department of Transport soon followed suit, announcing that it was eliminating a number of its own levies (*Kompas* 6 March 1996; 8 March 1996).

But the elimination of some costs related to the Departments of Manpower and Transport was unlikely to reduce significantly total bureaucracy-related business expenditure, and at best, was of only symbolic significance. Besides, as discussed earlier, a substantial portion of bureaucracy-related expenditure falls under the rubric of 'invisible' costs, which remain untouched by any reduction of official levies.

In spite of growing business protests about the increasing burden of wages, the popularly perceived disjuncture between profits and labour costs still makes 'business-bashing' a popular activity.[86] Manufacturing firms have also been very susceptible to criticism of high levels of ill-treatment of young, impoverished, and often predominantly female, workforces. Not surprisingly, because of their ostensible wealth and power, large multinationals have been a constant target of much of the criticism although there is little evidence that they treat workers worse than other firms. Firms like Levi-Strauss, Nike and

Reebok, for example, have often been attacked even though they do not operate their own production facilities in Indonesia but merely sub-contract to domestic or other foreign-owned firms – many of which are South Korean. Significantly, workers often point out that firms of South Korean origin are most guilty of ill-treatment.[87] Frequently, next on their list are firms owned by ethnic Chinese Indonesians of Medan origin, though in general, there does not seem to be a significant difference in the labour record of *pribumi* (indigenous Indonesian) and non-*pribumi*-owned firms.[88]

Interestingly, there has been very little evidence of concern by owners and managers of manufacturing firms to improve their labour record. The only exception has been represented by the kind of multinationals that sell the highly recognisable and popular brand-names mentioned earlier. This has to do with their need to maintain a favourable image with consumers in such lucrative markets as North America and Europe. The record of Nike's sub-contractors in Asia has, for example, even been the subject of an entire highly critical book (Katz 1994).[89] In response to similar criticisms, other multinationals, among them Levi-Strauss, have promoted a code of conduct that stipulates minimum conditions with which their numerous sub-contractors have to comply (*Far Eastern Economic Review* 14 April 1994: 56–60). In Indonesia, it was reported that Levi-Strauss cancelled a production agreement with one of its sub-contractors following a highly publicised strike in which workers complained about sub-standard working conditions and abuse (*Jakarta Post* 9 April 1995).[90] Notably, an effort was made by the company's representative in Jakarta to court the NGO community by offering to conduct consultations with YLBHI.[91]

In spite of the few exceptions, manufacturing firms have displayed little concern for their labour record for the same reasons that they have displayed little serious concern about the closely related issue of the rise of labour unrest. First, they are keenly aware of the way in which the continuing presence of a high level of surplus labour in the market acts as a contravening factor to the emergence of a strong labour movement in societies like Indonesia. Phil Knight, Chief Executive Officer of Nike, asked about the subsistence-level wages paid to workers, pointed out that 'there were thousands of Indonesians lined up outside the factory gates, waiting for jobs'.[92]

This lack of concern is also the result of a keen understanding of how state labour policy in Indonesia continues to present real political obstacles to genuine worker attempts to organise. In other words, businesses are aware that the growth of an independent labour movement contradicts the interests of a state that strives to preserve a social and political framework which precludes the development of strong society-based organisations – because of a proven near obsession with political order and stability. The manager of the European textiles firm mentioned earlier, for example, unhesitatingly pointed out that 'when it came to the crunch, we can rely on the security forces to restore order'. The phase of reformism, he added, will pass by.[93] Such business confidence seems to support the argument that, in spite of the escalation of labour unrest, and rising labour costs in recent years, Indonesia's attractiveness as a site for labour-intensive production has not been substantially eroded.

There is of course an additional reason that manufacturing firms have displayed little concern over their labour record and rising labour unrest in Indonesia – one which is related to the basic nature of firms which operate in the labour-intensive, export-oriented sector. Since the studies of Frobel *et al.* (1978; 1980) there have been numerous works that, though differing greatly in many respects, have recognised the essential geographical mobility of such firms and their consequent derived power. It was pointed out earlier that much of the foreign investment in Indonesia's manufacturing sector since the mid-1980s has come from NICs attempting to escape rising labour costs and labour unrest at home. In this connection, it is clear that the last option of moving out of Indonesia, for greener pastures, is one that continues to be open. Underscoring this point, the Koreans interviewed here emphasised that much of the foreign investment in Indonesia in the export sector is short term – firms will be looking to move out within five or ten years if operations do not prove to be profitable. Indeed, ultimately, it would not be too difficult to sustain the argument that, at this particular historical juncture, internationally mobile capital possesses an especially strong bargaining position *vis à vis* immobile states, many of which try to outcompete each other in providing favourable production environments. It is partly for this reason that (similarly geographically immobile) fledgling working-class movements in very late industrialising countries like Indonesia are emerging within an international context which is particularly unfavourable.

SUMMARY

State labour policy in the 1990s has primarily been shaped by the interplay of two broadly different strategies. One has been the limited reformism advocated by Cosmas Batubara and Abdul Latief, namely the revamping of the SPSI and raising the minimum wage. The second strategy, which involves the reassertion of a more security-oriented approach to labour affairs, was in the past particularly espoused by former head of KOPKAMTIB and Minister of Manpower Sudomo, although it has more recently been promoted by other senior ABRI figures.

The business community – comprising both foreign and domestic capital – has been an essentially conservative force. Because its short-term interests have been particularly well-served by the practice of the security approach, the business community has not yet been a source of a far-sightedness which might tip the balance in favour of more significant concessions to labour, in return for industrial peace. In fact, it has often had to be forced to comply with the limited reforms promoted by state officials. As long as businesses continue to view the state's repressive apparatus as the ultimate guarantor of industrial peace, there is little likelihood that they will come to regard concessions to labour as being necessary to safeguard their own longer-term interests. This interpretation of the situation is surely reinforced by the fact that the kind of foreign capital present in low-wage, labour-intensive indus-tries is the kind that is most geographically mobile.

The concern of the security-oriented approach has been the maintenance of the existing exclusionary corporatist social and political framework. Its principal feature has been the overriding concern for the preservation of social and political stability by ensuring the state's ability to monitor and control the workings of all society-based organisations and movements. The escalation of labour unrest has continued to be a major concern to ABRI, for example, because it calls into question the very legitimacy and relevance of this system. Demanding labour unions that can articulate and represent their constituencies rather than act as instruments of state control is not only a threat to the SPSI (or FSPSI, under its new name), but also clearly involves some degree of dismantling of the basic social and political framework put into place in the early 1970s by the army-dominated early New Order.

It has been shown that the rise of labour unrest initially resulted in the enhancement of the position of the proponents of limited reformism. However, the very limitations of limited reformism have been far too obvious. There is little impetus, for example, for the transformation of the F/SPSI from a vehicle which has been geared to ensure the continued control and demobilisation of labour to one that would play a greater role in representation and mobilisation. There is even less impetus – again, aside from the flirtation with non-F/SPSI enterprise unions – to allow for the establishment of alternative labour organisations which might better play such roles.

Because limited reformism has essentially involved not much more than window dressing, labour unrest has largely continued unabated. This has lately strengthened advocates of a more security-oriented approach. After the eruption of the Medan riots in April 1994, and again following the 27 July 1996 riots in Jakarta, we have seen the reassertion of a much tougher stance toward alternative labour-based organisations. At the same time, the state has shown renewed confidence in dealing with international pressure. While Latief's Department of Manpower continues to offer workers the 'carrot', largely in the form of periodic minimum wage rises, the security apparatus has come to wield the 'stick' against them with greater confidence than ever since the rise of labour unrest in 1990.

The situation described is partly attributable to the essential weakness of organised labour itself, which makes a strategy of repression a continuing viable option for the state. Indeed, the discussion has shown that, in spite of some state-led reforms, there has been little indication of moves toward a more fundamental redefinition of state–capital–labour relations in New Order Indonesia – one which would involve a substantially higher degree of political incorporation of the interests of labour.

9 Future directions

This study has been concerned with the politics of the working class in very late industrialising Indonesia. An approach which emphasises the historical and structural contexts within which working-class movements emerge has been combined with an interest in the influence of political legacies and of the concrete struggles of historical agencies.

The very process of industrialisation itself is inextricably related to the emergence of the urban industrial worker and may produce pressures for the development of working-class movements. In Indonesia, the gradual formation of a more distinctly urban industrial proletariat, shaped by the experiences and struggles of life and work in urban and peri-urban areas, accounts considerably for some of the recent, limited, resurgence in working-class organisation, in spite of the slow and not unambiguous nature of the process of class formation.

It has also been shown, however, that there is no simple correspondence between advancing industrialisation and the development of strong and effective working-class movements. In fact, the relationship between the two tends to be weaker the later that industrialisation has begun. Hence, later industrialisations tend to present less favourable political terrains for the development of strong working-class movements.

This in itself, ultimately, is the consequence of specific constellations of class and state power in different historical contexts and the institutions of state–society relations that derive from them. Thus, in the earlier industrialisers, the working class helped establish the model of accommodation between state, capital and labour which in this study has been called 'social democratic', linked to social and political frameworks we now refer to as liberal democracies. Working class struggles in later, Latin American, industrialisers played a role in the establishment of the more tenuous 'populist' model of accommodation, linked to inclusionary corporatist social and political frameworks. In still later industrialisers, both in East and Southeast Asia, working-class struggles take place within the confines of the 'exclusionary' model of accommodation, particularly characterised by the control and demobilisation of labour as a social force. The latter model is itself usually linked to an exclusionary corporatist social and political framework.

These models of accommodation should not be viewed as 'static objects' for they embody real and potential sources of tensions and contradictions. Those associated with the social democratic model are arguably reflected in the contemporary unravelling of the welfare state, which is taking place concurrently with the decline of organised labour. The many crises that the populist accommodation experienced in various Latin American countries in the 1960s and 1970s is a clear indicator of the potential shifts and changes within that model. Some contradictions in the exclusionary model (i.e. in South Korea) have become apparent with the greater development and maturation of the working class.

Great care has also been taken to present a dynamic picture of the struggles between the agencies representing the different social forces in Indonesia, and the way in which they may have some bearing on the social and political outcomes of the industrialisation process – though within the limits of possibilities offered in the specific context. Indeed, it is only by superseding an overly rigid, and formalistic, structural determinism, that the crucial role of political struggles can still be argued against those who suggest an essential helplessness of workers in the face of overwhelmingly powerful constraints.

But a simplistic voluntarism has also been as emphatically rejected for its analytical and political deficiencies. Historical agencies do not wage their struggles in a social vacuum in which anything is possible. Thus, although there is only a limited range of possible outcomes of the struggles waged by the working class within the Indonesian context, it is ultimately the advances and setbacks accrued in the process of concrete struggle that determine which specific outcome is the result.[1] The outcome of current struggles, in turn, helps to determine the range of possibilities available in the next round of struggles between historical agencies, and in that sense, also helps to shape the very context within which they will take place. Thus, future generations of South Korean workers, for example, will no doubt have inherited the legacy of the advances won by their predecessors in the late 1980s, making it that much more difficult for their foes to force a retreat to the conditions that existed earlier. In the same way, whatever advances that the contemporary workers' movement in Indonesia can achieve could act as a kind of bulwark against future incursions against space already won.[2]

Indeed, the impact of prior struggles of the working class on the nature of subsequent ones has been emphasised throughout this study. In the case of Indonesia, it has been demonstrated that the crucial legacy has been that of the struggles between the armed forces and the pro-communist SOBSI in the 1950s and 1960s in that they helped create the conditions for the long-lasting animosity that the armed forces, particularly the army, have held toward organised labour. It was shown that both the institutions and ideology which came to underpin the doctrine of HIP (Pancasila Industrial Relations) in the New Order have precursors in army attempts in the 1950s and 1960s to control and domesticate the radical stream of the labour movement. On the other hand, it was pointed out that a great part of the ideological baggage carried by the radical stream of the movement at the time was inherited from the anti-colonial struggle, considerably imbued with a largely imported set of revolutionary, socialist and Marxist ideas.

The way that structural constraints act to inhibit the options available to historical agencies was also demonstrated during the course of the study. In spite of the veneer of its radical political rhetoric, the labour movement of the 1950s and 1960s was shown to be just as vulnerable to the reaction of its foes as its pre-independence counterpart of the 1920s had been. This was attributed to the largely unaltered, inherited, colonial economy which ensured that no wide-ranging and deeply penetrating process of proletarianisation had occurred which might sustain a significant working-class movement. An agenda of proletarian-led revolution was extremely unlikely to succeed in that context. Indeed, by the early 1960s, the main thrust of the pro-PKI segment of the labour movement was represented by the policy of appeasement of party-identified 'progressive' elements in state and society under the banner of Soekarno's NASAKOM. The quick destruction of the PKI and its associated labour organisations by the Dutch colonial authorities in the 1920s, and again later, by the Indonesian military in the 1960s, was an indication of the essential weakness and vulnerability of that radical stream.

Nevertheless, radical labour organisations were able to temporarily enjoy some power and influence disproportionate to the actual strength of labour as a class. This was partly due to the long process involved in the consolidation of the post-colonial state and the absence from the scene of class adversaries that resembled anything more than a limited petty bourgeoisie. The political tide only began to turn against it as social forces opposed to the radical redistribution of economic and political power began to consolidate around the increasingly powerful military.

Thus, the establishment of the New Order represented the ascendance of a coalition of forces which was inherently hostile toward a militant, labour movement. Soon after the establishment of the New Order, the military component of this coalition secured its predominance and accelerated the process – already begun during Soekarno's Guided Democracy – of marginalising political parties and mass-based organisations. Eventually, under the direction of OPSUS, the fundamentals of the exclusionary, corporatist social and political framework was established, within which stringent controls over labour was an integral part. Thus, the specific institutional and ideological underpinnings of an exclusionary form of accommodation between state, capital and labour in Indonesia were consolidated at the same time as the principal elements of the wider framework of exclusionary corporatism were erected.

However, in contrast to more functionalist explanations, it was suggested that the continued political exclusion and demobilisation of labour had little direct relevance to the specific requirements of the ISI strategy – first based on consumer goods, and later, more capital intensive, resource-based industries – employed throughout the 1970s. Thus, the development of a system of stringent controls over labour reflected concerns which were, above all, political rather than economic in nature, and to a considerable degree, shaped by the experiences of the 1950s and 1960s. The establishment of these controls actually preceded the onset of EOI in Indonesia which was in itself not unique, given that a similar development could be identified in the experiences of the East Asian NICs, where they evolved over the post-World War II period in the name of forestalling communist incursion.

Other parts of the study have been concerned with the tensions and contradictions in the exclusionary model as manifested in the case of Indonesia. Attention was directed at the formation of a new industrial proletariat and the development of alternative, independent, working-class-based organisations. The discussion of class formation was geared to provide some insights into the nature of the complex processes involved in the growth and slow maturation of class identity among an increasing number of young Indonesians, male and female, within a tough, progressively urban and industrial milieu. While sustained industrialisation has only recently occurred, a more distinct working-class identity, full of contradictions, is in the process of formation. This process has been responsible for the conditions which have made organising among workers, even in the context of a vastly inhospitable political terrain, a much more viable activity in the 1990s than it was twenty years earlier.

Many caveats, however, were also advanced regarding the way in which the process of class formation is proceeding. Indeed considerable attention was given to the obstacles identified by Deyo with regard to the organisation of a working class emerging from low-wage, labour-intensive, export-oriented industries, with predominantly young, female, and highly mobile (between firms) workforces. Furthermore, the condition of chronic excess labour supply in Indonesia will continue to impose a serious constraining factor to the development of a substantial working-class movement, in spite of some tendencies of labour market tightening.[3]

In addition, the task of developing effective independent workers' organisations continues to be a daunting one, given the well-entrenched mechanisms of state control that essentially block off formal channels of political socialisation in general. The political environment is characterised, for example, by the absence of effective political parties generally, and any that would specifically find industrial workers a more or less natural constituency. Undoubtedly, there is much that can be said about the significance of less formal, everyday forms of political socialisation that take place in the homes and communities of workers, and the way in which they have contributed to independent, grassroots organising. However, the significance of the availability to workers of more formal and institutionalised channels of political socialisation should not be underestimated.

In lieu of such channels, the importance of labour-based NGOs in facilitating working-class organisation at the community level was suggested in the study. That such organisations (notwithstanding the trade union aspirations of the SBSI and others) have played a crucial role in the fledgling working-class movement is not altogether unusual. Non-trade union types of organisations, usually associated with the very early stage of industrialisation, and operating in repressive political environments, have often served as the basis for the later emergence of trade unionism.

In the case of contemporary Indonesia, the activities undertaken by workers in association with a wide array of NGOs have begun to pose a challenge to the rigidities of the exclusionary model. Questions, however, exist about the longer-term adequacy of these largely informal channels and vehicles in terms of developing a more fundamental challenge in the future. Though the informal organising that has often taken place in association with NGOs has been well-suited to the need of side-stepping stringent state regulations regarding trade union activities, the main problem that confronts contemporary activists is how to advance to a higher and more sophisticated level of organisation. This would imply the development of organisations which would have some resemblance to those that constituted the Korean *minju-no-jo* of the late 1980s, or perhaps, the KMU in the Philippines, whose presence was real and significant enough to deter efforts aimed toward their destruction via simple government fiat or repression.[4]

Meanwhile, state responses to escalating labour unrest and the proliferation of new forms of alternative labour organisation have been coloured by both a pragmatism that recognises the need for reforms and the strong penchant to opt for policies of outright repression. That the limited reformism of Batubara and Latief – like the security-oriented approach advocated by sections of ABRI – largely remains well within the confines of HIP, is a clear indication of the strong inclination within the state apparatus to maintain the status quo.

One external stimulus for reform in the labour area identified has been the international community of labour organisations, which is sometimes able to influence the policies of key governments on Indonesia. What underlies such overseas pressure, however, has not merely been lofty sentiments of 'international working-class solidarity', but the concrete interests of organised labour in such advanced industrial countries as the United States to, at the very least, slow down the process of relocation of manufacturing facilities to overseas sites which offer cheap labour and relatively trade union-free environments.

Nevertheless, the same development in the international division of labour is simultaneously a source of the essential weakness of labour as a class, globally, and the special difficulties confronted by fledgling working-class movements in very late industrialising countries: the international mobility of capital. Such international mobility, on the other hand, has been one of the important sources of strength of capital, particularly operating in labour intensive industries, forcing states to scramble to provide attractive conditions and environments of production, which often implies applying controls on organised labour. This is particularly the case in such countries as Indonesia, given that capital originating from the first NICs of East Asia – countries not particularly renowned for their pro-labour traditions – have predominated in the foreign investment in this sector. Meanwhile, Indonesian firms, long conditioned by an environment in which dealing with labour unrest has been the province of the state's repressive apparatus, have not seemed to develop an interest in reform in the labour area.

The discussion thus far seems to indicate that the odds at this particular historical juncture are heavily stacked against the fledgling independent working-class movement in Indonesia. Indeed, those that are involved in the battles of the working class, whether by choice or by force of circumstance, will need to be prepared for a protracted, even frustrating, struggle, perhaps devoid of clear-cut successes. This is not, however, an argument for the kind of structural 'fatalism' alluded to earlier in this study. It is further suggested here that, contingent on the 'preparedness' of actors engaged in the labour movement, opportunities may yet arise that could be exploited to build up a series of small, but not necessarily insignificant, advances.

For example, one 'window of opportunity' may be presented by the close of the Soeharto period. Indeed, whatever limited success that the labour movement can achieve in the short to medium term will in large part hinge on the ability significantly to improve organisational capacities to cope with a continually hostile but possibly increasingly unstable political environment. In the short to medium term, such an environment could in fact be produced by intra-elite struggles that take place in anticipation of, or following, the end of Soeharto's presidency. The uncertainty that current institutional arrangements of state–society relations can be sustained the way they are – indeed, the fragmentation of state power – can only work in favour of Indonesia's fledgling independent workers' movement.

Moreover, a turbulent process of political transition will almost certainly involve attempts by contending elites to mobilise sections of society, including workers, presently excluded from the officially delineated realm of politics. Under such a situation, it would be more likely, for example, for political parties and other organisations, representing particular sections of the elite, to attempt to enhance their position in the post-Soeharto political configuration by seeking a working-class constituency. Furthermore, how the process of transition affects the role of the military in politics is of crucial importance to labour, at the very least because of its direct implications to the security approach to industrial relations matters. Any retreat from the security approach will clearly create greater space for the development of an independent workers' movement. As discussed earlier, some have even envisaged an alliance between labour and disaffected members of the military, although we have also seen how the fundamental interests of the latter seem to ensure that any such alliance would be extremely fragile. Whatever alliances are forged, needless to say, the crucial problem is not only to be organised sufficiently as to be regarded a significant enough force to co-opt (the weak are only repressed, or worse, ignored), but also to be able actively and effectively to manipulate intra-elite struggles in a way that is amenable to the interests of the movement (as opposed merely to being exploited for the short-term political ends of particular elites).

Continuing industrialisation will ensure the presence of a growing and more aware constituency for the labour movement. There is no doubt that this constituency will continue to present pressures which may not be easily accommodated within the present framework of exclusionary corporatism. Moreover, though the employment of coercion and violence is still a strategy that the state can confidently use against organised labour, it will likely become a less viable one in the future. This in turn will affect business confidence in the coercive force of a state apparatus fixated on political stability, thus prompting more reformist inclinations in the business community in relation to labour unrest.

Perhaps the realistic question, therefore, is whether the struggles of the working class in Indonesia can eventually usher in a form of accommodation that embodies some of the more inclusionary features of the populist model, in place of the more confining and subordinating features of the exclusionary model. An alternative scenario would be a state of more-or-less permanent, or prolonged, tension in which labour is unable to win substantial concessions from state and capital, but in which its adversaries cannot subdue it completely either.

The supreme irony is that, if the exclusionary model unravels at all in very late industrialising countries like Indonesia, it may do so while organised labour in the advanced industrial countries continues its decline, perhaps forcing the social democratic accommodation eventually to evolve into something else. Some self-proclaimed 'visionaries' would hail the latter development as part of the dawning of a new 'post-industrial society' in which organised labour itself is virtually redundant. If such is the case, workers in the advanced industrial countries may very well see a part of their future reflected in the present conditions of currently industrialising 'Third World' countries – where organised labour has been historically weaker – rather than the other way around.

The latter observations suggest that Indonesian workers are on a historical trajectory which is in many ways substantially different from those of some of the earlier industrialisers. On the other hand, the trajectory that workers of the advanced industrialised countries are currently on, may lead to – if it has not already – a fresh round of struggles in which the main issue is the elimination or safeguarding of the rights, freedoms and privileges won in the prior struggles of organised labour.[5] In both cases, victories won – or losses suffered – today, will have an impact on the terms with which the struggles of tomorrow are fought. Notwithstanding the unfavourable terrain in which they have to operate, it is in this sense that workers in Indonesia, as anywhere else, can still make their own history.

Notes

1 INTRODUCTION

1 Data on the growth of an industrial working class, and on the importance of low-wage exports, is given in Chapter 6.
2 Deyo's case studies were South Korea, Taiwan, Singapore and Hong Kong.
3 One of the most important issues in Indonesian politics remains an uncertain political succession process (see Schwarz 1994).
4 Offe argues that these new social movements are primarily based on the 'new middle class' of 'human service professionals and the public sector', elements of the 'old' middle class, and on those peripheral to the labour market (students, etc.). Moreover, these movements do not practise class politics insofar as they tend to be 'highly class-unspecific' (Offe 1985: 828–833; see the discussion in Lebowitz 1991: 5).
5 Burawoy was specifically speaking of Marxist scholarship on the working class.
6 Block (1990: 118–119) recognises that debate over the issue of the efficient use of labour in the advanced industrial countries has been dominated by neo-classical assumptions. He observes that unions have been increasingly regarded as, at best, necessary evils because their role interferes with the allocation of resources by the market. This, Block adds, is the same argument that underlay the Combination Acts that outlawed trade unions in England in the early nineteenth century. He also suggests that research findings that point to the fact that unionised firms tend to be more productive than their non-unionised counterparts are likely to be ignored. Interestingly, there have been studies on very late industrialising countries, such as Malaysia, that have produced a similar result (e.g. Standing 1991).
7 A concept first popularised by Frobel *et al.* (1978; 1980) and treated critically by Jenkins and Southall. The latter, however, elects to substitute the term 'Changing International Division of Labour' or CIDL for NIDL.
8 Although Jenkins argues that the trade unions of the advanced industrialised countries have been misguided about the extent to which imports from 'less developed countries' have penetrated their markets, as well as about the implications of NIDL to employment and manufacturing decline (Jenkins 1984: 47–49, 53).
9 Interestingly, the mirror image of these assumptions is found in the endless supply of articles and features in the popular publications of the Indonesian media (e.g. *Matra, Eksekutif, Jakarta Jakarta*) which glorify the 'progressiveness' of entrepreneur-cum-yuppie lifestyles.
10 An exact date is now given to this abrupt end: 21 June 1994, when three popular news publications, *Tempo, Editor* and *Detik*, were banned by the government.

11 Thus, a recent debate in Indonesia, involving prominent local political scientists and the American Indonesianist, Bill Liddle, identified the weakness of the middle class as the source of the weakness of democracy in Indonesia (*Kompas* 5 June 1995). A dissenting view is given by Australian scholar Richard Robison, who argues that a middle class does exist in Indonesia, but one which is not necessarily interested in democracy (*Gatra* 8 July 1995: 35). Notably, the faith in the more or less democratic inclinations of the bourgeoisie and/or the middle class has been exhibited by scholars writing from a broadly Marxist perspective on Indonesia as much as by liberals. For examples, see Budiman (1990: 11) and Bulkin (1984: 3–22). Indeed, Rueschemeyer *et al.* (1992: 46–47) have rightly pointed out some of the similarities between the liberal and the Marxist literature on the politics of industrialisation.

12 This is not an argument that suggests the 'insignificance' of studying this more or less state-legitimated realm of politics, but one which implies a redefinition of the strict parameters of political inquiry.

13 Lloyd writes:

> if the urban poor of a Third World Metropolis see themselves as a proletariat, they will redouble their efforts in collective organisation; if they are seen as a proletariat by foreign or international working class movements, money and other assistance will be offered to them to pursue the revolutionary struggle.
>
> (Lloyd 1982: 12)

14 Resulting in at least one case (Erickson 1977), in the portrayal of workers as being at the total mercy of elite strategies (Munck 1988a: 9).

15 Haupt as quoted by Munck (1988a: 21).

16 In this sense, the position here on the relationship between structure and agency adheres to the spirit of Marx's own famous formulation:

> Men make their own history, but they do not make it just as they please; they do not make it under circumstances chosen by themselves, but under circumstances directly encountered, given, and transmitted from the past.
>
> (Marx 1963: 15)

> Indeed, according to one scholar, Marx's position was that 'The worker . . . is a political being with the capacity to resist oppression, and with the ability to speak back to history' (Chandoke 1994: 22).

17 Perhaps predictably, there has been a small resurgence in interest in the working class in Indonesia since the developments of the early 1990s – if the number of post-graduate students in various universities around the world tackling the subject is any indication.

18 One such criticism was conveyed by the labour activist Djati (1994).

19 The role of trade unions in the 'Third World' is, after all, one of the major preoccupations of students of labour movements (see Southall 1988a).

20 One such criticism was conveyed during a seminar on Indonesian labour at the Australian National University, Canberra, 28 August 1993.

21 Both objections were conveyed by labour activists in a seminar on 'Labour and Industrialisation', Jakarta, Yayasan SPES, 15 July 1994.

22 East Java and North Sumatra are discussed in the study in relation to the so-called 'Marsinah' case, and the Medan riots of April 1994.

2 THEORETICAL AND COMPARATIVE CONSIDERATIONS: LABOUR AND THE POLITICS OF INDUSTRIALISATION

1 The terms 'inclusionary' and 'exclusionary' corporatism were introduced by Stepan to look at the differences between Latin American countries. Within the former framework, according to Stepan, state elites attempt to 'incorporate salient working-class groups', while within the latter, they rely on coercive policies to deactivate and restructure them (Stepan 1978: 78).

2 Frenkel also discusses a variant in this approach which presents convergence with the Japanese model as the natural outcome of later industrialisation experiences.

3 The New Institutionalism owes an intellectual debt to both neo-classical economics and modernisation theory. Many of its tools and core concepts are derived from neo-classical economics, as is suggested by its origins in rational choice. At the same time, its concern with norms of behaviour is reminiscent of the structural-functional variant of the modernisation school of the 1950s and 1960s (for a good discussion of rational choice and the New Institutionalism, see Leys 1996, Chapter 4). Interestingly, the influence of rational choice is not confined to neo-classical economists or resurgent modernisation theorists. 'Rational Choice Marxism', for example, is to a large extent an attempt to apply such tools as mathematical 'game theory' – part of the rational choice repertoire – to address 'Marxian questions' (see Roemer 1986 and Elster 1986). In this approach ' . . . class membership becomes an endogenous feature of agents: people are not born into classes . . . but choose their own class position as a rational (i.e. preference maximising) response to their wealth constraints' (Roemer 1994: xi). For a critique, see Wood (1989; 1995: 110–121); for a defence, see Wright (1994).

4 Kurth reminds us, however, that 'in both the late and the late-late industrialisers, there have been monopolistic compacts among industrial producers, organised direction by investment banks, and substantial government assistance with subsidies and tariffs' (Kurth 1979: 323).

5 Therborn (1977) suggests that the dismissal of the role of the working class in Moore's analysis was due to his greater interest in bourgeois revolutions than the advance of democracy. Establishing a fixed set of criteria for democracy – including the attainment of universal suffrage – Therborn argues that democracy always came at a far later date than the establishment of bourgeois dominance over politics.

6 The proposition is that liberal democracies came into existence only when the working class had been strong and organised enough to press for the extension of political and economic rights, often beyond what the bourgeoisie were willing to support. Indeed, they also argue that the bourgeoisie, once successful in wresting political power from the traditional oligarchy, rarely fight for the extension of democracy after it has secured its own place (Rueschemeyer *et al.* 1992: 46).

7 Interestingly, in a more recent co-authored work on the 'democratisation' of Latin America, O'Donnell takes a position which emphasises the role of political actors (O'Donnell and Schmitter 1986).

8 It is possible to bring historical agency 'back in' without adopting the approach of rational choice, including its Marxist variant, represented in the work of Roemer, Elster and, to an extent, Przeworski (1991). Rational choice proponents, influenced by the economist Mancur Olson (1965), place the 'rational' weighing of cost and benefits by individuals at the centre of research into collective action. The methodological individualism employed substantially

modifies the traditional Marxist position on the social formation of the individual by shifting attention to choices made by the latter. The way rational choice theorists do this, however, reveals a preoccupation with a much too narrow 'economic' model of human nature (Wood 1989: 84) that forms the basis of an uncritical and a-historical view of what constitutes 'rationality'. There is no place here for passions, anger or zeal.

9 For a broad discussion on the issue, see Kurth (1979). In Russia, where much credit for the limited industrialisation which took place before the Bolshevik Revolution goes to foreign capital, no significant bourgeoisie independent of the state ever emerged.

10 Of the 'roughly five million occupied' people in 1801, two-thirds were wage earners, or partly dependent on wage labour. About a quarter of these were employed in manufacturing and mining, and 10 per cent in trade and transport. Even the large agricultural population was involved in industry as seasonal labourers (Phillips 1989: 14).

11 For example, while strikes were effectively legalised in Britain in 1824, with the repeal of the Combination Act, workers in France and Germany had to cope with the outlawing of strikes and workers' organisations. In France, the law against association was passed in 1791, and with additions that made it even more repressive until 1848, peaceful protest was effectively prevented. Thus, workers had to turn either to full-scale insurrection, or to revolutionary secret societies. In Germany, all forms of labour organisation were viewed with suspicion by authorities throughout the 1850s and 1860s. The semi-authoritarian Wilhelmine Empire also promulgated an anti-socialist law which was in operation from 1878 to 1890. Under this law, socialist literature was banned and labour leaders were imprisoned or exiled. Even after 1890, representatives of the German working class were harassed and forms of anti-socialist censorship remained (Geary 1981: 60–63).

12 In contrast to Britain, France had only experienced a great burst of industrial growth in the 1830s, with textiles developing in some areas and coal as well as metallurgical industries developing in others. Still, throughout the nineteenth and early twentieth centuries, France had a large and backward artisan sector. Even in 1914, 60 per cent of the population was classified as 'rural', while four million people were employed by industry in 1890 and five million by 1914. Trade unions were illegal until 1884 (Magraw 1989: 49–50), although, by 1848, various working-class organisations, in the form of clubs and societies, had been established (Geary 1981: 42, 44).

13 In the German states, rapid industrialisation only occurred after 1848, but at a quite exceptional rate. It was largely based on the coal, iron and steel industries where workers were concentrated in giant companies. In 1870, half of the active population was employed in agriculture, but by 1913, this had been cut to only one-third. In 1882, there were 6.4 million people employed in 'industry and manufacture', rising to 11.3 million in 1907. The trade and transport sector also grew rapidly (Geary 1989b: 102).

14 It may be fruitful to make a cursory comparison with Russia, where the social-democratic accommodation did not emerge. Here industrialisation came even later, and was more uneven. Most of the Russian population was not yet touched by industrialisation by the time of the great upheavals of 1848 (Geary 1981: 25–26). What industrialisation took place by the 1860s and 1870s was largely dependent on foreign capital and the tsarist state. Nevertheless, a growing number of industrial workers eventually came to be concentrated in giant establishments in the larger cities. As Moore observed, the repressive policies of the tsarist state not only heavily influenced the rate and character of

Russian industrial growth but also contributed to the radicalisation of Russian industrial workers in the early twentieth century. These policies, according to Moore, ensured that more moderate and reformist elements within the working-class movement were eventually sidelined by revolutionary elements (Moore 1978: 357–375).

15 To continue the comparison with Russia, the social-democratic accommodation did not present itself as a strong possibility to the weaker working-class of this country, which confronted an authoritarian state, a small bourgeoisie dependent on that state, and the dominance of foreign capital. Hence, the working-class movement was encouraged to adopt a more revolutionary political strategy.

16 These basically conform to what Rueschemeyer *et al.* have called 'formal democracy' (1992: 10).

17 These tensions are rooted in the fiscal crisis of the state, and growing unemployment in the advanced capitalist countries, which many suggest is partly owing to the greater international mobility of capital. Thus the survival of this model of accommodation, in its current form, is more under threat than it has ever been. As mentioned earlier, a kind of neo-liberal orthodoxy has emerged in which the legitimacy of trade unions is being increasingly questioned, thereby peripheralising organised labour as a social force. At the same time, the way that the nature of work itself is being reconstituted, in part through the introduction of flexible production systems, also undermines the strength of organised labour. How the social-democratic accommodation will change, however, is clearly beyond the scope of this current work. For a provocative analysis of the case of Britain, see the first Chapter in Panitch (1986).

18 In Brazil, factory employment, totalling 380,000 by 1925, only accounted for 3.7 per cent of total employment. In Argentina, where industrialisation was most pronounced and the working-class movement, strongest, only 340,000 people were employed in factories by 1925, accounting for 8.3 per cent of the economically active population (Collier and Collier 1991: 67).

19 The 'depoliticisation' that to an extent was attempted by Vargas is demonstrated in the purging of Communists in 1935.

20 Even the process of collective bargaining was completely taken over by the Ministry of Labour and Social Welfare (Alexander 1963: 164–165).

21 Of course, we can only fruitfully speak of this in relative terms. It is significant that in Imperial Germany, at the same time as the massive industrial expansion of Leipzig, Dresden, Chemnitz, Berlin and Hamburg, much of the country 'south of the River Main remained untouched by industrialisation, as did vast eastern provinces of Posen and Pomerania' (Geary 1989a: 6).

22 The possible exception is Bismarckian Germany.

23 Frobel *et al.* (1978, 1980) suggest that these countries embarked on the export-led strategy at a particularly appropriate time as such industries were then becoming increasingly uncompetitive in the advanced capitalist countries because of continually rising wage levels. This in turn reflected the success of the working class in the latter countries in claiming a larger share of the social surplus. They also essentially argue that the shift of capital to areas in the world providing cheap labour has resulted in the industrialisation of the global periphery and the simultaneous de-industrialisation of the core economies. For a critique, see Jenkins (1984 and 1991).

24 A fragmentation which is rooted in allegiance or opposition to Chinese communism.

25 Even by 1983, workers in production-related occupations already constituted 29 per cent of the total labour force in South Korea, 40 per cent in Taiwan, and 38

per cent in Singapore (Deyo *et al.* 1987: 50).

26 In the case of Hong Kong, this issue is of course complicated by the imminent transfer of sovereignty to China.

27 Although the movement, before the 1970s, had only been legal for short periods of time (Brown and Frenkel 1993: 82). There was, for example, a long period of illegality between 1958 and 1972.

28 It is for this reason, among others, that state-sector unions in Thailand opposed privatisation (Brown and Frenkel 1993: 101–102).

29 Deyo contrasts this with the way that flexible production systems in the advanced industrial countries have resulted in greater workforce participation in firm-level management (Deyo 1995: 2). Notably, flexible production systems have yet to make a mark in Indonesia.

30 Although Manning and Jayasuriya suggest that a gradual tightening of the labour market in Indonesia is already taking place, as the absolute numbers of workers employed in agriculture has declined in Java, and steadied in the outer islands (Manning and Jayasuriya 1996:32).

31 Though the growth of the industrial work force, for the most part, has been more gradual and modest. In Thailand for example, manufacturing employment rose from 3.4 per cent of the workforce in 1960 to 10 per cent in the end of the 1980s (Brown and Frenkel 1993: 85). In Malaysia, however, employment in manufacturing accounted for about one-third of the labour force in 1990 (Arudsothy and Littler 1993: 109). For data on Indonesia, see Chapter 6.

32 Between 1971 and 1985, the composition of employment in agriculture, industry and services was virtually unchanged (Hutchison 1993: 207).

33 Thus, in spite of the suppression of the *Hukbalahap* and the dismantling of communist labour organisations, as well as stringent anti-labour laws under Marcos in the 1970s, large sections of the labour movement remain politicised. A state-imposed peak labour organisation, the Trades Union Congress of the Philippines (TUCP) was created by Marcos in 1975, but challenged by the establishment of the KMU, a federation of more radically inclined, independent unions (Muntz 1992: 266). Labour played a part in the ascension of Corazon Aquino to power in 1986, although organised labour benefited little from her period in power (Hutchison 1993: 195–196, 202–208).

3 HISTORICAL LEGACIES: WORKING-CLASS POLITICS IN PRE-NEW ORDER INDONESIA

1 On the general 'anarchy' of the 1950s, as portrayed in the official orthodoxy, see Bourchier (1994b).

2 See the superficial way the subject is treated in SPSI (1990a: 2–3).

3 The KBKI was to suffer from internal divisions. One section already broke formal links with the PNI in 1959, which espoused President Soekarno's 'Marhaenism' or 'Socialism *à la* Indonesia'. This section kept the name KBKI, and was led by Minister of Labour Ahem Erningpradja, who maintained good relations with the military. Another section took the name KBM (*Kesatuan Buruh Marhaenist* ; Marhaenist Workers' Union), and emerged as the formal PNI union. It also adopted a line which was more sympathetic to SOBSI (KBM 1965: 7–9; Hawkins 1963b: 96; Hasibuan 1968: 135–136).

4 The KBSI claimed to be independent of political parties; Interview with Koeswari, former deputy secretary-general, 9 February 1994. Still, there were close, if informal, links to the PSI (Tedjasukmana 1958: 102–106).

5 The plantation-based economy was not confined to Java. North Sumatra, most

notably, where Javanese workers were imported in large numbers to work in agricultural estates, emerged as another centre (see Stoler 1985).

6   These included those working in sugar refineries, tea and coffee factories, etc., which 'form part of an agricultural estate' (Sitsen 1943: 14).

7   This followed a period of rapid growth of secondary industry from 1935 to 1939 (Sitsen 1943: 39), producing consumer goods for domestic consumption. Speaking of manufacturing workers, Sitsen writes:

> The majority . . . worked in small shops, either built on to the home of the owner of the business, or built on his land . . . probably 40–45 per cent of the total number of workers lived in villages. Besides these, there is a group . . . probably about 40 per cent of the total, who sell their products wholly or principally to middlemen, while 15 to 20 per cent work in hand operated factories with less than 50 workmen . . . only the factory workers can be considered actual wage earners.
>
> (Sitsen 1943: 23)

8   According to the 1930 census, 63,000 people were employed in the strategic 'railroads and tramways' sector.

9   The union was established, at first, by the European workers of three Semarang-based private railway companies. Earlier, in 1905, European workers of the state railway company had also formed a union (Ingleson 1981b: 53).

10   It was originally called the *Sarekat Dagang Islam*. The word *dagang*, meaning 'trade', was subsequently dropped.

11   Multiple membership in various organisations was then the norm. Reflecting an interesting aspect of the dynamics of the nationalist movement at that stage, the PKI itself, in a sense, had originally grown out of the SI, in that it was established in 1920 by individuals who were simultaneously affiliated to the latter's 'Red' wing, and the ISDV. The ISDV, in turn, was formed in 1914 by the VSTP leader, Sneevliet (McVey 1965: 14). The 'Red' SI was opposed to the 'Green' or more purely Islamic SI, led by Agus Salim, Tjokroaminoto, Abdoel Moeis and others. The 'cleansing' of 'Red' elements took place in 1921 (McVey 1965: 104–105).

12   Sitsen suggests that there were just under 73,000 trade-union members in 1935 and under 110,000 in 1939 (Sitsen 1943: 47). This was, however, as we shall see, long after the trade-union movement's political role had diminished.

13   As Reid (1974: 6) suggests:

> The importance of Marxism for Indonesian nationalists is difficult to exaggerate . . . . Marxist ideas were influential through the whole spectrum of politically active Intellectuals. Their appeal rested primarily on the analysis by Lenin and Bukharin of imperialism as the last stage of capitalism. This provided an intellectually satisfying rationale to deeply-rooted Indonesian hopes for an end to the seemingly impregnable colonial system. For the more westernised it also offered a non-racial basis for anti-colonialism, vividly demonstrated by the support and sympathy Indonesian nationalists found from Dutch Marxists in Indonesia (before 1926) and in Holland. Moreover, in the period up to about 1924, when the colonial government could be considered to be carrying out its relatively progressive 'ethical' policy, Marxism appeared to identify more surely than nationalism the real enemy – private Dutch commercial, planting and capitalist interests. No philosophy of liberalism is likely to emerge from a people without a bourgeoisie . . . . Even those who found a clear philosophical basis for anti-Marxism in modernist Islam were inclined to argue that socialist ideals were prefigured in Islam.

Tedjasukmana (1958: 63) remarks that the main trade unions saw themselves as 'schools of socialism'.

14 In March 1921, Agus Salim and Semaoen drew up a program for Sarekat Islam which appeared to accommodate Islamic and socialist principles (McVey 1965:96–97).

15 There were several attempts to bring together the numerous unions into a single federation. The aim was temporarily achieved in 1919 with the establishment of the *Persatuan Pergerakan Kaum Buruh* (PPKB), which represented virtually all of the existing trade unions, including those linked to the SI and the ISDV. The founders of this federation, originally envisaged a 'revolutionary socialist federation of labour unions' which would comprise the upper chamber of a true parliament, while the lower chamber would be comprised of political parties. Sosrokardono, the SI and PPPB leader, commented that if successful, the federation would be able to achieve self-government for Indonesians, and establish a socialist society (McVey 1965: 44).

Such amalgamations, however, lived a precarious life, and the PPKB eventually split into two when Semaoen took his followers into a new federation in 1921, the Revolutionary Trade Union Central (Tedjasukmana 1958: 10–11). This left the PPKB's leadership under more moderate leaders who favoured political representation of labour, social legislation and adequate wage regulation (Hawkins 1963b: 91), but opposed revolutionary class struggle. Again on the initiative of Semaoen, the two federations were eventually reunited under the name of the *Persatuan Vakbonden Hindia* (PVH), which included the VSTP, PPPB and PFB (SOBSI 1958: 48).

16 Both Tedjasukmana (1958: 12–13) and Shiraishi (1990: 241–242) argue that the strike was deliberately provoked by the colonial government to gain a pretence to crush the VSTP.

17 Later, the party will regard the failure of the 1926–27 uprising as the product of poor planning and coordination, and of a lack of a program that linked the demands of workers with that of the peasantry who 'were more exploited' (Aidit n.d.: 61).

18 Although the BBI was more of a mass organisation than a trade union, it was able to organise a labour congress in November 1945 (Tedjasukmana 1958: 18), which established the *Partai Buruh Indonesia* or Indonesian Labour Party.

The participation of workers' organisations in the nationalist revolution helped to legitimise their role in national politics in the immediate post-colonial period. Sandra, for example, mentions the emergence of worker-based fighting units (*Lasykar Buruh Indonesia*) which took an active part in the revolution, particularly in the defence of workplaces (Sandra 1961: 66). Partly because of the role workers played, forty trade-union leaders were appointed to the provisional national parliament in 1947 via a presidential decree (Tedjasukmana 1958: 24).

19 One source of tension was organised labour's rejection of the government's pledge to restore foreign property. Labour leaders viewed take-overs of foreign enterprises as necessary and opposed the idea of eventually returning large-scale export sector enterprises to foreign hands. Tensions between state and labour also emerged in mid-1948, when a PKI-dominated coalition of Left-wing groups, the *Front Demokrasi Rakyat* (People's Democratic Front), which included SOBSI, organised strike action among urban and agricultural workers, which President Soekarno denounced as being unpatriotic (King 1982: 96–97).

20 Supporters of industrial or 'vertical' unions wanted to establish unions at the national level which would then extend themselves downward to the regions. Supporters of the 'craft' or 'horizontal' idea wanted to establish grassroots

unions first which would then form some kind of loose federation. Ultimately, their aim was to form a political party. This aim was opposed by supporters of the 'vertical' concept (Brown 1994: 82–83).

21 Legge (1993: 113) writes that SOBSI had actually developed out of the oil workers' union, SBM (*Serikat Buruh Minyak*), which was organised in the 1940s primarily by Djohan Sjahroezah, a follower of the socialist Sjahrir. Sjahroezah was active in Sjahrir's 'underground' movement against the Japanese occupation of 1942–45, and was notable for his grassroots organising. When the Left parties led by Sjahrir, which included his own Socialist Party, the Labour Party and the PKI, split, Sjahrir formed the Indonesian Socialist Party (PSI), which Sjahroezah joined. But SOBSI clearly came to be within the orbit of the PKI, not of Sjahrir's more moderate socialist group. Sjahroezah was reportedly also responsible in the 1940s for the initial organising of dock-workers and seamen, as well as the peasantry, He was helped by some individuals (including Kamaruzzaman and Munir) who would later be associated with the PKI. Interview with a former official of the SOBSI-affiliated seamen and dockworkers union, the SBPP, 21 May 1995, in the Netherlands.

22 Another competitor was the *Gabungan Serikat Buruh Revolusioner Indonesia* (GASBRI; Amalgamated Revolutionary Trade Unions of Indonesia) led by Tan Malaka, a former PKI leader who headed a rival grouping of communists.

23 Tedjasukmana notes that the SBII rejects 'the theory of the class struggle' and stands for cooperation with management in improving the welfare of workers, though many members regarded themselves as 'religious socialists' (Tedjasukmana 1958: 46–47).

24 Prior to this, local military commanders had forbidden strikes in what they regarded as vital enterprises (Meek 1956: 153).

25 In fact there was an increasing push in the late 1950s and early 1960s for the development of upstream, import-substitution industry projects, primarily predicated on nationalist sentiment that emphasised economic self-reliance. Thus, a blueprint was produced in the 1950s for what Robison calls 'state-led capitalist development', which involved the use of foreign-exchange earnings from the export of primary commodities for investments in industry, combined with state protection and credit for national industrial capital. Overseas borrowing was also undertaken for investment in such industries as steel mills and shipyards (Robison 1990: 39).

26 The independence of SOBSI from the PKI was argued recently by Razif (1994b). The informal, though real, status of the link between them, however, was discussed, among others, in Tedjasukmana (1958: 96–102).

27 The presence of party apparatchik in leadership positions may have increased in the late 1950s. Interview with former official of the *Serikat Buruh Pelabuhan dan Pelayaran* (SBPP), 21 May 1994, in the Netherlands.

28 This was confirmed during interviews with a former official of the SBPP, 21 May 1994, in the Netherlands; and with a former official of the *Serikat Buruh Kereta Api,* (SBKA; the Railway Workers' Union), one of the best organised of the SOBSI unions, 13 July 1994.

29 It must be remembered too that the leaders of the SOBSI constituent unions had the task of maintaining the support of rank-and-file workers, who were, perhaps not surprisingly, less interested in some of the party's 'lofty' ideas about revolution or socialism; Interview with a former official of the SBKA, 13 July 1994. A former official of the SBPP claims that he only ever received rudimentary instruction in Marxism-Leninism; Interview, 21 May 1994.

30 Data from Hawkins (1963a: 260), based on 1958 claims.

31 *Himpunan Serikat-Serikat Buruh Indonesia* (Federation of Indonesian Trade

Unions). Though 'Marxist' (Tedjasukmana 1958: 61), it was later linked with the army-connected IPKI.

32 *Sentral Organisasi Serikat Buruh Republik Indonesia* (Central Workers' Organisation of the Indonesian Republic). Though upholding the 'class struggle' (Tedjasukmana 1958: 62), it was a SOBSI/PKI foe.

33 *Gabungan Organisasi Buruh Sjarikat Islam Indonesia* (Amalgamated Indonesian Islamic Workers' Organisation), linked to *the Partai Sjarikat Islam Indonesia*, a lowly SI descendant.

34 The *Gabungan Serikat Buruh Indonesia* (Amalgamated Indonesian Trade Unions), based on civil servants (Tedjasukmana 1958: 62).

35 The *Kongres Buruh Islam Merdeka* (Independent Islamic Labour Congress) was formed in 1957 by dissident SBII members (Tedjasukmana 1958: 27).

36 The *Serikat Buruh Kristen Indonesia* (Indonesian Christian Trade Union).

37 Data from Hawkins (1963b: 106), citing Department of Labour documents.

38 All of the above points were confirmed in interviews with former officials of the SBPP and SBKA; respectively 21 May 1994 and 13 July 1994.

39 This point was confirmed by Agus Sudono, formerly of the GASBIINDO; Interview, 18 January 1994.

40 Internal 'class struggle' was also rejected by the KBKI which urged the direction of all hostility toward 'foreign exploiters and oppressors' (Tedjasukmana 1958: 60).

41 Agus Sudono characterised the difference between SOBSI and the non-communist unions, particularly GASBIINDO, as follows: the former viewed capitalists as enemies in the class struggle, while the latter thought that capitalists and workers could work together for the interests of the nation as a whole. The latter tended to view strikes as detrimental to that interest, while the former actively sought confrontation with employers; Interview with Agus Sudono, 18 January 1994.

42 Although it is highly unlikely that the vast majority of the rank-and-file workers of a SOBSI-affiliated union espoused an atheistic world-view. In fact, the SOBSI and PKI leaderships would have easily risked alienating a large section of its workers' constituency by an open advocacy of Godlessness given the cultural context. Interview with former SBKA official, 13 July 1994.

43 These views were expressed during interviews with Koeswari, former deputy secretary general of the KBSI (9 February 1994); a high-ranking Ministry of Labour official of the early 1960s (24 February 1994); and an official of the PSI in the 1950s (9 February 1994). The last two prefer to remain anonymous. That the KBSI spent most of its energies on such political objectives perhaps reflects most clearly the mood of the times, as the KBSI's official position was to develop a workers' movement that was *independent* of the dictates of political parties.

44 The military actively courted the individual rivals of SOBSI. A 1957 KBSI internal document reports an invitation from the central army headquarters to discuss the possibility of cooperation between the military and labour. The document reports that no decision was made during the meeting, but that the idea of such cooperation was not rejected outright (KBSI 1957: 14–15). Eventually, such cooperation was to take place through military dominated labour institutions which are discussed below.

45 On these changes, and particularly on the period of the liberal parliamentary system, see Feith (1962).

46 Intended to weaken the position of political parties, the system encouraged mass-based organisations to take up political representation functions and to limit their association with political parties. Significantly, in this new scheme of

things, the army won a greater political role for itself. For example, it was provided representation in Soekarno's National Council, which consisted primarily of representatives of 'functional groups' (workers, peasants, entrepreneurs, youth, religious scholars, etc.).

47 According to Agus Sudono, the non-communist unions were alarmed at SOBSI's actions as they were caught unprepared. Fearful of growing SOBSI power they encouraged General Nasution, then army chief-of-staff, to persuade Soekarno that the army, not the unions, should take control of the seized enterprises; Interview, 18 January 1994. Another version was recounted by a former high-ranking Ministry of Labour official – who prefers to remain anonymous. In this version, the army had aimed to force Soekarno to hand over managerial control over these enterprises even before the SOBSI-led takeover, and that the takeover had actually facilitated the achievement of that aim; Interview 24 February 1994.

48 Boileau mentions that SOKSI initially drew much of its strength from the state plantation sector and was fearful of PKI competition in these sectors (Boileau 1983: 40–41). Indeed, SOKSI organised the formation of enterprise-level worker organisations called PTK (*Persatuan Tenaga Karyawan*; Union of *Karyawan* Forces) in the state companies which it managed (King 1982: 117; Reeve 1985: 192). Hasibuan suggests that those who joined SOBSI included enterprise managers who were anti-communists; those who did so because they regarded the army as capable of providing political protection and patronage; and those who 'would always play it safe'. He suggests that there was pressure from above to join SOKSI (Hasibuan 1968: 112).

49 For a discussion of this see Leclerc (1972); also see Hasibuan (1968: 142).

50 SOKSI deliberately created organisations whose names were similar to PKI mass organisations. For example, its women's organisation was called GERWASI, its artists' group was called LEKRI, and its peasants' group was called RTI (the PKIs were, respectively, GERWANI, LEKRA and BTI). The name 'SOKSI' itself was a clear jibe at the PKI's SOBSI. This was part of the overtly confrontational strategy that SOKSI adopted against the PKI; Interview with Soehardiman, 25 January 1994. Soehardiman also writes that 'SOKSI had taken up the policy that ideology must be confronted by ideology, physical force by physical force, doctrine by doctrine, and organisation by organisation' (Soehardiman 1993: 123).

51 He was to play an important role in the New Order's official labour movement. Adolf Rachman was a close associate of Soehardiman, founder of SOKSI, and was by the latter's own admission, his 'teacher' on labour matters (Soehardiman 1993: 112).

52 The BKS-BUMIL was one instrument the military was using to encourage the amalgamation of the existing trade unions (see BKS-BUMIL 1961b).

53 Interview with Soehardiman, 25 January 1994.

54 In an address to a 1960 SBII Congress, General Nasution, then Minister of Defence and Security/Chief of Staff of the Army, reminded participants that he had imposed severe restrictions on the right to strike because 'consultation is a way to resolve labour disputes', foreshadowing the army-dominated New Order's dismissal of the right to strike. See Nasution (1960: 10).

As we shall see, the vision of harmonious relations between employers and workers, under the guardianship of the state, was to develop into the doctrine of Pancasila Industrial Relations in the New Order. The latter is often presented by state officials as being the product of Indonesia's indigenous culture, and contrasted with 'foreign' liberalism and communism. Bourchier (1996: 211–212), however, suggests that the fundamentals of HIP were actually borrowed from Catholic doctrine, as espoused by the SOB Pantjasila, because it too emphasises industrial harmony. Whatever the cultural roots of HIP may be, we have already seen that opposition to the idea of class conflict was a characteristic of various labour organisations linked to political parties whose main constituencies were not labour.

55 Source: King (1982: 115).

4 RECONSTITUTING ORGANISED LABOUR: THE GENESIS OF NEW ORDER LABOUR POLICY

1 He quotes Schmitter, who writes that there is

> a consistent, interdependent and relatively stable set of political structures and practices that permit existing elites to manage, guide or manipulate the transformation of economic and social structures at minimal cost to themselves in terms of power, wealth and status. These regimes seek not so much to arrest change – in fact, they often promote it – as they seek to control its consequences from above. By changing, they avoid change.
>
> (Schmitter 1973: 205)

2 Because of the Old Order's catastrophic record on economic management, the New Order has legitimised its rule by promising to deliver economic development. At the same time, schemes which represented an 'egalitarian' bent, and which were promoted during the Old Order, fared badly in the early New Order. For example, land-reform policy – heavily supported by the PKI and its peasant organisation, the BTI – was one that was promptly forgotten. Enterprise Councils, discussed in Chapter 3, were also discredited for having been infiltrated by the SOBSI/PKI and were thus, by 1967, in limbo (Reeve 1985: 282).

3 Interview with Adolf Rachman, 28 June 1994.

4 Interview, 20 June 1994.

5 This is confirmed in interviews with Sjaiful DP, a former official of GASBI-INDO, on 25 March 1994; and with Sutanto Martoprasono, a former official of the SARBUMUSI, on 8 June 1994.

6 Interview, 8 June 1994.

7 Erningpradja's role in the attempt to form OPPI, for example, was noted in the previous Chapter.

8 Interview, 8 June 1994.

9 The government electoral vehicle won 62.8 per cent of the vote (Amal 1994: 217).

10 Interview with Sjaiful, 25 March 1994.

11 Interview with Sutanto, 8 June 1994.

12 Interview with Adolf Rachman, 28 June 1994.

13 Interview, 18 January 1994.

14 Interview with Adolf Rachman, 28 June 1994. Here we see the beginnings of an intermittent rivalry with Agus Sudono for the leadership of the labour movement in the New Order, which would go on well into the 1980s.

15 Significantly, SOBSI was a member of the rival, communist-dominated international trade-union organisation, the World Federation of Trade Unions (WFTU) (Tedjasukmana 1958: 53). The SOBSI leader, Nyono, was a vice-president of the organisation.

16 Sudono's MASYUMI, like the PSI, was effectively banned by Soekarno for alleged complicity in regional rebellions in Sumatra and Sulawesi. According to

Sudono, he was encouraged to take up an active role in the ICFTU by Ali Moertopo and Mohammad Sadli; Interview, 18 January 1994.

17 Goldberg was the author of a manuscript which was virulently anti-SOBSI and PKI, and very sympathetic to the non-communist labour organisations (Goldberg 1952).

18 Agus Sudono, for example, took a course in 1957 in 'Trade Union Leadership and Industrial Relations' at the American University in Washington D.C. and at St John College in Annapolis (Sudono 1985: 63).

19 Interview with Sjaiful, 25 March 1994.

20 Interview with Awaloeddin Djamin (20 June 1994), who still chairs the foundation at the time of writing.

21 Interviews with Valentin Suazo and Dieter Bielenstein, respectively AAFLI and FES representatives in Jakarta; 22 December 1993 and 28 February 1994.

22 Interview, 20 June 1994.

23 There were 21 member organisations of the MPBI: GASBIINDO (Muslim), KUBU Pantjasila (military-linked), PGRI (Teachers' Union), KONGKARBU (SOKSI-GOLKAR), GOBSII (Muslim), KBM (Nationalist), SARBUMUSI (Muslim), KBIM (Muslim), SSPTT (Postal, Telegraph and Telecommunications Workers' Union), PERKABI (KOSGORO-GOLKAR), KESPEKRI (Protestant), FBI INDONESIA (Muslim), PORBISI (Muslim), KBKI (Nationalist), SOB Pantjasila (Catholic), SOBRI (Socialist), GERBUMI (Muslim), GSBI (Socialist), IKM (Muslim), KBSI (Socialist) and KEKARBU (MKGR-GOLKAR).

24 The forced estrangement of state employees from trade unions signalled by the formation of these organisations was in fact a gradual process. In 1967, Minister of the Interior General Amir Machmud had established the precursor of KORPRI, an association of employees of the Department of the Interior, called KOKARMENDAGRI. Soon other KOKAR were established in various departments until KORPRI was decreed by President Soeharto, amalgamating all the KOKAR. The purpose of KORPRI was to ensure the 'monoloyalty' of state employees and ensure electoral success for GOLKAR.

25 Interview with Adolf Rachman, 28 June 1994.

26 Interview with Sjaiful, 25 March 1994.

27 This is confirmed in an interview with Sjaiful on 25 March 1994. Awaloeddin Djamin provides an interesting case which reveals the same situation. Unable to decide among themselves on who would be the Indonesian representative to an ILO conference in the late 1960s, labour leaders asked Awaloeddin, then Minister of Manpower, to make the decision for them. Interview with Awaloeddin Djamin, 20 June 1994.

28 Interview with Sutanto, 8 June 1994; and with Adolf Rachman, 28 June 1994.

29 Interview, 28 June 1994. Another idea expressed at the time was of the creation of three federations, respectively representing GOLKAR and the newly created PPP and PDI. This idea was advocated by Rasyid Sutan Radjamas of the KBM (SPSI 1990a: 14).

30 Interview with Sutanto, 8 June 1994; and with Adolf Rachman, 28 June 1994.

31 Rachman thinks that his own efforts at developing a more united labour front were ignored by Ali Moertopo. According to Rachman, he was opposed to Moertopo's efforts, and as a result, was labelled an 'obstacle'. Summoned by Moertopo to his office, he claims he was forced to lend grudging support to the process initiated by OPSUS. Interview with Adolf Rachman, 28 June 1994.

32 See 'Deklarasi Persatuan Buruh Seluruh Indonesia', 20 February 1973, as published in SPSI (1993a).

33 A board of advisers was also set up, comprising of Sadli, Awaloeddin, Subroto,

Oesman, as well as the economic technocrat Sumarlin, BAPPENAS official Sayuti Hasibuan, and the engineer Suhartojo.

34 Sadli himself attended, ostensibly as a member of the FBSI's new advisory board. However, as mentioned earlier, he was a key member of the team of economic technocrats responsible for the New Order's economic restructuring program of the late 1960s. Sudono credits Sadli for being very supportive of efforts to unite organised labour, thus placing him squarely on the side of Ali Moertopo's OPSUS on the issue. This reveals the degree to which different factions of the political elite were in agreement about the necessity of reconstituting and domesticating organised labour, even though they might have disagreed on other matters.

35 Source: Sudono (1981: 17–18) and Sjaiful DP.

36 This was the GOLKAR element which was officially responsible for cooperatives and entrepreneurial activities (Soehardiman 1993: 174–175; Boileau 1983: 61–64).

37 Even Agus Sudono does not deny the central directing role that OPSUS played in the process. Interview, 18 January 1994.

38 Interview with Agus Sudono, 18 January 1994.

39 Again by his own account, Sudono had turned down a position at the ILO office in Geneva, offered to him in late 1971. He did so because 'a close aide' of Soeharto informed him that he was being groomed to lead a labour federation which was soon to be established (Sudono 1985:39–41). It is not unreasonable to suspect that this 'close aide' would have been an OPSUS member, if not Ali Moertopo himself, then near the zenith of political influence.

5 POLITICS AND IDEOLOGY: EXCLUSIONARY CORPORATISM AT WORK

1 Freeman (1993), noted above, also considers the 'communist threat' an important factor.

2 For a contending view on the roots of integralism in Indonesia see Marsillam Simandjuntak (1994).

3 In 1969, oil and LNG taxes only constituted 19.7 per cent of total revenue; in 1974/75, after the oil 'boom', they constituted 48.4 per cent; in 1981/82 they constituted 61.7 per cent of total revenue and 70 per cent of domestic revenue. State expenditure through the development budget increased from Rp 450 billion in 1974/75 to Rp 6,940 billion in 1981/82 (Robison 1990: 103–104).

4 In late 1995 the SPSI yet again changed its name to become the FSPSI, or SPSI Federation (see Chapter 8).

5 KOPKAMTIB was the Command for the Restoration of Order and Security, a supra-national security agency intertwined with the structure of the military, set up in the early New Order. BAKORSTRANAS is the National Strategic Coordinating Body.

6 The use of capital letters, resulting in a conscious reification, is often contained in actual official documents.

7 'Keputusan Seminar Nasional Hubungan Perburuhan Pancasila', Jakarta 4–7 December 1974, in Sudono (1978: 175).

8 In a recent study, Bourchier (1996) has argued that the New Order's integralism owes more to nineteenth-century European – primarily German and Dutch – intellectual streams than to indigenous cultural traditions, being initially incorporated into conservative nationalist thought during colonial times by aristocratic legal scholars. The subject is of course too complex to be dealt with

here. But if Bourchier is right, the implication is that the whole business of identifying 'innate' Indonesian cultural traits, insofar as they are supposed to influence forms of social and political organisation, is quite contrived.

9   Agus Sudono claims that he conceived the idea of Pancasila Labour Relations; see interview in *Prisma*, no.3 1992: 75–79.

10   According to Bourchier (1996: 211), Moertopo's ideas were probably borrowed from Catholic social theory, given the similarities between HIP and papal encyclicals on labour. Such a source of ideas is suggested by the fact that Moertopo was also patron of the Centre of Strategic and International Studies (CSIS) a powerful thinktank dominated by Catholic and Chinese intellectuals, established in the early 1970s. The most influential Catholic intellectual in the early New Order was Father Beek, a Dutch missionary and an ardent opponent of communism, who saw cooperation with the military as a means of securing Catholic security in a Muslim-dominated country (Bourchier 1996: 204–213). As mentioned earlier, however, Muslim political parties were also historically uncomfortable with the idea of class conflict.

11   See Sudono (1978: 178).

12   This is from the English-language version of *Pedoman Pelaksanaan Hubungan Industrial Pancasila*, published by the Department of Manpower in 1985. All further references to the document will involve this version.

13   Later on, Agus Sudono declared that, in the interest of national stability, workers should not use their right to strike. Workers and employers, he said, should not confront one another, but instead meet as 'members of one family' (INDOC 1982: 4).

14   Interview with Sudomo, 9 May 1994.

15   Interview with Sudomo, 9 May 1994.

16   The use of 'KOPKAMTIB methods' is admitted by Sudomo himself, who states that his education was in KOPKAMTIB. Interview, 9 May 1994.
     INDOC (1984: 17) quotes an FBSI official as saying, shortly after Sudomo's appointment as Minister, that 'Sudomo should apply the same "shock treatment" to existing labour problems as that which he often resorted to when he was KOPKAMTIB (. . .) chief'.

17   Notably, the actual appointment of persons to them has wholly been a government prerogative: P4D members are appointed for a period of two years by the Minister of Manpower, while the P4P members are appointed by the President for the same period (Manulang 1990: 101–102).

18   These are the Departments of Manpower – whose representatives act as chair of the committees – Industries, Finance, Agriculture, and Transport (Manulang *ibid.*).

19   The organisation was originally set up in 1952 as PUSPI, the Employers' Council on Social and Economic Affairs, as a 'forum of communication and consultation' (APINDO n.d.). It changed its name in 1985 to APINDO. However, as its own officials admit, APINDO exercises very little influence in determining the policies and behaviour of individual companies; Interview with Hadi Topobroto, executive director, APINDO, 4 January 1994.

20   Also see *Antara* 1 April 1982; *Kompas* 13 August 1982. There have been instances in which the SPSI itself has admitted that its representatives in the committees have worked against the interests of workers (e.g. SPSI 1990a: 232).

21   Still, in theory the P4D/P4P have substantial enough powers: for example, employers formally have to seek approval of the P4D for the dismissal of individual workers, and the approval of the P4P for large-scale dismissals (Manulang 1990: 109). Such stipulations are often simply ignored. Numerous press reports suggests this, for example those that deal with the period of indus-

trial strife in the early 1980s. See *Merdeka* 3 March 1982; *Suara Karya* 5 March 1982; *Sinar Harapan* 3 April 1982; *Antara* 16 April 1982; *Antara* 19 April 1982; *Suara Karya* 2 June 198; *Sinar Harapan* 23 June 1982; *Kompas* 24 June 1982; *Kompas* 30 June 1982.

22 Interview with Sudomo, 9 May 1994.

23 My emphasis.

24 It could be further argued, of course, that all criticism of the defects of the various 'legal–formal' institutions must take into account the fact that they are all part of a wider system which is geared toward the control and demobilisation of labour as a social force.

25 Much of the same could probably be said about the other 'peak' corporatist organisations conjured up by Moertopo's OPSUS in the early 1970s.

26 This took place only on 11 April 1973; the FBSI was 'founded' on 23 February (INDOC 1981: 88).

27 All data on SBLPs based on Sukarno (1980: 35–36).

28 By this time the enterprise-level units were no longer attached to the SBLPs as they had been eliminated with the creation of the SPSI in 1985.

29 Sudomo claims that the change was not undertaken on his initiative but was the decision of the FBSI leadership; Interview with Sudomo, 9 May 1994. However, this is highly unlikely. The two major leaders of the FBSI before the change occurred, Agus Sudono and Adolf Rachman, have expressed their disapproval of the change, particularly Rachman; Interviews with Agus Sudono, 18 January 1994; and Adolf Rachman, 28 June 1994.

30 Indeed, the practice of dismissing workers who initiate the establishment of workplace units was a fairly common occurrence (*Kompas* 13 December 1986).

31 Interview with Sudomo, 9 May 1994.

32 Tornquist (1991: 180), among others, lends some credence to this observation of limited autonomy.

33 Still, attempts by workers at the enterprise-level to secure some measure of autonomy from the central organisation persisted: SPSI documents mention conflict between workers and the SPSI when the latter's officials have tried to replace already existing PUK (SPSI 1990a: 232).

34 In the 1980–85 composition of the central executive board of the FBSI, he held one of the positions of 'chairman'.

35 Also interviews with Saut Aritonang, 8 December 1993; Sjaiful, 25 March 1994; Adolf Rachman, 28 June 1994.

36 Interview with Sudomo, 9 May 1994. It is unclear when Adolf Rachman fell out of favour with Sudomo. He had definitely tried to ingratiate himself with Sudomo when the latter first became Minister of Manpower. Echoing Sudomo's well-known views, INDOC (1984: 18) quotes him declaring that

> Striking is forbidden in vital enterprises and there is general consensus in considering strikes as disturbing harmonious working conditions and social stability and the basic values of the Indonesian nation which give priority to development. That is why the FBSI actively prevents strikes, and if a strike does break out, tries to end it.

37 General Moertopo had died the previous year. Agus Sudono appears to have made an attempt to persuade Sudomo to back him, but failed (*Kompas* 30 November 1985).

38 Having substituted *karyawan* for *pekerja*.

39 Interview with Bomer Pasaribu, then secretary-general of the SPSI, 17 January 1994.

40 Interview with Imam Soedarwo, 3 January 1994. He admitted that employers would pay more heed to the Department of Manpower than the SPSI.

41 Interview with Imam Soedarwo, 3 January 1994.

42 One SPSI leader claimed that foreign assistance to the organisation has 'never been properly accounted for' (*Jakarta Post* 11 November 1995).

43 The program was called 'Legal Aid for Industrial Disputes Settlement' (LAIDS), and was aimed at non-unionised workers. See various editions of the bulletin *Berita LAIDS*.

44 The involvement of ACTU personnel in this program is denied by Alan Matheson, international officer of the Australian union (*Background Briefing*, ABC Radio National, 24 September 1995). However, the involvement of former ACTU official Peter Duncan, effectively as executive officer, was first confirmed to me by SPSI senior official Tosari Widjaja, who is himself involved in the project; Interview 22 June 1994. In response to earlier queries by an organisation called Australia Asia Worker Links, Matheson suggested that the Australian government was actually funding an ILO program to promote compliance with ILO conventions in the Asian region. According to Matheson, the ACTU 'was asked to comment on the design of the three year project' (Letter from AAWL to Martin Ferguson (ACTU), date unclear; Memorandum from Alan Matheson to Len Cooper (AAWL), 23 March 1994). Not surprisingly, the WEP was criticised by independent labour activists for bestowing international legitimacy on the SPSI (e.g. various NGOs 1995).

Independent labour activists initially received information that the WEP was worth about A$1 million over several years. The real value of the program is apparently A$8.1 million, of which A$7.4 million is provided by the Australian government (AUSAID 1996).

There have been problems, however, in the implementation of the WEP, at least according to Saut Aritonang, a former independent trade-union leader who works for the program. Scheduled to begin in April 1996, the WEP was perceived by Aritonang to be in a state of limbo as late as March of that year; Interview 7 March 1996.

45 Interviews with representatives in Indonesia of AAFLI, 22 December 1993; FES, 28 February 1994; and the ILO, 9 March 1994.

46 Interview with Imam Soedarwo, 3 January 1994.

47 Interviews with Saralen Purba, 20 December 1993; Agus Sudono, 18 January 1994; Sjaiful, 25 March 1994.

48 The continued 'existence' of the old trade unions for a prolonged period was tolerated, in part, for economic reasons (*Merdeka* 3, 16 and 23 April 1985). Their pre-established overseas links provided an important source of funds for the operations of some SBLPs, and in fact probably benefited the post-1985 SPSI 'departments' as well. An example is given by the late Saralen Purba, an SPSI official who was a leader of the pre-FBSI KESPEKRI. He claimed that he was able to secure financial assistance through the IFBWW (International Federation of Building and Woodworkers), to which the FBSI sectoral union covering timber workers belonged to; Interview, 20 December 1993. Both GASBIINDO and SARBUMUSI remain registered members of the ICFTU, as do smaller organisations such as GOBSII, GERBUMI and KBIM. Such is the case even though the ICFTU continues to refuse membership to the SPSI itself. The ICFTU's rival, the WCL, has among its members such organisations as SOB Pantjasila, KESPEKRI and KONGKARBU-SOKSI (*Merdeka* 3 April 1985). See also SPSI (1990c: 5).

49 Not surprisingly, it was the younger officials who tended less to associate them-

selves with earlier groupings, as they had little if any, experience in the pre-FBSI period (Nurbaiti 1986: 55; also see Tornquist 1991: 180–182).

50 The same was expressed by Minister of Manpower (1988–93) Cosmas Batubara; Interview 29 December 1993.

51 This defence was offered in an official communication of the SPSI, dated 8 August 1989, signed by General Chairman Imam Soerdarwo and Secretary General Arief Soemadji, to the President of the AFL-CIO, Lane Kirkland.

52 A retired military officer, Darmawan Eddy, was appointed in 1988 as head of the SPSI branch of the strategic industrial area of Tangerang, West Java (Government of Indonesia 1989: 25), suggesting that the allocation of posts to those with military backgrounds was far from uncalculated. Prior to that, he had served as a personnel officer at a local textiles factory (AFL-CIO 1989: 21).

53 This is confirmed by a number of Indonesian workers; e.g. interviews and discussions with workers in Penjaringan, Jakarta, 11 January 1994. As these (retired?) officers were company employees themselves, they could pass as workers and hence be 'elected' to SPSI positions at the level of the firm.

54 Interview with Sudomo, 9 May 1994.

55 In that year Agus Sudono estimated that 20,000 textile factory workers would lose their jobs (*Pelita* 21 December 1982).

56 This is according to Agus Sudono, who estimated that 75 per cent of these strikes occurred in PMDN (domestic investment) firms. He speculated that the reason for this was the experience that multinational firms, originating from advanced industrial countries, had in dealing with labour problems (*Sinar Harapan* 5 November 1982). As subsequent Chapters will show, this would not be the case during the wave of strikes that occurred in the 1990s. By that time there had been a great deal of investment in low-wage industries that originated from NICs such as South Korea.

57 Significantly, Sudomo was referring to NGO activists.

58 Statements to that effect were made by Sudomo more than once. See *Jakarta Post* 18 June 1986.

59 Although his statement has been widely documented, Sudomo now takes pride in the number of CLAs which he says increased during his tenure as Minister. Interview with Sudomo, 9 May 1994.

60 The beverage producer was Teh Botol Sosro, manufacturer of the popular 'bottled tea' soft drink. This case precipitated a rare discussion in the national media about the right to strike. See *Kompas* 2 June 1987; 3 June 1987; 4 June 1987; 6 June 1987; 8 June 1986; 9 June 1987; 6 August 1987; *Jakarta Jakarta* 21 August–3 September 1987.

6 A CLASS IN THE MAKING: THE NEW URBAN PROLETARIAT

1 At the same time, it was also estimated that manufacturing could account for 23 per cent of Indonesia's GDP by 2000, and up to 33 per cent by 2010.

2 Hutchison (1992) discusses this subject in a study of the Philippines. For a general discussion of gender and export-led industrialisation, see Elson and Pearson (1980).

3 See, for example, Lambert 1993; Manning 1993, 1995; Bourchier 1994a; Hadiz 1993, 1994a and b.

4 For example, an official source mentions that 277 cases of strike action took place in Jakarta-proper between 1990 and 1994 (*Jakarta Post* 27 September 1995). *Kompas* (6 November 1992) estimated that between January and October

1992, 82 strikes, involving 45,000 workers, took place in Tangerang, and a further 52 strikes in Bekasi.

5 According to a survey by the Department of Manpower (1992–93: 67–68).

6 The case became notorious not only for the brutality that was inflicted on Marsinah but also because of the elaborate way in which the involvement of the local military apparatus appeared to be covered up. The East Java-based Yayasan Arek estimates that 533 strikes occurred in the area between 1989 and 1993 (*Koeli* no.3), thus casting further doubt on official statistics.

7 Potter (1993), however, while largely applying the framework developed by Rueschemeyer *et al.* (1992) to the East Asian experience, suggests that the working-class movement of South Korea has been an essential element in the growing pro-democracy movement in the country.

8 Compiled from various sources, including Manning (1993: 81), who quotes official reports. The figures presented in such reports constitute a very conservative estimate, as many strikes go unreported. One labour activist puts the number of strikes from 1989 to 1994 at an amazing 3,000 (Razif 1994b). An estimate of industrial action in West Java alone, for 1991, held that 195 strikes occurred there, far exceeding the figure for that year in Table 6.1 for all of Indonesia (Wibowo 1992). An American Embassy report (1994: 29–30) also notes that official statistics on strikes need to be approached with caution, noting how, according to the SPSI, over 340 strikes occurred in both 1992 and 1993. Another source (Jordan 1995: viii) quotes SPSI estimates that 1,130 strikes took place in Indonesia in 1994, which contrasts starkly with the much smaller figure presented in this table.

9 Up to October 1994 (*Reuters* 14 October 1994).

10 In his famous 'What is to be Done?' for example, he criticises the shortcomings of the 'economism' of the Western European trade union strategy. See Lenin (1976).

11 Presumably, women too.

12 I am borrowing heavily from Aldon Morris' (1992) very neat summary and discussion of Thompson's great work.

13 Interview and discussion with workers and labour organisers, Penjaringan, Jakarta, 11 January 1994.

14 However, this can simultaneously be a source of strength. Many young, female workers indicated that they were not too afraid of losing their jobs. The reason they cited was the ease with which they might acquire another. Apparently, this was more the case for the very young, age between 18–21. It was suggested by some of these workers that employers thought that such young women were easier to control. This subject was especially discussed during interviews and discussions with groups of workers in Bogor, 23 January 1994, and in Cengkareng, 1 February 1994.

15 This was highlighted during discussions with workers in Bogor, 23 January 1994; Cengkareng, 1 February 1994, and Tangerang, 18 June 1994. During these discussions many examples were provided of cases in which the leaders of strike action were subsequently dismissed, in a way that contravened officially stipulated procedures.

16 Saut Aritonang, for example, a founder of the *Setiakawan* independent union, suggests that the 'social justice' appeal of Pancasila is personally important to him; Interview, 8 December 1993. In a similar vein, Deyo himself notes that 'the Confucianism among politically active South Korean students' stresses such things as morality and justice' (Deyo 1989: 88–89).

17 Andriyani, however, who argues strongly that patriarchal values hinder the

working-class movement, relates an experience which suggests the passivity of women on similar occasions (Andriyani 1996: 161).

18 Interview with Chung Dong Jin, President Director of PT Bintang Busanajaya and PT Bintang Adibusana, Korean-owned garments manufacturers in Jakarta, and chairman of an association of Korean garments manufacturers operating in Indonesia, 30 March 1994.

19 Interviews and discussions, Penjaringan, Jakarta, 11 January 1994.

20 *Rukun Tetangga* and *Rukun Warga*; neighbourhood-level administrative units.

21 Interview with Arist Merdeka Sirait, 30 November 1993.

22 This is argued by Andriyani (1996).

23 Hanagan (1986) discusses the importance of workers' perception of the permanence of their life in urban industry to the initial development of working-class protest.

24 As was argued by a group of workers in Bogor, they can hardly expect to eke out much of a living in their home villages on the basis of agricultural activities, given the little access their families had to land; Discussion, 31 January 1994. The prospect of working as farm-labour did not appeal to any of these workers at all. Some of the statistics on land-ownership in West Java, bear out the apprehension of these workers. According to one study of the area, 50 per cent of 5.3 million 'rural' households currently do not have access to agricultural land at all, and a further 30 per cent controlled marginal holdings of less than half a hectare; Juni Thamrin (1993: 141), citing a 1986 Indonesian Central Bureau of Statistics report.

25 However, this is not something which is a working-class monopoly. For example, a large proportion of middle-class Jakartans, perhaps among the most cosmopolitan inhabitants of Indonesia's most cosmopolitan city, make a similar yearly trip to the *kampung*. Even these 'sophisticates' continue to display regional and ethnic loyalties, which does not mean that they lack a middle-class identity.

26 During one discussion, in answer to a question relating to the desirability of returning to his home village, a young, male, Javanese worker exclaimed: 'What for? None of my relatives there are alive; they're all in the city.' Discussion with Bogor workers, 31 January 1994.

27 A large majority of the urban industrial workforce in Indonesia consists of relatively recent migrants who have come from places quite a distance from their places of employment, although in some areas, the local population has furnished much of the workforce of local factories. Citing a study by Braadbart, White (1993: 132) suggests that employment in the eastern periphery of Bandung, in West Java, has been filled by workers of overwhelmingly local origins. Quoting Yusuf, White suggests that workers in the western and southern periphery of Bandung tend to come from other areas in Greater Bandung. By contrast, for the great Tangerang and Bogor industrial areas, White notes that the vast majority of workers came from decidedly more distant areas, citing the towns of Sukabumi and Cianjur, in West Java, and the southern parts of Central and East Java as common places of origins. In Tangerang, I encountered a large number of workers who came from the southern part of Sumatra. According to White, factories in the above industrial areas have favoured an in-migrant workforce in the expectation that such workers would be easier to control and are less likely to make trouble than local workers. However, the fact that Tangerang, in particular, has recently been a virtual hotbed of industrial unrest, does not seem to support such expectations. One South Sumatran worker in Tangerang suggested to me that she and her colleagues were often considered troublemakers by employers because they were

more openly confrontational than their Javanese colleagues; Interview, 4 June 1994.

28 Like Young and Hull, White also recognises that the rural–urban distinction is neither precise nor particularly relevant to characterise the environment of the new factories or other complexes where industrial workers live, which are largely best characterised as 'urban fringe' or 'peri-urban' areas (White 1993: 127–131).

29 This is supported by the macro-level data. See Manning (1992: 33) for figures on rising educational levels of urban population.

30 Though primary-level education is still the norm. During fieldwork I encountered cases of workers who had tertiary education experience. One Tangerang factory worker told me of a co-worker who had a *sarjana* (BA) degree in economics; Interview, 3 July 1994.

31 Thus workers have written their own accounts of personal experiences of life and work, which are often used as discussion material among workers' groups. See various editions of *Cerita Kami*, for some examples, and Moktar (1992).

32 From 'Masalah Bredel, Masalah Buruh', by Moktar, a former factory worker in West Java. It appears in *Media Kerja Budaya*, 1 November 1994. Many workers read secondhand newspapers or magazines.

33 This is somewhat different from my impression of the industrial areas that lie south of Jakarta, where West Javan workers seem to predominate, including those that originate from villages and towns that are relatively close by.

34 Before finding employment they would have stayed with relatives or friends in and around Jakarta and Tangerang, possibly with those who had encouraged them to relocate to the city in the first place (Roesli 1992: 34). Though there are other forms of recruitment of workers, connections through relatives and friends continue to be an important form of fulfilling demand for factory workers.

35 Interview with Arist Merdeka Sirait, 30 November 1993.

36 Writing about past European labour protests, Geary (1981: 17–18) suggests that workers who lived in houses owned by their bosses were less likely to be engaged in strike activity, because of the possibility of eviction. He also argues that workers living in socially homogeneous communities were more likely to be involved in strikes because such areas stimulated class solidarity.

37 Though taking place in a completely different social and historical setting, it is hard not to think about various descriptions of the conditions of the working classes of earlier industrialisers. On England alone, the work of Engels (1993) and Orwell (1986) come to mind, as well as, of course, the various works of Dickens.

38 Djati (1994: 9), writing on industrial areas in East Java, cites examples of how worker groups have had to disband or relocate because of pressure applied by such local-level officials.

39 One is reminded of Thompson's observation of the consequences to the English worker's life of the great changes that took place between 1790 and 1840. He writes that

> there was a slight improvement in average material standards. Over the same period there was intensified exploitation, greater insecurity, and increasing human misery. By 1840 most people were 'better off' than their fore-runners fifty years before, but they had suffered and continued to suffer this slight improvement as a catastrophic experience.
>
> (Thompson 1968: 231)

40 I thank Fauzi Abdullah for first raising this with me.

41 See various editions of *Cerita Kami, Koeli, PHK,* and other labour activist publications.

42 Many examples of such confrontations may be given. Perhaps one of the first cases of strike action that underlined the seriousness of labour unrest in the early 1990s was the PT Gadjah Tunggal strike of August 1991. This strike involved no less than 14,000 workers employed by 14 companies that operated under the banner of the huge conglomerate owned by Chinese businessman Sjamsul Nursalim. These companies produce a diverse range of rubber goods including automobile and bicycle tyres. For an account, see Jakarta Social Institute (1992).

7 DISTURBING THE PEACE: ORGANISATION AND STRUGGLE

1 The reference is particularly to the state-sponsored trade union organisation, set up in the context of the Cold War.

2 It was only during the latter half of the 1980s that the pro-democracy student movement joined forces with the independent labour movement. Before that, students and workers generally carried out separate struggles, partly because students thought little of the 'bread and butter' issues that workers were pursuing. The alliance of students and workers, especially after 1987, however, was of great importance to the pro-democracy movement that eventually succeeded in pressing for some degree of political reform. Nevertheless, the question of whether the student movement should actively play a role in the emerging independent labour movement, or a more limited facilitating role, continued to be debated (AMRC 1987:37–39).

3 For example seven workers of a commercial shrimp farm were dismissed in Medan in June 1993 for being involved with the SBSI. The head of the Medan branch of the organisation was arrested by the military, without a warrant, at about the same time and interrogated and tortured (Human Rights Watch/Asia 1993: 46–47). As mentioned, the fate that befell Marsinah in East Java, is but one of numerous examples that can be cited.

4 Muchtar Pakpahan and other SBSI officials claim than several workplace units of the organisation called *komisariat* have actually been recognised by employers and taken part in negotiating workplace agreements. This claim, interestingly, is disputed by representatives of various NGOs. Interview with Muchtar Pakpahan, 8 and 10 January 1994.

5 As in the case of workers' discussion groups that I encountered in Bogor, and in Cengkareng, West Jakarta. Members of these groups claim that they were already organising strike action before linking with SBM *Setiakawan* in 1990–91.

6 Many workers have claimed that in some industrial areas, heads of personnel departments cooperate with each other in developing a common list of notoriously 'troublesome' workers. Discussions with workers, Cengkareng, 1 February 1994.

7 As in the case of young women I met in Cengkareng, Tangerang, and Bogor who had been repeatedly involved in strike action and now serve as organisers and advisers to their colleagues in cases of industrial dispute. Occasionally, as in the case of Sadisah (see YAKOMA n.d.), the former Nike factory worker associated with the NGO YAKOMA; and Sunarty, secretary-general of the SBSI, they have even become international spokespersons for the labour movement.

8 These observations are made on the basis of visiting some of these groups and participating in their meetings during the course of fieldwork.

9 Workers that I talked to at a meeting in Depok, south of Jakarta, immediately identified knowledge of existing labour laws and regulations as the most valuable gain from interaction with NGOs. These workers were part of cultural group organised by the NGO, SISBIKUM (*Saluran Informasi dan Bimbingan Hukum*; Information Channel and Legal Assistance). Interviews, 23 January 1994.

10 I witnessed preparations for strike action that were undertaken by workers of a Korean doll-manufacturing factory in Bogor, in January 1994, arranged to coincide with similar action taken by workers of other factories in the area. This particular case involved a demonstration by workers in front of the Department of Manpower central office in Jakarta, an exercise requiring careful logistical planning. Another recent case involved strikes taking place in Bekasi in solidarity with workers on strike at PT Great River Industries in Bogor, in mid-July 1995 (*AKSI News Service* 1 August 1995).

11 During numerous discussions I had with workers in the industrial areas around and in Jakarta, Korean supervisors, managers, or employers have especially been cited as being particularly harsh. This view is supported even by government reports (e.g. Department of Manpower 1992–93: 84–85). Harshness toward workers by Taiwanese superiors has also been cited (e.g. *Jakarta Post* 20 June 1994).

12 It is for this reason that many workers' theatre groups have been banned from performing. A recent banning in Solo, Central Java, was reported in *Kompas* (25 September 1995). This case is interesting because it involved a touring workers' cultural group from faraway Tangerang. The 'Us' and 'Them' attitude is emphasised by Roesli (1992).

13 One such activist told me of an instance in which a worker decided to keep the word *buruh* as the description of mode of employment in his identity card. Earlier, he had been determined to exchange *buruh* for *karyawan*, which he thought was more prestigious. Apparently, what he subsequently learned about the 'heroics' of past workers' organisations persuaded him to be quite proud of being a *buruh*.

14 One such organiser, Arist Merdeka Sirait, notes that many NGOs stretch their resources by operating in widely dispersed industrial areas. He laments that there is no coordination that would allow a division of spheres of operation; Interview, 30 November 1993.

15 Of course, this kind of disagreement to some degree flows naturally from political differences, given that they involve particular 'readings' of the contemporary situation.

16 The 'corporatist' tag is due to the implication in their position of basically maintaining the status quo in terms of the institutional arrangements of the industrial relations system.

17 YBM also claims to coordinate the work of groups in West Java, and the central Java cities of Yogyakarta and Semarang; Interview with YBM organisers, 10 January 1994.

18 For a time the sectoral union also published the journal *Dinamika*, which was subsequently banned by the government.

19 Interview with YBM labour organisers, 10 January 1994.

20 At about the same time, the bulletin *Independen*, produced by AJI (*Asosiasi Jurnalis Independen*; the Association of Independent Journalists) was banned. 'Semi-clandestine' refers to publications that do not have official licences.

21 Interview with YBM organisers, 10 January 1994. During that same period, as similarly small but influential parties, the PSI and the Catholic PARKINDO had an especially close relationship, one that would have certainly been repli-

cated in the relationship between their respective labour arms. I am indebted to George Aditjondro for this observation.

22 These include Prof. Sarbini Sumawinata, a respected economist and critic of the New Order, and Koeswari, a high-ranking officer of the KBSI. One YBM labour organiser called these PSI figures her 'teachers'; Interview with YBM organisers, 10 January 1994.

23 It was on this basis that it attacked the link between SOBSI and the PKI, in particular.

24 Interview with Ari Sunaryati, LWR officer, 21 January 1994.

25 Although the 'liberalism' implied in their attention to human and labour rights is regarded as less threatening than 'communism', it is also considered anathema to Pancasila. An ingenious way of invoking both 'threats' is found by former Minister of Manpower Sudomo, who suggests that labour unrest is the product of liberals who have adopted 'New Left' tactics; Interview with Sudomo, 9 May 1994.

26 Interviews with Saut Aritonang, 8 December 1993 and Princen, 3 March 1994; also personal correspondence from David Bourchier, 27 January 1995. Whether by intention or not, its launching came at the heels of the annulment by President Soeharto in August of that year of a 1963 Presidential Instruction which banned strike action in vital institutions and projects. Notably, it also took place just prior to an SPSI Congress which was scheduled for November of the same year. Its inception process, however, was rather protracted: talks toward the organisation's establishment reportedly began as early as February 1990.

27 The reference to Poland's Solidarity was deliberate, according to H.J.C. Princen, one of the founders of *Setiakawan*. Poland's 'Solidarity', he says, did much to overthrow the repressive communist regime of that country. Indonesia's integralistic state, he also says, has more than a passing resemblance to the East European communist state; Interview 3 March 1994.

28 Saut Aritonang, secretary-general of *Setiakawan* suggests that it received assistance from the Dutch NGOs, HIVOS and NOVIB, the Dutch Union, FNV, and the American AAFLI. Princen himself claims that the organisation mainly operated with overseas funds already acquired by LPHAM and which he personally allocated for *Setiakawan*; Interviews with Saut Aritonang, 8 December 1993 and Princen, 3 March 1994.

29 Aritonang was opposed to the transformation of the FBSI into the SPSI after the organisation's 1985 Congress, which entailed the elimination of the SBLPs. Thus, for a time he was in the same camp as Adolf Rachman, the organiser of the SEKBER SBLP that for several years challenged the SPSI. In many ways, Aritonang typified the disenchantment of many well-intentioned, and often idealistic, local-level FBSI/SPSI activists with the powerlessness of that union. A passionate and outspoken North Sumatran, he showed a talent for organising and maintaining the loyalty of rank-and-file workers over whom he projected a considerable measure of charisma, even long after *Setiakawan's* subsequent demise – and although he had by then been largely ostracised by other NGO activists.

30 As discussed in the next Chapter, it was mainly pressure from the US government that the Indonesian government was concerned about.

31 General Moerdani, notably, was a one-time protégé of the late General Ali Moertopo.

32 It was at this time that it became clear that ABRI had lost much of its control over GOLKAR. In the mid-1980s GOLKAR was chaired by Sudharmono, the Minister of the State Secretariat who was despised by much of the ABRI

leadership because he had encroached on some of ABRI's vested economic interests. In spite of Moerdani's protests, Sudharmono was appointed Vice-President by Soeharto in 1988. See Schwarz (1994: 285).

33 As part of its fruitless attempt to gain government recognition, *Setiakawan* tried to organise meetings both with the Minister of the Interior, Rudini (*Media Indonesia* 28 November 1990) and the Director-General of Social and Political Affairs of that department, Hari Sugiman. Neither official met the *Setiakawan* delegations, citing the official commitment to the idea of a single union organisation.

34 SPSI leaders also did not welcome the competition that *Setiakawan* represented, as would be expected. Imam Soedarwo claimed that *Setiakawan* sought glory for itself rather than to defend workers. Agus Sudono was unsympathetic as well, calling the initiative an effort 'aimed at undermining workers' unity'. He also called on workers not to be easily incited by the organisation, as it had no legal basis (*Jakarta Post* 20 November 1990).

   The displeasure with the establishment of *Setiakawan* extended to the very top levels of the state. Making what was then an unusual intervention into labour affairs, President Soeharto himself asserted that an additional union was not required in Indonesia (*Indonesia Times* 29 January 1991). Clearly, the involvement of various well-known critics of the government in *Setiakawan*, such as Princen, as well as Chris Siner Teymu and Jopie Lasut of the so-called *Petisi 50 Group*, did little to endear it to the government. On the latter group, see Effendi (1989).

35 He was also instrumental in the formation of a taxi drivers' union that was active for some time. See Bourchier (1994a: 60).

36 Cahyono also accused Aritonang of fabricating an incident in which he was reportedly kidnapped and interrogated for several days by security personnel (*Tempo* 28 September 1991).

37 Interview with Saut Aritonang, 8 December 1993.

38 Interview, 8 December 1993.

39 After the demise of *Setiakawan*, Princen continued his human-rights advocacy through LPHAM, while Cahyono was involved with a radical organisation called INFIGHT. Aritonang lost his place at the forefront of labour activism, largely because he was perceived to have been compromised through a personal accommodation he reached with state officials. By Aritonang's own admission, he was approached in 1991 by the Department of Manpower – at that time under Cosmas Batubara. He is now provided with an office in the YTKI complex and is involved in the workers' education program mentioned earlier.

40 The request for recognition is contained in an SBSI document numbered 69/SBSI/IV/1993, dated 29 April 1993, in which the organisation claimed 75 branches in 27 provinces.

41 Linked to the HMI (*Himpunan Mahasiswa Islam*; Islamic Students Association), traditionally the largest campus-based student organisation in the country.

42 The GMKI (*Gerakan Mahasiswa Kristen Indonesia*, Indonesian Christian Students Movement).

43 One worker explained that she had joined the SPSI because she thought it would do some good for her colleagues, but was quickly disappointed by what she saw. She hoped that by joining the SBSI, she could do more, and expressed her willingness to risk losing her job, 'for the sake of the SBSI' (*Tempo* 2 May 1992: 24).

44 Interview with Muchtar Pakpahan, 10 January 1994.

45 Interview with Payaman Simanjuntak, Adviser to the Minister of Manpower, 6

December 1993. He argues that such organisations are led by politically ambitious individuals.

46 A term which, in this case, seems to reveal an attachment toward Western-style trade unionism which is not unaccompanied by some degree of acceptance of HIP, similar to Aritonang's. Interview with Muchtar Pakpahan, 10 January 1994.

47 Interview, 10 January 1994.

48 Interview, 10 January 1994. Hendropriyono was closely associated with General Wismoyo Arismunandar, who was then one of the army's rising stars and considered a future presidential prospect. Among the other generals that Pakpahan claimed to have close contact with was General Sembiring, a member of parliament who once lashed out at what he saw as the reduction of the armed forces' influence in GOLKAR. Hendropriyono and Wismoyo were later transferred to positions of marginal importance, while Sembiring was ejected from parliament.

49 Interviews with Muchtar Pakpahan, 8 and 10 January 1994.

50 He did have cause, however, to harbour resentment toward the Department of Manpower. Not only had it ignored the SBSI's application for registration as a legitimate trade union, but it had also condoned the closing down of the SBSI's first congress in mid-1993, in spite of the fact that the occasion was attended by officials of foreign embassies and international organisations. Adding insult to injury, on 8 January 1994, Minister of Manpower Abdul Latief also reneged on an appointment to meet Pakpahan and other SBSI officials, sending director-general Suwarto instead in his place, merely to repeat the government's position on the illegitimacy of trade unions outside of the SPSI; Interview with Muchtar Pakpahan, 10 January 1994.

51 See SBSI (1994), which contains a call to engage in a general strike.

52 Notes taken during SBSI meeting with labour activists, 8 February 1994.

53 The SBSI itself claimed that 750,000 workers in the major industrial cities of Java and Sumatra joined the call (*Jakarta Post* 14 February 1994), though this is a rather gross exaggeration.

54 The unwillingness to support Pakpahan was expressed to me in private conversation by some NGO leaders.

55 Interview, 10 January 1994.

56 To his credit, Pakpahan began to make gestures of reconciliation with other labour-based NGOs after the February débâcle.

57 Much of the tension was attributable to workers demanding Muslim holiday bonuses (Human Rights Watch/Asia 1994: 60–63). Also see *Analisa* 8 February 1994; 12 February 1994; 28 February 1994; 1 March 1994; *Mimbar Umum* 9 March 1994; 12 March 1994; 13 March 1994; 17 March 1994; *Medan Pos* 20 March 1994; *Garuda* 22 March 1994; *Waspada* 3 March 1994; 6 March 1994.

58 It is notable that, according to the official version of events, the Medan riots were spurred by anti-Chinese sentiments. While this interpretation serves to undermine the claim that the riots erupted on the basis of legitimate workers' grievances, it also demonstrates the continuing greater aversion of the New Order to recognise class-related sources of conflict in society. For a discussion of the links between class and race in the Medan riots, see *Far Eastern Economic Review* 16 June 1994: 30.

59 Personal communication with SBSI officials, 15 July 1994.

60 The spirit of 1973 was a reference to the year of the 'Declaration of Unity' which marked the establishment of the FBSI. See Chapter 4.

61 These points were made at an SBSI evaluation meeting, on 19 March 1994, in which various labour NGO activists were invited.

62 Pakpahan received from a lower court a term of three years in jail, which was later increased to four years by a higher court on appeal (*Reuters* 24 January 1995). He was only subsequently released by the Supreme Court in October 1995.

63 Sirait is another North Sumatran who came to the Jakarta area in his youth, where he scrounged a living as a street musician, and later, as a worker at the PT Fairchild factory in Bogor. By his own admission, he was introduced to labour organising by Fauzi Abdullah of YLBHI. Joining SISBIKUM in 1985, and with experience in another NGO, YAKOMA, Sirait has become a well-known spokesman for workers' rights. Interview, 30 November 1993.

64 Interviews with Father Sandyawan of *Institut Sosial*, 15 December 1993; and Indera Nababan of YAKOMA, 28 March 1994.

65 Interview with Indera Nababan, 28 March 1994. A problem with the position of NGOs discussed here, however, is that their rejection of both current attempts at alternative trade unionism, and state-sponsored unionism, appears to be unaccompanied by a well thought-out conceptual scheme about how their own activities might pave the way for the emergence of an independent trade union movement (Etty 1993).

66 Who at one time was a *Setiakawan* activist.

67 A new generation of students began to be politically active in the mid- and late 1980s after large scale repressive policies were enacted in the late 1970s to curb student involvement in social and political affairs. With few links to political elites, the experiences of some of these students in helping organise peasant and worker protests have resulted in a distinct radicalisation process. Aspinall (1994: 17) describes such student activists as those

> who deliberately strive to avoid elite politics, thus do not employ any specific stratagem to make use of the opportunities afforded by intra-regime disunity. Rather, they simply continue to engage in political activity, make increasingly bold and confrontational actions and demands, and by doing so, strive to widen the space available for political action.

68 Dita Indah Sari, of the PPBI, during a talk in Perth, Western Australia, 7 December 1994.

69 See FORSOL (1993).

70 Interviews with Johnson Pandjaitan (IS), 6 March 1996, and Amiek and Prapto, labour activists and former workers, 12 March 1996.

8 STATE RESPONSES: REFORM OR REPRESSION?

1 To the extent that even the respected liberal economist, Kwik Kian Gie (*Kompas* 7 June 1994), attacked the decision for contradicting laws on foreign investment and the egalitarian ideals of the nation. Sectors newly opened to foreign capital included electricity, telecommunications and railways. In response to such critics, cabinet members assured the public that PP20/1994 was not intended 'to sell-off' Indonesia (*Kompas* 7 July 1994).

2 In particular, Taiwanese attraction to China was widely reported in the press. Taiwan is the third largest foreign investor in Indonesia (after Japan and Hong Kong), with total cumulative investment valued at US$3.5 billion in the early 1990s (*Jakarta Post* 20 July 1992).

3 Immediate developments following the announcement of the deregulation measure seemed to allay some of these fears. Primarily because of a year-end surge, plans for new foreign investment projects worth US$23.7 billion

prompted Investment Minister Sanyoto Sastrowardoyo to proclaim that he was no longer worried about competition from China (*Far Eastern Economic Review*, 18 May 1995: 56).

4 That some investment decline had taken place in China at the end of 1994, for example, was partly attributed to uncertainties about its post-Deng political course (*Far Eastern Economic Review* 18 May 1995: 56; *Jakarta Post* 20 July 1992). Investment Minister Sanyoto has dismissed as 'groundless' reports that Indonesia has been assessed as representing a greater political risk than such countries as Pakistan and Bangladesh (*Jakarta Post* 25 April 1995).

5 Complaints reported include those pertaining to such vital public services as the provision of electric power (*Prospek* 21 September 1991: 10, 34).

6 Interviews with officials of KOTRA and JETRO, respectively the Korean and Japanese trade offices, in Jakarta, 9 June 1994; 13 April 1994.

7 In South Korea, for example, the nominal annual wage increased by an average of 16.3 per cent between 1987 and 1992, which, according to Song, was the direct result of workers' victories against a 'repressive labour regime' (Song 1994: 11).

8 Interview with Chung Dong-Jin, President Director of PT Bintang Busanajaya and PT Bintang Adibusana, and Chairman of Korea Industrial Garments Association, 30 March 1994.

9 Interview with KOTRA official, 9 June 1994.

10 Indonesian manufacturing workers were paid US$0.28 per hour in 1993, compared to US$0.71 in Thailand, US$1.80 in Malaysia, US$0.68 in the Philippines and US$0.54 in China (*Kompas* 23 June 1994, citing Morgan Stanley Research). Productivity growth in manufacturing in Indonesia also outstripped that of Thailand and the Philippines, where similar data are available for the same period (World Bank 1993b: 251–252).

11 Episodes such as MALARI in 1974 and the student protests of 1978 come to mind, as do the Tanjung Priok affair of 1984, during which soldiers shot at and killed Muslim demonstrators, and cases of peasant protests in the late 1980s.

12 Interview with Cosmas Batubara, 29 December 1993.

13 Interview with Cosmas Batubara, 29 December 1993.

14 Interview with Cosmas Batubara, 29 December 1993.

15 A strike which took place because of the unwillingness of the employer to grant a pay rise in accordance to new minimum wage stipulations.

16 Interview with Cosmas Batubara, 29 December 1993. He suggested that methods utilised when Sudomo was Minister were no longer appropriate.

17 Interview with Cosmas Batubara, 29 December 1993.

18 The GSP program, enacted in 1974, provides duty-free entry to the US market of eligible products from beneficiary developing countries. A provision in the US GSP law requires that such countries have taken or are taking steps to ensure internationally recognised worker rights (GSP Information Centre 1993: 1).

19 However, the same source notes that Indonesia actually exported goods at a value of under US$1.2 billion to the US in 1992. Of the remainder over US$500 million worth of goods, 'competitive need limits restrictions' prevented US$302 million worth of goods (mainly plywood) from entering duty-free under GSP. 'Administrative' duty was paid on the remaining US$206-worth of GSP-eligible products, because the Indonesian exporters and/or US importers did not complete the administrative requirements for those goods to enter under the program (American Embassy 1994: 39).

20 For Batubara, by taking a more active part in the global economy, 'Indonesia

was taking part in the world'. Interview with Cosmas Batubara, 29 December 1993.

21 Interview with Cosmas Batubara, 29 December 1993.

22 This was quite an outstanding incident since that director, Valentino Suazo, was a replacement for Jeffrey Ballinger, who was an outspoken critic of state labour policy. Ballinger was expelled from the country in 1991 due to his public mocking of the labour practices of a well-known and well-connected domestic entrepreneur, Dewi Motik.

23 A politics and security meeting of the cabinet is reported to have concluded that the government needs to maintain the SPSI's monopoly as a trade union because 'labour issues have political and security aspects that demand vigilance' (*Kompas* 30 July 1993).

24 Interview with Cosmas Batubara, 29 December 1993.

25 Government calculations in 1992 held that it met approximately 60 per cent of such needs.

26 As Batubara himself claims; Interview 29 December 1993.

27 Although Batubara himself cites his background as a 1960s student activist. Interview with Cosmas Batubara, 29 December 1993.

28 Even so, Batubara continued to maintain that the exercise of this right should accord with existing regulations – thus deeming virtually all industrial action since 1990 to be illegal. At the end of Batubara's tenure, Payaman Simanjuntak issued a new, draconian policy which allowed employers to assume the voluntary resignation of workers absent from work due to strike action. Circular dated 5 February 1993, numbered B.62/M/BW/1993.

29 This was an interpretation that, interestingly, was proposed by Sudomo; Interview, 9 May 1994.

30 However, to the government's displeasure, the SBSI was to claim that it had fulfilled the new formal requirements when applying for government recognition in 1993 (American Embassy 1994: 36). In any case, there was no way that the SBSI could get past an accompanying 'Catch-22' in the regulation: a further requirement that any newly established union obtain a recommendation from the existing union, the SPSI. In addition, as *Asiawatch* observed, the formation of alternative union federations continued to be hampered by yet another requirement that they have at least ten registered industrial unions as members, all of which must meet the individual membership requirements and each of which would need approval of the SPSI to register (*Asiawatch* 23 January 1993:5).

31 Notably, a 1986 Ministerial Decree (No. 1109/MEN/1986) which defined a labour union at the company level as an organisation of workers 'organised by the SPSI', had been rescinded in 1992, adding some ammunition to the 'autonomy' argument (American Embassy 1994: 32).

32 The formal relationship between the SPSI-proper and the industrial unions is described in FSPSI 1996: 52–68.

33 Still, the Department of Manpower will be expected to act as 'supervisor' of the new system (FSPSI 1996: 108).

34 Interviews with Teten Masduki (YLBHI), Johnson Pandjaitan (IS) and Arist Merdeka Sirait (SISBIKUM), respectively on 4, 6 and 8 March 1996.

35 Interview 12 March 1996.

36 English word and quotation marks used in the original Indonesian.

37 In a 'Memorandum' to Coordinating Minister of Industry and Trade Hartarto, White and Case presented an outline of arguments in support of Indonesia's existing legal framework of workers' rights. In it, the firm's representatives also report a meeting with a staff-member of the USTR, during which it was

suggested that the USTR was willing to 'sacrifice Indonesia' to ensure that the NAFTA agreement was approved by Congress and supported by labour groups in the US. 'In order for this not to happen', she further suggested, 'there must be specific milestones that Indonesia meets that the USTR can point to to (*sic*) appease the labour groups'. The same memorandum also mentions, rather detachedly, USTR concern about the 'alleged "rape/murder" of a labour organiser allegedly by the army', an obvious reference to the Marsinah case (see White and Case 1993a). In another 'Memorandum', addressed to Minister of Manpower Abdul Latief, Ambassador to the US Arifin Siregar, as well as Hartarto, White and Case offered extensive working drafts of separate briefing papers on the history of the Indonesian trade union movement and the SPSI, Indonesian laws governing the formation of trade unions, the basis for the non-recognition of the SBSI, and 'point-by-point suggested responses to the principal issues raised by the GSP Subcommittee . . . ' (see White and Case 1993b). In still another 'Memorandum', addressed to fifteen top Indonesian government officials, the firm pointed to the preparation, on behalf of Minister of Trade S.B. Joedono, of a document which 'explains how the Government of Indonesia may ask private companies to express support for Indonesia regarding GSP and other matters (lobbying) without requiring these companies to officially register as foreign agents under United States law' (see White and Case 1993c).

38 It is notable, however, that the regulation was basically a spill-over from a debate that took place during the Batubara period. It was then that Payaman Simanjuntak, director-general of industrial relations and labour standards, proposed the formation of in-house unions in emulation of the Japanese model, as a way of overcoming the impasse on the politically charged question of freedom of organisation. Interestingly, he was attacked on nationalistic grounds, mainly from within the SPSI, for seeking to replace Indonesia's existing model of industrial relations with that of a foreign country (*Kompas* 25 February 1993).

39 This point was raised by Cosmas Batubara, who claims that, as Minister, he rejected similar proposals made by various businesspeople. According to Batubara, these proposals were only in the interest of big business; Interview with Cosmas Batubara, 29 December 1993.

40 For example, Indera Nababan of YAKOMA, who pointed out the difficulty with which even SPSI units are formed. Personal communication.

41 This was stated in a talk he delivered to a LEM-SPSI seminar, 26 January 1994.

42 It claimed that 744 such unions had been established, 24 of which had negotiated collective labour agreements (see Suwarto 1995). These figures have not been corroborated.

43 An official document (Government of Indonesia n.d.: 2–3), conveyed to the US government in defence of Indonesia's labour record, prominently mentions this policy as proof of on-going improvements in the labour area. In a 'preliminary statement' to the US GSP Subcommittee made on 3 November 1993, Indonesian Ambassador to the US, Arifin Siregar, mentions the establishment of in-house unions as part of government policy (Correspondence, Arifin Siregar to Michael Kantor, dated 20 October 1993). In-house unions are again mentioned in a document prepared by the Department of Foreign Affairs, Republic of Indonesia (1993), outlining the views of the Indonesian government on labour problems and reform.

44 A report subsequently written on the basis of the mission criticised, among other things, an 'exceedingly complex industrial relations legal framework, and ineffective enforcement procedures' (ILO Mission 1993: 9).

45 Also notes taken during meeting between labour activists and US State Department official, Jakarta, 5 February 1994.

46 Latief, appearing on the TV program, *Aneka Dialog RCTI*, 15 February 1994. A draft law may increase the fine to Rp 50 million (Suwarto 1995) – then about US$23,000. Latief also undertook the notable step of developing a new major nationwide employer-funded health insurance scheme, JAMSOSTEK (McLeod 1993).

47 *Aneka Dialog RCTI*, 15 February 1994.

48 Sources: *Warta Ekonomi* (25 February 1991: 17); and *Economic and Business Review Indonesia* (15 May 1996: 9).

49 Citing *Merdeka* 20 April 1994.

50 Taking the case of West Java as an example, they argued in 1994 that even by the government's criteria, the minimum physical needs of a male worker with a family would be far from adequately fulfilled. Moreover, they suggested that minimum wage levels are set according to gender-biased criteria in that they are calculated solely according to the needs of male workers. In special reference to Central and East Java, they have argued that minimum wage levels still fall short of even fulfilling the minimum physical needs of a single, male worker; See various NGOs (1994) for these arguments.

51 Nationally, there was a rise averaging 10.63 per cent.

52 This may also indicate that employers had been cutting costs by not conferring regular permanent employment status on a large part of their workforce.

53 The actual number of strikes was probably much higher given that, as noted in Chapter 6, official estimates tend to be very conservative.

54 Interview with Sudomo, 9 May 1994.

55 The official was Winston Lord, US Assistant Secretary of State for East Asian and Pacific Affairs.

56 Latief also justified the continued use of troops to maintain order in Medan long after the riots by suggesting that Indonesia 'could not afford more worker protests' that 'scared off foreign investors'. Moreover, he claimed that foreign investment in North Sumatra had dropped by 40 per cent following the riots, which, he said, created 'the image that Indonesia is not stable'. Latief also claimed that his Department had moved quickly since the riots to 'remove several . . . officials, including the local department head' (*Reuters* 1 November 1994).

57 Interestingly, during large-scale military exercises in East Java in late 1992, one of the imaginary targets of ABRI action was a mob of protesting workers (*Kompas* 4 November 1992).

58 A good example is the case of academic George Aditjondro, who, in 1995, relocated to Australia to avoid arrest and possible imprisonment for critical comments made at a seminar (*Merdeka* 7 June 1995).

59 *Voice of America*, 30 January 1995. Amosi Telaumbanua's sentence was increased from fifteen months to three years. Other SBSI officials received lighter prison sentences (*Reuters* 12 October 1994 and 14 October 1994).
  The renewed ascendance of a tougher approach toward labour unrest was also represented by President Soeharto's declaration that Pakpahan's case had nothing to do with labour rights, but involved a criminal offence (*Reuters* 16 October 1994). Predictably, Pakpahan rejected the characterisation of his activities as 'criminal' (*Reuters* 18 October 1994).

60 Letter from Enzo Friso to Lewis Preston, 12 September 1994.

61 Letter from Representative Lane Evans of Illinois to US Trade Representative, dated 9 September 1994.

62 Arguably, the mood of confidence was not only attributable to the dissipation

of the GSP issue, but also to the realisation that Indonesia was a key element in the economic and trade plans of the US and Australian governments. Prime Minister Keating, whose plan for greater Australian economic integration with the East Asian region involved courting the Soeharto government, reportedly even urged President Clinton to 'soften' his human rights stance on Indonesia (*United Press International* 26 October 1993). Not surprisingly, Keating was vehemently criticised by independent labour activists in Indonesia, including the YMB, a labour-based NGO (*Green Left Review* 22 September 1993). At about the same time, US trade unionists also attacked the Australian government's lacklustre support for efforts to link trade and labour rights issues in the GATT forum (*The Australian* 23 October 1993).

Indonesian independent labour activists also expressed their disappointment at what they perceived to be a lack of overt support from the Australian peak union, the ACTU (*West Australian* 15 December 1994). A focus of concern were statements made by some ACTU officials in relation to Indonesia. Though critical of the SPSI central leadership, ACTU chief Martin Ferguson, for example, made startlingly dismissive public remarks about the SBSI, while the organisation was under siege from the Indonesian government. At the same time, Ferguson argued that the 'new' industrial sector unions' establishment represented a possible significant reform, and that they should be distinguished from the SPSI-proper (SBS *Dateline* program, aired 3 December 1994). Essentially the same view was voiced by Ferguson at a meeting with independent labour activists in Jakarta, 3 December 1993.

In a memorandum to the AAWL dealing with Indonesia, ACTU senior official Alan Matheson suggested that 'the ACTU believes that current moves toward free, democratic and independent unions need to be supported. Those moves include the development of sectoral streams'. He also maintained that 'most international unions view with caution the development of SBSI: e.g. is it a trade union or is it being driven by lawyers and academics?'; Memorandum to Len Cooper (AAWL), 23 March 1994.

63 USIA East Asia Wireless File, 7 April, 1995.
64 Interview, *Prisma* (No. 3 1992: 62–74).
65 Although workers have often reported their distress at being labelled 'PKI' for protesting. A colleague of the slain Marsinah, for example, claimed that factory security guards had called her striking co-workers communists. Notes taken during YAPUSHAM Award ceremony, Jakarta, 10 December 1993.
66 A public debate developed when it was suggested, in late 1995, that 'formless' organisations were a manifestation of new PKI activities (*Forum Keadilan* 23 October 1995: 12–19). This vague accusation could be read to refer to NGOs, radical student organisations, or labour groups.
67 See YLBHI (1994a).
68 This was noted in a tentative YLBHI report on the Medan riots (1994b).
69 Commenting on his relationship with ABRI, he suggested that 'in order to provide prosperity to the common people, he is obliged to cooperate with various parties' (*Detik* 4–10 May 1994:7).
70 Citing an interview with the officers in the local daily, *Sinar Harapan Pagi*.
71 These claims are consistent with those of Medan NGOs who argue that 'third parties' were responsible for instigating the riots, as well as for disseminating anti-Chinese leaflets (*Jakarta Post* 7 September 1994). Paid thugs and hoodlums, in particular, have been cited for being responsible for initiating destructive actions.
72 Evidence has been presented by a leading labour activist to me in the form of

photocopied company documentation indicating payments to Department of Manpower officials and to personnel of a local military command.

73 See YLBHI (1994b).

74 In December 1995, for example, the PPBI helped to organise a strike by 14,000 workers at the giant PT Sritex textile factory in Solo, Central Java – manufacturer of GOLKAR uniforms – which was violently broken up by military personnel (*Forum Keadilan* 17 June 1996: 61). In June 1996, the PPBI organised a rally involving 5,000 factory workers at Jakarta's parliament building, during which PRD leader Budiman Sudjatmiko announced that workers required their own political party. Just prior to the Jakarta riots, the PPBI organised well-publicised strikes in East Java, after which three of its leaders, including chairperson Dita Sari, were charged with inciting hatred toward the government (newspaper accounts of the latter strikes are found in *Surya, Jawa Pos,* and *Surabaya Pos*, 9 July 1996).

75 Those alleged to have been responsible for the July rioting, including various PRD members, may be charged with subversion, an offence which carries the maximum penalty of death. In another blow to the labour movement, the Catholic priest Sandyawan, head of the *Institut Sosial*, was later implicated in the matter for allegedly harbouring PRD fugitives (*Kompas* 20 August 1996).

76 Already the government has pushed further its stated intention of controlling and circumventing the activities of NGOs in general, by announcing the aim of 'imposing order' (*menertibkan*) on these types of organisations. From the viewpoint of the government, many such organisations 'have undertaken activities that cannot be detected' (*Republika* 12 August 1996), and therefore are a threat to political stability.

77 There is, of course, also the influence that is exercised 'instrumentally', in the form of personal links with government officials.

78 *Aneka Dialog RCTI*, 15 February 1994.

79 Interview, with Hadi Topobroto, 4 January 1994.

80 The identity of this resource person is undisclosed upon request.

81 An exception, however, was again the manager of the European manufacturing firm. Asked why employers do not pay higher than subsistence wages to their workers, he simply suggested that they didn't because 'they don't have to'.

82 Interview with Chung Dong Jin, Korean entrepreneur, 30 March 1994.

83 Interview with Baik Doo-Chun, Assistant Director, KOTRA Jakarta, 9 June 1994.

84 Interview with Chamroel Djafri, President Director of PT Mayer Florex Indonesia, Director of PT Mayertex Indonesia, and Vice-Chairman of API, 29 March 1994.

85 Dhanani suggests that in 'incorporated' manufacturing firms, profits averaged near 80 per cent. The *Jakarta Post* quotes an 'international labour observer' who argues that 'what [Indonesian employers] mean by bankruptcy may be a decrease in profits to 50 percent', pointing out that net profits of textiles firms in Indonesia range between '54 and 58 per cent' compared to the US, where they range between '14 and 16 per cent' (*Jakarta Post* 19 February 1995). The picture painted by the businesspeople interviewed, however, stressed falling profits caused by increasing production costs.

86 Much has been said also about the stark contrast between the trifling sum paid to workers who produce Nike shoes, and the millions of dollars paid 'in sponsorship' to sports superstars. (See *Harpers Magazine* August 1992: 47; and *Nike in Indonesia*, volume 1, no. 2, February 1995.)

87 This assessment concurs with that of Cosmas Batubara, who noted that companies originating from 'Western' countries with strong trade union tradi-

tions were more easily persuaded to fall in line with his reforms, while South Korean firms were most difficult to deal with. This view is also supported by Hadi Topobroto, executive director, APINDO. He suggested that Korean firms are the most 'rotten'. Interviews with Batubara, 29 December 1993; and Hadi Topobroto, 4 January 1994.

88 As was also suggested by Cosmas Batubara. Interview 29 December 1993.

89 Nike sub-contractors in Indonesia – five Korean-owned and one Indonesian owned, but Korean-managed – have often been criticised for their labour practices (see *Inside Indonesia*, no. 27, June 1991: 7).

90 The sub-contractor was PT Duta Busana Danastri. Levi-Strauss also reportedly moved out of its production facilities in China over non-compliance with this code of conduct on the part of sub-contractors.

91 Although, in the end, the multinational rejected a request from YLBHI that it provide assistance in acquiring access to its sub-contractors' factories, for inspection purposes. Notes taken during discussions between YLBHI and Levi-Strauss Representative in Indonesia, 16 February and 25 March 1994.

92 Quoted in 'Nike in Indonesia', see note 86.

93 He admitted that a prior case of strike action at one of the two factories operated by his firm was resolved after local security forces were 'invited' to settle the problem.

9 FUTURE DIRECTIONS

1 After all, referring to the labour movement in England in the nineteenth century, Marx once wrote that 'The English have all the *material pre-requisites* for the social revolution. What they lack is a *spirit for generalisation and revolutionary fervour*' (Marx quoted in Levin 1989: 148).

2 In the advanced industrial countries, however, current incursions against organised labour demonstrate that even such bulwarks are not necessarily impregnable in the context of continuing struggles.

3 Manning and Jayasuriya (1996: 30–32), as mentioned earlier, suggest that the labour market is undergoing an historical transformation, as the absolute numbers of workers employed in agricultural activities declined sharply in the 1990s for the first time in Java, and stabilised in the Outer Islands. They link this to the earlier decline in fertility rates, continuing increases in school enrolments, and to the rapid growth in urban jobs.

4 As pointed out, one negative aspect of the involvement of NGOs in the labour movement has been a resultant fragmentation rooted in competing political orientations and strategic inclinations. Three distinct clusters of labour NGOs have been identified in this study: the corporatist reformist; the liberal/social democratic reformist; and the radical.

5 As in the current and bitter struggle in France, for example.

Bibliography

BOOKS, ARTICLES IN BOOKS AND ACADEMIC JOURNALS, UNPUBLISHED PAPERS AND DOCUMENTS

AAWL (Australia Asia Workers Links) (1994) letter to Martin Ferguson (ACTU), exact date unclear.

AFL-CIO (American Federation of Labor-Congress of International Organizations) (1989) 'A Petition to the US Trade Representative Regarding Workers Rights', submitted to the Chairman of the GSP Subcommittee, Trade Policy Staff Committee, 1 June.

Aidit, D.N. (n.d.) *Sedjarah Gerakan Buruh Indonesia: (Dari Tahun 1905 Sampai Tahun 1926), Vol. I*, Jakarta: Jajasan Pembaruan.

——(1958) *Indonesian Society and the Indonesian Revolution*, Jakarta: Jajasan Pembaruan.

Alexander, Robert J. (1963) 'Brazil, Argentina and Chile', in Walter Galenson (ed.) *Labour in Developing Economies*, Berkeley: University of California Press.

Amal, Ichlasul (1994) 'Dilemmas of Decentralisation and Democratisation', in David Bourchier and John Legge (eds) *Democracy in Indonesia: 1950s and 1990s*, Clayton: Centre of Southeast Asian Studies, Monash University.

American Embassy (1994) 'Labour Trends in Indonesia', unpublished report, Jakarta.

AMRC (Asia Monitor Resource Centre) (1987) *Minju No-Jo, South Korea's New Trade Unions: The Struggle for Free Trade Unions*, Hong Kong.

Anderson, Benedict (1994) 'Rewinding Back to the Future', in David Bourchier and John Legge (eds), *Democracy in Indonesia: 1950s and 1990s*, Clayton: Centre of Southeast Asian Studies, Monash University.

Andriyani, Nori (1996) 'The Making of Indonesian Women Worker Activists', MWS Thesis, Women's Studies Program, Memorial University of Newfoundland, St. Johns.

Anonymous (1994) 'Nasakomisasi dan Trade Unionisme', unpublished paper, Jakarta, 15 July.

APINDO (Asosiasi Pengusaha Indonesia) (n.d.) *APINDO: The Employers Association of Indonesia*, Jakarta.

Arudsothy, Ponniah and Craig R. Littler (1993) 'State Regulation and Union Fragmentation in Malaysia', in Stephen Frenkel (ed.) *Organised Labour in the Asia Pacific Region: A Comparative Study of Trade Unionism in Nine Countries*, Ithaca: ILR Press.

Asiawatch (1992) 'Petition Before the US Trade Representative on Labour Rights in Indonesia', June.

Aspinall, Edward (1994) 'Intra-regime Conflict and Civilian Dissent in Indonesia:

The Case of Students', paper prepared for the Asian Studies Association of Australia Biennial Conference, Murdoch University, Western Australia, 13–16 July.

AUSAID (Australian Agency for International Development) (1996), 'Executive Project Summary', attached to message addressed to Mr Teten Masduki (YLBHI), dated 10 January.

BAKORSTRANAS (Badan Koordinasi Strategis Nasional) (1990) 'Technical Guidance: Guidelines for Dealing with Industrial Relations Cases' (no. 02/Stanas/XII/1990: Pedoman Penanggulangan Kasus Hubungan Industrial).

Batubara, Cosmas (1991) 'Kebijaksanaan Penyelesaian Perselisihan Perburuhan', unpublished paper, 15 October.

Bello, Walden and Stephanie Rosenfeld (1992) *Dragons in Distress: Asia's Miracle Economies in Crisis*, London: Penguin.

Berger, Mark (1994) 'The End of the Third World?', *Third World Quarterly*, 15, 2: 257–275.

Bergquist, Charles (1984) *Labour in the Capitalist World Economy*, Beverly Hills: Sage.

Bjorkman, Maja, Laurids S. Lauridsen and Henrik Secher Marcussen (1988) 'Types of Industrialization and the Capital–Labour Relation in the Third World', in Roger Southall (ed.) *Trade Unions and the New Industrialization of the Third World*, London: Zed Press.

BKS-BUMIL (Badan Kerjasama Buruh-Militer) Seluruh Indonesia (1961a) 'Keputusan Ketudjuh tentang Resolusi Pembentukan Dewan Perusahaan', internal document, BKS-BUMIL Conference, Lembang, 1 February.

——(1961b) 'Keputusan Kedelapan Tentang Penggalangan Persatuan Organisasi Buruh Indonesia', internal document, BKS-BUMIL Conference, Lembang, 1 February.

Block, Fred (1990) *Post Industrial Possibilities: A Critique of Economic Discourse*, Berkeley: University of California Press.

Boileau, Julien M. (1983) *GOLKAR: Functional Group Politics in Indonesia*, Jakarta: Center for Strategic and International Studies.

Bourchier, David (1994a) 'Solidarity: The New Order's First Free Trade Union', in David Bourchier (ed.), *Indonesia's Emerging Proletariat: Workers and Their Struggles*, Indonesia Annual Lecture Series, Clayton: Centre of Southeast Asian Studies, Monash University.

——(1994b) 'The 1950s in New Order Ideology and Politics', in David Bourchier and John Legge (eds), *Democracy in Indonesia, 1950 and 1990s*, Monash Papers on Southeast Asia no. 31, Clayton: Centre of Southeast Asian Studies, Monash University.

——(1996) 'Lineages of Organicist Political Thought in Indonesia', Ph.D. thesis, Department of Politics, Monash University, Melbourne.

Boyd, Rosalind, Robin Cohen, and Peter C.W. Gutkind (eds) (1987), *International Labour and the Third World: The Making of a New Working Class*, Brookfield: Averbury.

BPS (Biro Pusat Statistik) (1993) *Statistik Indonesia*, Jakarta.

Breman, Jan (1982) 'The Village on Java and the Early Colonial State', *Journal of Peasant Studies*, 9, 4: 189–240.

Brown, Andrew and Stephen Frenkel (1993) 'Union Unevenness and Insecurity in Thailand', in Stephen Frenkel (ed.) *Organised Labour in the Asia Pacific Region: A Comparative Study of Trade Unionism in Nine Countries*, Ithaca: ILR Press.

Brown, Colin (1994) 'The Politics of Trade Union Formation in the Java Sugar Industry, 1945–1949', *Modern Asian Studies*, 28, 1: 77–98.

Budiman, Arief (1990) 'Introduction: From Conference to a Book', in Arief

Budiman (ed.) *State and Civil Society in Indonesia*, Monash Papers on Southeast Asia, no. 22, Clayton: Centre of Southeast Asian Studies, Monash University.

Bulkin, Farchan (1984) 'Kapitalisme, Golongan Menengah dan Negara: Sebuah Catatan Penelitian', *Prisma*, 2, February: 3–22.

Burawoy, Michael (1985) *The Politics of Production: Factory Regimes Under Capitalism and Socialism*, London: Verso.

Business International Corporation (1968) *Doing Business in Indonesia*, New York.

Cahyono, Edi (1992) 'Labour Movement: From *Unjuk Rasa* and Strikes to Class Consciousness', paper contributed to Second Indian Ocean Region Trade Union Conference, Perth, 4–12 December.

Callinicos, Alex (1995) *Theories and Narratives: Reflections on the Philosophy of History*, Cambridge: Polity Press.

Capizzi, Elaine (1974) 'Trade Unions Under the New Order', in *Repression and Exploitation in Indonesia*, Spokesman Books.

Chandoke, Neera (1994), 'Marxian Political Economy as Method: How Political is Political Economy?' *Economic and Political Weekly*, XXIX, 5, 29 January: 15–24.

Chu, J.J. (1993), 'Political Liberalization and the Rise of Taiwanese Labour Radicalism', *Journal of Contemporary Asia*, 23, 2: 173–187.

CIWCS (Centre for Indonesian Working Class Struggle) (1994) leaflet.

Cohen, Jean L. (1982) *Class and Civil Society: The Limits of Marxian Critical Theory*, Amherst: University of Massachusetts.

Cohen, Robin, Peter C.W. Gutkind, Phyllis Brazier (eds) (1979) *Peasants and Proletarians: The Struggles of Third World Workers*, London: Hutchinson and Co.

Collier, Ruth Berins and David Collier (1991) *Shaping the Political Arena*, Princeton: Princeton University Press.

Cribb, Robert (1985) 'The Indonesia Marxist Tradition', in Colin Mackeras and Nick Knight (eds) *Marxism in Asia*, London: Croom Helm.

Cumings, Bruce (1989) 'The Abortive Abertura: South Korea in the Light of the Latin American Experience', *New Left Review*, 173, January–February: 5–32.

Department of Foreign Affairs of the Republic of Indonesia (1993) 'Workers' Rights: Issues and Perspectives', September.

Department of Manpower of the Republic of Indonesia (1985) *Pedoman Pelaksanaan Hubungan Industrial Pancasila*, Jakarta.

Department of Manpower of the Republic of Indonesia (1992–93), *Laporan Akhir Penelitian Dampak Pemogokan terhadap Perusahaan dan Kesejahteraan Pekerja*, Pusat Penelitian dan Pengembangan Tenaga Kerja, Jakarta.

Deyo, Frederic C. (1987) 'State and Labour: Modes of Political Exclusion in East Asian Development', in Frederic C. Deyo (ed.) *The Political Economy of the New Asian Industrialism*, Ithaca: Cornell University Press.

——(1989) *Beneath the Miracle: Labour Subordination in the New Asian Industrialism*, Berkeley: University of California Press.

——(1995) 'Labour and Post-Fordist Industrialisation in Southeast Asia', paper prepared for a workshop on the Political Economy of Southeast Asia, Asia Research Centre on Social, Political and Economic Change, Murdoch University, Western Australia, 18 August.

—— (1987) Stephan Haggard and Hagen Koo, 'Labour in the Political Economy of East Asian Industrialisation', *Bulletin of Concerned Asian Scholars*, 19, 2: 42–53.

Dhanani, Shafiq (1992) 'Estimating Informal Sector Employment and Incomes in Indonesia', BAPPENAS/RMPT (Regional Manpower Planning and Training Project), Technical Report no. 1, Jakarta.

——(1994) 'Training Needs in Manufacturing Sector: Findings of 1992 Manufacturing Survey', paper presented at a seminar on Vocational Training, Labour Market and Economic Development in Indonesia, Bali, 10–12 February.

Directorate of International Trade (HPI), Department of Foreign Affairs of the Republic of Indonesia (1993), 'Ancaman Pencabutan GSP AS Apabila Tidak Terjadi Perbaikan Dalam Hak-hak Perburuhan di Indonesia', Internal Report, 27 August.

Djajusman, D. Suziani (1992) 'Di Seberang Gerbang Pabrik: Asrama Buruh Perempuan', *Prisma*, 3: 51–58.

Djati, Arief W. (1994) 'Buruh, Resistensi dan Politik', unpublished paper.

Effendi, M. Tohir (1989) 'Oposisi di Indonesia: Studi Kasus Kelompok Petisi 50', *Sarjana* thesis, Faculty of Social and Political Sciences, University of Indonesia, Jakarta.

Elson, Diane and Ruth Pearson (1980) *The Latest Phase in the Internationalisation of Capital and its Implications for Women in the Third World*, discussion paper, Institute of Development Studies, University of Sussex, Brighton.

Elster, Jon (1986) 'Further Thoughts on Marxism, Functionalism, and Game Theory', in John Roemer (ed.), *Analytical Marxism*, Cambridge: Cambridge University Press.

Engels, Friedrich (1993) *The Condition of the Working Class in England*, Oxford: Oxford University Press.

Erickson, Kenneth (1977) *The Brazilian Corporative State and Working Class Politics*, Berkeley: University of California Press.

Etty, Tom (1990) 'Trade Union Rights in Indonesia: Problems, Concerns and Challenges for (Inter)national Labour', paper presented to an SPSI/ICFTU-APRO seminar on International Labour Standards, Jakarta, 9–12 September.

——(1993) 'Report on Working Visit to Indonesia, 9 September–19 September', unpublished paper, 5 October.

——(1994) 'Indonesia in 1993: The Labour Year', unpublished paper.

Farid, Hilmar (1992) 'Covering Strikes: Indonesian Workers and "Their" Media', paper contributed to Second Indian Ocean Region Trade Union Conference, Perth, 4–12 December.

Feith, Herbert (1962) *The Decline of Constitutional Democracy in Indonesia*, Ithaca: Cornell University Press.

FORSOL (Forum Solidaritas Buruh) (1993) 'Noted Action to GSP Subcommitteee Fact Finding Mission', Jakarta.

Freeman, Richard B. (1993) 'Does Suppression of Labor Contribute to Economic Success? Labour Relations and Markets in East Asia', unpublished paper.

Frenkel, Stephen (1993) 'Theoretical Frameworks and Empirical Contexts of Trade Unionism', in Stephen Frenkel (ed.) *Organised Labour in the Asia Pacific Region: A Comparative Study of Trade Unionism in Nine Countries*, Ithaca: ILR Press.

——, Jon-Chao Hong, and Bih-Ling Lee (1993), 'The Resurgence and Fragility of Trade Unions in Taiwan', in Stephen Frenkel (ed.) *Organised Labour in the Asia Pacific Region: A Comparative Study of Trade Unionism in Nine Countries*, Ithaca: ILR Press.

Friso, Enzo (ICFTU) (1994), correspondence with Lewis Preston (World Bank), 12 September.

Frobel, Folker, Juergen Heinrichs and Otto Kreye (1978) 'The New International Division of Labour', *Social Science Information*, 17, 1: 123–142.

——(1980) *The New International Division of Labour*, Cambridge: Cambridge University Press.

FSPSI (Federasi Serikat Pekerja Seluruh Indonesia) (1996) *Buku Saku Federasi Serikat Pekerja Seluruh Indonesia Periode 1995–2000, Vol. II*, Jakarta.

Furnivall, J.S. (1944) *Netherlands India: A Study of a Plural Economy*, Cambridge, Cambridge University Press.

GASBIINDO (Gabungan Serikat Buruh Islam Indonesia) (1967) *Sokoguru Revolusi Indonesia.*

Geary, Dick (1981) *European Labour Protest, 1848–1939*, New York: St. Martin's Press.

——(1989a) 'Introduction', in Dick Geary (ed.) *Labour and Socialist Movements in Europe before 1914*, Oxford: Berg.

——(1989b) 'Socialism and the German Labour Movement', in Dick Geary (ed.) *Labour and Socialist Movements in Europe before 1914*, Oxford: Berg.

Gerschenkron, Alexander (1962) *Economic Backwardness in Historical Perspective*, Cambridge: Harvard University Press.

Goldberg, Harry (1952) 'Gerakan Buruh di Indonesia', unpublished paper.

Goodman, David and Michael Redclift (1981) *From Peasant to Proletarian: Capitalist Development and Agrarian Transitions*, Oxford: Basil Blackwell.

Gorz, Andre (1982) *Farewell to the Working Class: An Essay on Post-Industrial Socialism*, London: Pluto Press.

Government of Indonesia (1989) 'Statement of the Government of Indonesia Before the Office of the United States Trade Representative, Trade Policy Staff Committee, Generalized System of Preferences Subcommittee', 18 October.

——(1990) 'Answers to the Questions Raised by the Office of the United States Trade Representative and the Generalised System of Preference Subcommittee', 6 February.

——(n.d.) 'Summary of Additional Steps Taken by the Government of Indonesia to Improve Worker Rights.'

GSP Information Centre (1993) 'GSP Subcommittee of the Trade Policy Staff Committee 1992 GSP Annual Review: Worker Rights Review Summary, Case 007-CP-92, Indonesia', Washington, July.

Hadiz, Vedi R. (1993) 'Workers and Working Class Politics in the 1990s', in Chris Manning and Joan Hardjono (eds) *Indonesia Assessment 1993, Labour: Sharing in the Benefits of Growth?*, Canberra: Department of Political and Social Change, Research School of Pacific Studies, Australian National University.

——(1994a), 'The Political Significance of Recent Working Class Action in Indonesia', in David Bourchier (ed.) *Indonesia's Emerging Proletariat: Workers and Their Struggles*, Annual Indonesia Lecture Series, Clayton: Centre of Southeast Asian Studies, Monash University.

——(1994b), 'Challenging State Corporatism on the Labour Front: Working Class Politics in the 1990s', in David Bourchier and John Legge (eds) *Democracy in Indonesia, 1950s and 1990s*, Monash Papers on Southeast Asia no. 31, Clayton: Centre of Southeast Asian Studies, Monash University.

Hanagan, Michael (1986) 'Agriculture and Industry in the Nineteenth-Century Stephanois: Household Employment Patterns and the Rise of a Permanent Proletariat', in Michael Hanagan and Charles Stephenson (eds) *Proletarians and Protest: The Roots of Class Formation in an Industrializing World*, New York: Greenwood Press.

Hancock, Peter James (1994) 'West Java: A Demographic Anomaly'. B.A. Honours Thesis, School of Social Sciences and Asian Languages, Curtin University of Technology, Perth, September.

Hasibuan, Sayuti (1968) 'Political Unionism and Economic Development in Indonesia: Case Study, North Sumatra', Ph.D. thesis in Business Administration, University of California, Berkeley.

Hawkins, Everett D. (1963a) 'Labour in Transition', *Indonesia*, Ruth McVey (ed.), New Haven: Yale University Press.

——(1963b) 'Indonesia', in Walter Galenson (ed.) *Labour in Developing Economies*, Berkeley: University of California Press.

Hewison, Kevin and Andrew Brown (1992) 'Labour and Unions in Industrialising Thailand: A Brief History', paper presented at Second Indian Ocean Region Trade Union Conference, Perth, 4–12 December.

——, Garry Rodan and Richard Robison (1993) 'Introduction: Changing Forms of State Power in Southeast Asia', in Kevin Hewison, Richard Robison and Garry Rodan (eds), *Southeast Asia in the 1990s: Authoritarianism, Democracy, Capitalism*, Sydney: Allen and Unwin.

Hill, David T. (1994) *The Press in New Order Indonesia*, Asia Paper no. 4, Asia Research Centre on Social, Political and Economic Change, Murdoch University, Perth: University of Western Australia Press.

Hill, Hal (1994) 'The Economy', in Hal Hill (ed.), *Indonesia's New Order: the Dynamics of Socio-Economic Transformation*, St. Leonards: Allen and Unwin.

Hirschman, Albert O. (1968) 'The Political Economy of Import-Substituting Industrialisation in Latin America', *The Quarterly Journal of Economics*, 82, 1, February: 2–32.

Hofheinz, Roy, Jr., and Kent Calder (1982) *The Eastasia Edge*, New York: Basic Books.

Hull, Terence H. (1994) 'Workers in the Shadows: A Statistical Wayang', in David Bourchier (ed.) *Indonesia's Emerging Proletariat: Workers and Their Struggles*, Annual Indonesia Lecture Series, Clayton: Centre of Southeast Asian Studies, Monash University.

Human Rights Watch/Asia (1994) *The Limits to Openness: Human Rights in Indonesia and East Timor*, New York.

Hutchison, Jane (1992) 'Women in the Philippines Garments Exports Industry', *Journal of Contemporary Asia*, 22, 4: 471–489.

——(1993) 'Class and State Power in the Philippines', in Kevin Hewison, Richard Robison, and Garry Rodan (eds) *Southeast Asia in the 1990s: Authoritarianism, Democracy, Capitalism*, Sydney: Allen and Unwin.

INDOC (Indonesian Documentation and Information Centre) (1981) *Indonesian Workers and Their Right to Organise*, Leiden.

——(1982) *Indonesian Workers and Their Right to Organise*, Update, Leiden, February.

——(1983) *Indonesian Workers and Their Right to Organise*, Update, Leiden, March.

——(1984) *Indonesian Workers and Their Right to Organise*, Update, Leiden, March.

Ingleson, John (1981a) 'Worker Consciousness and Labour Unions in Colonial Java', *Pacific Affairs*, 54, 31: 485–501.

——(1981b) 'Bound Hand and Foot: Railway Workers and the 1923 Strike in Java', *Indonesia*, 31, April: 53–87.

——(1986) *In Search of Justice: Workers and Unions in Colonial Java, 1908–1926*, Singapore: Oxford University Press.

ILO (International Labour Office) (1994) *Lists of Ratifications by Convention and by Country (as at 31 December 1993)*, Report III (Part 5), International Labor Conference, 81st Session.

——(1995) 'Draft Project Document: Workers Education Assistance to the Indonesian Trade Union Movement', 15 August.

International Labor Organization Mission to Indonesia (1993) 'Indonesia: Report of the Direct Contacts Mission on Implementation of Convention no. 98'.

ILRERF (International Labor Rights Education and Research Fund) (1992) 'Petition Before the Inter-Agency Trade Policy Committee, Subcommittee on the Generalized System of Preferences, Requesting the Review of the Beneficiary Status of Indonesia', 1 June.

Jakarta Social Institute (1992) 'Strike on PT Gajah Tunggal Group – Tangerang', paper presented at Eighth International NGO Forum on Indonesia Conference on People's Participation in Economic Liberalisation, Odawara, Japan, 21–23 March.

Jenkins, Rhys (1984) 'Divisions Over the International Division of Labour', *Capital and Class*, 22: 28–57.

——(1991) 'The Political Economy of Industrialization: A Comparison of Latin America and East Asian Industrializing Countries', *Development and Change*, 22, 2: 197–231.

Jordan, Bill (1995) 'Preface', in David R. Harris (ed.) *Prisoners of Progress: A Review of the Current Indonesian Labour Situation*, INDOC, FNV, INFID, Leiden.

Kahin, Audrey (1994) 'Regionalism and Decentralisation', in David Bourchier and John Legge (eds) *Democracy in Indonesia, 1950s and 1990s*, Monash Papers on Southeast Asia no. 31, Clayton: Centre of Southeast Asian Studies, Monash University.

Katz, Donald R. (1994) *Just Do It: The Nike Spirit in the Corporate World*, Holbrook: Adams.

Katznelson, Ira (1986) 'Working Class Formation: Constructing Cases and Comparisons', in Ira Katznelson and Aristide R. Zolberg (eds), *Working Class Formation: Nineteenth Century Patterns in Western Europe and the United States*, Princeton: Princeton University Press.

KBM (Kesatuan Buruh Marhaenis) (1965) 'Laporan Umum Dewan Pimpinan Pusat Kesatuan Buruh Marhaenis pada Kongres Nasional ke IV Kesatuan Buruh Marhaenis', 25 July–1 August, Jakarta.

KBSI (Kongres Buruh Seluruh Indonesia) (1957) 'Laporan Dewan Pimpinan Harian Kongres Buruh Seluruh Indonesia Kepada Konperensi Kilat KBSI', Bandung, 3–5 December.

——(1961) 'Perkembangan Keadaan Politik Sosial Ekonomi Perburuhan Djuni 1956–April 1961', Second KBSI Working Conference, Bandung, 14–16 April.

Keck, Margaret E. (1989) 'The New Unionism in the Brazilian Transition', in Alfred Stepan (ed.) *Democratizing Brazil: Problems of Transition and Consolidation*, New York: Oxford University Press.

Kelly, John (1988) *Trade Unions and Socialist Politics*, London: Verso.

Kiely, Ray (1995) 'Third World Relativism: A New Form of Imperialism', *Journal of Contemporary Asia*, 25, 2: 159–178.

Kim, Hwang-Joe (1993) 'The Korean Union Movement in Transition', in Stephen Frenkel (ed.) *Organised Labour in the Asia Pacific Region: A Comparative Study of Trade Unionism in Nine Countries*, Ithaca: ILR Press.

King, Dwight Y. (1979) 'Defensive Modernization: The Structuring of Economic Interests in Indonesia', in Gloria Davies (ed.) *What is Modern Indonesian Culture*, Southeast Asia Series no. 52, Ohio Center for International Studies.

——(1982) *Interest Groups and Political Linkage in Indonesia 1800–1965*, Special Report no. 20, Centre for Southeast Asian Studies, Northern Illinois University.

Komisi Upah (1996) 'Pernyataan Komisi Upah tentang Ketentuan Upah Minimum tahun 1996', 12 January, Jakarta.

Koo, Hagen (1993) 'The State, *Minjung*, and the Working Class in South Korea', in Hagen Koo (ed.) *State and Society in Contemporary Korea*, Ithaca: Cornell University Press.

Krueger, Anne O. (1982) 'Newly Industrializing Economics', *Economic Impact*, 40: 26–32.

Kurth, James (1979) 'Industrial Change and Political Change: A European Perspective', in David Collier (ed.) *The New Authoritarianism in Latin America*, Princeton: Princeton University Press.

Labour Research Association (1984) *Labour Confronts the Transnationals*, New York: International Publishers.

Lambert, Rob (1993) 'Authoritarian State Unionism in New Order Indonesia', Working Paper no. 25, Asia Research Centre on Social, Political and Economic Change, Murdoch University, Western Australia.

Lebowitz, Michael (1991) *Beyond Capital: Marx's Political Economy of the Working Class*, London: Macmillan.

Leclerc, Jacques (1972) 'An Ideological Problem of Trade Unionism in the Sixties: Karyawan versus Buruh', *Review of Indonesian and Malayan Affairs*, 6, 1: 76–91.

Legge, John (1993) *Kaum Intelektual dan Perjuangan Kemerdekaan*, Jakarta: Grafitipers.

Leggett, Chris (1993a) 'Singapore's Industrial Relations in the 1990s', in Garry Rodan (ed.) *Singapore Changes Guard: Social, Political and Economic Direction in the 1990s*, Melbourne: Longman Cheshire.

——(1993b) 'Corporatist Trade Unionism in Singapore', in Stephen Frenkel (ed.) *Organised Labour in the Asia Pacific Region: A Comparative Study of Trade Unionism in Nine Countries*, Ithaca: ILR Press.

Lenin, Vladimir Ilyich (1976) 'The Vanguard Party' (original title: 'What is to be Done?'), in Irving Howe (ed.) *Essential Works of Socialism*, New Haven: Yale University Press.

Lev, Daniel S. (1994) 'On the Fall of the Parliamentary System', in David Bourchier and John Legge (eds) *Democracy in Indonesia, 1950s and 1990s*, Monash Papers on Southeast Asia no. 31, Clayton: Centre of Southeast Asian Studies, Monash University.

Levin, David A. and Stephen Chiu (1993) 'Dependent Capitalism, a Colonial State, and Marginal Unions: The Case of Hong Kong', in Stephen Frenkel (ed.) *Organised Labour in the Asia Pacific Region: A Comparative Study of Trade Unionism in Nine Countries*, Ithaca: ILR Press.

Levin, Michael (1989) *Marx, Engels and Liberal Democracy*, London: Macmillan.

Levinson, Charles (1974) *International Trade Unionism*, London: Allen and Unwin.

Lewis, Lane (1994) (US Representative, Illinois), letter to USTR, 9 September.

Leys, Colin (1996) *The Rise and Fall of Development Theory*, Bloomington: Indiana University Press.

Limqueco, Peter, Bruce McFarlane and Jan Odhnoff (1989) *Labour and Industry in ASEAN*, Manila: Journal of Contemporary Asia Publishers.

Lloyd, Peter (1982) *A Third World Proletariat?*, London: George Allen and Unwin.

Lubis, T. Mulya, Fauzie Abdullah and Mulyana W. Kusumah (1981) *Laporan Keadaan Hak Asasi Manusia di Indonesia 1981*, Jakarta: Sinar Harapan.

MacIntyre, Andrew (1991) *Business and Politics in Indonesia*, Sydney: Allen and Unwin.

Magraw, Roger (1989) 'Socialism, Syndicalism and French Labour', in Dick Geary (ed.) *Labour and Socialist Movements in Europe Before 1914*, Oxford: Berg.

Manning, Chris (1992) 'Survey of Recent Developments', *Bulletin of Indonesian Economic Studies*, 28, 1, April 1992: 3–38.

——(1993) 'Structural Change and Industrial Relations during the Soeharto Period: An Approaching Crisis', *Bulletin of Indonesian Economic Studies*, 29, 2, August: 59–95.

——(1995) 'Approaching the Turning Point?: Labour Market Change Under Indonesia's New Order', *The Developing Economies*, XXXIII, 1, March 1995: 52–81.

——and Sisira Jayasuriya (1996) 'Survey of Recent Developments', *Bulletin of Indonesian Economic Studies*, 32, 2, August: 3–43.

Mansvelt, W.M.F. and P. Creutzberg (1979) *Changing Economy in Indonesia: A Selection of Statistical Source Material from the Early 19th Century up to 1940, Volume 5, National Income*, Amsterdam: Royal Tropical Institute.

Manulang, Sendjun H. (1990) *Pokok-Pokok Hukum Ketenagakerjaan Indonesia*, Jakarta: Rineka Cipta.

Marx, Karl (1963) *The 18th Brumaire of Louis Bonaparte*, New York: International Publishers.

Mather, Celia (1983) 'Subordination of Women and Lack of Industrial Strife in West Java', in John G. Taylor and Andrew Turton (eds) *Sociology of 'Developing Societies'*, New York: Monthly Review Press.

Matheson, Alan (1994) (ACTU) memorandum to Len Cooper (AAWL), 23 March 1994.

McLeod, Ross (1993) 'Workers' Social Security Legislation', in Chris Manning and Joan Hardjono (eds), *Indonesia Assessment 1993, Labour: Sharing in the Benefits of Growth?*, Canberra: Department of Political and Social Change, Research School of Pacific Studies, Australian National University.

McVey, Ruth (1965) *The Rise of Indonesian Communism*, Ithaca: Cornell University Press.

Meek, John Paul (1956) 'The Government and Economic Development in Indonesia, 1950–1954', Ph.D. thesis, Graduate Faculty, University of Virginia.

Moertopo, Ali (1972) *Akselarasi Modernisasi Pembangunan 25 Tahun*, Jakarta: Center for Strategic and International Studies.

——(1974) *Strategi Politik Nasional*, Jakarta: Center for Strategic and International Studies.

——(1975) *Buruh dan Tani dalam Pembangunan*, Jakarta: Center for Strategic and International Studies.

Moktar (1992) 'Citeureup', paper contributed to Second Indian Ocean Region Trade Union Conference, Perth, 4–13 December.

Moore, Barrington (1966) *The Social Origins of Dictatorship and Democracy*, Harmondsworth: Penguin.

——(1978) *Injustice: Social Bases of Obedience and Revolt*, London: Macmillan.

Morris, Aldon D. (1992) 'Political Consciousness and Collective Action', in Aldon D. Morris and Carol McClurg Morris, *Frontiers in Social Movement Theory*, New Haven: Yale University Press.

Munck, Ronaldo (1988a) *The New International Labour Studies: An Introduction*, London: Zed Books.

——(1988b) 'Capital Restructuring and Labour Recomposition Under a Military Regime: Argentina (1976–83)', in Roger Southall (ed.) *Trade Unions and the New Industrialization of the Third World*, London: Zed Books.

Munslow, Barry and Henry Finch (eds) (1984) *Proletarianisation in the Third World: Studies in the Creation of a Labour Force Under Dependent Capitalism*, London: Croom Helm.

Muntz, Bob (1992) 'Nagkakaisang Manggagawa: A Philippine Case Study in Trade Unionism, Class Conflict and Foreign Investment', in Michael Pinches and Salim Lakha (eds) *Wage Labour and Social Change: The Proletariat in Asia and the Pacific*, Quezon City: New Day Publishers.

Nasution, A.H. (1960) 'Sambutan Menteri Keamanan & Pertahanan/KSAD dalam Kongres ke-VI Serikat Buruh Islam Indonesia, 23–26 January 1960', in *Buku Kenang-kenangan Kongres SBII ke-VI di Jogjakarta 23–26 January 1960*, Jakarta: PB SBII Bagian Penerangan.

NGOs, various (1994) 'Kondisi Umum Upah dan Pengupahan', unpublished paper.

——(1995) 'Klarifikasi, Sikap dan Posisi NGOs tentang Program Workers' Education Project', addressed to Mr Peter Duncan (WEP) and Mr Herman van der Laan (ILO Jakarta), dated 18 January.

Novo, Lendo (n.d.) 'Biaya Produksi dan Upah Bagi Pengusaha Indonesia', unpublished paper.

Nurbaiti, Ati (1986) 'Pengaturan Perburuhan dalam Penataaan Struktur Politik Orde Baru: Kasus Buruh Industri Tekstil di PT ITM, Kec. Tangerang, Kabupaten Tangerang', S-1 Thesis, University of Indonesia, Jakarta.

——(n.d.) 'Potret Keterlibatan Aparat Keamanan dalam Konflik Buruh-Majikan', unpublished paper.

Nusantara, Abdul Hakim G. (1995) in David R. Harris (ed.) 'Law and the Right to Organise', in *Prisoners of Progress: A Review of the Current Indonesian Labour Situation*, Leiden: INDOC, FNV, INFID.

O'Brien, Leslie (1988) 'Between Capitalism and Labour: Trade Unionism in Malaysia', in Roger Southall (ed.) *Labour Unions in Asia and Africa: Contemporary Issues*, London: Macmillan.

O'Donnell, Guillermo A. (1973) *Modernization and Bureaucratic Authoritarianism*, Berkeley: Institute of International Studies.

O'Donnell, Guillermo A. and Philip C. Schmitter (1986) *Tentative Conclusions about Uncertain Democracies*, Baltimore: Johns Hopkins University Press.

Offe, Claus (1985) 'New Social Movements: Challenging the Boundaries of Institutional Politics', *Social Research*, 52, 4, Winter.

Ofreneo, Rene (1993) 'Labor and the Philippine Economy', Ph.D. Thesis, College of Social Sciences and Philosophy, University of the Philippines.

Ogle, George E. (1990) *South Korea: Dissent Within the Economic Miracle*, London: Zed Books.

Olle, Werner and Wolfgang Schoeller (1987) 'World Market Competition and Restrictions Upon International Trade Union Policies', in Rosalind E. Boyd, Robin Cohen and Peter C.W. Gutkind (eds) *International Labour and the Third World*, Aldershot: Avebury.

Olson, Mancur (1965) *The Logic of Collective Action*, Cambridge: Harvard University Press.

Orwell, George (1986) *The Road to Wigan Pier*, London: Penguin.

Pakpahan, Muchtar (1993) 'Peradilan Perburuhan dalam Sistem Hukum Nasional', unpublished paper.

Pangaribuan, Robinson (1995) *The Indonesian State Secretariat, 1945–1993*, Perth: Asia Research Centre on Social, Political and Economic Change, Murdoch University.

Panitch, Leo (1986) *Working Class Politics in Crisis: Essays on Labour and the State*, London: Verso.

Pasaribu, Bomer (1994) 'Perwujudan Hak Berserikat dan Berunding dalam Hubungan Industrial Pancasila', in Adi Sasono, Soetrisno, Tosari Widjaja, R. Moedjianto, Moh. Djumhur Hidayat (eds), *Membangun Hubungan Industrial Pancasila*, Jakarta: Department of Manpower of the Republic of Indonesia and Centre for Information and Development Studies.

Petras, James and Dennis Engbarth (1988) 'Third World Industrialization and Third World Trade Union Struggles', in Roger Southall (ed.) *Trade Unions and the New Industrialization of the Third World*, London: Zed Press.

Phillips, Gordon (1989) 'The British Labour Movement Before 1914', in Dick Geary (ed.) *Labour and Socialist Movements in Europe Before 1914*, Oxford: Berg.

Potter, David (1993) 'Democratization in Asia', in David Held (ed.) *Prospects for Democracy: North, South, East, West,* Cambridge: Polity Press.

Przeworski, Adam (1991) *Democracy and the Market: Political and Economic Reforms in Eastern Europe and Latin America*, Cambridge: Cambridge University Press.

Razif (1994a) 'The Working Class: Defeated by History, Mobilised by History', in David Bourchier (ed.) *Indonesia's Emerging Proletariat: Workers and Their*

Struggles, Annual Indonesia Lecture Series, Clayton: Centre of Southeast Asian Studies, Monash University.

——(1994b) 'Sejarah Pemikiran Serikat Buruh Indonesia', unpublished paper.

Reeve, David (1985) *Golkar of Indonesia: An Alternative to the Party System*, Singapore: Oxford University Press.

Reid, Anthony (1974) *The Indonesian National Revolution, 1945–1950*, Hawthorn: Longman.

Robison, Richard (1982) 'The Transformation of the State in Indonesia', *Bulletin of Concerned Asian Scholars*, 14, 1: 48–60.

——(1986) *Indonesia: The Rise of Capital*, Sydney: Allen and Unwin.

——(1990) *Power and Economy in Suharto's Indonesia*, Manila: Journal of Contemporary Asia Publishers.

——(1993) 'Tensions in State and Regime', in Kevin Hewison, Richard Robison and Garry Rodan (eds) *Southeast Asia in the 1990s: Authoritarianism, Democracy and Capitalism*, Sydney: Allen and Unwin.

—— and Vedi R. Hadiz (1993) 'Privatization or the Reorganisation of Dirigism: Indonesian Economic Policy in the 1990s', *Canadian Journal of Development Studies*, Special Issue: 13–32.

Roemer, John (1986) 'Introduction', in John Roemer (ed.) *Analytical Marxism*, Cambridge: Cambridge University Press.

Roemer, John (1994) 'Introduction', in John Roemer (ed.) *Foundations of Analytical Marxism*, Aldershot: Edward Elgar Publishing Limited.

Roesli, M. Arief (1992) 'Buruh dan Kesadaran Kelas', unpublished paper.

Rudiono, Danu (1992) 'Kebijaksanaan Perburuhan Pasca Boom Minyak', *Prisma*, 1: 61–80.

Rueschemeyer, Dietrich, Evelyne Huber Stephens, and John D. Stephens (1992) *Capitalist Development and Democracy*, Cambridge: Polity Press.

Sabarno, Hari (1994) 'Pelaksanaan HIP yang Mantap, Aman, dan Dinamis Menciptakan Stabilitas Nasional', in Adi Sasono, Soetrisno, Tosari Widjaja, R. Moedjianto, Moh. Djumhur Hidayat (eds) *Membangun Hubungan Industrial Pancasila*, Jakarta: Department of Manpower of the Republic of Indonesia and Centre for Information and Development Studies.

Sandra (1961) *Sedjarah Perkembangan Buruh Indonesia*, PT Pustaka Rakyat.

SARBUMUSI (Sarekat Buruh Muslimin Indonesia) (1968) 'Keputusan-keputusan Sidang Pleno ke-II', 1–5 November.

——(1971) 'Memorandum' (addressed to the President of the Republic of Indonesia and to the Chief of the Supreme Court of the Republic of Indonesia), Jakarta, 23 April 1971.

SBM (Serikat Buruh Merdeka) Setiakawan (1990) 'Program Kerja Serikat Buruh Merdeka Setiakawan (Periode 1990–1995)', internal document.

SBSI (Serikat Buruh Sejahtera Indonesia) (1993a) *Serikat Buruh Sejahtera Indonesia*, Jakarta.

——(1993b) letter no. 69/SBSI/IV/1993, on application as a registered trade union, 29 April.

——(1994) 'Seruan Mogok/Unjuk Rasa', leaflet, 28 January.

Schmitter Phillip (1973) 'The Portugalization of Brazil?' in Alfred Stepan (ed.), *Authoritarian Brazil*, New Haven: Yale University Press.

Schwarz, Adam (1994) *A Nation in Waiting: Indonesia in the 1990s*, St. Leonards: Allen and Unwin.

Scott, James C. (1985) *Weapons of the Weak*, New Haven: Yale University Press.

Shin, Yoon-Hwan (1989) 'Demystifying the Capitalist State: Political Patronage, Bureaucratic Interests and Capitalists-in-Formation in Soeharto's Indonesia', Ph.D. thesis, Yale University.

——and You-il Lee (1995) 'Korean Direct Investment in Southeast Asia', *Journal of Contemporary Asia*, 25, 2: 179–196.

Shiraishi, Takashi (1990) *An Age in Motion*, Ithaca: Cornell University Press.

Siregar, Arifin (Indonesian Ambassador to US) (1993) correspondence with Michael Kantor (USTR), 20 October .

Simandjuntak, Marsillam (1994) *Pandangan Negara Integralistik*, Jakarta: PT Pustaka Utama Grafiti.

Simanjuntak, Payaman (1993) Director General of Industrial Relations and Labour Standards, Department of Manpower of the Republic of Indonesia, Circular B.62/m/BW/1993, 5 February.

Sitsen, Peter H.W. Sitsen (1943) *Industrial Development of the Netherlands Indies*, Bulletin 2, New York: The Netherlands and Netherlands Indies Council of the Institute of Pacific Relations.

Sjahrir (1989) 'Indonesian Financial and Trade Deregulation: Government Policies and Society Responses', paper presented at a Workshop on Dynamics of Economic Policy Reform in Southeast Asia and Australia, Center for the Study of Australia–Asia Relations, Griffith University, Queensland, 7–9 October.

SOB (Sentral Organisasi Buruh) Pantjasila (1960) *Tuntunan Bagi Kader Buruh Pantjasila*, Jakarta.

SOBSI (Sentral Organisasi Buruh Seluruh Indonesia) (1958) *Sedjarah Gerakan Buruh Indonesia*, Jakarta: Badan Penerbit Dewan Nasional.

Soedarwo, Imam and Arief Soemadji (SPSI) (1989) correspondence with Lane Kirkland (AFL-CIO), 8 August.

Soehardiman (1993) *Kupersembahkan Kepada Pengadilan Sejarah*, Yayasan Bina Produktivitas.

Soeharto (1990) *Pidato Kenegaraan Presiden Republik Indonesia Soeharto 16 Agustus 1990*, Department of Information, Republic of Indonesia.

Soepomo, Iman (1989) *Hukum Perburuhan: Undang-undang dan Peraturan-peraturan*, Jakarta: Djambatan.

Soewarsono (1991) 'Pemogokan Buruh dan Negara Kolonial', unpublished paper, 21 March.

Song, Ho Keun (1994) 'The State and Wage Policy: Some Implications for Corporatism', paper presented at a conference on Capitalism and Corporatism in Korea: Comparative Perspectives, Georgetown University, Washington D.C., USA, 15 May.

Southall, Roger (ed.) (1988a) *Trade Unions and the New Industrialization of the Third World*, London: Zed Books.

——(1988b), 'Introduction', in Roger Southall (ed.) *Trade Unions and the New Industrialization of the Third World*, London: Zed Books.

Spalding, Hobart A. (1977) *Organized Labour in Latin America: Historical Case Studies of Workers in Dependent Societies*, New York: New York University Press.

SPSI (Serikat Pekerja Seluruh Indonesia) (1990a) *Bunga Rampai Dalam Lintasan Sejarah Pembangunan*, Jakarta: DPP-SPSI and PERUM ASTEK.

——(1990b) 'Komposisi dan Personalia Dewan Pimpinan Pusat Serikat Pekerja Seluruh Indonesia 1990–1995', 30 November.

——(1990c) 'Pertanggungjawaban DPP SPSI Periode 1985–1990', internal document.

——(1993a) *Deklarasi Persatuan Buruh Seluruh Indonesia*, Jakarta.

——(1993b) *Keputusan Rapat Kerja Nasional II Serikat Pekerja Seluruh Indonesia, Caringin, Bogor, 6–9 Desember 1993*, Jakarta: DPP-SPSI.

——(1993c) *Check Off System Serikat Pekerja Seluruh Indonesia November 1992–Oktober 1993*, Jakarta: SPSI.

Standing, Guy (1991) 'Do Unions Impede or Accelerate Structural Adjustment?

Industrial Versus Company Unions in an Industrialising Labour Market', Labour Market Analysis and Employment Planning, Working Paper no. 47, World Employment Programme, Geneva: International Labour Office.

Stepan, Alfred (1978) *The State and Society: Peru in Comparative Perspective*, Princeton: Princeton University Press.

Stoller, Ann Laura (1985) *Capitalism and Confrontation in Sumatra's Plantation Belt, 1870–1979*, New Haven: Yale University Press.

Sudono, Agus (1978) *Gerakan Buruh Indonesia dan Kebijaksanaannya: Kumpulan Pidato/Ceramah/Sambutan*, Jakarta: FBSI-AAFLI.

——(1981) *FBSI Dahulu, Sekarang dan Yang Akan Datang*, Jakarta: FBSI.

——(1985) *30 Tahun Agus Sudono Mengabdi Gerakan Buruh*, Jakarta: FBSI.

Sukarno (1980) *Pembaharuan Gerakan Buruh di Indonesia dan Hubungan Perburuhan Pancasila*, Bandung: Penerbit Alumni.

Suwarto (1995) 'Statement of the Director General of Industrial Relations and Labour Standards to the USTR', 27 July.

Tanjung, Feisal (1993) 'Ceramah Panglima Angkatan Bersenjata Republik Indonesia pada Rakernas II Serikat Pekerja Seluruh Indonesia (SPSI)', paper presented at SPSI conference, Bogor, 7 December.

Tanter, Richard (1990) 'The Totalitarian Ambition: Intelligence and Security Agencies in Indonesia', in Arief Budiman (ed.) *State and Civil Society in Indonesia*, Monash papers on Southeast Asia no. 22, Clayton: Centre of Southeast Asian Studies, Monash University.

——and Kenneth R. Young (eds) (1990) *The Politics of Middle Class Indonesia*, Clayton: Centre of Southeast Asian Studies, Monash University.

Tedjasukmana, Iskandar (1958) *The Political Character of the Indonesian Trade Union Movement*, Ithaca: Cornell University Modern Indonesia Project.

Thamrin, Juni (n.d.) 'Kebijaksanaan Pengupahan Buruh pada Masa Orde Baru', unpublished paper.

——(1993) 'Labour in Small Scale Manufacturing', in Chris Manning and Joan Hardjono (eds) *Indonesia Assessment 1993, Labour: Sharing in the Benefits of Growth?*, Canberra: Department of Political and Social Change, Research School of Pacific Studies, Australian National University.

Thee, Kian Wie (1993) 'Foreign Investment and the ASEAN Economies with Special Reference to Indonesia', *The Indonesian Quarterly*, 21, 4: 434–460.

Therborn, Goran (1977) 'The Rule of Capital and the Rise of Democracy', *New Left Review*, 103, May-June: 3–41.

Thompson, E.P. (1968) *The Making of the English Working Class*, London: Pelican Books/Penguin.

Todd, Trish (1992) 'The Development of the Labour Movement in Malaysia', paper presented at the Second Indian Ocean Region Trade Union Conference, Perth, 4–12 December.

Tornquist, Olle (1991) *What's Wrong with Marxism Vol.II: On Peasants and Workers in India and Indonesia*, New Delhi: Manohar.

Ungpakorn, Ji (1995) 'The Tradition of Urban Working Class Struggle in Thailand', *Journal of Contemporary Asia*, 25, 1: 366–379.

Wad, Peter (1988) 'The Japanisation of the Malaysian Trade Union Movement', in Roger Southall (ed.) *Trade Unions and the New Industrialization of the Third World*, London: Zed Books.

White, Benjamin (1983) 'Agricultural Involution and its Critics: Twenty Years After', *Bulletin of Concerned Asian Scholars*, 15, 2: 18–31.

White, Benjamin (1993) 'Industrial Workers in West Java's Urban Fringe', in Chris Manning and Joan Hardjono (eds) *Indonesia Assessment 1993, Labour: Sharing in the Benefits of Growth?*, Canberra: Department of Political and Social Change, Research School of Pacific Studies, Australian National University.

White and Case (1993a) 'Memorandum' addressed to H.E. Hartarto, Coordinating Minister for Industry and Trade, 6 August.

——(1993b) 'Memorandum' addressed to H.E. Ministers Hartarto and Latief and Ambassador Siregar, 21 August.

——(1993c) 'Memorandum' addressed to H.E. Prof. S.B. Joedono, Minister of Trade, 4 September.

Wibowo, Harry (1992) 'Subordination and Resistance: Notes on the Working Class-in-Formation and labour strikes in the early 1990s', paper presented at a Conference on Indonesian Democracy, 1950s and 1990s, Monash University, 17–21 December, Clayton.

Widjaja, Tosari (1969) 'Sedjarah Singkat SARBUMUSI', unpublished paper, 20 August.

Wood, Ellen Meiksin (1989) 'Rational Choice Marxism: Is the Game Worth the Candle', *New Left Review*, 77: 41–88.

——(1995) *Democracy Against Capitalism*, Cambridge: Cambridge University Press.

World Bank (1993a) *Indonesia: Sustaining Development*, Report no. 11737-IND, 25 May.

——(1993b) *World Development Report 1993: Investing in Health*, New York: Oxford University Press.

——(1994) *Indonesia: Stability, Growth and Equity in Repelita VI*, Country Department III, East Asia Pacific Region, 27 May.

——(1995) *World Development Report 1995: Workers in an Integrating World*, New York: Oxford University Press.

—— (1996) *Indonesia: Dimensions of Growth*, Report no. 15383-ND, 7 May.

Wright, Erik Olin (1994) *Interrogating Inequality: Essays on Class Analysis, Socialism and Marxism*, London: Verso.

YAKOMA (Yayasan Komunikasi Massa) (n.d.) 'Life Story of Sadisah', unpublished paper.

YAPUSHAM (Yayasan Pusat Studi Hak Asasi Manusia) (1996) 'Index Pelanggaran Hak Asasi Manusia', no. 5.

YBM (Yayasan Buruh Membangun) (1994) 'Pengalaman Yayasan Buruh Membangun Sebagai Suatu Gerakan Buruh dalam Menemani Kaum Buruh', unpublished paper.

YLBHI (Yayasan Lembaga Bantuan Hukum Indonesia) (1994a) *Laporan Pendahuluan Kasus Pembunuhan Marsinah*, Fact-finding Team, March.

——(1994b) 'Catatan Kasus Medan', unpublished preliminary report.

——(1994c) *Indonesian Labour News: Repression and Violence Against Labour Continues*, Jakarta.

Young, Kenneth R. (1994) 'A New Political Context: The Urbanisation of the Rural', in David Bourchier and John Legge (eds) *Democracy in Indonesia, 1950s and 1990s*, Monash Papers on Southeast Asia no. 31, Clayton: Centre of Southeast Asian Studies, Monash University.

LABOUR LAWS AND MINISTER OF MANPOWER OF THE REPUBLIC OF INDONESIA REGULATIONS AND DECREES

Emergency Law no. 16, 1951.

Labour Law no. 22, 1957 on the Settlement of Labour Disputes.

Presidential Instruction no. 7, 1963 on the Banning of Strikes and Lockouts in Vital Government Enterprises, Institutions and Bodies.

Basic Manpower Law no. 14, 1969.

Ministerial Regulation no. 1/MEN/1975 on the Registration of Workers' Organisations.

Ministerial Decree no. 1109/MEN/1986 on Guidelines for the Establishment, Promotion and Development of Labour Unions at Companies.

Ministerial Decree no. 342/1986 on Guidelines for the Mediation of Industrial Disputes.

Ministerial Regulation no. 05/MEN/1987 on the Registration of Workers' Unions.

Ministerial Regulation no. 03/MEN/1993 on the Registration of Workers' Organisations.

Ministerial Decree no. 15A/MEN/1994 on Guidelines Regarding the Resolution of Industrial Disputes and Dismissals at the Enterprise and Mediation Levels.

Ministerial Regulation no. 01/MEN/1994 on Enterprise Level Unions.

Ministerial Regulation no. PER01/MEN/1996 on Regional Minimum Wages.

NEWSPAPERS, NEWS MAGAZINES, PERIODICALS, WIRE SERVICES, ELECTRONIC BROADCASTS

Abadi
Aksi News Service
Analisa
Aneka Dialog RCTI
Angkatan Bersendjata
Antara
Asian Wall Street Journal
Asiawatch
Australian
Background Briefing, ABC Radio
Berita Buana
Berita LAIDS
Berkala SARBUMUSI
Bisnis Indonesia
Cerita Kami
Dateline, SBS
Detik
Economic and Business Review Indonesia
Editor
El Bahar
Far Eastern Economic Review
Forum Keadilan
Garuda
Gatra
Green Left Weekly
Harian Terbit
Harpers Magazine
Indonesia Raya
Indonesia Times
Indonesian Observer
Inside Indonesia
Jakarta Jakarta
Jakarta Post
Jawa Pos

Koeli
Kompas
Medan Pos
Media Indonesia
Media Kerja Budaya
Merdeka
Mimbar Umum
Nike in Indonesia
Nusantara
Pedoman
Pelita
PHK
Pos Kota
Prisma
Prospek
Republika
Reuters
Sinar Harapan
Suara Karya
Suara Merdeka
Suara Pembaruan
Surabaya Pos
Surya
Tempo
United Press International
USIA East Asia Wireless File
Voice of America
Warta Ekonomi
Waspada
West Australian

Index

DATE DUE

ILL (MRS)		
8168908		
FEB 2 6 1999		